ESSENTIALS FOR design

XHTML

comprehensive

Michael Brooks

D1717247

PEARSON

Prentice Hall

Prentice Hall
Upper Saddle River, New Jersey 07458

Library of Congress Cataloging-in-Publication Data

Brooks, Michael.
   XHTML comprehensive / Michael Brooks.
      p. cm. — (Essentials for design)
   Rev. ed. of: XHTML, level one and level two / Kelly L. Valqui.
   Includes index.
   ISBN 0-13-187796-8
   1. XHTML (Document markup language)   I. Valqui, Kelly. XHTML.   II. Title.
   QA76.76.H94V358 2006
   006.7'4 — dc22
                                 2006024112

Vice President and Publisher: Natalie E. Anderson
Executive Acquisitions Editor: Chris Katsaropoulos
Product Development Manager: Eileen Bien Calabro
Editorial Supervisor: Brian Hoehl
Editorial Assistant: Kaitlin O'Shaughnessy
Executive Producer: Lisa Strite
Content Development Manager: Cathi Profitko
Senior Media Project Manager: Steve Gagliostro
Media Project Manager: Alana Meyers
Director of Marketing: Sarah Loomis
Senior Marketing Manager: Jason Sakos

Marketing Assistant: Ann Baranov
Sr. Customer Service Representative: Joseph Pascale
Managing Editor: Lynda Castillo
Production Project Manager/Manufacturing Buyer: Lynne Breitfeller
Art Director/Cover Design: Blair Brown
Interior Design: Thistle Hill Publishing Services, LLC.
Cover Illustration/Photo: FoodPix®
Composition/Full-Service Project Management: Progressive Publishing Alternatives
Cover Printer: Coral Graphics
Printer/Binder: Von Hoffman Press

Credits and acknowledgments borrowed from other sources and reproduced, with permission, in this textbook appear on the appropriate page within the text.

Macromedia Flash, Generator, FreeHand, Dreamweaver, Fireworks, and Director are registered trademarks of Macromedia, Inc. Photoshop, PageMaker, Acrobat, Adobe Type Manager, Illustrator, InDesign, Premiere, and PostScript are trademarks of Adobe Systems Incorporated. QuarkXPress is a registered trademark of Quark, Inc. Macintosh is a trademark of Apple Computer, Inc. CorelDRAW!, procreate Painter, and WordPerfect are trademarks of Corel Corporation. FrontPage, Publisher, PowerPoint, Word, Excel, Office, Microsoft, MS-DOS, and Windows are either registered trademarks or trademarks of Microsoft Corporation.

Other product and company names mentioned herein may be the trademarks of their respective owners.

10 9 8 7 6 5 4 3 2 1

ISBN 0-13-187796-8

ABOUT THE AUTHOR

Michael Brooks is a senior instructional designer with Lowe's Corporation and an instructor in the Interactive Media Department at the Art Institute of Charlotte; he is also a co-owner of Web-Answers, a multimedia design firm.

Michael has an MPA from Appalachian State University. His professional duties require a great deal of time working in XHTML, JavaScript, and Flash. He has an intimate knowledge of the business and strategic aspects of Web design.

Raised in the foothills of Western North Carolina, Michael enjoys photography and occasionally teaches classes in business management and political science.

ACKNOWLEDGMENTS

I would like to thank the professional writers, artists, editors, students, and educators who have worked long and hard on the *Essentials for Design* series.

Ellenn Behoriam, Kelly Valqui, and the entire crew of Against The Clock, Inc., made substantial contributions to this text. And thanks to the dedicated teaching professionals and technical editors: Kara Hardin, Visual Arts Department, Pensacola Junior College; Lynn Bowen, Internet Specialist Coordinator, Valdosta Technical College; and Lindsey Allen, Austin Community College. Your insightful comments and expertise have certainly contributed to the success of the *Essentials for Design* series.

And to Melissa Sabella, Anne Garcia, and Eileen Calabro — I appreciate your contribution to the continued success of this wonderful series.

CONTENTS AT A GLANCE

TABLE OF CONTENTS

HOW TO USE THIS BOOK

Essentials for Design courseware from Prentice Hall is anchored in the practical and professional needs of all types of students. The *Essentials for Design* series presents a learning-by-doing approach that encourages you to grasp application-related concepts as you expand your skills through hands-on tutorials. As such, it consists of modular lessons that are built around a series of numbered step-by-step procedures that are clear, concise, and easy to review.

Essentials for Design books are divided into chapters. A chapter covers one area (or a few closely related areas) of application functionality. Each chapter consists of several lessons that are related to that topic. Each lesson presents a specific task or closely related set of tasks in a manageable portion that is easy to assimilate and retain.

Each element in the *Essentials for Design* book is designed to maximize your learning experience. A list of the *Essentials for Design* chapter elements, and a description of how each element can help you, begins on the next page. To find out more about the rationale behind each book element and how to use each to your maximum benefit, take the following walk-through.

WALK-THROUGH

Chapter Objectives. Starting with an objective gives you short-term, attainable goals. Each chapter begins with a list of objectives that closely match the titles of the step-by-step tutorials. ▶

Chapter 6 Creating XHTML Forms **211**

Why Would I Do This?

Site designers willingly spend considerable time and effort on the presentation of information to their viewers; but they often overlook the benefits of acquiring information from viewers. As the Web is an interactive medium, it can be used as a tool to collect significant amounts of data, on a variety of topics, from all types of users.

Forms can help Web designers gather information from users for any number of important reasons including:

- Asking users for their preferences to customize the information they enter.
- Using online surveys about users' tastes and interests.
- Processing information for e-commerce transactions. When processing an e-commerce transaction, we need a variety of information such as item numbers, quantity, and shipping address.
- Allowing users to search using simple text boxes where keywords can be entered.

In this chapter, you learn how to create forms for your Web pages, which allow you to collect useful information from your viewers, and ultimately use that information to enhance the content on your sites.

VISUAL SUMMARY

The purpose of an online form is to acquire information from the user and send it to the server. HTML is a *client-side language*, which means the user's computer or browser interprets the code and does the work. For many practical purposes, it is necessary to send information from a Web page to a server. A computer language used by a Web server is called a *server-side language*. A server is simply a computer that performs a specific management function, such as making Web

◀ Why Would I Do This? Introductory material at the beginning of each chapter provides an overview of why these tasks and procedures are important.

Visual Summary. A series of illustrations introduces the new tools, dialog boxes, and windows you will explore in each chapter. ▼

---

24 Chapter 1 Creating XHTML Documents

LESSON 7 Indenting Text

It is sometimes necessary to indent entire paragraphs of information on a Web page. You do this to emphasize the material and to make it stand out from the rest of the copy. Direct quotes are oftentimes set off in this manner.

You can create indented paragraphs with the `<blockquote>` tag, which is similar to pressing the Tab key on your keyboard. *Blockquotes* provide convenient and consistent indentation in a document. The container tags `<blockquote>` and `</blockquote>` enclose the section to be indented (usually paragraphs of text).

Indent Elements on a Web Page

1 Continue working in the open headings.htm file in your text editor.

2 Choose File>Save As, and save the file as "indenting.htm" in your WIP_01 folder.

Indenting.htm is the active file in your text editor window.

3 Change the text file by including the `<blockquote>` container tags as follows:

```
<html>
<head>
<title>Recommended Books</title>
</head>
<body>
<h1 align="center">Dr. Know-It-All Recommendations</h1>

<blockquote>
<p>These days, Dr. Know-It-All is reading several books by
Dr. C. Little, including his Latest, Why Don't Chickens Have
Lips? Dr. Know-It-All has also been engrossed in My Life In
Australia, by Alligator Al.</p>

<p>Dr. Know-It-All recommends books on a weekly basis, or
whenever we get around to it.</p>

</blockquote>
<h2 align="center">Upcoming Books</h2>
<p>At the urging of Mrs. Know-It-All, the next book Dr. Know-It-All
reviews will be Weight Loss Secrets, by Sally Slinky.</p>
</body>
</html>
```
This indents the first two paragraphs of text that follow the first heading.

Forms can contain many different types of input fields, including text boxes and drop-down menus. In Figure 6.1, you see a basic form with input fields that collect and submit user data. Certain types of input fields are more appropriate in one situation than another. You explore a number of these input options in this chapter.

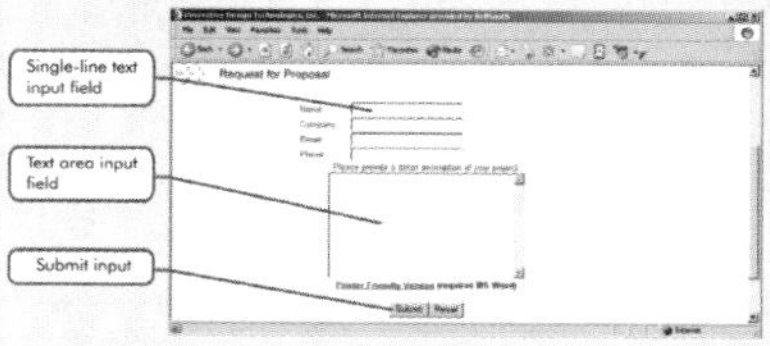

Single-line text input field
Text area input field
Submit input

FIGURE 6.1

Standard forms, similar to the one shown above, are created using XHTML or HTML. CSS, however, provides additional control over the presentation of forms because it allows you to change the field colors, background colors, and so forth.

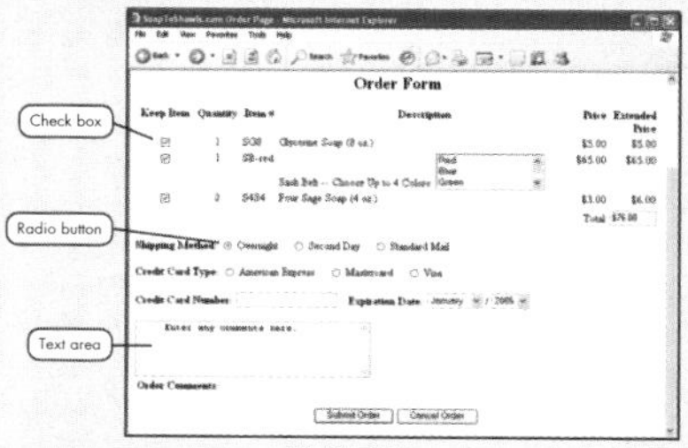

Check box
Radio button
Text area

FIGURE 6.2

◀ Step-by-Step Tutorials. Hands-on tutorials let you learn by doing and include numbered, bold, step-by-step instructions.

? ◀ **If You Have Problems.** These short troubleshooting notes help you anticipate or solve common problems quickly and effectively.

CAREERS IN DESIGN

BASICS FOR WEB PAGE DESIGNERS

You can choose from a number of exciting job categories within the Web-publishing industry. Depending on the diversity of your skill set, you may be able to apply your talents in many different areas. When considering a career in Web publishing, you need to be familiar with the following general skills.

Programming. If you are going to enter a career in Web site design/development, you must know how to program in XHTML. It might be useful to learn an advanced programming language, such as Perl, PHP, ColdFusion, and/or ASP. Knowing how to use JavaScript is an excellent skill as well.

Graphic Design. You should also be able to use a graphics program, such as Photoshop or Fireworks, even if you only use the program for basic techniques such as cropping an image or saving it as a particular format for the Web.

Design and Layout. In order to create professional-looking Web pages, it is essential that you understand the basic design principles and methodologies for Web design. These methodologies include design considerations for a variety of platforms, how to apply color effectively, how to develop effective copy, and other valuable visual techniques.

Webmaster. It is useful to possess a general understanding of how a Web server operates, even if you have no desire to become a full-blown Webmaster. To enhance your effectiveness as a Web site designer/developer, you should know what happens to a file when you upload it to the server, how to manage files, and be familiar with some of the technology behind the Web server — at the very least.

◀ **Careers in Design.** These features offer advice, tips, and resources that will help you on your path to a successful career.

To Extend Your Knowledge . . .

XHTML 2.0 NAVIGATION LISTS

To date, Web designers have built navigation lists from virtually any element or script. XHTML 2.0 includes a new kind of list, represented by the `<nl>` element. The XHTML 2.0 draft states that navigation lists are "intended to define collections of selectable items for presentation."

In an XHTML 2.0 document, a navigation list would resemble the following:

```
<nl>
 <name>Title Number 1</name>
 <li href="#link">List Item</li>
 <li>
   <nl>
     <name> Title Number 2</name>
     <li href="#link">List Item</li>
     <li href="#link">List Item</li>
   </nl>
 </li>
</nl>
```

To Extend Your Knowledge. These features provide extra tips, alternative ways to complete a process, and special hints about using the software. ▶

End-of-Chapter Exercises. Extensive end-of-chapter exercises emphasize hands-on skill development. You'll find two levels of reinforcement: Skill Drill and Challenge. ▼

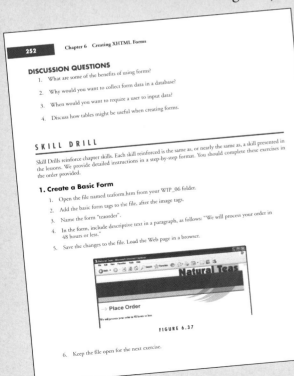

DISCUSSION QUESTIONS

1. What are some of the benefits of using forms?
2. Why would you want to collect form data in a database?
3. When would you want to require a user to input data?
4. Discuss how tables might be useful when creating forms.

SKILL DRILL

Skill Drills reinforce chapter skills. Each skill reinforced is the same as, or nearly the same as, a skill presented in the lessons. We provide detailed instructions in a step-by-step format. You should complete these exercises in the order provided.

1. Create a Basic Form

1. Open the file named teaform.htm from your WIP_06 folder.
2. Add the basic form tags to the file, after the image tags.
3. Name the form "teaorder".
4. In the form, include descriptive text in a paragraph, as follows: "We will process your order in 48 hours or less."
5. Save the changes to the file. Load the Web page in a browser.

FIGURE 6.37

6. Keep the file open for the next exercise.

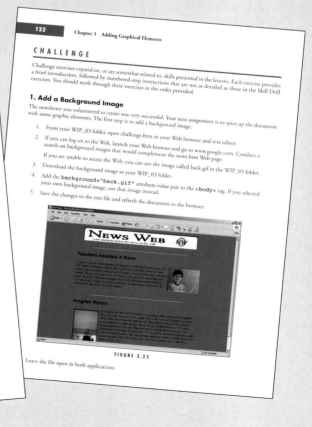

CHALLENGE

Challenge exercises expand on, or are somewhat related to, skills presented in the lessons. Each exercise provides a brief introduction, followed by numbered-step instructions that are not as detailed as those in the Skill Drill exercises. You should work through these exercises in the order provided.

1. Add a Background Image

The newsletter you volunteered to create was very successful. Your next assignment is to spice up the document with some graphic elements. The first step is to add a background image.

1. From your WIP_03 folder, open challenge.htm in your Web browser and text editor.
2. If you can log on to the Web, launch your Web browser and go to www.google.com. Conduct a search on background images that would complement the news.htm Web page.
   If you are unable to access the Web, you can use the image called back.gif in the WIP_03 folder.
3. Download the background image to your WIP_03 folder.
4. Add the `background="back.gif"` attribute-value pair to the `<body>` tag. If you selected your own background image, use that image instead.
5. Save the changes to the text file and refresh the document in the browser.

FIGURE 3.23

Leave the file open in both applications.

Portfolio Builder. At the end of every chapter, these exercises require creative solutions to problems that reinforce the topic of the chapter. ▶

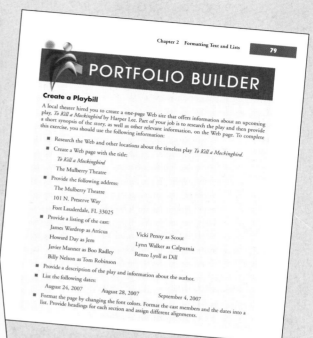

PORTFOLIO BUILDER

Create a Playbill

A local theater hired you to create a one-page Web site that offers information about an upcoming play, *To Kill a Mockingbird* by Harper Lee. Part of your job is to research the play and then provide a short synopsis of the story, as well as other relevant information, on the Web page. To complete this exercise, you should use the following information:

- Research the Web and other locations about the timeless play *To Kill a Mockingbird*.
- Create a Web page with the title:

  To Kill a Mockingbird

  The Mulberry Theatre
- Provide the following address:

  The Mulberry Theatre

  101 N. Preserve Way

  Fort Lauderdale, FL 33025
- Provide a listing of the cast:

  James Wardrop as Atticus

  Howard Day as Jem

  Javier Manner as Boo Radley

  Billy Nelson as Tom Robinson

  Vicki Penny as Scout

  Lynn Walker as Calpurnia

  Renzo Lyoll as Dill
- Provide a description of the play and information about the author.
- List the following dates:

  August 24, 2007   August 28, 2007   September 4, 2007
- Format the page by changing the font colors. Format the cast members and the dates into a list. Provide headings for each section and assign different alignments.

467

INTEGRATING PROJECT

This Integrating Project is designed to reflect a real-world XHTML programming job, drawing on the skills you learned throughout this book. The files you need to complete this project are located in the RF_XHTML_L1>IP folder.

Build the Backwater's Web Site

In this Integrating Project, you create a three-page Web site for a restaurant. The home page includes information about the restaurant; the menu page allows viewers to see the variety of foods offered at the restaurant; and the form page allows users to submit inquiries to the owner of the restaurant. Once the site is complete, you prepare it for publishing by providing meta information for search engines, as well as validate the document.

◀ **Integrating Project.** The integrating project is designed to reflect real-world graphic-design jobs, drawing on the skills you have learned throughout this book.

489

TASK GUIDE

Element	Strict	Transitional	Frameset	Basic	XHTML1.1	Empty
a	x	x	x	x	x	
abbr	x	x	x	x	x	
acronym	x	x	x	x	x	
address	x	x	x	x	x	
applet		x	x			
area		x	x			x
b	x	x	x			
base	x	x	x		x	x
basefont		x	x			x
bdo	x	x	x	x	x	
big	x	x	x			
blockquote	x	x	x		x	
body	x	x	x	x	x	
br	x	x	x	x	x	x
button	x	x	x		x	
caption	x	x	x	x	x	
center		x	x			
cite	x	x	x		x	
code	x	x	x	x	x	
col	x	x	x	x	x	x
colgroup	x	x	x	x	x	
dd	x	x	x	x	x	
del	x	x	x		x	
dfn	x	x	x	x	x	
dir		x	x			
div	x	x	x	x	x	
dl	x	x	x	x	x	
dt	x	x	x	x	x	
em	x	x	x	x	x	
fieldset	x	x	x		x	
font		x	x			
form	x	x	x	x	x	
frame			x			x

Task Guides. These charts, found at the end of each book, list alternative ways to complete common procedures and provide a handy reference tool. ▶

STUDENT INFORMATION AND RESOURCES

Companion Web Site (www.prenhall.com/essentials). This text-specific Web site provides students with additional information and exercises to reinforce their learning. Features include: additional end-of-chapter reinforcement material, online Study Guide, easy access to *all* resource files, and much, much more!

Before completing most chapters within this text, you will need to download the Resource files from the Student CD or from Prentice Hall's Companion Web site for the Essentials for Design Series. Check with your instructor for the best way to gain access to these files or simply follow these instructions:

If you are going to save these files to an external disk, make sure it is inserted into the appropriate drive before continuing.

1. Start your web browser and go to http://www.prenhall.com/essentials

2. Select your textbook or series to access the Companion Web site. We suggest you bookmark this page, as it has links to additional Prentice Hall resources that you may use in class.

3. Click the Student Resources link.

4. Locate the files you need from the list of available resources and then click the link to download.

   Moving forward the process will vary depending upon which operating system (OS) you are using. Please select your OS and follow the instructions below:

   Windows OS:

5. Locate the files you need from the list of available resources and click the link to download.

6. When the File Download box displays, click the **Save** button.

7. In the Save As dialog box, select the location to which you wish to save the file. We recommend you saving the file to the Windows desktop or TEMP folder so it is easy to locate, but if you are working in a lab environment this may not be possible. To save to an external disk, simply type in or select your disk's corresponding drive. Example: a:\ where "a" designates an external disk drive.

8. Click the **Save** button to begin the downloading process.

9. Once the download is complete, navigate to the file using Windows Explorer.

10. Double click on the file to begin the self extraction process and follow the step-by-step prompts.

    Mac OS with Stuffit Expander 8.0.2 or greater:

5. Locate the files you need from the list of available resources and click the link to download.

6. With default settings the file will be downloaded to your desktop.

7. Once Download Manager shows status as "complete", double-click on the file to expand file.

    NOTE: Stuffit Expander can be downloaded free at <http://www.stuffit.com/>

    Mac OS with Stuffit Expander 8:

5. Locate the files you need from the list of available resources and click the link to download.

6. With default settings the file will be downloaded to your desktop.

7. Once Download Manager shows status as "complete", double-click on the file and choose Stuffit Expander as the application to expand file.

    NOTE: Stuffit Expander can be downloaded free at <http://www.stuffit.com/>

    Need help? Contact Tech Support Online at <http://247.prenhall.com>

Resource CD.   If you are using a Resource CD, all the files you need are provided on the CD. Resource files are organized in chapter-specific folders (e.g., Chapter_01, Chapter_02, etc.), which are contained in the RF_XHTML_L1 folder. You can either work directly from the CD, or copy the files onto your hard drive before beginning the exercises.

Before you begin working on the chapters or lessons in this book, you should copy the Work_In_Progress folder from the Resource CD onto your hard drive or a removable disk/drive.

Resource Files. Resource files are organized in chapter-specific folders. Words are separated by an underscore, and all file names include a lowercase three-letter extension. For example, if you are directed to open the file "mysite.htm" in Chapter 2, the file can be found in the RF_XHTML_L1>Chapter_02 folder. We repeat these directions frequently in the early chapters.

The Work In Progress Folder. This folder contains individual folders for each chapter in the book (e.g., WIP_01, WIP_02, etc.). When an exercise directs you to save a file, you should save it to the appropriate folder for the chapter in which you are working.

The exercises in this book frequently build upon work that you have already completed. At the end of each exercise, you will be directed to save your work and either close the file or continue to the next exercise. If you are directed to continue but your time is limited, you can stop at a logical point, save the file, and later return to the point at which you stopped. In this case, you will need to open the file from the appropriate WIP folder and continue working on the same file.

Typeface and Code Conventions. Computer programming code appears in a monospace font that `looks like this`. In many cases, you only need to change or enter specific pieces of code; in these instances, the code you need to type or change appears in a second color and `looks like this`.

Rather than include every line of code in the exercises in Chapters 2–8, we use ellipses (...) to show you where we truncated the code. We show you three or more lines of code before and after each section of code that you should modify in the step. This ensures that you place the new code in the correct location within the script.

INSTRUCTOR'S RESOURCES

Instructor's Resource Center.   This CD-ROM includes the entire Instructor's Manual for each application in Microsoft Word format. Student data files and completed solutions files are also on this CD-ROM. The Instructor's Manual contains a reference guide of these files for the instructor's convenience. PowerPoint slides with more information about each project are also available for classroom use. All instructor resources are also available online via the Companion Web site at www.prenhall.com/essentials.

TestGen Software.   TestGen is a test generator program that lets you view and easily edit test bank questions, transfer them to tests, and print the tests in a variety of formats suitable to your teaching situation. The program also offers many options for organizing and displaying test banks and tests. A built-in random number and text generator makes it ideal for creating multiple versions of tests. Powerful search and sort functions let you easily locate questions and arrange them in the order you prefer.

QuizMaster, also included in this package, enables students to take tests created with TestGen on a local area network. The QuizMaster utility built into TestGen lets instructors view student records and print a variety of reports. Building tests is easy with TestGen, and exams can be easily uploaded into WebCT, Blackboard, and CourseCompass.

Prentice Hall has formed close alliances with each of the leading online platform providers: WebCT, Blackboard, and our own Pearson CourseCompass.

NTRODUCTION

HyperText Markup Language, better known as HTML, has come a long way since it was first standardized in the early 1990s. Unlike other hypertext systems that required authors to possess programming skills, this language allows people who have little or no programming experience to successfully create Web pages. HTML "programmers" can use different programs, operating systems, and file formats to exchange information.

Tim-Berners Lee is the visionary programmer who developed the theory behind HTML and the Web. His idea was to create a global information system that would be available to anyone with a computer. His system would allow people to link information on disparate systems using a common addressing method, which is what we know as the Uniform Resource Locator (URL), or Web address.

As the Web evolved and gained commercial popularity, Web authors began to express the desire for more than simple methods of structuring content; they wanted presentational control, as well. This gave rise to new HTML formatting techniques that delivered more design capabilities — as well as frustrating compatibility issues.

To resolve those compatibility issues, and to satisfy the content and presentational requirements of Web authors, a new language was developed: the eXtensible Hypertext Markup Language. XHTML begins the migration from non-compatible hypertext documents to Web pages that contain both structural and presentational elements, while offering universal accessibility across platforms.

This book is designed to introduce you to the tools and features of XHTML, as well as teach you how to produce professional-looking documents for the Web. We encourage you to look at the big picture — what you're actually creating — and make design decisions based on that reality, rather than establishing a blanket rule for production. You can apply the skills you learn to virtually any document, from a one-page gallery, to a multi-tiered corporate site.

As you progress through this book, pay attention not only to the step-by-step tasks within the chapters, but also to the principles behind them. Most hands-on exercises and Skill Drills demand absolute attention to detail; but many of the Challenges and Portfolio Builders provide opportunities to express your personal creativity. In addition, we encourage you to go beyond the projects and experiment on your own, rather than limit yourself solely to the ideas presented in this book.

CHAPTER 1

Creating XHTML Documents

OBJECTIVES

In this chapter, you learn how to:

- Identify key differences between HTML and XHTML

- Create hypertext documents

- Apply document tags

- Format text into paragraphs

- Align paragraphs

- Create line breaks

- Add headings

- Align headings

- Indent sections of text

Why Would I Do This?

HTML is a simple technology. Part of the reason the Web gained popularity so quickly was that virtually anybody could use HTML to build a Web page. Non-programmers and programmers alike were able to build and post sites on the Web — and you will, too, after you complete the lessons and exercises in this book. Before you begin the lessons on XHTML, it's important that you know a bit about the Hypertext Markup Language (HTML), the framework upon which XHTML is built.

HTML is a simple scripting language that instructs a Web ***browser*** how to display a Web page. A ***scripting language*** is similar to a traditional programming language but is usually less powerful and is often designed for a specific function. Scripting languages run from or within other programs; they are not stand-alone applications. HTML was designed to run with different programs (such as the various Web browsers) and operating systems to exchange information through a large heterogeneous network (the Internet).

HTML has recently evolved into ***XHTML (eXtensible Hypertext Markup Language)***, which is very similar to traditional HTML but contains new standards that will make the language more compatible with new technologies such as XML and Cascading Style Sheets (CSS). These standards, in turn, will make Web sites more compatible with mobile devices and new software applications. Minor changes are needed to allow existing HTML code to coexist within the XHTML standards.

Strict adherence to XHTML standards cannot be easily accomplished in most browsers. For this reason, the content of this book conforms to the transitional form of XHTML. ***Transitional XHTML*** allows most XHTML syntax rules to be implemented without requiring rules that would cause incompatibilities in common browsers. Transitional XHTML also allows developers to keep using HTML presentation elements, such as the <table> tag, which will be eventually removed from the language.

XHTML is, essentially, a newer version of HTML. HTML 4.01 is likely the final version of HTML. For the most part, the terms "HTML" and "XHTML" are used interchangeably in this book, although they are slightly different languages.

Transitional XHTML is essentially HTML 4.01 that includes minor code changes and stricter structural rules and syntax. The ***syntax*** of a scripting language is the set of rules that dictates how the language is written. HTML and XHTML pages are written using strings and characters. A ***string*** is a line of code that instructs the program to complete a specific task. A ***character*** is a part of the code, such as a letter or a semicolon (;).

XHTML is designed to offer ***backward compatibility***, which is the ability to support older technology and browsers, even though it was designed for newer technology and browsers. A new standard called "XHTML 2.0" is on the horizon, however. This newer version does not offer support for older browsers. (You'll learn more about browser compatibility issues as you work through this book.)

The focus of this book is on XHTML 1.1 and how you can use it to create compelling content for the Web. When necessary, we note specific examples of when it makes better sense to use HTML. As you complete the exercises and build Web-based content, you receive sneak peeks at what's new in XHTML 2.0.

VISUAL SUMMARY

XHTML can be written in a text editor such as Microsoft's Notepad or Macintosh's TextEdit application. The text file is then saved with a .htm or .html extension. The file extension tells the operating system and Web browser to treat the file as a Web page.

A Web page is a ***hypertext document***, which is a text document that allows users to jump to various points in a nonsequential manner. In this situation, ***hyper*** means that users can choose a link to jump to another point within the same document, to jump to another Web page, or to view a different type of file. Users are not necessarily forced to go to a specific point, such as the next slide in a slide show.

In this book, we used Notepad to write the XHTML documents, and we used Internet Explorer (IE) to view them. The following illustration shows Microsoft's Notepad program window with a simple Web page. You can find this program by clicking the Start button and navigating to All Programs>Accessories>Notepad.

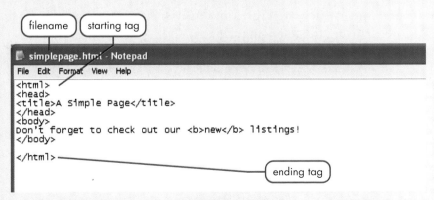

FIGURE 1.1

The XHTML language is comprised of tags that define items and describe how they appear on the Web page. A *tag* is a character or set of characters, enclosed in less-than (<) and greater-than (>) signs, that tells the Web browser what to do with specific pieces of information. Tags define the structure of the Web page. Here are some commonly used XHTML tags:

- `<b>` `</b>` are the bold tags
- `<i>` `</i>` are the italic tags
- `<h1>` `</h1>` are the tags for Level 1 headings

Tags generally come in pairs, with an opening and a closing tag. The *opening tag*, as in `<b>`, indicates the start of a section. The *closing tag*, as in `</b>`, indicates the end of a section. Note the forward slash used in the closing tag.

Compare the following line of code with Figure 1.2 to see how the code displays.

```
Don't forget to check out our <b>new</b> listings!
```

FIGURE 1.2

As you can see, only the word "new" is bold because it is the only word inside the tags. XHTML also allows you to use *nested tags*, which are tags contained within other tags. For instance, you could italicize the entire sentence using the following tags:

```
<i>Don't forget to check out our <b>new</b> listings!</i>
```

This line of code displays as follows:

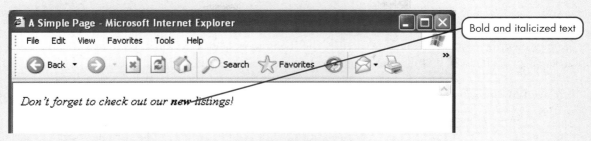

FIGURE 1.3

In HTML, it doesn't matter how you order the nested tags. For example, if you opened with a **<b>** tag and followed it with an opening **<i>** tag, you could choose to close the **<b>** tag first or the **<i>** tag — either way, you would achieve the same result. For example:

```
<i><b>Content here.</i></b>
```

creates the same result as

```
<i><b>Content here.</b></i>
```

It is better practice to close tags in the reverse order you opened them. This is required in XHTML:

```
<i><b>Content here.</b></i>
```

The above examples are simple illustrations, but you can begin to see how XHTML elements will display on a Web page. An *element* is an object that can contain text, such as a paragraph or an image. We examine elements in more detail throughout this book.

LESSON 1 Understanding a Hypertext Document

On the most basic level, a Web page is simply a text file that refers to other files (text and images). The browser knows how to interpret a hypertext document because it understands the system of tags that describes the content. Tags describe each string of text, whether the string represents a headline, an image, a name rendered in bold typeface, or the overall body of content. Every page uses the same standard structure.

You don't need to buy an expensive layout program to create Web pages. All you need to know is how to apply the XHTML scripting language to your content. A text editor and browser are all you need to get started.

Create a Web Page

1 Create a folder named "Work_In_Progress" on your hard drive.

2 In the Work_In_Progress folder, create a subfolder named "WIP_01".

Save all of the files in this chapter to your WIP_01 folder.

3 Open the RF_XHTML_L1 folder. Copy the contents of your Chapter_01 folder to the WIP_01 folder in your Work_In_Progress folder.

The RF_XHTML_L1 folder contains the files you need to complete the exercises in this book.

4 Open a simple text editor, such as Text Edit or Notepad.

The text-editing program launches. Do not use a word-processing program, such as Microsoft Word or Corel WordPerfect. Using a word-processing program causes unpredictable results.

5 Type the following on the first line of the document:

`Hello World!`

FIGURE 1.4

6 Save the document as "hello.htm" in your WIP_01 folder. Make sure to choose Save as type All Files from the Save As dialog box. Mac user's using TextEdit should use its Preferences to set the text format to Plain Text.

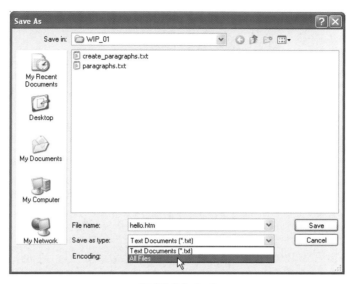

FIGURE 1.5

This ensures that the .txt extension is excluded from the file name. Web browsers recognize .htm and .html extensions as Web pages. The difference between the two extensions dates back to Windows 3.x, which only recognized three-letter extensions, and the Macintosh, which used the four-letter extension. Today's platforms recognize both extensions. Remember to always save your documents in lowercase letters. This prevents any issues with case sensitivity and linking.

? If You Have Problems

You want this to be a text file, but you want it to include the .htm extension — not .txt. Occasionally, Windows adds .txt to a file name, which would rename the file hello.htm.txt. If this happens, manually rename the file, and then reopen it.

7 Open your browser.

We used Microsoft Internet Explorer (IE) for the illustrations in this book. If you use another browser, there may be slight differences in button names and/or how the page renders.

8   **Choose File>Open (or Open File) in the browser window.**

The Open dialog box displays. If you do not see a hypertext file in the Open dialog box, pull down the Files of Type menu and choose All Files. By default, the browser opens .htm or .html files. If you do not see the file you saved in the Open dialog box, pull down the Files of Type menu.

FIGURE 1.6

9   **Click the Browse button in the Open dialog box. Navigate to WIP_01>hello.htm.**

10   **Double-click hello.htm.**

The path to hello.htm displays in the Open dialog box.

11   **Click OK.**

The Web page displays in the browser. Even though you created a Web page, it is not considered an XHTML document. In the next lesson, you learn some of the requirements for creating a valid XHTML document.

FIGURE 1.7

12   **Leave the file open in both windows.**

To Extend Your Knowledge . . .

BROWSER WARS

Until recently, Netscape and Microsoft, the two primary browser manufacturers, released products that included nonstandard functionality. Each acted in the best interests of their users and their company; but for Web designers, this cross-platform incompatibility created far-reaching problems. When a designer used IE to develop a site, and a viewer used Navigator to view that site, any nonstandard features that were used to develop the page caused unsightly errors in the Navigator window. It was quite common for a page to look perfect in IE and be completely blank, off centered, or out of alignment in Navigator.

A REFORMULATION OF HTML 4.01 INTO XML

The **W3C** (World Wide Web Consortium) was organized in 1994 to bring order to a rapidly changing industry — namely, the Web. The W3C issues recommendations (standards) that development companies should make every attempt to honor.

According to the W3C, there are three basic purposes behind XHTML:

> Clean up sloppy, nonstandard HTML
>
> Provide ways to extend HTML and add new features
>
> Separate content from presentation

You explore all of these purposes in this book. The W3C's official Web site is http://www.w3c.org.

LESSON 2   Document Tags and Elements

Tags are the underlying foundation of Web pages. Tags tell the browser what to do with specific pieces of information and define the structure of a Web page. **Document tags** specify each section of an XHTML document. HTML did not require the use of all document tags, but the stricter XHTML requires that opening and closing document tags must be applied to every document. Additionally, *all* tags must be written in lowercase.

Document tags are as follows:

- `<html></html>`. The html tags define the beginning and end of an XHTML document. A requirement for a valid XHTML page is that all other tags (including document tags) are contained between the `<html>` and `</html>` tags.

- **`<head></head>`**. The head section of a page is where you place information that is not generally displayed on the page but is still important to the page. For instance, ***meta data*** (hidden information about the author, date, and document) is placed in the **`<head>`** section. In other situations, the **`<head>`** section may include scripts that will be run by the browser.

- **`<title></title>`**. The title, which is included in the head of the document, doesn't actually appear on the page but typically controls the text that displays in the Title bar of the browser window.

- **`<body></body>`**. You place the content of your page between the **`<body>`** tags. All text, images, and other items the user sees are located in this section of the document.

Elements

As you learned earlier, an element is a type of object that can contain text or other objects. For example, a Web page might consist of an HTML element that contains many other elements, including a body element. The body element might contain text. When one element (such as the above body element) is contained within another element, it is called a "nested element." The text element is nested within the body element, and the body element is nested within the html element.

Add Document Tags to a Web Page

1   **Continue working in the open text editor window that contains hello.htm.**

2   **Place your cursor before the words "Hello World!" Press the Enter/Return key three times.**

This positions "Hello World!" three lines farther down in the window, allowing you to type the first document tag at the top of the page (above "Hello World!").

3   **Reposition your cursor at the top of the page and type the following tag:**

`<html>`

The **`<html>`** document tag (element) defines the entire page as an HTML document. All of the page's content must be placed within the **`<html>`** and **`</html>`** elements.

FIGURE 1.8

4   **Press Enter/Return. Type the following:**

`<head>`

Remember that important information about the document is placed in the head section of a page. This information does not display in the browser.

5   **Press Enter/Return. Type the following:**

`<title>This is my first Web page.</title>`

The title typically displays in the Title bar of the browser window. The **`<title>`** tag is also used when indexing your Web page with search engines. You learn more about search-engine indexing later in this book.

6   **Press Enter/Return. Type the following:**

`</head>`

This closes the head section of the document.

7   **Press Enter/Return. Type the following:**

`<body>`

The content of the page is contained within the body section of the document. Content can include text, images, and any other items the user sees.

8   **Position your cursor after the words "Hello World!" Type the following:**

`</body>`

This closes the body section of the document.

9   **Press Enter/Return and type the following:**

`</html>`

This ends the XHTML document.

FIGURE 1.9

10   **Choose File>Save from the main Menu bar in the text editor.**

This saves your XHTML file.

11   **Click your browser window to activate it. Click the Refresh button on the browser toolbar.**

The document refreshes in the browser. The only visual change you see is the addition of a Title bar. Even though you can't see it on your screen, the document tags added more structure to the XHTML document.

FIGURE 1.10

12   **Close hello.htm in your text editor and browser.**

To Extend Your Knowledge . . .

XHTML VALIDATION

Unlike HTML documents, XHTML documents must be validated. **Validating** an XHTML document confirms that the document adheres to one of the three Document Type Definitions (DTDs) defined by the W3C. A **DTD** tells the browser the type of document that will be used (and the type of tags that will be encountered). You can use the validation process to ensure that you didn't make any structural or typing mistakes in the content of a page.

The three types of XHTML are:

1. **XHTML Strict**. To comply with this recommendation, you must not only follow the XML rules that prevent you from creating sloppy code, you must also remove any HTML that is focused on presentation. A different technology, such as CSS is used to format the presentation of the page.

Cascading Style Sheets (CSS) allow Web designers to control the style and layout appearance of a Web page. CSS can be used to format multiple Web pages at the same time, without making individual page adjustments.

XML (eXtensible Markup Language) is a markup language designed to create customized tags, enabling the definition, transmission, and validation of data between applications. XML is designed to make it easy for different computer systems, mobile devices, and computer software applications to exchange data in a simple, easy-to-understand format that is similar to HTML.

2. **XHTML Transitional** is literally a reformulation of HTML 4.01. Virtually every tag is reproduced in entirety, but all of the loopholes for which browsers have been compensating have been removed. Some pages require minor modifications to conform to the new rules; some **deprecated** features (those marked for extinction) must be removed. It should take a short amount of time to bring any properly written page into conformance with this standard. XHTML Transitional documents are closest in form and function to the vast majority of Web pages that already exist. XHTML Transitional is sometimes needed to compensate for browsers that don't fully support CSS. We use and discuss this version of XHTML throughout this book, with certain noted exceptions.

3. **XHTML Frameset**. HTML frames enable you to create a window-in-a-window effect on a Web page.

LESSON 3 Creating Paragraphs

White space, the empty area on a page that makes it easier to read, is an important design element, one that is often taken for granted when working with word-processing or page-layout programs. With those programs, you can press the Enter/Return key to add as many blank lines as you prefer and immediately see the result on the screen.

In XHTML, however, adding a blank line is not such a simple matter. Browsers ignore the white space in the text of a file. If you want to display white space in the final document, you must instruct the browser to do so. You can use several methods to add white space to a Web page. Adding a new paragraph, for example, creates an empty line between the preceding paragraph and the new one. To create a paragraph, you enclose a section of text inside the `<p>` and `</p>` tags.

Work with Paragraphs

1   **In your text editor, open paragraphs.txt from your Work_In_Progress>WIP_01 folder.**

This text file contains two typed paragraphs.

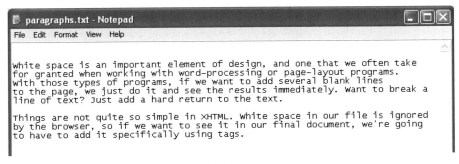

FIGURE 1.11

2   **Before the beginning of the first paragraph, insert the following code:**

```
<html>
<head>
<title>Creating Paragraphs.</title>
</head>
<body>
```

White space is an important element of design, and one that we often take for granted when working with word-processing or page-layout programs. With those types of programs, if we want to add several blank lines . . .

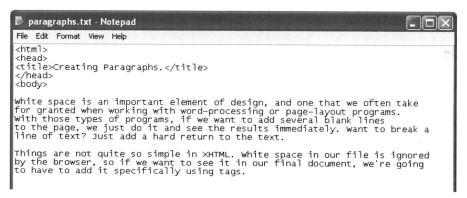

FIGURE 1.12

3   **Insert the following code at the end of the document:**

Things are not quite so simple in XHTML. White space in our file is ignored by the browser, so if we want to see it in our final document, we're going to have to add it specifically using tags.

```
</body>
</html>
```

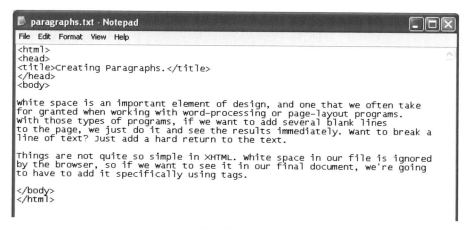

FIGURE 1.13

This will end the document tags.

? If You Have Problems

Throughout this book, you will find several sections that may require significant typing. To save time, we provide some of these lengthy files. These files are organized by chapter; you can find them in the RF_XHTML_L1 folder.

4 Save the document as "paragraph.htm" in your WIP_01 folder. Display the file in your browser.

The Web page displays in your browser without the blank space between the two sections of text, because there are no instructions to separate the text into paragraphs.

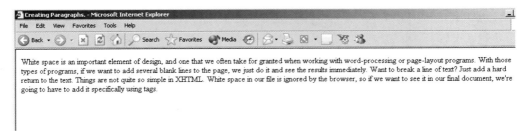

FIGURE 1.14

5 Return to the document in the text editor. Enclose the two sections of text with the `<p></p>` tags, as follows:

```
<p> White space is an important element of design, and one that we
often take for granted when working with word-processing or page-
layout programs. With those types of programs, if we want to add
several blank lines to the page, we just do it and see the
results immediately. Want to break a line of text? Just add a
hard return to the text. </p>

<p> Things are not quite so simple in XHTML. White space in our
file is ignored by the browser, so if we want to see it in our
final document, we're going to have to add it specifically using
tags.</p>
```

6 Save the changes to the document. Refresh paragraph.htm in your browser.

The `<p></p>` tags separate the sections of text into paragraphs.

FIGURE 1.15

7 Leave paragraph.htm open in your text editor.

To Extend Your Knowledge . . .

CLOSING CONTAINER TAGS

One of the changes from HTML to XHTML is stricter coding. For instance, HTML 4.01 states that paragraph tags (`<p></p>`) should be placed at the beginning and end of a block of text to set it off from the text around it. Both major browsers, however, allow developers to leave off the ending `</p>` tag, effectively using the `<p>` tag as a double line break. In XHTML, however, the `<p>` tag must be accompanied by a closing `</p>` tag. All **container tags** have a similar requirement.

LESSON 4 Aligning Paragraphs

Before you learn how to align paragraphs on a Web page, it's important to understand that there is more to a tag than the command itself. For instance, the paragraph element (`<p>`), which adds a blank line before and after a section of text, can offer more instruction than the basic command; it can also contain **attributes**, which are pieces of information in the opening tag that provide details about the tag and what it is supposed to do. For example:

```
<p align="center">
```

In this case, you have a `<p>` element. The element contains an align attribute, which has a **value** (option) of "center". This is known as an **attribute-value pair** (also called **name-value pair**). The value is enclosed in double quotes so the browser knows where it begins and ends. In XHTML, name-value pairs must be surrounded by quotes; quotes are not required in HTML. The align attribute offers three value options: right, left, or center.

The align attribute for the paragraph tag has been deprecated (replaced with a newer method) in the current XHTML standard; style sheets are now the preferred method of alignment. In future versions of XHTML, the align attribute will not be available. The align attribute conforms to the XHTML Transitional document type.

Align Paragraphs on a Web Page

1   **Open the text editor window that contains the paragraph.htm document.**

The document becomes active in the text editor.

2   **Add the `align="center"` name-value pair to the first `<p>` tag:**

```
<p align="center"> White space is an important element of design,
and one that we often take for granted when working with word-
processing or page-layout programs. With those types of programs,
if we want to add several blank lines to the page, we just do it
and see the results immediately. Want to break a line of text?
Just add a hard return to the text. </p>
```

The **`align="center"`** attribute instructs the browser to align the paragraph in the center of the page. Make sure there is a space between the "**p**" and the **`align="center"`** attribute. There is always a space after the tag command and the tag's attributes.

3   **Add the `align="right"` attribute to the second paragraph:**

```
<p align="right"> Things are not quite so simple in XHTML. White
space in our file is ignored by the browser, so if we want to see
it in our final document, we're going to have to add it
specifically using tags. </p>
```

The **`align="right"`** name-value pair aligns the paragraph on the right of the Web page.

4   **Save the changes to the document. Refresh the document in your browser.**

The document reflects the alignment changes in the paragraphs.

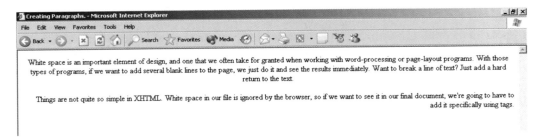

FIGURE 1.16

5   **Leave paragraph.htm open in your text editor.**

To Extend Your Knowledge . . .

DEPRECATED TAGS

Deprecated tags are included in the current HTML 4.01 standard but might become obsolete in the next approved standard or substandard. These tags have been deprecated because newer, easier ways of rendering the same Web page elements have been established. Many presentational tags and attributes have been deprecated in favor of style sheets because they allow HTML authors to design with more flexibility, without sacrificing accessibility. Even though deprecated features might become obsolete in future versions of HTML, browsers that support the features will likely continue to do so.

LESSON 5 Creating Line Breaks

The **<p></p>** tags separate sections of text into paragraphs; but what if you want to force a line of text onto the next line without creating a space? Rather than use the **<p></p>** tags, you can create a line break to achieve the same result.

You create a line break with the **
** tag. The **
** tag is different from the other tags you've examined so far — it's an *empty tag* (there's no actual content within the tag).

To boldface someone's name, as we did to Bunny Hop in the following example, the name is placed between the opening and closing bold tags. "Bunny Hop" is the content for those tags. (You learn more about boldface tags and other formatting tags later in this book.) For example:

```
<b>Bunny Hop</b>
```

The **
** tag, however, works differently. It simply forces a line break; no content is associated with the tag. In HTML, the tag reads **
** (without a slash). One of the requirements of XHTML is that you use complete pairs of tags; technically, the XHTML tag should read **
**.

Since there's no actual content in the **
** tag, using a closing tag might look rather awkward. In addition, if a browser understands only HTML (and not XHTML), it may display the result of the **
** tag incorrectly. The designers of XML (and XHTML) understood this browser problem and defined a "shorthand" for empty elements; this shorthand combines both the opening and closing tag in one tag. Unfortunately, older browsers don't understand the shorthand. To prevent errors in these browsers, you must add a space before the slash. The tag becomes:

```
<br />
```

Older browsers, and current browsers and programs designed to read XHTML, can interpret the **
** tag.

Create a Line Break

1   **Open linebreaks.htm in your text editor.**

This is essentially the same file you created in a previous exercise.

2   **Position your cursor after the first section of text and type "`<br />`". The body text displays as follows:**

```
White space is an important element of design, and one that we
often take for granted when working with word-processing or page-
layout programs. With those types of programs, if we want to add
several blank lines to the page, we just do it and see the
results immediately. Want to break a line of text? Just add a
hard return to the text.

<br />

Things are not quite so simple in XHTML. White space in our file
is ignored by the browser, so if we want to see it in our final
document, we're going to have to add it specifically using tags.
```

This removes the space between the two sections of text and forces a line break.

3   **Save the changes to the document. Refresh your browser.**

The **`<br />`** tag forces a line break but does not separate the sections into paragraphs.

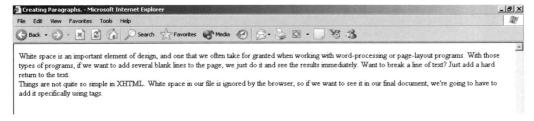

FIGURE 1.17

4   **Close linebreaks.htm in your text editor.**

To Extend Your Knowledge . . .

LINE BREAK TAG DEPRECATED IN 2.0

The line break tag (`<br />`) has been deprecated in XHTML 2.0 in favor of the `<line></line>` tags. The `<line>` tag encloses text that should display on its own line. For example:

<p>HTML 4.01 is no longer the recommended standard for the Web.

`<line>`Transitional XHTML is the current working standard.`</line>`

As of this writing, XHTML 2.0 is in draft form — it is not yet the recommended version. We mention it as a sneak peek of what's likely to come in the next version of XHTML.

MORE REASONS TO USE THE LINE BREAK

The `<br />` tag is useful in situations where the `<p>` tag would not be well suited, such as when you need to insert an address. If you add an address to a Web page, using the `<p>` tag creates a space between each line of the address. Using the `<br />` tag allows you to format an address more appropriately. For example:

Jane Doe`<br />`

1000 Your Avenue`<br />`

Your Town, ST 11111`<br />`

This creates an address that appears on a Web page, as follows:

Jane Doe
1000 Your Avenue
Your Town, ST 11111

LESSON 6 Creating Headings

At times, you may want to display topic headings within your documents. Browsers identify headings as important content, so they normally display headings in larger sizes and bolder typeface than the rest of the text in the document. Adding headings makes it easier to read a document, and the content appears more organized.

The different sizes (levels) of section headings in documents allow readers to understand the relative importance of the information presented in each section. For example, an article might include the title at the beginning and smaller subtitles throughout the document. XHTML headings come in six sizes, `<h1></h1>` through `<h6></h6>`, so you can present an extensive hierarchy of information when necessary.

It might seem logical that the h6 heading would be the largest and h1 the smallest — but the opposite is true. Heading levels indicate the importance of the text, not its size. An h1 heading is of highest importance, and an h6 heading is of least importance.

Add Headings to a Web Page

| 1 | **In your text editor, choose File>Open. Navigate to the RF_XHTML_L1>Chapter_01 folder.** |

| 2 | **Double-click the headings.htm file** |

The headings.htm file displays in the browser. Notice the existing XHTML code in the document. Remember, to see a file with a .html or .htm extension, change your Files of type from the default *.txt to All Files.

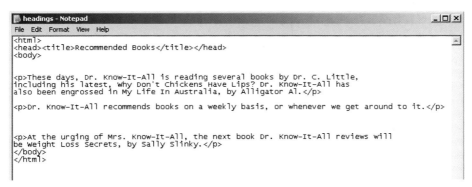

FIGURE 1.18

| 3 | **Add the following headings to the headings.htm document.** |

```
<html>
<head>
<title>Recommended Books</title>
</head>
<body>

<h1>Dr. Know-It-All Recommendations</h1>

<p>These days, Dr. Know-It-All is reading several books by
Dr. C. Little, including his Latest, Why Don't Chickens Have
Lips? Dr. Know-It-All has also been engrossed in My Life In
Australia, by Alligator Al.</p>

<p>Dr. Know-It-All recommends books on a weekly basis, or
whenever we get around to it.</p>

<h2>Upcoming Books</h2>

<p>At the urging of Mrs. Know-It-All, the next book Dr. Know-It-
All reviews will be Weight Loss Secrets, by Sally Slinky.</p>
</body>
</html>
```

Adding a heading to each section of the Web page makes it easier to read.

4 **Choose File>Save As from the text editor. Save the document as "headings.htm" in your WIP_01 folder.**

This saves the new version of the file in your WIP_01 folder.

5 **Switch to the browser window. Navigate to the WIP_01>headings.htm file. Display the document in your browser.**

Notice the first heading is a Level 1 heading, and the second is a Level 2 heading.

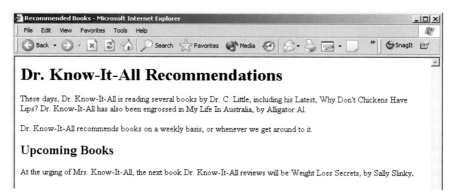

FIGURE 1.19

6 **Switch back to the text document and add the align="center" name-value pair to the headings, as follows:**

```
<html>
<head>
<title>Recommended Books</title>
</head>
<body>

<h1 align="center">Dr. Know-It-All Recommendations</h1>

<p>These days, Dr. Know-It-All is reading several books by
Dr. C. Little, including his Latest, Why Don't Chickens Have
Lips? Dr. Know-It-All has also been engrossed in My Life In
Australia, by Alligator Al.</p>

<p>Dr. Know-It-All recommends books on a weekly basis, or whenever
we get around to it.</p>

<h2align="center">Upcoming Books</h2>

<p>At the urging of Mrs. Know-It-All, the next book Dr. Know-It-All
reviews will be Weight Loss Secrets, by Sally Slinky.</p>
</body>
</html>
```

In an earlier lesson, you learned how to use the align attribute to align paragraphs on a Web page. You can also use the align attribute with a heading tag to align a heading left, right, or center on the page.

7 **Save the changes in the text document. Refresh headings.htm in the browser.**

The headings are center-aligned on the page.

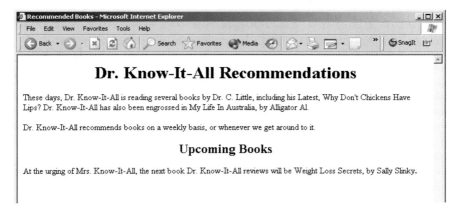

FIGURE 1.20

8 **Leave headings.htm open in the text editor.**

To Extend Your Knowledge . . .

XHTML 2.0 STRUCTURED HEADINGS

XHTML includes six levels of numbered headings. XHTML 2.0 offers another method called "structured headings." Structured headings use the single `<h>` element in combination with the section element to indicate the structure of the document. The importance of a heading is determined by its nesting order, and headings are rendered according to this order. For example:

```
<h>This is a top-level heading because it is listed first</h>
<p>...</p>
<section>
<p>...</p>
<h>This is a second-level heading because it is nested below the top-level heading</h>
<p>...</p>
<section>
<h>This is a third-level heading because it is nested within the second-level heading</h>
<p>...</p>
</section>
</section>
```

LESSON 7 Indenting Text

It is sometimes necessary to indent entire paragraphs of information on a Web page. You do this to emphasize the material and to make it stand out from the rest of the copy. Direct quotes are oftentimes set off in this manner.

You can create indented paragraphs with the **<blockquote>** tag, which is similar to pressing the Tab key on your keyboard. *Blockquotes* provide convenient and consistent indentation in a document. The container tags **<blockquote>** and **</blockquote>** enclose the section to be indented (usually paragraphs of text).

Indent Elements on a Web Page

1 **Continue working in the open headings.htm file in your text editor.**

2 **Choose File>Save As, and save the file as "indenting.htm" in your WIP_01 folder.**

Indenting.htm is the active file in your text editor window.

3 **Change the text file by including the <blockquote> container tags as follows:**

```
<html>
<head>
<title>Recommended Books</title>
</head>
<body>

<h1 align="center">Dr. Know-It-All Recommendations</h1>

<blockquote>

<p>These days, Dr. Know-It-All is reading several books by
Dr. C. Little, including his Latest, Why Don't Chickens Have
Lips? Dr. Know-It-All has also been engrossed in My Life In
Australia, by Alligator Al.</p>

<p>Dr. Know-It-All recommends books on a weekly basis, or
whenever we get around to it.</p>

</blockquote>

<h2 align="center">Upcoming Books</h2>

<p>At the urging of Mrs. Know-It-All, the next book Dr. Know-It-All
reviews will be Weight Loss Secrets, by Sally Slinky.</p>
</body>
</html>
```

This indents the first two paragraphs of text that follow the first heading.

4   **Save the changes in the text editor window. Open indenting.htm in your browser.**

The first two paragraphs are indented from the rest of the body text.

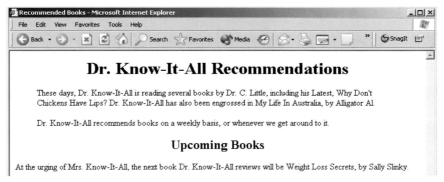

FIGURE 1.21

5   **Place your cursor before the second paragraph in the blockquoted section. Nest an additional section of text using a blockquote tag, as follows.**

```
<html>
<head>
<title>Recommended Books</title>
</head>
<body>

<h1 align="center">Dr. Know-It-All Recommendations</h1>

<blockquote>

<p>These days, Dr. Know-It-All is reading several books by
Dr. C. Little, including his Latest, Why Don't Chickens Have
Lips? Dr. Know-It-All has also been engrossed in My Life In
Australia, by Alligator Al.</p>

<blockquote>

<p>Dr. Know-It-All recommends books on a weekly basis, or
whenever we get around to it.</p>

</blockquote>
</blockquote>

<h2 align="center">Upcoming Books</h2>

<p>At the urging of Mrs. Know-It-All, the next book Dr. Know-It-All
reviews will be Weight Loss Secrets, by Sally Slinky.</p>
</body>
</html>
```

The second blockquote indents the section of text to a greater degree. This is a nested block quote.

6 **Save the changes in the document. Refresh the page in the browser.**

The changes display in the Web browser.

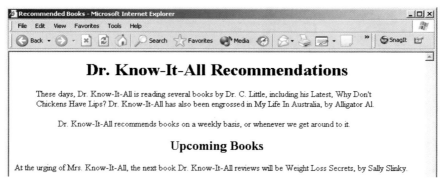

FIGURE 1.22

7 **Leave indenting.htm open in both applications.**

Cite Text Using Blockquotes

The `cite=""` attribute allows you to indicate the source of a quote. The attribute's value should be a quote-enclosed URL that points to the online document and, if possible, the exact location of the quote within the document.

1 **In the text editor window of the open file, add a `cite=""` attribute in the second set of blockquote tags, as follows:**

```
<html>
<head>
<title>Recommended Books</title>
</head>
<body>

<h1 align="center">Dr. Know-It-All Recommendations</h1>

<blockquote>

<p>These days, Dr. Know-It-All is reading several books by
Dr. C. Little, including his Latest, Why Don't Chickens Have
Lips? Dr. Know-It-All has also been engrossed in My Life In
Australia, by Alligator Al.</p>

<blockquote cite="http://www.web-answers.com">

<p>Dr. Know-It-All recommends books on a weekly basis, or
whenever we get around to it.</p>
```

```
</blockquote>

</blockquote>

<h2 align="center">Upcoming Books</h2>

<p>At the urging of Mrs. Know-It-All, the next book Dr. Know-It-All
reviews will be Weight Loss Secrets, by Sally Slinky.</p>
</body>
</html>
```

This provides the source of the information that was quoted. In this case, we used Web Answer's Web site as an example, even though it is not the source for the text. Most authors use the blockquote tags to indent content, but its intended purpose is for quoted text.

2   **Save the changes to indenting.htm. Refresh the file in your browser.**

You see no difference in the display of the document in the browser. The cite attribute provides the source of information in the code only. In IE, the source code of the page loaded in the browser can be seen by choosing View>Source.

3   **Close indenting.htm in both applications.**

To Extend Your Knowledge . . .

JUSTIFY HEADINGS AND TEXT

If you set the align value to `align="justify"`, all lines except the last are stretched to fill the entire width of the page. The justify option has been deprecated in XHTML. (The justify alignment option has no effect on one-line headings.)

SUMMARY

In Chapter 1, you began your study of XHTML by exploring the use of hypertext documents and the evolution of XHTML from HTML. You learned how to create hypertext documents in a text editor and view your work in a Web browser.

You learned how the XHTML scripting language is comprised of a series of tags and how the use of tags is one of the key structural differences between XHTML and HTML. While learning some of the commonly used XHTML tags, you discovered that some tags offer attributes that further define how an element displays on a Web page.

KEY TERMS

Attributes

Attribute-value

Backward compatibility

Blockquotes

Browser

Cascading Style Sheets (CSS)

Characters

Closing tag

Container tag

Deprecated

Document tags

Document Type Definition (DTD)

Element

Empty tag

HTML

Hyper

Hypertext document

Meta data

Name-value pair

Nested tag

Opening tag

Scripting language

String

Syntax

Tag

Validation

Value

W3C

White space

XHTML (eXtensible Hypertext Markup Language)

XHTML Frameset

XHTML Strict

XHTML Transitional

XML (eXtensible Markup Language)

CHECKING CONCEPTS AND TERMS

MULTIPLE CHOICE

Circle the letter of the correct answer for each of the following questions.

1. A container tag _____.
   a. is an opening and closing tag, such as <p></p>, where the closing tag is required in the XHTML standard
   b. is an opening and closing tag, such as <p></p>, where the closing tag is not required in the XHTML standard

2. To create a paragraph on a Web page, use the following tag/s:
   a. <h1></h1>
   b.
   c. <p></p>
   d. <para></para>

3. When using an empty tag, you create a space between the command and the slash (/) to _____.
   a. make the command more readable
   b. ensure proper support with older browsers
   c. conform to the XHTML standard
   d. allow the use of an escape character

4. The align attribute for the <p> tag _____.
   a. has been deprecated in favor of style sheets
   b. was added to the XHTML standard as a new method of alignment
   c. only left- and right-aligns sections of text
   d. only center-aligns sections of text

5. Headings _____.

   a. are all at the same level of importance

   b. are only used to make text bold

   c. come in six different levels and make a Web page more readable

   d. indent sections of text

6. XHTML was designed to clean up sloppy HTML code and _____.

   a. conform to a standard to provide better support across applications

   b. become the crossover to XML applications

   c. make it easier to extend the language

   d. All of the above.

7. Document tags are required to create a valid XHTML document.

   a. True

   b. False

8. The <head></head> tags _____.

   a. contain information about the document, including the title and meta information

   b. enclose the body content

   c. create a new paragraph in your Web page

   d. enclose the first paragraph of content shown on the page

9. Line breaks force a break to the next line without creating a blank line between the sections of text.

   a. True

   b. False

10. What is the purpose of the Title tag?

   a. To provide a description of the document in the source file

   b. To provide the name of the person who wrote the document

   c. To provide the title of the document in the browser's Title bar

   d. To make the text appear in 36 point bold text

DISCUSSION QUESTIONS

1. What are some of the key differences between XHTML and HTML?

2. Why is it important to create standards for creating Web pages?

3. How did the browser wars influence the way Web pages were/are designed?

SKILL DRILL

Skill Drill exercises reinforce chapter skills. Each skill reinforced is the same as, or nearly the same as, a skill we presented in the chapter. Detailed instructions are provided in a step-by-step format. You should work through these exercises in order.

1. Create an XHTML Template

You are about to create a rather large Web site that consists of several documents. To save time and effort, you decide it would be best to create a template with HTML document tags.

1. Launch a text editor.

2. Type the following document tags in the text editor.

```
<html>
<head>
<title>Template</title>
</head>
<body>
</body>
</html>
```

FIGURE 1.23

3. Save the document as "template.htm" in your WIP_01 folder.

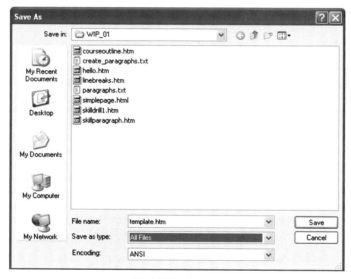

FIGURE 1.24

You can open this template and choose File>Save As each time you want to create a new HTML document.

4. Keep the file open for the next Skill Drill.

2. Create a Page from a Template

In this drill, you create a new Web page from the template you created in the previous exercise.

1. With template.htm open in the text editor, choose File>Save As.

2. Save your file as "skilldrill1.htm" in your WIP_01 folder.

3. Delete the word "Template" between the **<title></title>** tags, and replace it with "Page 1" (without the quotation marks).

4. Insert the words "Page 1 text" between the **<body>** and </body> tags.

5. Save your file and open it in your Web browser.

FIGURE 1.25

6. Close the file in your browser and text editor.

3. Align Paragraphs

Left-aligned text is the default alignment in a Web browser window. You can change the alignment to right or center. In this exercise, you center-align and left-align the paragraphs.

1. In your text editor, open skillparagraph.html from your WIP_01 folder.

2. Center-align both paragraphs, as follows:

```
<p align="center">

When you really come down to it, a Web page is just a text file
that refers to other files, such as images. The browser knows how
to interpret this file because it understands the system of tags
that describes the content. Each string of text is described by
tags, whether it represents a headline, an image, someone's name
rendered in bold or the overall body of content. Every page uses
a standard structure.

</p>
<p align="center">
```

```
Tags are the foundation of a Web page. They describe how items
should look and what they are. Tags tell the browser what to do
with specific pieces of information, and they define the structure
of a page.

</p>
```

3. Save the changes to skillparagraph.htm and open the file in your browser.

4. Return to the text editor and change the alignment value to left in the bottom paragraph, as follows:

```
<p align="center">

When you really come down to it, a Web page is just a text file
that refers to other files, such as images. The browser knows how
to interpret this file because it understands the system of tags
that describes the content. Each string of text is described by
tags, whether it represents a headline, an image, someone's name
rendered in bold or the overall body of content. Every page uses
a standard structure.

</p>
<p align="left">

Tags are the foundation of a Web page. They describe how items
should look and what they are. Tags tell the browser what to do
with specific pieces of information, and they define the structure
of a page.

</p>
```

5. Save the changes to the file in the text editor. Refresh the file in your browser.

   The bottom paragraph should now be left-aligned.

6. Leave the file open and continue to the next exercise.

4. Create Headings

Headings add visual structure to a document, allow for easier reading, and help to organize content. Headings are available in six levels, with h1 at the top of the hierarchy and h6 at the bottom. In this exercise, you add a main (h1) heading and a subheading.

1. In the open skillparagraph.htm in the text editor, position your cursor on the line below the **<body>** tag.

2. Press Enter/Return and then type the following:

```
<h1>Working with Hypertext</h1>
```

3. Position your cursor below the first closing </p> tag and press Enter/Return.

4.   Type the following:

```
<h2>Tags</h2>
```

5.   Save the changes to skillparagraph.htm. Refresh your browser to render the headings.

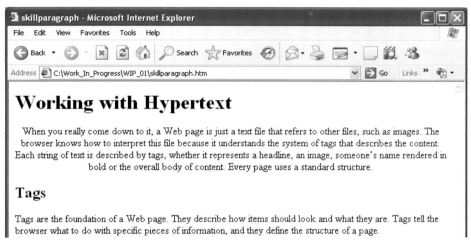

FIGURE 1.26

Adding headings makes it easier to read the document, and the content appears more organized.

6.   Leave the file open for the next exercise.

5. Indent Paragraphs of Text

Indenting sections of text can make a document easier to read. In this exercise, you indent both of the paragraphs in skilldrill1.htm.

1.   In the open skillparagraph.htm in the text editor, enclose both paragraph sections (exclude the headings) in blockquotes, as follows:

```
<blockquote>

<p align="center">

When you really come down to it, a Web page is just a text file
that refers to other files, such as images. The browser knows how
to interpret this file because it understands the system of tags
that describes the content. Each string of text is described by
tags, whether it represents a headline, an image, someone's name
rendered in bold or the overall body of content. Every page uses
a standard structure.

</p>

</blockquote>
```

```
<h2>Tags</h2>

<blockquote>

<p align="left">

Tags are the foundation of a Web page. They describe how items
should look and what they are. Tags tell the browser what to do
with specific pieces of information, and they define the structure
of a page.

</p>

</blockquote>
```

2. Save the changes to skillparagraph.htm. Refresh your browser and view the result.

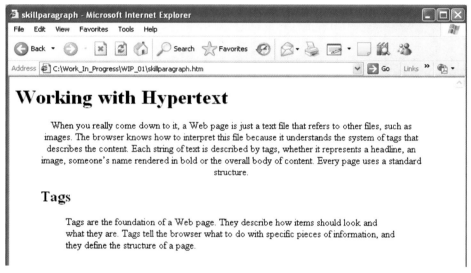

FIGURE 1.27

3. Switch back to the text editor. Remove the alignment on the paragraphs so they return to the default alignment (left) and are indented.

```
<blockquote>

<p>

When you really come down to it, a Web page is just a text file
that refers to other files, such as images. The browser knows how
to interpret this file because it understands the system of tags
that describes the content. Each string of text is described by
tags, whether it represents a headline, an image, someone's name
rendered in bold or the overall body of content. Every page uses
a standard structure.
```

```
</p>

</blockquote>

<h2>Tags</h2>

<blockquote>

<p>

Tags are the foundation of a Web page. They describe how items
should look and what they are. Tags tell the browser what to do
with specific pieces of information, and they define the structure
of a page.

</p>

</blockquote>
```

4. Save the changes in the text file and refresh the document in the browser.

5. Close the file in your text editor and browser.

C H A L L E N G E

Challenge exercises expand on, or are somewhat related to, skills presented in the lessons. Each exercise provides a brief introduction, followed by numbered-step instructions that are not as detailed as those in the Skill Drill exercises. You should work through these exercises in order.

1. Format a Document and Correct Nested Tags

You offered to format your instructor's course outline so it's easier to read. You decide to format the heading alignment. You know that tags must be nested correctly, so you correct the nesting in the document as well.

You might notice some unfamiliar tags in this exercise. You learn more about them later.

1. From your WIP_01 folder, open courseoutline.htm in a Web browser.

2. Open this file in your text editor. If your browser does not allow editing of the viewed source file, such as Firefox or Mac users, please open the file in your text editor.

3. Change the heading at the top of the page to a Level 2 heading (h2).

4. Scan through the document carefully. Note how the tags are nested. Correct the order of any nested tags that appear to be out of place.

5. Save your changes and display the document in the browser.

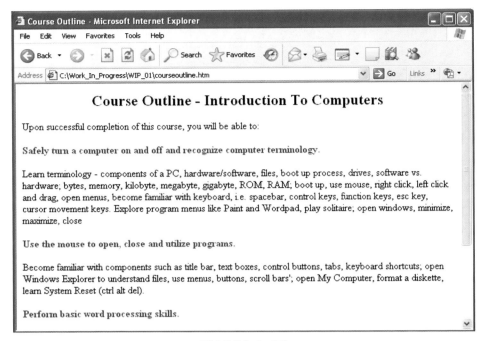

FIGURE 1.28

6. Keep the file open for the next exercise.

2. Use Line Breaks to Format an Outline

Now that the tags are nested correctly, and you applied a better heading size, you can use line breaks to group sections of text and apply additional formatting to enhance the outline.

1. In the open file, activate the text editor.

2. Blockquote the sections of text beneath each of the paragraphs (the sections of text enclosed by the `<p></p>` tags). Currently, no tags enclose these sections of text.

3. Cite each blockquoted section to the Web Answers URL (http://www.web-answers.com).

4. Center-align the paragraphs above the blockquoted text.

5. Underline the centered paragraphs of text using the `<u></u>` tags.

6. Save the changes to the source file (text file). Refresh the document in the browser to view the formatting.

7. Close the document in both applications.

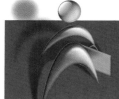

PORTFOLIO BUILDER

Create an Online Résumé

Résumé For You, Inc. hired you to create online samples of their résumé styles. Although they do not publish résumés online, they want to show the different layout styles they offer to as wide an audience as possible.

Your assignment is to work on two of the most popular résumé styles. Create two résumé examples using standard formatting tags. To complete this exercise, you should use the following information:

- Create a sketch on paper that illustrates the layout styles you are going to design.

- Use your name and contact information as the owner of the document. You can include your work experience and history, or you can invent the résumé content, perhaps choosing two different professions. Search the Web for samples of different types of résumés.

- The résumés must show formatting, including bolding, underlining, and italics. Include heading sizes, indentation, and text alignment. You can use your paper sketches to identify where to place the formatted elements before you begin the actual coding.

CHAPTER 2

Formatting Text and Lists

OBJECTIVES

In this chapter, you learn how to:

- Create basic text effects
- Change text color
- Work with different text sizes

- Apply font styles
- Create ordered and unordered lists
- Create definition lists

Why Would I Do This?

When HTML was first created, the intent was to define the nature of each section of text, such as a heading or a paragraph, and make that information computer-readable. The ability to control the appearance of the text (i.e., its presentation on the page) was an afterthought — one that has recently received significant attention. Consider this line of code as an example, where the `<h1>` tag is used to describe the content as a Level 1 headline.

```
<h1>Frogs from South America </h1>
```

FIGURE 2.1

It is important to note that this code does not tell the browser how to display the content of the tag. It simply describes the content of the enclosed text. This was really the intent of HTML and all markup languages — to describe the information.

When designers demanded more control over the appearance of Web pages, tags and attributes were added to the language. This was a poor solution, however, since HTML did not have the necessary functionality to fulfill this requirement. Therefore, the W3C later implemented new methods to separate content description from appearance, namely XHTML and CSS.

When Web designers reviewed the plans for XHTML, some were alarmed to discover that certain tags, such as underline (`<u>`) and strikethrough (`<s>`), were being eliminated. Many designers wondered how they were going to control the appearance of text on their Web pages without these and other related tags.

Tags determine the structure of the document, defining such items as the headers, individual paragraphs, and tables. *Style*, on the other hand, such as *font* color and size, must be handled separately; Cascading Style Sheets were designed to do just that.

In this chapter, you learn how to format text with XHTML Transitional. Later in the book, you explore other methods of achieving the same effect.

VISUAL SUMMARY

Formatting tags allow you to change the *default* appearance of the text that displays in a Web browser. A default is the assumed value when no other value is provided. Default text usually displays in a Web browser as 12-point, black, Times New Roman unless the default settings have been changed in the browser.

Web designers can use a variety of formatting tags to change the appearance of default text. As mentioned earlier, some of these formatting tags have been deprecated in favor of CSS. Consider the following examples. Figure 2.2 shows how text displays in a browser without any formatting. Figure 2.3 shows the same Web page after formatting tags were applied.

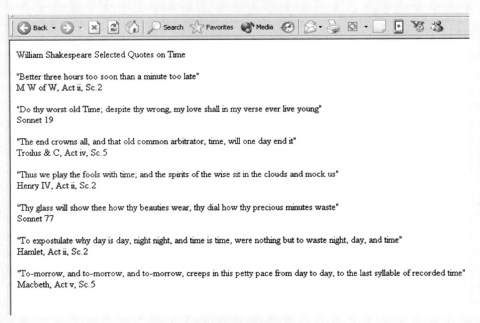

FIGURE 2.2

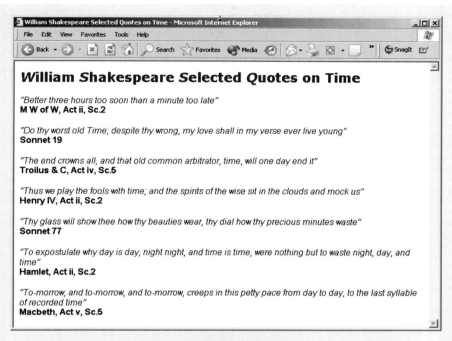

FIGURE 2.3

The preceding illustration demonstrates how text is rendered when formatting tags are applied. Some tags emphasize the text (bold and italics), while others change the appearance of text (color and size). We discuss several formatting tags in this chapter.

LESSON 1 Basic Text Effects

The XHTML 1.0 standard includes several methods to change the typographic settings of the text on Web pages. You can change the typeface, color, text effects, and size. ***Typeface*** refers to the name of the font, such as Arial, Times, or Helvetica.

You can choose from three basic text effects when using XHTML Transitional, much the same as you would in a word processor. The three basic effects are:

- **<b></b>** applies boldface type
- **<i></i>** applies italic type
- **<u></u>** underlines the type</ul>

The following illustration demonstrates how the **<b>**, **<u>**, and **<i>** tags render text in a Web browser.

FIGURE 2.4

The underline (**<u></u>**) tags were not well supported by many browsers when they were introduced in the HTML 3.2 standard. They have since been deprecated in the HTML 4.01 reference. The deprecated **<u></u>** tags are accepted in XHTML Transitional but not in XHTML Strict. Keep in mind that underlined text could be mistaken for a hyperlink, as viewers have grown accustomed to associating underlined text with hyperlinks.

At times, you may want to draw attention to important points within your text. Boldfaced text allows you to do so. Italics are often used for single-word emphasis. There are more advanced text effects you can create using CSS.

To Extend Your Knowledge . . .

In Chapter 1, the example code was very simple. In Chapters 2–8, however, the example code is longer and more complex. Rather than include every line of code in the exercises in Chapters 2–8, we use ellipses (. . .) to indicate where we truncated the code. We show you three or more lines of code before and after each section of code that you should modify in the step. This ensures that you place the new code in the correct location within the script.

Apply Basic Formatting to a Web Page

1 **In your text editor, open basic_formatting.htm from your RF_XHTML_L1>Chapter_02 folder.**

The basic_formatting.htm file displays in the text editor window. Notice the existing content and tags. You work with this document in the next several exercises.

For the remainder of the book, rather than include the complete path of RF_XHTML_L1> Chapter_0x folder, we simply refer to the Chapter_02 folder, Chapter_03 folder, and so forth.

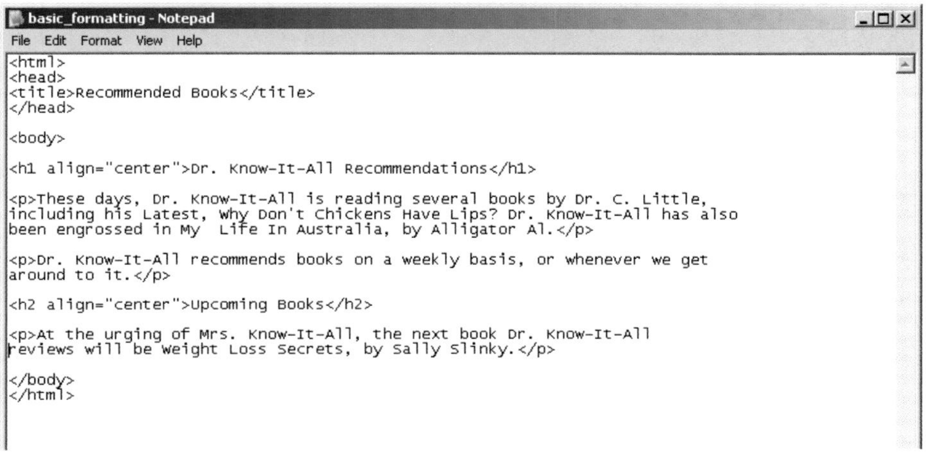

```
basic_formatting - Notepad
File  Edit  Format  View  Help
<html>
<head>
<title>Recommended Books</title>
</head>

<body>

<h1 align="center">Dr. Know-It-All Recommendations</h1>

<p>These days, Dr. Know-It-All is reading several books by Dr. C. Little,
including his Latest, Why Don't Chickens Have Lips? Dr. Know-It-All has also
been engrossed in My  Life In Australia, by Alligator Al.</p>

<p>Dr. Know-It-All recommends books on a weekly basis, or whenever we get
around to it.</p>

<h2 align="center">Upcoming Books</h2>

<p>At the urging of Mrs. Know-It-All, the next book Dr. Know-It-All
reviews will be Weight Loss Secrets, by Sally Slinky.</p>

</body>
</html>
```

FIGURE 2.5

2 **Change the text in basic_formatting.htm by underlining, bolding, and italicizing parts of the content as follows:**

. . .

```
<h1 align="center">Dr. Know-It-All Recommendations</h1>

<p>These days, <b> Dr. Know-It-All</b> is reading several books by
<b> Dr. C. Little</b>, including his Latest, <i> Why Don't
Chickens Have Lips?</i> <b>Dr. Know-It-All</b> has also been
engrossed in <i>My Life In Australia</i>, by <b> Alligator
Al</b>.</p>

<p><b>Dr. Know-It-All </b> recommends books on a <u> weekly
basis</u>, or whenever we get around to it.</p>

<h2 align="center">Upcoming Books</h2>

<p>At the urging of <b>Mrs. Know-It-All</b>, the next book <b>
Dr. Know-It-All</b> reviews will be <i>Weight Loss Secrets</i>,
by <b>Sally Slinky</b>.</p>
```

. . .

This applies the effects to selected text. It enhances the display of the document when viewed in a browser.

3   Choose File>Save As from your text editor. Save the document in your WIP_02 folder as "basic_formatting.htm".

This creates a new version of the file in your WIP_02 folder.

4   Launch your Web browser. Navigate to the WIP_02 folder. Double-click basic_formatting.htm.

Basic_formatting.htm displays in your browser with the new text effects you applied. You can begin to see how you can subtly (or dramatically) change the appearance of your Web pages by adding text effects.

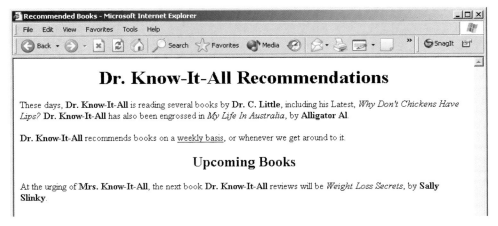

FIGURE 2.6

5   Close the file in your text editor and browser.

To Extend Your Knowledge . . .

ELIMINATION OF THE <B>, <U>, AND <I> TAGS

Users who are familiar with HTML might realize that there is a relatively small transition from HTML 4.x to XHTML Transitional. This is not the case with XHTML 2.0, however, which represents a significant divergence from HTML 4.x.

The <b>, <u>, and <i> tags have been completely dropped in XHTML 2.0. The <strong> tag is expected to replace the <b> tag; style sheets offer another possible replacement for the <b> tag. The <u> tag currently has no replacement tag. The <em> tag will replace the <i> tag.

The <strong> and <em> tags are considered structural tags rather than presentational tags and were included in the original HTML standard.

LESSON 2 Changing Font Color

You can change text color with the **`<font></font>`** container tags and with the **`color=""`** attribute (adding a value between the quotes). Please note that the **`<font>`** container tag is not a stand-alone tag. It requires one or more attributes to change the appearance of text.

Let's explore the **`color=""`** attribute. You can choose from two options when changing the color of text with the **`<font color=""></font>`** tags. The first option is to use one of the 16 color names that are universal across Web browsers. Four of those color names are listed here:

- `<font color="red">Red Text</font>`
- `<font color="green">Green Text</font>`
- `<font color="purple">Purple Text</font>`
- `<font color="blue">Blue Text</font>`

Figure 2.7 illustrates how the preceding code changes text color in a Web browser.

FIGURE 2.7

The 16 color names are defined in Figure 2.8.

Color Name:	Hex Number:	Color Name:	Hex Number:
Black	#000000	Green	#008000
Silver	#C0C0C0	Lime	#00FF00
Gray	#808080	Olive	#808000
White	#FFFFFF	Yellow	#FFFF00
Maroon	#800000	Navy	#000080
Red	#FF0000	Blue	#0000FF
Purple	#800080	Teal	#008080
Fuschia	#FF00FF	Aqua	#00FFFF

FIGURE 2.8

Although all browsers allow you to use these color names, they are inconsistently implemented and should be used with caution. In the preceding chart, notice how a code is listed for each color, such as "#FFFFFF" for white. These are hexadecimal numbers. A **_hexadecimal number_** is a number where each digit can represent a number between 1 and 16. Computer programmers use hexadecimal numbers because they are easier to write than zeros and ones to describe how individual memory bits are stored.

Hexadecimal color codes are written in a form describing the amount of red, green, and blue. For example, if we take the code "#FFCC00", the "FF" represents the amount of red, the "CC" represents the amount of green, and the "00" represents the amount of blue.

In other words, a hexadecimal color code is a six-character figure, such as "RRGGBB". It is an alternate value for a color name. For example, `<font color="#008000">` produces the color green on a Web page. The advantage of this method is that in addition to using the 16 color names, you have access to many more color choices.

Hexadecimal color codes allow greater consistency than color names when Web pages are viewed on different browsers in different operating systems. For this reason, it is recommended that Web designers use hexadecimal color codes instead of color names. Since Web designers will occasionally see color names used, this chapter includes them in the discussion.

In the Chapter_02 folder is a file named color.htm. It lists all the hexadecimal codes and their respective colors, as shown in Figure 2.9.

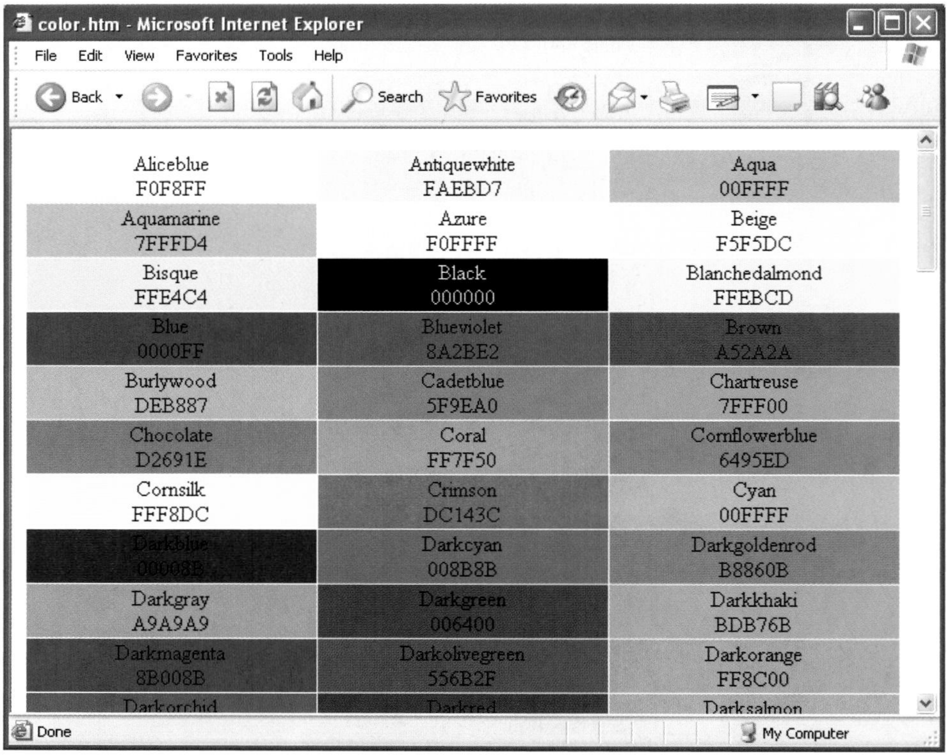

FIGURE 2.9

Change Font Color

1   In your text editor and browser, open color_formatting.htm from your Chapter_02 folder.

2   Save your file under the same filename in your Work_In_Progress>WIP_02 folder.

3   Change the color of the text in the document by adding the `<font color="">` tags to the sections of text as follows:

```
. . .

<h1 align="center"><font color="maroon">Dr. Know-It-All
Recommendations</font></h1>

<p><font color="#808080">These days, <b>Dr. Know-It-All</b> is
reading several books by<b> Dr. C. Little</b>, including his
Latest, <i>Why Don't Chickens Have Lips?</i> <b>Dr. Know-It-All
</b>has also been engrossed in <i>My Life In Australia</i>, by
<b>Alligator Al</b></font></p>

<p><font color="#808080"><b>Dr. Know-It-All </b>recommends books
on a <u>weekly basis</u>, or whenever we get around to
it.</font></p>

<h2 align="center"><font color="maroon">Upcoming
Books</font></h2>

<p><font color="#808080">At the urging of <b>Mrs. Know-It-
All</b>, the next book <b>Dr. Know-It-All</b> reviews will be
<i>Weight Loss Secrets</i>, by <b>Sally Slinky</b>.</font></p>

. . .
```

Notice that you used the color name value for the headings and the hexadecimal value for the paragraphs. You can use either method interchangeably. The "#" is required in the XHTML Transitional standard, but it is not required in HTML. Remember to always include the quotes around the value.

4   **Save the changes to the file. Refresh the document in your browser.**

The document reflects the color changes you applied to the text. Use the colors in the color.htm chart in the Chapter_02 folder to ensure that the color displays as intended across browsers. Avoid using custom colors, because they might not render as desired on other machines/platforms.

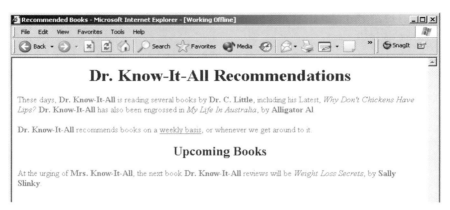

FIGURE 2.10

5   **Close the file in your text editor and browser.**

To Extend Your Knowledge . . .

FONT ISSUES

A lot of controversy surrounds the use of the `<font>` tag when creating Web pages. Some browsers provide poor support for the `<font>` tag. In addition to restrictions on using the `<font>` tag, remember that it has been deprecated since HTML 4.0. Nonetheless, if you do use the `<font>` tag, most browsers still support it, providing you follow the rules outlined in this book. If you want to comply with the XHTML standards, however, you should create your pages using XHTML Transitional.

LESSON 3 Changing Font Size

You can use the `size=""` attribute to change the size of your font. The `size=""` attribute can range from `size="1"` to `size="7"`, with 1 being the smallest and 7 being the largest. The default setting for text size in most browsers is 3. The size system for using the font tag is based on the assumption that the user's browser has not been changed from the default setting. If the user changes the setting on his browser, a Web page might not display as intended.

Using absolute values of the **size=""** attribute (**<font size="1">**) can be risky. Assigning relative values is often a better choice if you decide to use XHTML to change the size of text on your Web page. For instance, assigning the relative value of **<font size="+1">** or **<font size="-1">** produces more predicable results than assigning the absolute value of **<font size="1">** or **<font size="7">**. The "+" indicates by how many values of size you want to increase the default font size (which in most cases is 3). For instance, **<font size="+2">** increases the font size to 5, whereas **<font size="-2">** decreases the font size to 1.

As you gain experience, you will begin to use CSS for formatting and XHTML for content display. CSS provides excellent control over the display of your documents and produces predictable results across platforms.

Change the Font Size

1   **In your text editor, open size_formatting.htm from your Chapter_02 folder.**

2   **Save the file in your Work_In_Progress>WIP_02 folder.**

3   **Change the font size in the paragraphs to 4, as follows:**

. . .

```
<p><font color="#808080" size="4">These days, <b>Dr. Know-It-
All</b> is reading several books by<b> Dr. C. Little</b>, including
his Latest, <i>Why Don't Chickens Have Lips?</i> <b>Dr. Know-It-All
</b>has also been engrossed in <i>My Life In Australia</i>, by
<b>Alligator Al</b>.</font></p>

<p><font color="#808080" size="4"><b>Dr. Know-It-All </b>recom-
mends books on a <u>weekly basis</u>, or whenever we get around
to it.</font></p>

<h2 align="center"><font color="maroon">Upcoming Books</font></h2>

<p><font color="#808080" size="4">At the urging of <b>Mrs. Know-
It-All</b>, the next book <b>Dr. Know-It-All</b> reviews will be
<i>Weight Loss Secrets</i>, by <b>Sally Slinky</b>.</font></p>
```

. . .

Additional attributes can be included in the same tag. Notice that you simply added a space and the attribute **size="4"** to the existing **<font color="">** opening tag. This increases the text size to 4 in the browser window.

? If you have problems

When using a word processor, text size usually changes in increments of 2, starting at 8, then 10, 12, 14, and so on. In XHTML, standard text size starts at 1, which is typically the same as 8 in a word processor, and increases in increments of 1.

---

4   **Save the changes to size_formatting.htm. Open the document in your browser and view the result.**

The paragraph text displays one size larger in the browser. This is based on the default setting of most browsers. Some users may see a larger change or no change, depending on their current browser settings.

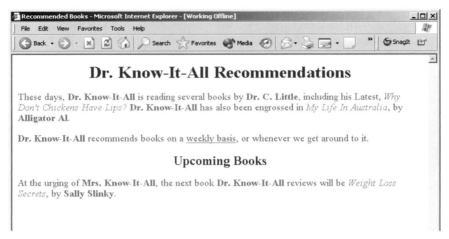

FIGURE 2.11

5   **Close the file in your text editor and browser.**

LESSON 4   Changing the Font Style

You can use the **face=""** attribute to change the typeface from the default, which is Times New Roman on Windows-based systems, and Times on a Macintosh. You can set the typeface to any valid font style that is installed on your computer. In practical use, however, only three styles are more or less guaranteed to be displayed on every computer: Courier, Times, and Helvetica.

When choosing a typeface for your text, keep in mind that while you have this typeface on your machine, your viewers may not have it on their computers. Make sure the appearance of your text is acceptable in the default system font, as well as any other font you choose. If a viewer does not have the specified font installed on her machine, the page displays in a different font; this could significantly alter the appearance of your Web page on the viewer's screen.

You can specify alternate font faces by adding commas between font names. For example, **<font face="Helvetica, Verdana, Arial">** tells the computer that when Helvetica is not available, it should display Verdana. When both Helvetica and Verdana are not supported, it should display Arial. The browser displays the default font when no matching font can be found.

Change the Font Face

1 In your text editor, open font_formatting.htm from your Chapter_02 folder.

2 Save the file as font_formatting.htm in your Work_In_Progress>WIP_02 folder.

3 Add the attribute `face="arial"` to the `<font>` tag containing the heading, as follows:

```
. . .

<p><font color="#808080" size="4">These days, <b>Dr. Know-It-
All</b> is reading several books by<b> Dr. C. Little</b>,
including his Latest, <i>Why Don't Chickens Have Lips?</i> <b>Dr.
Know-It-All </b>has also been engrossed in <i>My Life In
Australia</i>, by <b>Alligator Al</b>.</font></p>

<p><font color="#808080" size="4"><b>Dr. Know-It-All
</b>recommends books on a <u>weekly basis</u>, or whenever
we get around to it.</font></p>

<h2 align="center"> <font color="maroon" face="arial">Upcoming
Books</font></h2>

<p><font color="#808080" size="4">At the urging of <b>Mrs. Know-
It-All</b>, the next book <b>Dr. Know-It-All</b> reviews will be
<i>Weight Loss Secrets</i>, by <b>Sally Slinky</b>.</font></p>

. . .
```

This instructs the browser to change the font from the default typeface to Arial. Arial may already be the default font on your computer.

4 Save the changes in the text file and open the document in the browser.

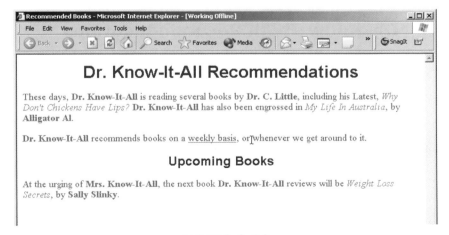

FIGURE 2.12

5 Switch back to the file in the text editor. Add comma-separated typeface styles to the heading, as follows:

```
. . .

<p><font color="#808080" size="4">These days, <b>Dr. Know-It-
All</b> is reading several books by<b> Dr. C. Little</b>,
including his Latest, <i>Why Don't Chickens Have Lips?</i> <b>Dr.
Know-It-All </b>has also been engrossed in <i>My Life In
Australia</i>, by <b>Alligator Al</b>.</font></p>

<p><font color="#808080" size="4"><b>Dr. Know-It-All
</b>recommends books on a <u>weekly basis</u>, or whenever
we get around to it.</font></p>

<h2 align="center"><font color="maroon" face="verdana, arial,
helvetica"> Upcoming Books</font></h2>

<p><font color="#808080" size="4">At the urging of <b>Mrs. Know-
It-All</b>, the next book <b>Dr. Know-It-All</b> reviews will be
<i>Weight Loss Secrets</i>, by <b>Sally Slinky</b>.</font></p>

. . .
```

This provides three options for font support. You can use any typeface you prefer, but remember that the more rare the typeface, the less likely the end user has it installed on his machine.

6 Save the changes. Refresh the document in your Web browser and view the result.

In this case, the text displays in Verdana (which is similar to Arial) since the font is installed on the computer.

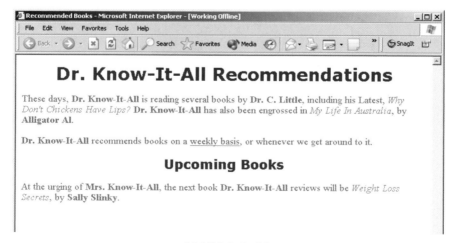

FIGURE 2.13

7 Close the file in your browser and text editor.

To Extend Your Knowledge . . .

WHY NOT XHTML 2.0 NOW?

Even though XHTML 2.0 is not currently supported by any of the major browsers, it is important to understand how the new standard will affect the Web. XHTML 2.0 offers many advantages to developers, but until browser-makers release browsers that support the new standard—and a critical mass of viewers use those browsers—XHTML Transitional will remain in effect. Learning about XHTML 2.0 now, however, will ease the transition from the old standard to the new.

LESSON 5 Formatting the Body

You can add attributes to the **\<body>** tag to format the body text. Body attributes are used to assign colors to the ***foreground*** (text), the ***background*** (the canvas of your Web page), and to unvisited, active, and visited links. You can use the **text=""** attribute to change the default text color, and you can use the **bgcolor=""** attribute to change the background color.

For instance, to change the text color throughout the Web page, you would apply the following tags:

\<body text="blue"> or \<body text="#3399cc">

To change the solid background color on the page, you would apply:

\<body bgcolor="blue"> or \<body bgcolor="#3399CC">

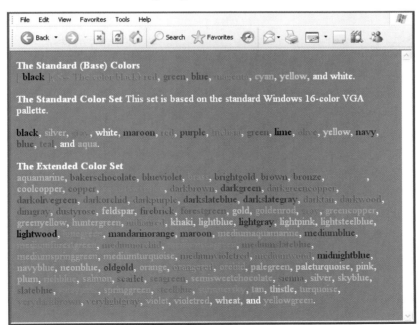

FIGURE 2.14

Figure 2.14 illustrates a blue background with text of various colors in the foreground. You can find this Web page (color_example_background.htm) in the Chapter_02 folder.

Format the Body of a Web Page

1   In your text editor, open body_formatting.htm from your Chapter_02 folder.

2   Save the file in your Work_In_Progress>WIP_02 folder.

3   Open the file in your browser.

With the exception of the headings, most of the text displays in the default color (black) since no color has been specified.

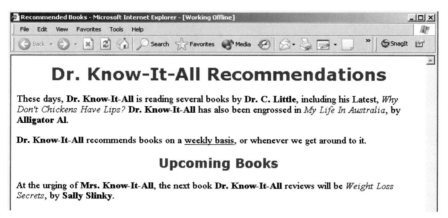

FIGURE 2.15

4   Switch back to the text editor window and add `text="#006699"` to the `<body>` tag, as follows:

```
<body text="#006699">
```

This globally changes the color of text that does not have local instructions applied through a **`<font>`** tag.

5 Save the changes to the file. Refresh the document in the browser and view the result.

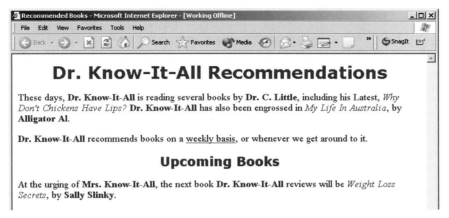

FIGURE 2.16

6 Switch back to the text editor window and apply the attribute `bgcolor="#ffffcc"` to the `<body>` tag.

```
<body text="#006699" bgcolor="#ffffcc">
```

The Web page background color changes to light yellow. Even if you decide to leave the Web page background color white, you should still define the hexadecimal code for white (`bgcolor="#ffffff"`) in the body tag. Some browsers display a default gray background unless you specify the `bgcolor=""` attribute.

7 Save the changes to the file. Refresh the document in the browser and view the result.

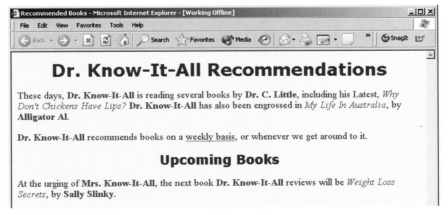

FIGURE 2.17

8   **Close the file in your text editor and browser.**

To Extend Your Knowledge . . .

MORE FONT ISSUES

Even though they are still widely supported, body attributes have been deprecated in favor of style sheets. As long as you conform to the XHTML Transitional standard, however, you can still use the body attributes. In fact, when you become more familiar with Cascading Style Sheets, we suggest you use both CSS and XHTML Transitional to ensure you comply with both older and newer Web browsers.

In the XHTML 2.0 draft, the font tag is replaced with a CSS equivalent.

LESSON 6   Creating Unordered Lists

A *list* is a collection of items. Those items can be either ordered or unordered. You can apply attributes to the list tags to control how the *list items* are presented on the Web page. An *unordered list* is not numbered; it contains items preceded by bullets in the shape of small filled circles (the default shape), solid squares, or open circles. You can use the `<ul></ul>` container tags to create an unordered list, as follows:

```
<ul>
<li>List Item 1</li>
<li>List Item 2</li>
<li>List Item 3</li>
<li>List Item 4</li>
<li>List Item 5</li>
</ul>
```

The preceding code creates the following list in a browser:

FIGURE 2.18

You can change the default bullet type of an unordered list (**<ul type="circle">**) by adding the **type=""** attribute to the **<ul>** tag. You can choose from the following values:

- **Disc** creates a bullet in the shape of a disc.

- **Square** creates a bullet in the shape of a square.

- **Circle** creates a bullet in the shape of a circle.

FIGURE 2.19

The **<li></li>** tags designate list items. You must use the **<li>** tags in conjunction with the **<ul>** tags to create an unordered list. By default, each list item appears on a separate line, so there is no need to insert line breaks as you advance from one list item to the next.

Create an Unordered List

1 **In the text editor, open casserole.htm from your Chapter_02 folder.**

The file displays with existing content and tags. Notice that the **
** tag is used in two of the paragraphs in the file.

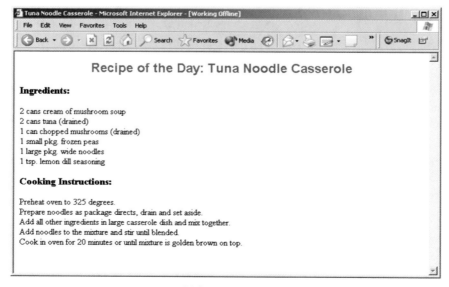

```
casserole - Notepad
File  Edit  Format  View  Help
<title>Tuna Noodle Casserole</title>
</head>

<body>

<h2 align="center">
<font face="Arial" color="#008000">Recipe of the Day: Tuna Noodle Casserole</font>
</h2>

<h3>
Ingredients:
</h3>

<p>
2 cans cream of mushroom soup<br />
2 cans tuna (drained)<br />
1 can chopped mushrooms (drained)<br />
1 small pkg. frozen peas<br />
1 large pkg. wide noodles <br />
1 tsp. lemon dill seasoning
</p>

<h3>
Cooking Instructions:
</h3>

<p>
Preheat oven to 325 degrees.<br />
Prepare noodles as package directs, drain and set aside.<br />
Add all other ingredients in large casserole dish and mix together.<br />
Add noodles to the mixture and stir until blended.<br />
Cook in oven for 20 minutes or until mixture is golden brown on top.
</p>

</body>
</html>
```

FIGURE 2.20

2   **Open casserole.htm in your Web browser and view the document.**

The document displays with limited formatting. Even though the items on the page are relatively easy to read, XHTML lists would provide better organization and presentation.

Tuna Noodle Casserole - Microsoft Internet Explorer - [Working Offline]
File   Edit   View   Favorites   Tools   Help

Back · · · · Search · Favorites · Media · · · · · · · · SnagIt

Recipe of the Day: Tuna Noodle Casserole

Ingredients:

2 cans cream of mushroom soup
2 cans tuna (drained)
1 can chopped mushrooms (drained)
1 small pkg. frozen peas
1 large pkg. wide noodles
1 tsp. lemon dill seasoning

Cooking Instructions:

Preheat oven to 325 degrees.
Prepare noodles as package directs, drain and set aside.
Add all other ingredients in large casserole dish and mix together.
Add noodles to the mixture and stir until blended.
Cook in oven for 20 minutes or until mixture is golden brown on top.

FIGURE 2.21

3   **Switch back to casserole.htm in the text editor. In the first paragraph section, remove the `<p>` tags and the `<br />` tags and replace them as follows:**

```
. . .
<h3>Ingredients:</h3>
<ul>
<li>2 cans cream of mushroom soup</li>
<li>2 cans tuna (drained)</li>
<li>1 can chopped mushrooms (drained)</li>
<li>1 small pkg. frozen peas</li>
<li>1 large pkg. wide noodles</li>
<li>1 tsp. lemon dill seasoning</li>
</ul>
. . .
```

This creates a bulleted (unordered) list of the items. You can change the default bullet format by using the `type=""` attribute.

4   **Save your changes. Refresh the document in your Web browser and view the result.**

An unordered bulleted list is designed to list items in random order. This list of ingredients requires no step-by-step instruction, so a bulleted list serves the purpose well.

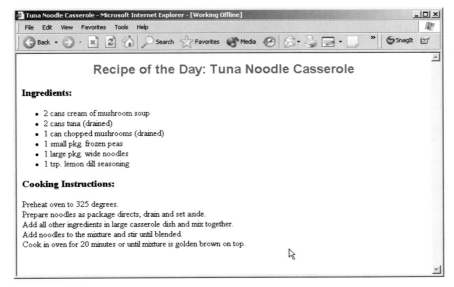

FIGURE 2.22

5 Leave the file open for the next exercise.

LESSON 7 Creating Ordered Lists

Ordered lists (numbered lists) contain items that must be listed in a particular order. You create an ordered list with the **<ol></ol>** container tags. You must use the **<li>** tags in conjunction with the **<ol>** tags to create an ordered list. You can use traditional Arabic numerals, Roman numerals, or letters to identify each item.

Figure 2.23 illustrates the default Arabic numeral display of an ordered list. Figure 2.24 demonstrates the uppercase-letter style.

 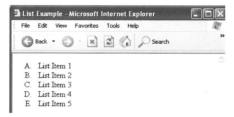

FIGURE 2.23   **FIGURE 2.24**

Available types for ordered lists include:

1 Arabic Numerals (default)

A Uppercase letters   **a** Lowercase letters

I Uppercase Roman numerals   **i** Lowercase Roman numerals

Create an Ordered List

1 In the open casserole.htm, switch to the text editor. Remove the **<p>** tags and the **
** tags from the last paragraph. Replace the tags as follows:

```
. . .

<h3>Cooking Instructions:</h3>
<ol>
<li>Preheat oven to 325 degrees.</li>
<li>Prepare noodles as package directs, drain and set aside.</li>
<li>Add all other ingredients in large casserole dish and mix
together.</li>
<li>Add noodles to the mixture and stir until blended.</li>
<li>Cook in oven for 20 minutes or until mixture is golden brown
on top. </li>
</ol>

. . .
```

This creates a numbered list of the items. You can change the default number style by using the `type=""` attribute. For example, the `type="I"` attribute changes the default number list to upper-case Roman numerals.

2   **Save your changes. Refresh the document in your Web browser and view the result.**

The Cooking Instructions section displays as a numbered list. This type of list is appropriate because the reader is following step-by-step instructions.

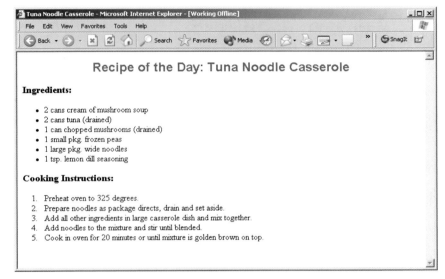

FIGURE 2.25

3   **Close the file in both applications.**

LESSON 8   Creating Definition Lists

Definition lists are slightly different from other lists because they contain a term and its definition. This type of list is most useful for FAQs or defining terms on a Web page. Definition lists are comprised of the following elements: `<dl>` (begin definition list), `<dt>` (definition term), `<dd>` (definition), and their corresponding closing tags. Below is an example of a definition list:

```
<dl>
    <dt>Geek</dt>
    <dd> A person who is single-minded or accomplished in scientific or
    technical pursuits but is felt to be socially inept. </dd>
    <dt>Hacker</dt>
    <dd>a clever programmer.</dd>
</dl>
```

The preceding code displays in a browser, as follows:

FIGURE 2.26

Create a Definition List

1 In your text editor, open definition.htm from your RF_XHTML_L1 folder.

2 Create a definition list as follows:

```
<html>
<head>
<title>My Definition Page</title>
</head>
<body>
<h3>Hypertext Definitions</h3>
<dl>
<dt>XHTML</dt>

<dd>eXtensible Hypertext Markup Language. A scripting language
used to create hypertext documents for the Web.</dd>

<dt>URL</dt>

<dd>Universal Resource Locator. A Web address, or file path to a
file on the World Wide Web.</dd>

</dl>
</body>
</html>
```

This creates a definition list.

3 **Save the document as "definition.htm" in your Work_In_Progress>WIP_02 folder. Open the document in a Web browser.**

The definition list displays in the browser window. The term displays above the definition, which is indented slightly to allow for easy reading.

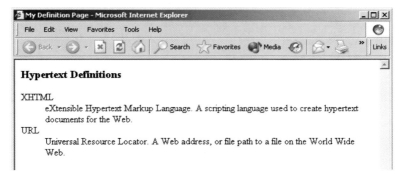

FIGURE 2.27

4 **Switch to the text editor. Apply bold formatting to the terms.**

You can format any part of the definition list, but the most popular element to format is the term itself. This creates contrast between the term and its definition.

```
<html>
<head>
<title>My Definition Page</title>
</head>
<body>
<h3>Hypertext Definitions</h3>
<dl>
<dt><b>XHTML</b></dt>

<dd>eXtensible Hypertext Markup Language. A scripting language
used to create hypertext documents for the Web.</dd>

<dt><b>URL</b></dt>

<dd>Universal Resource Locator. A Web address, or file path to a
file on the World Wide Web.</dd>

</dl>
</body>
</html>
```

5	**Save the changes and refresh the document in the browser.**

The terms display in boldface type.

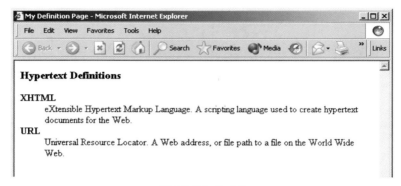

FIGURE 2.28

6	**Close the file in both applications.**

To Extend Your Knowledge . . .

XHTML 2.0 NAVIGATION LISTS

To date, Web designers have built navigation lists from virtually any element or script. XHTML 2.0 includes a new kind of list, represented by the `<nl>` element. The XHTML 2.0 draft states that navigation lists are "intended to define collections of selectable items for presentation."

In an XHTML 2.0 document, a navigation list would resemble the following:

```
<nl>
 <name>Title Number 1</name>
 <li href="#link">List Item</li>
 <li>
     <nl>
       <name> Title Number 2</name>
       <li href="#link">List Item</li>
       <li href="#link">List Item</li>
     </nl>
 </li>
</nl>
```

SUMMARY

In this chapter, you learned that in addition to structural tags, HTML offers presentational tags. Even though the presentational tags have been deprecated in the HTML 4.01 standard in favor of Cascading Style Sheets, you can still use them in XHTML Transitional. Using the basic text effect tags, you can apply bolding, underlining, and italics to Web page content. This allows you to draw the viewer's attention to key points in your text.

You also learned how to make aesthetic changes to your text, such as how to change the text color, size, and typeface. You discovered that some of the formatting features, such as color values, include multiple options.

You discovered that lists provide an excellent way to display key points of information. You learned how to create ordered lists to present information in a step-by-step manner, unordered lists to present information in a random order, and definition lists to present a term and its associated definition.

CAREERS IN DESIGN

BASICS FOR WEB PAGE DESIGNERS

You can choose from a number of exciting job categories within the Web-publishing industry. Depending on the diversity of your skill set, you may be able to apply your talents in many different areas. When considering a career in Web publishing, you need to be familiar with the following general skills.

Programming. If you are going to enter a career in Web site design/development, you must know how to program in XHTML. It might be useful to learn an advanced programming language, such as Perl, PHP, ColdFusion, and/or ASP. Knowing how to use JavaScript is an excellent skill as well.

Graphic Design. You should also be able to use a graphics program, such as Photoshop or Fireworks, even if you only use the program for basic techniques such as cropping an image or saving it as a particular format for the Web.

Design and Layout. In order to create professional-looking Web pages, it is essential that you understand the basic design principles and methodologies for Web design. These methodologies include design considerations for a variety of platforms, how to apply color effectively, how to develop effective copy, and other valuable visual techniques.

Webmaster. It is useful to possess a general understanding of how a Web server operates, even if you have no desire to become a full-blown Webmaster. To enhance your effectiveness as a Web site designer/developer, you should know what happens to a file when you upload it to the server, how to manage files, and be familiar with some of the technology behind the Web server — at the very least.

KEY TERMS

Background

Default

Definition list

DTD

Font

Foreground

Global settings

Hexadecimal color code

Hexadecimal number

List

List item

Local settings

Ordered list

Style

Typeface

Unordered list

CHECKING CONCEPTS AND TERMS

MULTIPLE CHOICE

Circle the letter of the correct answer for each of the following questions.

1. Which of the following tags is not widely supported?

  a. <b> tag

  b. <i> tag

  c. <u> tag

  d. None of the above

2. The **<font>** tag is not a stand-alone tag. In order for the tag to affect text, you must use an attribute with it.

  a. True

  b. False

3. The **<font>** tag offers three formatting attributes. They are _____.

  a. align, type, and color

  b. color, face, and size

  c. color, size, and height

4. You can use hexadecimal numbers (codes) and color names when selecting a color for text.

  a. True

  b. False

5. The **<font>** tag has been deprecated in favor of equivalent capabilities in _____.

  a. XML

  b. CSS

  c. JavaScript

  d. None of the above

6. Using the Times, Helvetica, or Courier typeface ensures that the font style displays as intended on most machines.

  a. True

  b. False

7. Ordered lists _____.

  a. provide a step-by-step numbered list of items

  b. provide two options of bullet styles

  c. are not part of XHTML

  d. are designed to display names and definitions

8. Unordered lists _____.

    a. are bulleted lists that use a standard black dot next to each list item

    b. allow you to change the bullet list style with the type="" attribute

    c. present a term and its definition

    d. are not part of XHTML

9. Definition lists consist of two parts: a term and its description.

    a. True

    b. False

10. XHTML 2.0 suggests that the presentational tags, including `<b>`, `<u>`, and `<i>`, should be eliminated.

    a. True

    b. False

DISCUSSION QUESTIONS

1. Why were most of the formatting tags deprecated in XHTML 2.0?

2. When would it be beneficial to use the `<font>` tag, and why?

3. Why would it be wise to apply both Cascading Style Sheets and the `<font>` tag to text on your Web pages?

SKILL DRILL

Skill Drill exercises reinforce chapter skills. Each skill reinforced is the same as, or nearly the same as, a skill we presented in the chapter. We provide detailed instructions in a step-by-step format. You should work through these exercises in order.

1. Add Basic Text Effects to an Existing Web Page

Your task is to create a Web page for a community program that offers free courses to the citizens of Pembroke, Florida.

1. Copy course.htm from your Chapter_02 folder to your WIP_02 folder.

2. Open course.htm in a text editor and a browser.

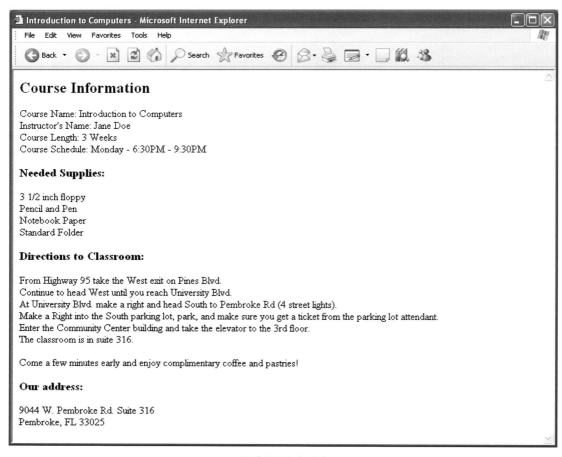

FIGURE 2.29

3. Add basic text effects to course.htm in the text editor, as follows:

```
. . .
<h2>Course Information</h2>
<p>
<b>Course Name:</b> Introduction to Computers<br />
<b>Instructor's Name: </b>Jane Doe<br />
<b>Course Length: </b>3 Weeks<br />
<b>Course Schedule:</b> Monday - 6:30PM - 9:30PM
</p>
<h3>Needed Supplies:</h3>
<p>
3 1/2 inch floppy<br />
Pencil and Pen<br />
Notebook Paper<br />
Standard Folder
</p>
```

```
<h3>Directions to Classroom:</h3>
<p>
From Highway 95 take the West exit on Pines Blvd. <br />
Continue to head West until you reach University Blvd.<br />
At University Blvd. make a right and head South to Pembroke Rd
(4 street lights).<br />
Make a Right into the South parking lot, park, and make sure you
get a ticket from the parking lot attendant. <br />
Enter the Community Center building and take the elevator to the
3rd floor. <br />
The classroom is in suite 316.</p>
<p>
Come a few minutes early and enjoy <b>complimentary</b> coffee and
pastries!
</p>
<h3>Our address:</h3>

. . .
```

4.   Save course.htm in your text editor. Refresh the document in the browser and view the result.

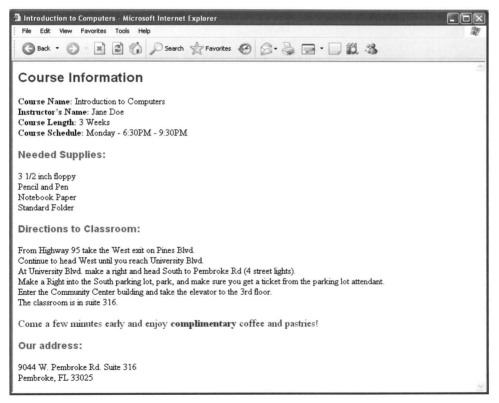

FIGURE 2.30

5. Keep the file open for the next exercise.

2. Add Font Formatting

You decide the typeface in your community program Web page requires enhancements. You need to change the color, size, and typeface of the text to make it more interesting.

1. In the open file, switch to course.htm in the text editor.

2. Apply the following font changes:

```
...
<h2<>font color="#800000" face="Arial">Course
Information</font></h2>
<p>
<b>Course Name:</b> Introduction to Computers<br />
<b>Instructor's Name: </b>Jane Doe<br />
<b>Course Length: </b>3 Weeks<br />
<b>Course Schedule:</b> Monday - 6:30PM - 9:30PM
</p>
<h3><font color="#008080" face="Arial">Needed Supplies:
</font></h3>
<p>
3 1/2 inch floppy<br />
Pencil and Pen<br />
Notebook Paper<br />
Standard Folder
</p>
<h3><font color="#008080" face="Arial">Directions to Classroom:
</font> </h3>
<p>
From Highway 95 take the West exit on Pines Blvd. <br />
Continue to head West until you reach University Blvd.<br />
At University Blvd. make a right and head South to Pembroke Rd
(4 street lights).<br />
Make a Right into the South parking lot, park, and make sure you
get a ticket from the parking lot attendant.<br />
Enter the Community Center building and take the elevator to the
3rd floor. <br /></p>
<p>The classroom is in suite 316.</p>
<p>
<font size="4" color="#800000">Come a few minutes early and enjoy
<b>complimentary</b> coffee and pastries! </font> </p>
<h3> <font color="#008080" face="Arial"> Our address: </font>
</h3>
<p>9044 W. Pembroke Rd. Suite 316<br />
Pembroke, FL 33025</p>
...
```

3. Save the file in the text editor. Refresh your browser and view the result of your changes.

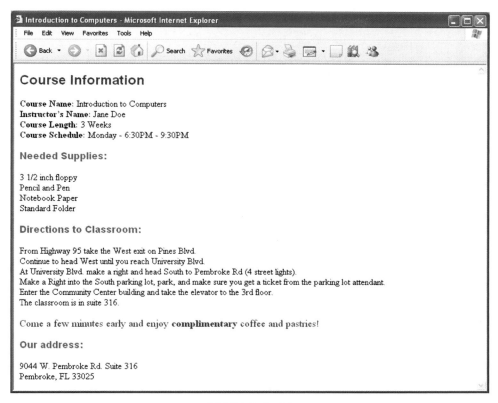

FIGURE 2.31

4. Keep the file open for the next exercise.

3. Create Ordered and Unordered Lists

The information on your community chapter Web page lacks organization. Turning some of the content into lists would make the information easier to read. You decide to make the class supplies section an unordered list and make the driving instructions section an ordered list.

1. In the open document, switch to course.htm in the text editor.

2. Create an ordered and unordered list, as follows:

```
. . .
<h3><font color="#008080" face="Arial">Needed
Supplies:</font></h3>
<ul>
<li>3 1/2 inch floppy</li>
<li>Pencil and Pen</li>
<li>Notebook Paper</li>
<li>Standard Folder </li>
```

```
</ul>
<h3><font color="#008080" face="Arial">Directions to
Classroom:</font></h3>
<ol>
<li>From Highway 95 take the West exit on Pines Blvd.</li>
<li>Continue to head West until you reach University Blvd.</li>
<li>At University Blvd. make a right and head South to Pembroke
Rd (4 street lights).</li>
<li>Make a Right into the South parking lot, park, and make sure
you get a ticket from the parking lot attendant.</li>
<li>Enter the Community Center building and take the elevator to
the 3rd floor. </li>
</ol>
<p>The classroom is in suite 316.</p>

. . .
```

3. Save the changes to the file. Refresh the document in your browser and view the result.

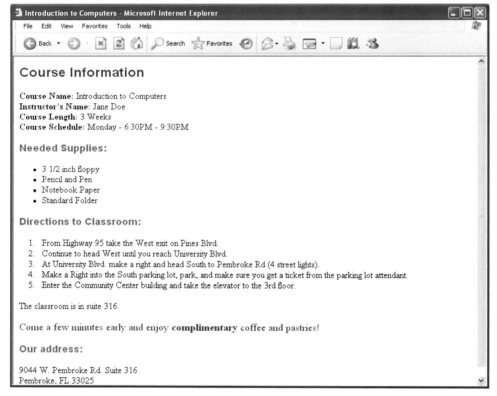

FIGURE 2.32

4. Keep the file open for the next exercise.

4. Create a Definition List

A definition list is an excellent choice when creating an FAQ. You can apply formatting for questions and answers quickly and easily, whereas using other elements might require more coding. In this exercise, you provide answers to frequently asked questions about the course.

1. In the open document, switch to the text editor.

2. Add a definition list that outlines two popular questions that are asked about the course.

```
. . .
<li>3 1/2 inch floppy</li>
<li>Pencil and Pen</li>
<li>Notebook Paper</li>
<li>Standard Folder </li>
</ul>
<h3><font color="#008080" face="Arial">FAQs:</font></h3>
<dl>
<dt>Can the course be counted toward college credits?</dt>
<dd>No. The course is not a college credited course.</dd>
<dt>Are there any prerequisites?</dt>
<dd>No. The course is an introductory course and therefore no
knowledge of computers is required.</dd>
</dl>
. . .
```

3. Bold the definition terms.

```
. . .
<h3><font color="#008080" face="Arial">FAQs:</font></h3>
<dl>
<dt><b> Can the course be counted toward college credits?</b></dt>
<dd>No. The course is not a college credited course.</dd>
<dt><b>Are there any prerequisites?</b></dt>
<dd>No. The course is an introductory course and therefore no
knowledge of computers is required.</dd>
</dl>
. . .
```

4. Save the changes to the file. Refresh the document in your browser and view the result.

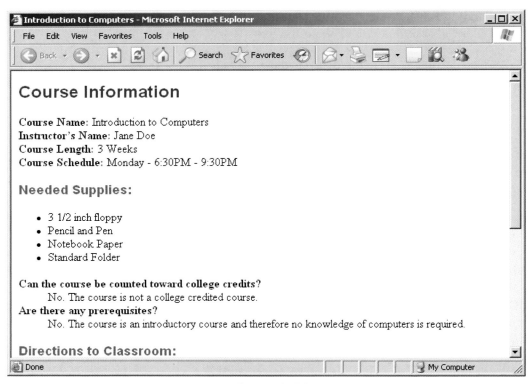

FIGURE 2.33

5. Close the file in both applications.

CHALLENGE

Challenge exercises expand on, or are somewhat related to, skills presented in the lessons. Each exercise provides a brief introduction, followed by numbered-step instructions that are not as detailed as those in the Skill Drill exercises. You should work through the exercises in order.

1. Replace Text Enhancement Tags with Structural Tags

Your instructor asked you to enhance the formatting of a course outline. You decide to convert some of the formatting tags to structural tags and to change the size of some sections of text.

1. Copy numoutline.htm from your Chapter_02 folder to your WIP_02 folder and open the file in your text editor and browser.

2. Choose View>Source from the browser's main Menu bar.

3. The first line of each paragraph uses the **`<b>`** and **`</b>`** tags to make these lines bold. This tag is not supported in XHTML 2.0 (but **`<strong>`** and **`<em>`** are). Replace all bold tags **`<b>`** and **`</b>`** with **`<strong>`** and **`</strong>`**.

4. Add the Level 2 heading "Hypertext Today" to the top of the document.

5. Using the **`<font>`** tag, increase the bolded text (**`<strong>`**) to a relative size of 4.

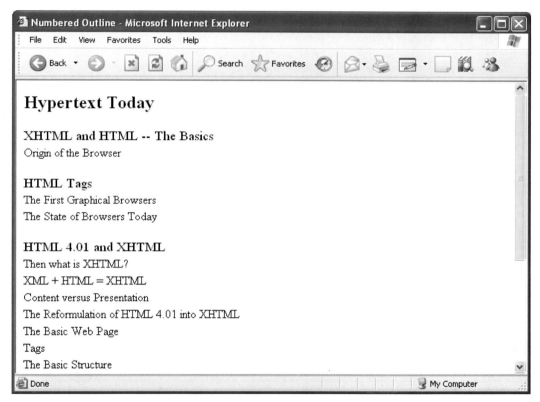

FIGURE 2.34

6. Save the changes and close the file in your browser and text editor.

2. Create an Ordered Outline

You were asked to place the content of the short outline in sequential order. Some of the items in the outline need to be nested.

1. Copy challenge2.htm from your Chapter_02 folder to your WIP_02 folder.

2. Add an opening ordered list tag directly beneath "<h2>Hypertext Today</h2>" in the source document.

3. Add a closing ordered list tag directly before the closing body tag in the source document.

4. Each section is enclosed in a paragraph tag. Replace every **\<p>** tag with an **\<li>** tag to make each section a list item.

5. Replace every ending paragraph tag **\</p>** with a **\</li>** tag to finish converting each section to a list item.

6. Save the changes to the text file and view the document in your Web browser.

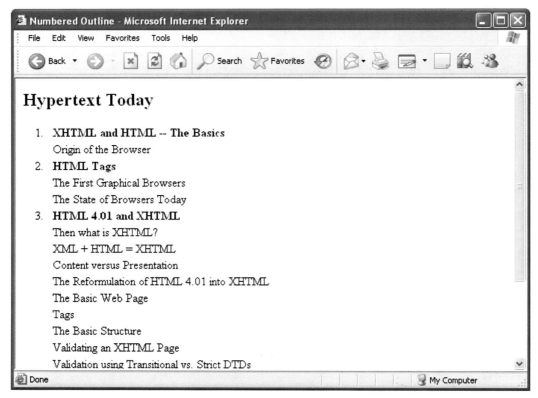

FIGURE 2.35

7. Close the file in your text editor and browser.

3. Create a Nested List

You created the main portion of an ordered list, but it's not very readable, nor is it structured properly. To resolve these problems, create nested ordered lists.

1. Copy challenge3.htm from your Chapter_02 folder to your WIP_02 folder and open the file in your text editor and browser.

2. Remove all of the line break tags in the file. The line breaks are forcing the text to the next line; you achieve the same effect using a nested list, only in an ordered format.

3. Place an opening ordered list tag directly below each bold sentence that is enclosed in list item tags. You use these items to begin creating a list. The bolded text, such as "XHTML", "HTML", and "HTML Tags", act as the list headings.

4. Add list item tags to each sentence (such as "Origin of the Browser") that follows the ordered list tag you just inserted.

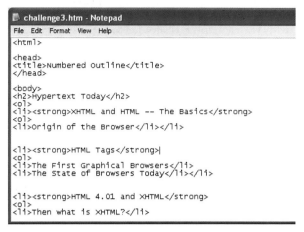

FIGURE 2.36

5. Place a closing ordered list tag after the last list item of each section and before the bolded sentence of the next section.

6. Save the changes to the text file and view the document in your browser.

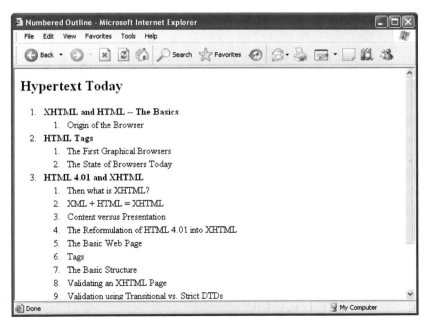

FIGURE 2.37

7. Close the file in your browser and text editor.

4. Change List Values and Apply Formatting

The structure of your instructor's outline is much improved, and the subheadings are nested below the main headings. The next challenge is to change the subheading values to lowercase letters.

1. Copy challenge4.htm from your Chapter_02 folder to your WIP_02 folder and open the file in your text editor and browser.

2. Add the **type** attribute with the lowercase letter value to the ordered list **<ol>** tags.

3. Change the **<ol>** tags to lowercase Roman numerals.

4. Change the color of the main ordered list's items to green.

5. Save your changes and view the result in a browser.

FIGURE 2.38

6. Close the file in both applications.

Why Would I Do This?

Text formatting is an important element in creating the overall look and feel of a Web site; but let's not overlook another critical Web page design element — graphical images. Virtually every site on the Web includes images of one sort or another, including corporate logos, pictorial site directories, navigation buttons, illustrated page content, and banners.

Designers sometimes take the use of images to the extreme, which leads to excessively large Web pages with long download times. Remember that every image on a page adds to its size; the bigger the page, the longer viewers must wait for it to download. For every additional second a viewer must wait to see an image, the greater the chance he will become frustrated and move to another site.

In Chapter 3, you discover how to work with images to enhance text-based Web pages. Don't worry if your graphical abilities are limited — a plethora of image resources is available on the Web.

VISUAL SUMMARY

Several types of images can be added to a Web page, and each has its own strengths and weaknesses. Figure 3.1 highlights a few common reasons to use images.

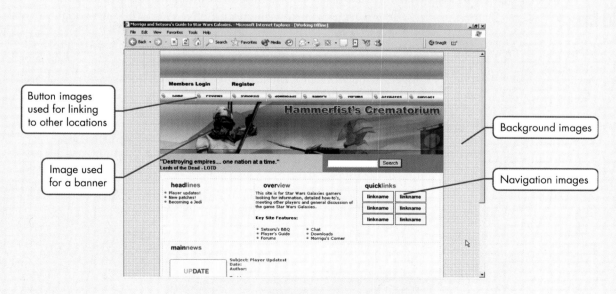

FIGURE 3.1

Images for Web pages are typically saved in three file formats: GIF, JPEG, and PNG. GIF and JPEG are the most common file formats used for Web pages and are the ones that are best supported by most browsers. *PNG* is a newer format that combines some of the best aspects of GIF and JPEG files but is less widely supported in browsers. GIF, JPEG, and PNG are all bitmap graphic formats, meaning that images are represented as grids of dots known as *pixels*.

Due to the need to download images quickly, all three file types incorporate compression. *Compression* is the process by which data is converted into a form that minimizes the space required to store or transmit it. Compression can be *lossy*, meaning that it reduces the image's quality as the file size becomes smaller, or *lossless*, meaning that the image quality is not changed as the file size is made smaller.

Web Imagery File Types

File Extension	Number of Colors Supported	Transparency	Compression Type
GIF	256	Yes	Lossless
JPG	Millions	No	Lossy
PNG	Millions	Yes	Lossless

Graphics Interchange Format (*GIF*) is the original Web graphics format. It uses *indexed color*, meaning that each pixel in the image is assigned a number from 0 to 255. This number represents the pixel's color on a color look-up table. Indexed color is limited to a maximum of 256 colors. This format works best with images that have large areas of a single color, such as logos or *line art*. GIF images use lossless compression to allow for quicker download and have two other advantages:

- GIF images can use *transparency*. When a color is transparent, you can see through it. In a GIF file, one color is designated as the transparent color, and any pixels of that color allow the background to show through. This is useful for several reasons, not the least of which is that it allows you to create a single image that can be used on different backgrounds.

- GIFs can be animated. The result is similar to a flipbook: multiple still images are viewed in rapid succession to create the appearance of movement. GIF animations can *loop* (repeat). Be aware that while animated GIFs can enliven a page when used properly, they can also be distracting when overused. Animated GIFs annoy many users and are rarely used by modern Web designers.

Figure 3.2 is an example of a Web page that uses a transparent GIF.

The logo image is transparent so the background shows through.

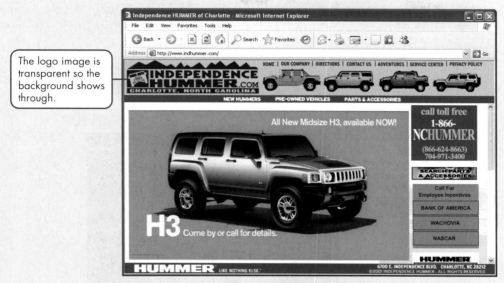

FIGURE 3.2

The *JPEG* (or JPG) format was created by the Joint Photographic Experts Group. This group realized that they needed an alternative to GIFs because the GIF file format could not successfully render the subtle color changes and complex gradients found in photographs. The JPEG format was created specifically for photographic images.

Any image with gradual color changes looks better and renders at smaller file sizes in the JPEG format. JPEG uses lossy compression and compression that reduces the number of colors in the image as the file size is reduced.

JPEG images with too much compression appear to have distortions in the image, particularly in areas of highly saturated colors such as yellow or red. Photographic images should always be saved in the JPEG format, which offers the smallest file sizes at reasonable image-quality levels. Graphic design programs such as Adobe Photoshop allow Web designers to pick the optimal compression for a particular image.

Photographic imagery should always be in a JPEG format

FIGURE 3.3

The PNG (Portable Network Graphics) format generates files that are similar to GIFs. PNG supports photographic images without distortion, although it is not widely used because it cannot reduce file sizes to the same degree as JPEG images and is not as widely supported in Web browsers.

PNG was created in response to a legal issue. Most GIF images are based on *LZW compression*, a specific type of file compression that is covered by a patent issued to Unisys Corporation. This patent states that any graphics program that reads or creates images with LZW compression must be licensed. The major software companies, such as Adobe and Macromedia, obtained licenses for their programs and can freely use the LZW compression technique.

Small developers and independent Web site operators, however, could not afford the high price of the LZW license. They needed a low-cost alternative. The PNG image format fulfilled this need and was standardized in 1996. PNG files can generate a strange blue tint in some Web browsers and are not yet used by most Web developers.

LESSON 1   Inserting an Image in a Web Page

You can add images to a Web page with the **`<img />`** tag, which is an empty tag. In the code **`<img src="logo.gif" />`**, "src" refers to the ***source attribute***; it specifies which file appears on the page. When we "add" an image to a Web page, we don't actually add it—we reference it.

HTML references files that are used on a Web page, and the files are never actually included in the Web page file. Essentially, a Web page is text, or code, that includes references to external media such as images, sounds, animations, or movies. Web sites are simply collections of text files and associated media.

This is confusing for students learning to create Web pages. Many computer users are already familiar with software such as Microsoft Word. When they insert an image, they choose the image file and it is embedded into the Word file. If they e-mail the Word file to another user, the image appears—without the user needing a separate copy of the image file on their machine. The Word file contains everything the recipient needs to view the text and image.

In a Web page, you add a link that points to an external image that is not embedded in the file. If you link the image to the Web page file, all you add is a reference to where the browser can find the image. If you then send the Web page file to a friend without including the image file, she will see a large "X" where the image should be located.

When you add an image to a Web page, all you actually add is a reference to the image's location that tells the browser where it is located. The image can be located on your hard drive or on any server you choose. As long as the ***path*** (specific directory location) to the file is correct, the browser can find the image and load it correctly.

When your image and its associated Web page are located in the same directory, you do not need to include a complete path when you reference the image. If your image is located in a ***remote directory*** (a directory other than the directory where the Web page resides), you must define the path within the **`src=""`** attribute.

The following is a reference to an image file in a remote directory:

```
<img src="images/picture.gif" />
```

This type of link is often referred to as a ***relative link***, which shows the path relative to the location of the Web page. For example, to find the image mentioned in the preceding source attribute, the computer must start in the same folder where the Web page exists, then go to a subfolder named "images".

Absolute links show the exact location of an image or file. This is an example of an image file that the computer can locate using an absolute link:

```
<img src="http://www.web-answers.com/images/picture.gif" />
```

In this example, the starting point isn't important—the computer knows exactly where to find the file. Generally speaking, Web designers prefer to use relative links whenever possible. This makes it easy to move Web sites to different locations. For example, if we decide to change the name of our URL to www.web-answers-education.com, we could move our entire Web site to the new location. If we have a relative link such as **`src="images/picture.gif"`**, the image should still show up on the page.

Using relative links requires designers to keep all files together in one primary site folder. Subfolders are often created, such as an images folder. Assume we are working with images; if a designer accidentally moves a file or forgets to include a file or subfolder when moving a Web site, a blank area will be shown instead of the image.

Forgetting a file or accidentally moving a file to the wrong location is a very common mistake among new Web designers. Testing your Web pages in a browser will help you find these errors. If you have an image that is missing, check the source attribute for the missing file's location, then make sure it is present in the location specified. The examples in this book will use relative links unless otherwise specified.

In the following exercises, you add an image to a Web page, add a border to the image, and view the result in your browser.

Add an Image

1   **Copy all the files from your Chapter_03 folder into your WIP_03 folder.**

2   **From the WIP_03 folder, open images.htm in both the text editor and the browser.**

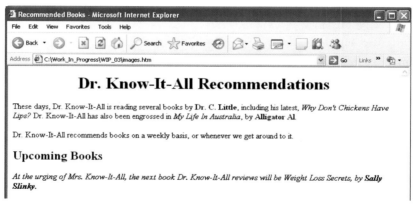

FIGURE 3.4

The page loads in the browser. It displays some formatted text.

3   **Apply the `<img />` tag to add the images, as follows:**

```
. . .
<h1 align="center">Dr. Know-It-All Recommendations</h1>

<p><img src="book1.jpg" />These days, Dr. Know-It-All is reading
several books by <b>Dr. C. Little</b>, including his latest,
<i>Why Don't Chickens Have Lips?</i> Dr. Know-It-All has also
been engrossed in <i>My Life In Australia</i>, by <b>Alligator
Al</b>.</p>

<p>Dr. Know-It-All recommends books on a weekly basis, or whenever
we get around to it.</p>
```

```
<h2>Upcoming Books</h2>

<p><img src="book2.jpg" /><i>At the urging of Mrs. Know-It-All,
the next book Dr. Know-It-All reviews will be <i>Weight Loss
Secrets</i>, by <b>Sally Slinky</b>.</i></p>

. . .
```

Remember that you do not need to add a file path to the image directory because the images are in the same directory as the Web page.

4   **Save the file in the text editor. Refresh the document in your browser and view the result.**

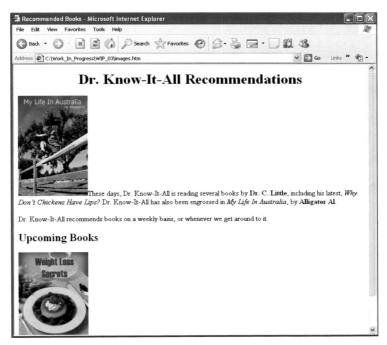

FIGURE 3.5

The images display in the predefined location. Notice how the text is positioned. You learn how to control the image's positioning later in this chapter.

5   **Leave the file open for the next exercise.**

Add a Border to an Image

Unless an image is used as a link, the image displays by default without a border on a Web page. You can use the `border=""` attribute to add a border to an image. Doing so creates a black border around the image. You can specify the border's width, depending on the size of the image and how it is used. Image border widths are measured in pixels.

1 In the open document, switch to the text editor. Add a border width of 1 pixel to the first image, as follows:

```
...

<h1 align="center">Dr. Know-It-All Recommendations</h1>

<p><img src="book1.jpg" border="1" />These days, Dr. Know-It-All
is reading several books by <b>Dr. C. Little</b>, including his
latest, <i>Why Don't Chickens Have Lips?</i> Dr. Know-It-All has
also been engrossed in <i>My Life In Australia</i>, by
<b>Alligator Al</b>.</p>

<p>Dr. Know-It-All recommends books on a weekly basis, or whenever
we get around to it.</p>

<h2>Upcoming Books</h2>

<p><img src="book2.jpg" /><i>At the urging of Mrs. Know-It-All,
the next book Dr. Know-It-All reviews will be <i>Weight Loss
Secrets</i>, by <b>Sally Slinky</b>.</i></p>

...
```

This instructs the browser to display a border size of 1 pixel around the image.

2 Add a border width of 8 pixels to the second image, as follows:

```
...

<h1 align="center">Dr. Know-It-All Recommendations</h1>

<p><img src="book1.jpg" border="1"  />These days, Dr. Know-It-All
is reading several books by <b>Dr. C. Little</b>, including his
latest, <i>Why Don't Chickens Have Lips?</i> Dr. Know-It-All has
also been engrossed in <i>My Life In Australia</i>, by
<b>Alligator Al</b>.</p>

<p>Dr. Know-It-All recommends books on a weekly basis, or whenever
we get around to it.</p>

<h2>Upcoming Books</h2>

<p><img src="book2.jpg" border="8" /><i>At the urging of
Mrs. Know-It-All, the next book Dr. Know-It-All reviews will be
<i>Weight Loss Secrets</i>, by <b>Sally Slinky</b>.</i></p>

...
```

This instructs the browser to display a border size of 8 pixels around the image.

3 | Save the changes to the text file and refresh the document in the browser.

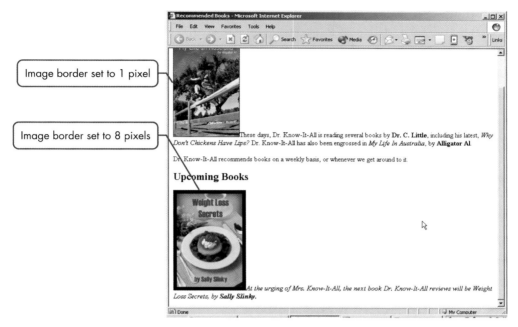

Image border set to 1 pixel

Image border set to 8 pixels

FIGURE 3.6

The first image displays on the page with a 1-pixel black border. The second image displays with an 8-pixel black border.

4 | Switch to the text editor. Change the image borders to zero, as follows:

```
. . .

<h1 align="center">Dr. Know-It-All Recommendations</h1>

<p><img src="book1.jpg" border="0" />These days, Dr. Know-It-All
is reading several books by <b>Dr. C. Little</b>, including his
latest, <i>Why Don't Chickens Have Lips?</i> Dr. Know-It-All has
also been engrossed in <i>My Life In Australia</i>, by
<b>Alligator Al</b>.</p>

<p>Dr. Know-It-All recommends books on a weekly basis, or whenever
we get around to it.</p>

<h2>Upcoming Books</h2>

<p><img src="book2.jpg" border="0" /><i>At the urging of Mrs.
Know-It-All, the next book Dr. Know-It-All reviews will be
<i>Weight Loss Secrets</i>, by <b>Sally Slinky</b>.</i></p>

. . .
```

The images display without borders. If you don't want borders to appear around your images, you can exclude the **border="0"** attribute altogether. Web authors set the border attribute to 0 to eliminate the border around a linked image in most browsers. The border attribute has been deprecated since HTML 4.0.

5   **Save the changes to the document.**

6   **Close the file in your Web browser and text editor.**

To Extend Your Knowledge . . .

FILE ORGANIZATION

When you plan a Web project, you must determine how to organize your files. Organizing your Web site files makes it easier to reference specific items, including your images. Some designers create a top-level folder for the hypertext documents and a subfolder for the images. Organize your files according to your personal workflow.

LESSON 2   Adding Alternate Text

Even though **bandwidth** (the speed of a user's connection to the Internet) is getting faster every year, many users still turn off images in their Web browsers. This is particularly true with users outside the United States, many of whom do not enjoy the benefits of high-speed connections. Other viewers use text-only browsers. To provide a positive experience for those viewers who have limited bandwidth, Web developers add alternate text to the image tag.

Alternate text (usually abbreviated **alt text**) is intended as a textual alternative to the image. Alt text describes the purpose of the image, rather than the appearance of the image, if the graphic fails to download. More importantly, alt text allows visually impaired visitors to "hear" the site rather than see it; a screen reader reads the alt text to the user. Alt text is specified with the **alt=""** attribute.

With the advent of XHTML, alt text is a requirement. You must include the **alt=""** attribute for every **<img />** tag you place on a Web page. The browser displays alt text under five circumstances:

- The user turned off images.
- The image is not yet downloaded.
- The image is not available.
- The browser is not capable of displaying images.
- The browser is part of specialized hardware used by persons with disabilities.

Add Alternate Text

1 | **In your text editor and browser, open alttext.htm from your WIP_03 folder.**

2 | **Add alt text to the image tags as follows:**

```
. . .

<h1 align="center">Dr. Know-It-All Recommendations</h1>

<p><img src="book1.jpg" alt="My Life In Australia"/> These days,
Dr. Know-It-All is reading several books by <b>Dr. C. Little</b>,
including his latest, <i>Why Don't Chickens Have Lips?</i> Dr.
Know-It-All has also been engrossed in <i>My Life In
Australia</i>, by <b>Alligator Al</b>.</p>

<p>Dr. Know-It-All recommends books on a weekly basis, or whenever
we get around to it.</p>

<h2>Upcoming Books</h2>

<p><img src="book2.jpg" alt="Weight Loss Secrets"/><i>At the urging
of Mrs. Know-It-All, the next book Dr. Know-It-All reviews will be
<i>Weight Loss Secrets</i>, by <b>Sally Slinky</b>.</i></p>

. . .
```

Alt text is now in place, in case the image does not display in the browser window or the user turns off images.

3 | **Save the changes to the file. Refresh the document in the browser.**

4 | **Position your cursor over the image.**

This activates a tool tip that displays the text in the **alt=""** attribute. If the image is unavailable, the text displays on the page instead of the image. The rollover text does not display in all browsers.

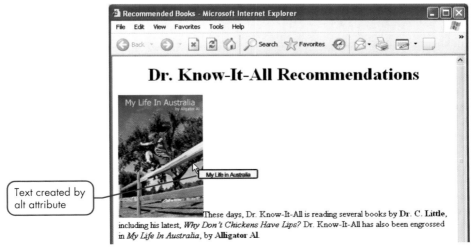

FIGURE 3.7

5   **Close the file in your text editor and browser.**

To Extend Your Knowledge . . .

NO IMAGE TAG IN XHTML 2.0

XHTML 2.0 doesn't have an `<img>` element; the tag is obsolete in this draft of the specification. The replacement is the `<object></object>` tags. The object element allows you to supply more information about the image and actually format the display of the alternate text.

For example:

```
<object id="baby"
  type="image/jpeg"
  data="baby.jpg"
  width="152"
  height="160">
<p>A baby in a cradle.</p>
</object>
```

LESSON 3   Controlling the Image

You added images to your Web page in Lesson 1, but you didn't arrange the images in an attractive manner. Similar to body copy and headings, images can carry a number of attributes that affect the image's appearance. These attributes allow you to control alignment, how text wraps around the image, the size of the image, and the appearance of a small temporary image that appears on screen while the final image loads. In this lesson, you focus on image alignment and text wrapping.

In the graphic in the previous exercise, notice that the bottom of the image and the first line of text are located on the same line. Until recently, this was the only way to display text and images on the same line. Today, you can control the relationship of text and images using the **`align=""`** attribute.

The **`align=""`** attribute has five possible values:

- Top
- Bottom
- Middle
- Left
- Right

If you don't indicate a preference, the browser applies the default value of bottom. Bottom alignment was applied to the image in the previous exercise. While you may assume that "bottom" means the image is placed at the bottom of the page, it actually means that the text is aligned along the bottom of the image.

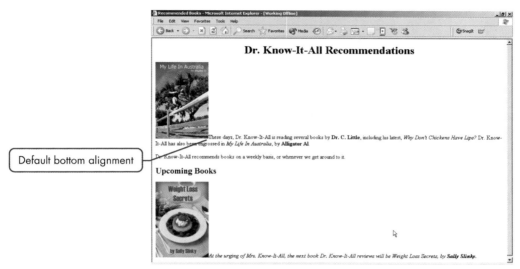

FIGURE 3.8

As you see above, the text aligns along the bottom of the image by default.

If you apply top, bottom, or middle alignment, only a single line of text appears next to the image, no matter how much available space is on the page. If you want to wrap text around an image, the image must be aligned to the left or right.

When you apply left or right alignment, situations will arise when you must move your content below an image. To do that, you can add a **clear=""** attribute to the **
** tag. For instance, if you apply **<br clear="left" />** next to the image, the text moves down the page until there are no more images on the left.

By default, text or other images display next to an embedded image, even if that image is contained in a **<p>** tag (unless the image is placed in a table; you'll learn more about tables later). The **clear=""** attribute is designed to separate text from images, allowing the reader to focus first on the image, and then on the accompanying text.

Align the Images

1   **In your text editor and browser, open alignimages.htm from your WIP_03 folder.**

2   **Set the first image to middle alignment, and set the second image to top alignment, as follows:**

. . .

```
<h1 align="center">Dr. Know-It-All Recommendations</h1>
```

```
<p><img src="book1.jpg" align="middle" alt="My Life In Australia" />
These days, Dr. Know-It-All is reading several books by <b>Dr. C.
Little</b>, including his latest, <i>Why Don't Chickens Have
Lips?</i> Dr. Know-It-All has also been engrossed in <i>My Life
In Australia</i>, by <b>Alligator Al</b>.</p>

<p>Dr. Know-It-All recommends books on a weekly basis, or whenever
we get around to it.</p>

<h2>Upcoming Books</h2>

<p><img src="book2.jpg" align="top" alt="Weight Loss Secrets" />
<i>At the urging of Mrs. Know-It-All, the next book Dr. Know-It-
All reviews will be <i>Weight Loss Secrets</i>, by <b>Sally
Slinky</b>.</i></p>

. . .
```

The first image has one line of text aligned at its middle. The second image has one line of text aligned at its top.

3   **Save the file in the text editor. Refresh the browser and view the result.**

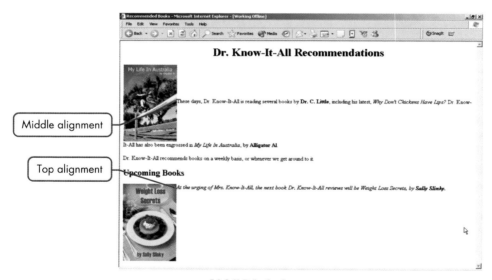

FIGURE 3.9

Even though you moved the text up and there's plenty of space next to the image, only one line of text displays next to the image. It would look much better with wrapped text. To wrap the text, you must apply left and right alignment.

4 Set right alignment on "My Life In Australia" and left alignment on "Weight Loss Secrets," as follows:

```
. . .

<h1 align="center">Dr. Know-It-All Recommendations</h1>

<p><img src="book1.jpg" align="right" alt="My Life In Australia"
/>These days, Dr. Know-It-All is reading several books by <b>Dr.
C. Little</b>, including his latest, <i>Why Don't Chickens Have
Lips?</i> Dr. Know-It-All has also been engrossed in <i>My Life
In Australia</i>, by <b>Alligator Al</b>.</p>

<p>Dr. Know-It-All recommends books on a weekly basis, or whenever
we get around to it.</p>

<h2>Upcoming Books</h2>

<p><img src="book2.jpg" align="left" alt="Weight Loss Secrets"
/><i>At the urging of Mrs. Know-It-All, the next book Dr. Know-
It-All reviews will be <i>Weight Loss Secrets</i>, by <b>Sally
Slinky</b>.</i></p>

. . .
```

5 Save the file in the text editor. Refresh the document in the browser and view the result.

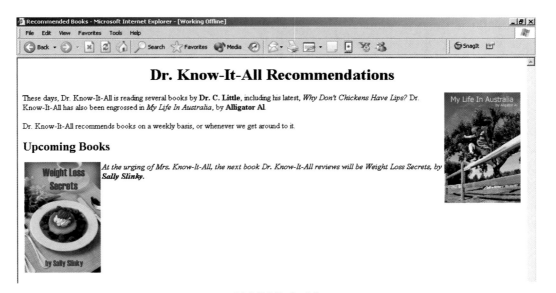

FIGURE 3.10

Once you align an image to the left or right, the remaining content (including other images) wraps around the image. If this is not your intended result, you can use the **<br clear="" />** attribute to instruct the browser to move down to the next clear area after the image.

6 Leave the file open for the next exercise.

Clear a Break after an Image

1 In the open file, insert the **
** tag before the Upcoming Books heading, as shown here:

```
. . .

<h1 align="center">Dr. Know-It-All Recommendations</h1>

<p><img src="book1.jpg" align="right" alt="My Life In Australia"
/>These days, Dr. Know-It-All is reading several books by <b>Dr.
C. Little</b>, including his latest, <i>Why Don't Chickens Have
Lips?</i> Dr. Know-It-All has also been engrossed in <i>My Life
In Australia</i>, by <b>Alligator Al</b>.</p>

<p>Dr. Know-It-All recommends books on a weekly basis, or whenever
we get around to it.</p>

<br clear="right" />

<h2>Upcoming Books</h2>

<p><img src="book2.jpg" align="left" alt="Weight Loss Secrets" />
<i>At the urging of Mrs. Know-It-All, the next book Dr. Know-It-
All reviews will be <i>Weight Loss Secrets</i>, by <b>Sally
Slinky</b>.</i></p>

. . .
```

2 Save the file in the text editor.

3 Refresh the browser and view the result.

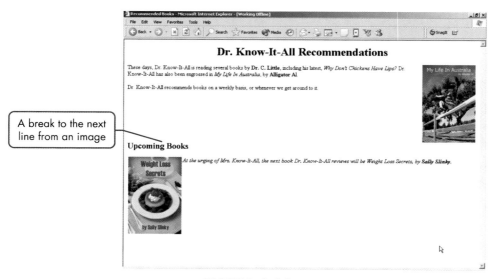

FIGURE 3.11

Notice that the clear attribute forces the browser to move the next section of content down, clearing the space next to the image above it. You could have used the **`<br clear="all">`** name-value pair to render the same effect. The **`clear="all"`** attribute clears all sides of an element.

4   **Close the file in your text editor and browser.**

LESSON 4   Specifying Image Height and Width

Two of the most important image attributes are height and width. The XHTML standard requires that these attributes be applied to every image. Without a specified height and width in the **`<img>`** tag, the browser must download the entire image before it can format the layout of the screen — this happens because the browser does not know how big the image will be and how much space it should set aside for the image to be displayed. Providing the width and height allows the page to display faster.

The dimensions you provide represent the size of the image as it appears on the Web page; these dimensions do not necessarily reflect the actual size of the original image. Please note that ***scaling*** (reducing or enlarging) the height and width attributes does not affect the size of the file. You might expect an image that has been scaled to 50% of its original dimensions would be 50% smaller in every way. This, however, is not the case. A 300 kb file is a 300 kb file, no matter how small or large it appears on your Web page.

You should only use this scaling technique during the initial planning of the site, while you are trying to identify proper image placement and size on the page. Remember that when you scale up an image, you sacrifice image quality because the image becomes ***pixilated*** (you can see the individual pixels in the image). Pixelation results in lower quality and ***resolution*** (clarity and definition of the file).

When you scale down an image, it becomes distorted because you are forcing all of the pixels to occupy too small a space; this forces the browser to hide many of the pixels in the image. This often results in an image getting a "jagged" appearance, where straight lines in the image become distorted as parts of them are hidden.

When a Web site is ready to ***post*** (place the final version on the Web for public viewing), all images should be edited in a graphics-manipulation program to achieve the optimum size and best level of compression. Designers must often choose between varying sizes and quality levels to lower the file size of images to acceptable levels.

Resize an Image's Display

1   **In your text editor and browser, open widthandheight.htm from your WIP_03 folder.**

2   **In your text editor, set the images' widths to 180 px, and set the heights to 269 px, which is 120% of the images' original sizes.**

. . .

```
<h1 align="center">Dr. Know-It-All Recommendations</h1>
```

```
<p><img src="book1.jpg" align="right" alt="My Life In Australia"
width="180" height="269"/> These days, Dr. Know-It-All is reading
several books by <b>Dr. C. Little</b>, including his latest,
<i>Why Don't Chickens Have Lips?</i> Dr. Know-It-All has also
been engrossed in <i>My Life In Australia</i>, by <b>Alligator
Al</b>.</p>

<p>Dr. Know-It-All recommends books on a weekly basis, or whenever
we get around to it.</p>

<br clear="right" />

<h2>Upcoming Books</h2>

<p><img src="book2.jpg" align="left" alt="Weight Loss Secrets"
width="180" height="269"/><i>At the urging of Mrs. Know-It-All,
the next book Dr. Know-It-All reviews will be <i>Weight Loss
Secrets</i>, by <b>Sally Slinky</b>.</i></p>

...
```

3   **Save the file in your text editor.**

4   **Refresh the browser and view the result.**

The instructions you gave the browser force the images to display at the larger dimensions.

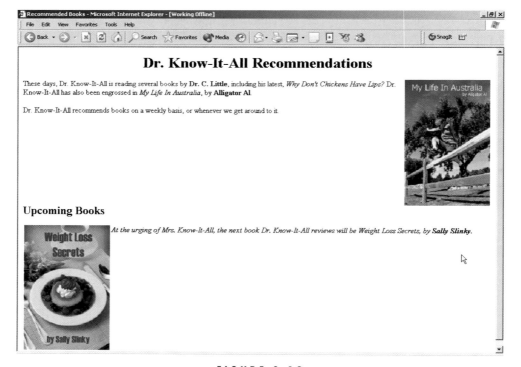

FIGURE 3.12

5   **Change the width and height values to the actual size of the images, as follows:**

```
. . .

<p>

<img src="book1.jpg" align="right" alt="My Life In Australia"
width="150" height="224" />These days, Dr. Know-It-All is reading
several books by <b>Dr. C. Little</b>, including his latest,
<i>Why Don't Chickens Have Lips?</i> Dr. Know-It-All has also
been engrossed in <i>My Life In Australia</i>, by <b>Alligator
Al</b>.</p>

<p>Dr. Know-It-All recommends books on a weekly basis, or whenever
we get around to it.</p>

<br clear="right" />

<h2>Upcoming Books</h2>

<p>

<img src="book2.jpg" align="left" alt="Weight Loss Secrets"
width="150" height="223" /><i>At the urging of Mrs. Know-It-All,
the next book Dr. Know-It-All reviews will be <i>Weight Loss
Secrets</i>, by <b>Sally Slinky</b>.</i></p>

. . .
```

6   **Save the file in your text editor.**

7 **Refresh the browser and view the result.**

The images display at their original sizes. Adding the height and width values decreased the download time from the server to the user's browser because the attributes tell the browser how many pixels to reserve. When using the `height=""` and `width=""` attributes, the browser does not have to calculate the space needed for the image, which saves time.

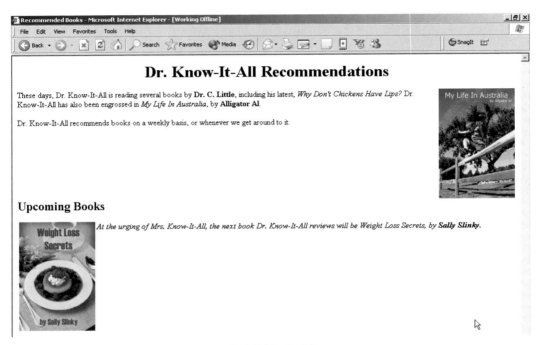

FIGURE 3.13

8 **Close the file in your text editor and browser.**

To Extend Your Knowledge . . .

DETERMINING IMAGE SIZE

You can determine the size of an image in several ways, including opening the image in a graphics-editing program such as Adobe Photoshop or Macromedia Fireworks. In certain situations, you can determine this information from the browser.

In the Netscape Navigator for Macintosh, you can place your mouse over the image and hold down the mouse button. When the menu pops up, you can choose View Image In New Window. The height and width of the image appears in the Title bar. You can gather the same information in Navigator for Windows by right-clicking the image and choosing View Image from the context-sensitive pop-up menu.

On Internet Explorer for Windows, you can right-click the image and choose Properties. The height and width are listed under Dimensions. Unfortunately, this does not work with IE for Macintosh.

LESSON 5 Working with Space around an Image

You can add space between an image and other elements, such as text, using the **hspace=""** and **vspace=""** attributes. The **hspace=""** attribute allows you to change the *horizontal space* between an image and other objects on a Web page. The **vspace=""** attribute allows you to change the *vertical space* between an image and other objects on a Web page.

Even though these attributes provide control over the display of an image relative to other objects on a Web page, we recommend that you do not use **hspace=""** or **vspace=""** attributes; both have been deprecated. Instead, you can use the nonbreaking space character entity to add space between elements.

Nonbreaking Space

A *character entity* is a code in HTML/XHTML that produces a symbol, such as the copyright symbol. In this case, however, an empty space the size of one character is created when you add a *nonbreaking space*. (You learn more about character entities later in this book.) By default, XHTML allows for only one character space between elements, no matter how many spaces you provide in your source code. When you use the nonbreaking space, however, you can add as many additional character spaces as necessary.

The format of the nonbreaking space is a bit different than what you've worked with so far. It does not use the open and close carats (< and >) to contain the command. Rather, the ampersand (&) character is used to start the character entity command, followed by the command name, and then the semicolon is used to end the command. For example:

```
 
```

The nonbreaking space character entity acts exactly as a normal text space, except that the browser addresses each one individually. If you place four nonbreaking spaces in your code, the browser puts four spaces between objects. This type of space can be applied to any object, not just an image.

Add Vertical Space to an Image

1   **In your text editor and browser, open spacing.htm from your WIP_03 folder.**

2   **Add 20 pixels of vertical space to the bottom image, as follows:**

```
. . .

<img src="book1.jpg" align="right" alt="My Life In Australia"
width="150" height="224" />These days, Dr. Know-It-All is reading
several books by <b>Dr. C. Little</b>, including his latest,
<i>Why Don't Chickens Have Lips?</i> Dr. Know-It-All has also
been engrossed in <i>My Life In Australia</i>, by <b>Alligator
Al</b>.</p>

<p>Dr. Know-It-All recommends books on a weekly basis, or whenever
we get around to it.</p>
```

```
<br clear="right" />
<h2>Upcoming Books</h2>
<p>
<img src="book2.jpg" align="left" alt="Weight Loss Secrets"
width="150" height="223" vspace="20"/><i>At the urging of Mrs.
Know-It-All, the next book Dr. Know-It-All reviews will be
<i>Weight Loss Secrets</i>, by <b>Sally Slinky</b>.</i></p>
. . .
```

This instructs the browser to place 20 pixels of vertical space above and below the image.

3   **Save the changes to the text file and refresh the document in the browser.**

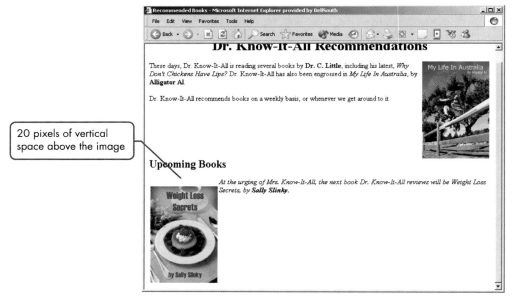

FIGURE 3.14

4   **Leave the file open in both applications.**

Add Horizontal Space to an Image

1   **In the open file, switch to the text editor.**

2   **Add 50 pixels of horizontal space to the bottom image, as follows:**

```
. . .
<img src="book1.jpg" align="right" alt="My Life In Australia"
width="150" height="224" />These days, Dr. Know-It-All is reading
several books by <b>Dr. C. Little</b>, including his latest,
```

```
<i>Why Don't Chickens Have Lips?</i> Dr. Know-It-All has also
been engrossed in <i>My Life In Australia</i>, by <b>Alligator
Al</b>.</p>

<p>Dr. Know-It-All recommends books on a weekly basis, or whenever
we get around to it.</p>

<br clear="right" />

<h2>Upcoming Books</h2>

<p>

<img src="book2.jpg" align="left" alt="Weight Loss Secrets"
width="150" height="223" vspace="20" hspace="50"/><i>At the urging
of Mrs. Know-It-All, the next book Dr. Know-It-All reviews will be
<i>Weight Loss Secrets</i>, by <b>Sally Slinky</b>.</i></p>

. . .
```

This instructs the browser to place 50 pixels of horizontal space between the image and other elements.

3   **Save the changes to the text file and refresh the document in the browser.**

There are 50 pixels of space to the left and right of the bottom image. Notice that there is a space between the image and the edge of the Web page (on the left).

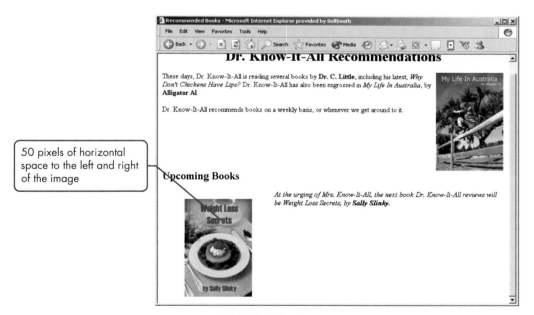

FIGURE 3.15

4   **Leave the file open in both applications.**

Add Nonbreaking Space

1   **In the open file, switch to the text editor.**

2   **Add 10 nonbreaking spaces between the words "Upcoming" and "Books", as follows:**

```
. . .

<p>

<img src="book1.jpg" align="right" alt="My Life In Australia"
width="150" height="224" />These days, Dr. Know-It-All is reading
several books by <b>Dr. C. Little</b>, including his latest,
<i>Why Don't Chickens Have Lips?</i> Dr. Know-It-All has also
been engrossed in <i>My Life In Australia</i>, by <b>Alligator
Al</b>.</p>

<p>Dr. Know-It-All recommends books on a weekly basis, or whenever
we get around to it.</p>

<br clear="right" />

<h2>Upcoming             
       Books</h2>

<p>

<img src="book2.jpg" align="left" alt="Weight Loss Secrets"
width="150" height="223" vspace="20" hspace="50" /><i>At the
urging of Mrs. Know-It-All, the next book Dr. Know-It-All reviews
will be <i>Weight Loss Secrets</i>, by <b>Sally
Slinky</b>.</i></p>

. . .
```

Although the use of the nonbreaking space is not practical in this example, it illustrates how you can create empty spaces between elements on a Web page. As you work more with Web pages, you will discover other (more appropriate) uses for the nonbreaking space.

Note that the nonbreaking space code is in all lowercase letters. In XHTML, this is required. If capital letters were used (such as), the tag would fail to work and it would display as text in the browser window.

3   **Save the changes to the text file and refresh the document in the browser.**

There are 10 spaces between the words "Upcoming" and "Books". You can use as many nonbreaking spaces as you need to separate elements. If you use the nonbreaking space to render a specific page layout, keep in mind that your page might display differently on other machines (depending on the screen's resolution settings).

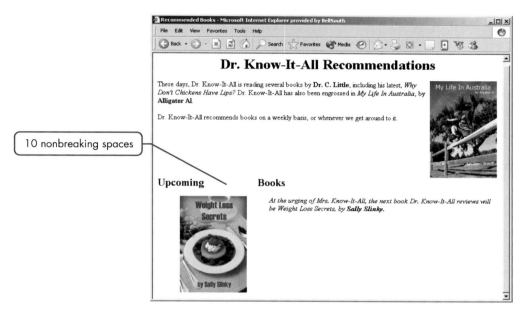

FIGURE 3.16

4   **Remove the 10 nonbreaking spaces from the code in the text editor.**

5   **Save the changes to the text file and refresh the document in the browser.**

The additional space is removed.

6   **Close the file in your text editor and browser.**

LESSON 6 Lowsrc (Low Source) Images

Another image attribute you should be familiar with is *lowsrc*, which is a smaller version of the final image. The smaller image is downloaded and displayed while the full image continues to download. A temporary lowsrc image gives the viewer something to look at while he waits for the final image to download and appear on his screen. This attribute it not widely used due to ever-increasing amounts of bandwidth; but even when bandwidth was scarce, developers did not take full advantage of this feature.

Originally, lowsrc images were low-quality or black-and-white versions of the actual images. Today, however, designers apply creativity to their lowsrc images and develop interesting line-art wire frames or skeletal versions of the final images. JPEG images load from the top down, so the effect of filling a wire frame can be quite striking. Adding a compelling lowsrc image might make the difference between a viewer leaving your site during a long boring download or staying on your site to watch the lowsrc image metamorphose into the final image.

Specify a Lowsrc Image

1 In your text editor and browser, open lowsrc.htm from your WIP_03 folder.

2 Specify the lowsrc image you want to display for each image on the Web page, as follows:

```
. . .
<h1 align="center">Dr. Know-It-All Recommendations</h1>

<p><img src="book1.jpg" align="right" alt="My Life In Australia"
width="150" height="224" lowsrc="book1_low.jpg"/> These days, Dr.
Know-It-All is reading several books by <b>Dr. C. Little</b>,
including his latest, <i>Why Don't Chickens Have Lips?</i> Dr.
Know-It-All has also been engrossed in <i>My Life In
Australia</i>, by <b>Alligator Al</b>.</p>

<p>Dr. Know-It-All recommends books on a weekly basis, or whenever
we get around to it.</p>

<br clear="right" />

<h2>Upcoming Books</h2>

<p><img src="book2.jpg" align="left" alt="Weight Loss Secrets"
width="150" height="223" lowsrc="book2_low.jpg"/><i>At the urging
of Mrs. Know-It-All, the next book Dr. Know-It-All reviews will
be <i>Weight Loss Secrets</i>, by <b>Sally Slinky</b>.</i></p>

. . .
```

3 Save the changes to the file. Refresh the document in the browser and view the result.

A lowsrc image only appears if the full image isn't available, usually because the full image hasn't yet loaded. Since your files are local and load rapidly, you may have difficulty seeing the lowsrc image before the final image displays. If you had to download the page from a Web server, you would see the lowsrc image.

4 Close the file in your text editor and browser.

LESSON 7 Horizontal Rules

Horizontal rules (lines) are often used to create visual dividers on a Web page. The horizontal rule is a straight line that goes from the left side of the screen to the right side. To divide sections with horizontal rules, you can apply the `<hr />` empty tag.

You can apply several different attributes to change the default appearance of horizontal rules. You can change the width, thickness, alignment, and style of a horizontal rule. The `size=""` attribute sets the thickness, and the `width=""` attribute sets the width. The width can be specified as pixels or as a percentage of the screen size.

The `align=""` attribute aligns horizontal rules to the left, right, or center. By default, horizontal rules possess a three-dimensional "cutout" appearance. If you prefer your rules to appear without the default shading, you can apply the `noshade=""` attribute. If the default color of the horizontal rules interferes with the colors on your Web page, you can use the `color=""` attribute to assign a predefined color (color name) or hexadecimal color to the rules.

The `align=""`, `size=""`, and `width=""` attributes were deprecated in the HTML 4 standard in favor of style sheets. You can use the attributes in XHTML Transitional, but we recommend that you avoid them whenever possible.

Add a Horizontal Line

1 In your text editor and Web browser, open hr.htm from your WIP_03 folder.

2 Position your cursor below the first heading. Insert a horizontal rule, as follows:

```
. . .
<h1 align="center">Dr. Know-It-All Recommendations</h1>
<hr />
. . .
```

3 **Save your file and refresh in the browser.**

A gray bar displays across the Web page. It separates the heading from the page content. Notice that the `<hr />` tag is empty.

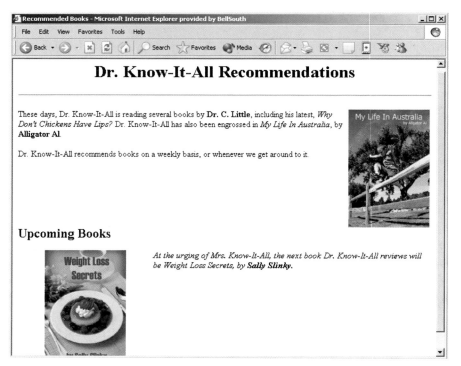

FIGURE 3.17

4 **Leave the file open in your text editor and browser.**

Modify a Horizontal Line

1 **In the open file, switch to the text editor.**

2 **Modify the horizontal rule by adding the following attributes:**

```
. . .
<h1 align="center">Dr. Know-It-All Recommendations</h1>
<hr width="50%" noshade="noshade" color="blue" />
. . .
```

A blue horizontal line that is 50% of the screen width displays on the Web page. The horizontal line has no shading. Keep in mind that these attributes were deprecated in favor of style sheets, but they work if you are using XHTML Transitional.

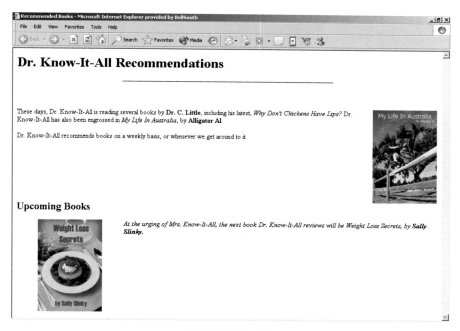

FIGURE 3.18

3   **Close the file in both applications.**

SUMMARY

In Chapter 3, you learned about the types of images you can use within your Web pages. You learned to use the `src=""` attribute to reference images. You also learned about the other attributes the XHTML standards require you to use when referencing images on a Web page.

You discovered that some viewers browse the Web with the graphics feature turned off in their browsers; other users are unable to display graphics on their systems due to slow Internet connections. You learned how to apply alt text to your images to resolve both of these issues for your viewers.

You explored how to control image alignment relative to text and other content to create a visually pleasing Web page layout. With these basic design elements, you should feel confident in your ability to modify text and images on a Web page.

KEY TERMS

Absolute link	Line art	Post
Alt text	Loop	Relative link
Bandwidth	Lossless	Remote directory
Character entity	Lossy	Resolution
Compression	Lowsrc	Scaling
GIF (Graphics Interchange Format)	LZW compression	Src/Source attribute
Horizontal rule	Nonbreaking space	Transparency
Horizontal space	Path	Vertical space
Indexed color	Pixel	
JPEG/JPG (Joint Photographic Experts Group)	Pixelated	
	PNG	

CHECKING CONCEPTS AND TERMS

MULTIPLE CHOICE

Circle the letter of the correct answer for each of the following questions.

1. Which image format supports only 256 colors?
   a. GIF
   b. JPG
   c. PNG
   d. None of the above.

2. Why is the `alt=""` attribute so important?
   a. It provides information to the viewer in the event an image does not display. It is required in XHTML 1.1.
   b. The alt="" attribute provides helpful tool tips.
   c. It allows you to include an alternate image on the page.

3. What additional tag can you use to control how an image aligns with text?
   a. <h2>
   b. <font>
   c. <br clear="all">

4. The `<img>` tag offers five possible values for alignment.
   a. True
   b. False

5. To avoid a gap of white space when aligning text with an image, use the following value/s:
   a. Bottom
   b. Top
   c. Left
   d. Right
   e. c and d

6. The height and width attributes are required when using the `<img />` tag.
   a. True
   b. False

7. Horizontal rules _____.

   a. separate content on a Web page

   b. have been deprecated completely from XHTML

   c. display as gray lines across a Web page

   d. cannot be created in XHTML

8. You can add space between any types of elements on a Web page by _____.

   a. inserting the clear="" attribute with the paragraph tag

   b. inserting nonbreaking space/s

   c. adding empty spaces in the source code

   d. using the <space> tag

9. The image tag is eliminated in the XHTML 2.0 draft in favor of the `<object>` element.

   a. True

   b. False

10. A lowsrc image is a larger image file than the `src=""` image.

   a. True

   b. False

DISCUSSION QUESTIONS

1. How can you prevent slow download times when you include images on your Web pages?

2. Why do you think the height, width, and alt tags are required in the XHTML standard?

3. Besides the obvious aesthetic reasons, why is it important to display images on a Web page?

SKILL DRILL

Skill Drill exercises reinforce chapter skills. Each skill reinforced is the same as, or nearly the same as, a skill we presented in the chapter. We provide detailed instructions in a step-by-step format. You should work through these exercises in the order provided.

1. Add Images to a Web Page

A community service organization hired you to create an online newsletter. They want you to develop a simple text page with a few images to highlight each story.

1. From your WIP_03 folder, open news.htm in a text editor and browser.

This document displays two headings and two paragraphs of text that have been indented (block-quoted) multiple times.

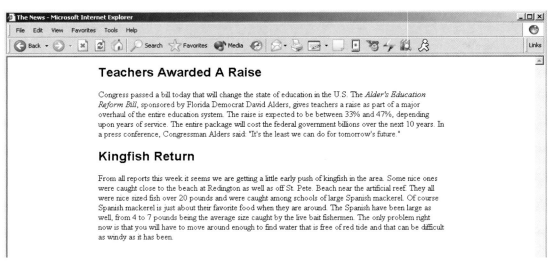

FIGURE 3.19

2. Insert the images and required attributes, as follows:

```
...
<title>The News</title>
</head>
<body>
<p align="center">
<img src="header.gif" width="590" height="68" alt="Newsletter" />
</p>
<blockquote>
<blockquote>
<blockquote>
<blockquote>
<h2><font face="Arial">Teachers Awarded A Raise</font></h2>
<p>
<img src="teachers.jpg"  />
Congress passed a bill today that will change the state of educa-
tion in the U.S. The <i>Alder's Education Reform Bill</i>, spon-
sored by Florida Democrat David Alders, gives teachers a raise as
```

part of a major overhaul of the entire education system. The raise is expected to be between 33% and 47%, depending upon years of service. The entire package will cost the federal government billions over the next 10 years. In a press conference, Congressman Alders said: "It's the least we can do for tomorrow's future."

```
</p>

</blockquote>

</blockquote>

</blockquote>

</blockquote>

<blockquote>

<blockquote>

<blockquote>

<blockquote>

<h2><font face="Arial">Kingfish Return </font></h2>

<p>

<img src="boat.jpg" />
```

From all reports this week it seems we are getting a little early push of kingfish in the area. Some nice ones were caught close to the beach at Redington as well as off St. Pete. Beach near the artificial reef. They all ...

3. Provide the height and width information to decrease the time it takes for the images to download to the viewer's browser.

```
...

<p>

<img src="teachers.jpg" width="165" height="125" />
```

Congress passed a bill today that will change the state of education in the U.S. The <i>Alder's Education Reform Bill</i>, sponsored by Florida Democrat David Alders, gives teachers a raise as part of a major overhaul of the entire education system. The raise is expected to be between 33% and 47%, depending upon years of service. The entire package will cost the federal government billions over the next 10 years. In a press conference, Congressman Alders said: "It's the least we can do for tomorrow's future."

```
</p>
```

```
</blockquote>

</blockquote>

</blockquote>

</blockquote>

<blockquote>

<blockquote>

<blockquote>

<blockquote>

<h2><font face="Arial">Kingfish Return </font></h2>

<p>

<img src="boat.jpg" width="125" height="187" />
```

From all reports this week it seems we are getting a little early push of kingfish in the area. Some nice ones were caught close to the beach at Redington as well as off St. Pete. Beach near the artificial reef. They all ...

4. Provide alternate text in case the images do not display properly.

```
   ...

   <p>

   <img src="teachers.jpg" width="165" height="125" alt="Teachers
   Awarded A Raise">
```

Congress passed a bill today that will change the state of education in the U.S. The <i>Alder's Education Reform Bill</i>, sponsored by Florida Democrat David Alders, gives teachers a raise as part of a major overhaul of the entire education system. The raise is expected to be between 33% and 47%, depending upon years of service. The entire package will cost the federal government billions over the next 10 years. In a press conference, Congressman Alders said: "It's the least we can do for tomorrow's future."

```
   </p>

   </blockquote>

   </blockquote>

   </blockquote>

   </blockquote>

   <blockquote>
```

```
<blockquote>

<blockquote>

<blockquote>

<h2><font face="Arial">Kingfish Return </font></h2>

<p>

<img src="boat.jpg" width="125" height="187" alt="Kingfish
Return" />
```

From all reports this week it seems we are getting a little early push of kingfish in the area. Some nice ones were caught close to the beach at Redington as well as off St. Pete. Beach near the artificial reef. They all ...

5. Save news.htm in your text editor. Refresh the document in the browser to view the changes.

    Notice that the code in the **<blockquote>** tag is nested. You can nest **<blockquote>** tags to add multiple indentations. Be sure there is an ending **</blockquote>** tag for every opening **<blockquote>** tag.

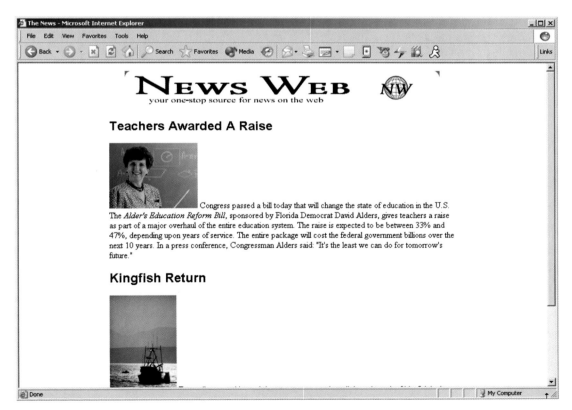

FIGURE 3.20

6. Leave the file open for the next exercise.

2. Align Images

The images display on the community service Web page, but the layout is less than ideal. To enhance the page's aesthetic appeal, align the images with the appropriate section of text.

1. In the open document, switch to the text editor.

2. Apply the following image attribute changes.

```
. . .

<p>

<img src="teachers.jpg" align="right" width="165" height="125"
alt="Teachers Awarded A Raise" />

Congress passed a bill today that will change the state of
education in the U.S. The <i>Alder's Education Reform Bill</i>,
sponsored by Florida Democrat David Alders, gives teachers a
raise as part of a major overhaul of the entire education system.
The raise is expected to be between 33% and 47%, depending upon
years of service. The entire package will cost the federal
government billions over the next 10 years. In a press
conference, Congressman Alders said: "It's the least we can
do for tomorrow's future."

</p>

</blockquote>

</blockquote>

</blockquote>

</blockquote>

<blockquote>

<blockquote>

<blockquote>

<blockquote>

<h2><font face="Arial">Kingfish Return </font></h2>

<p>

<img src="boat.jpg" align="left" width="125" height="187"
alt="Kingfish Return" />

From all reports this week it seems we are getting a little early
push of kingfish in the area. Some nice ones were caught close to
the beach at Redington as well as off St. Pete. Beach near the
artificial reef. They all ...
```

3. Save the file in the text editor. Refresh the document in your browser and view the result.

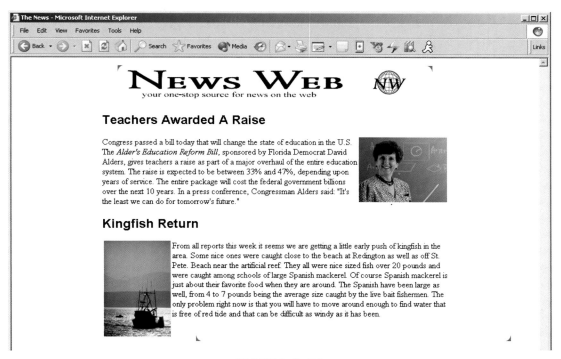

FIGURE 3.21

4. Leave the file open for the next exercise.

3. Clear a Break between Aligned Images

The page is coming along nicely, but the text and image alignment are causing the content to run together. Fix this problem with the **<br clear="all" />** tag.

1. In the open file, switch to the text editor.

2. Add two **<br clear="all" />** tags as follows:

```
. . .

Congress passed a bill today that will change the state of
education in the U.S. The <i>Alder's Education Reform Bill</i>,
sponsored by Florida Democrat David Alders, gives teachers a
raise as part of a major overhaul of the entire education system.
The raise is expected to be between 33% and 47%, depending upon
years of service. The entire package will cost the federal
government billions over the next 10 years. In a press
conference, Congressman Alders said: "It's the least we can
do for tomorrow's future."

</p>
```

```
</blockquote>

</blockquote>

</blockquote>

</blockquote>

<br clear="all" />

<blockquote>

<blockquote>

<blockquote>

<blockquote>

<h2><font face="Arial">Kingfish Return </font></h2>

<p>

<img src="boat.jpg" align="left" width="125" height="187"
alt="Kingfish Return" />

From all reports this week it seems we are getting a little early
push of kingfish in the area. Some nice ones were caught close to
the beach at Redington as well as off St. Pete. Beach near the
artificial reef. They all were nice sized fish over 20 pounds and
were caught among schools of large Spanish mackerel. Of course
Spanish mackerel is just about their favorite food when they are
around. The Spanish have been large as well, from 4 to 7 pounds
being the average size caught by the live bait fishermen. The
only problem right now is that you will have to move around
enough to find water that is free of red tide and that can be
difficult as windy as it has been.

</p>

</blockquote>

</blockquote>

</blockquote>

</blockquote>

<br clear="all" />

<p align="center">

<img src="footer.gif" width="590" height="25" alt="Newsletter" />

</p>

...
```

3. Save the changes to news.htm. Refresh the document in your browser and view the result.

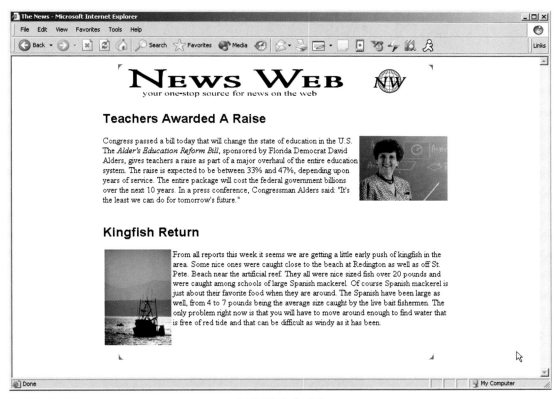

FIGURE 3.22

4. Save the changes and keep the file open.

4. Add Horizontal and Vertical Space

The text is too close to the bottom image. You need to add some space between the text and the image.

1. In the open file, switch to your text editor.

2. Add horizontal spacing to the bottom image, as follows:

```
. . .
<h2><font face="Arial">Kingfish Return </font></h2>
<p>
<img src="boat.jpg" align="left" width="125" height="187"
alt="Kingfish Return" hspace="10" />
From all reports this week it seems we are getting a little early
push of kingfish in the area. Some nice ones were caught close to
the beach at Redington as well as off St. Pete. Beach near the
artificial reef. They all ...
```

3. Add vertical spacing to the bottom image, as follows:

```
. . .

<h2><font face="Arial">Kingfish Return </font></h2>

<p>

<img src="boat.jpg" align="left" width="125" height="187"
alt="Kingfish Return" hspace="10" vspace="10" />
```

From all reports this week it seems we are getting a little early push of kingfish in the area. Some nice ones were caught close to the beach at Redington as well as off St. Pete. Beach near the artificial reef. They all . . .

4. Save the changes to news.htm. Refresh the document in your browser and view the result.

5. Close the file in your text editor and browser.

5. Add a Horizontal Line

The newsletter is almost complete, but you decide to add several horizontal rules to provide a more organized appearance on the page.

1. Open skillhr.htm in your browser and text editor.

2. At the page's top, add a basic horizontal rule that is 50 percent of the screen width. This rule separates the heading from the content.

```
. . .
<p align="center">
<img src="header.gif" width="590" height="68" alt="Newsletter" />
</p>
<hr width="50%" />
<blockquote>
<blockquote>
<blockquote>
<blockquote>
<h2><font face="Arial">Teachers Awarded A Raise</font></h2>
<p>
<img src="teachers.jpg" align="right" width="165" height="125"
alt="Teachers Awarded A Raise" />
```

Congress passed a bill today that will change the state of education in the U.S. The <i>Alder's Education Reform Bill</i>, sponsored by Florida Democrat David Alders, gives teachers a raise as part of a major overhaul . . .

3. Add another horizontal line between the two sections of content. It should be 50 percent of the screen width.

    . . .

    ```
    Congress passed a bill today that will change the state of
    education in the U.S. The <i>Alder's Education Reform Bill</i>,
    sponsored by Florida Democrat David Alders, gives teachers a
    raise as part of a major overhaul of the entire education system.
    The raise is expected to be between 33% and 47%, depending upon
    years of service. The entire package will cost the federal
    government billions over the next 10 years. In a press
    conference, Congressman Alders said: "It's the least we can do
    for tomorrow's future."

    </p>

    </blockquote>

    </blockquote>

    </blockquote>

    </blockquote>

    <br clear="all" />

    <hr width="50%" />

    <blockquote>

    <blockquote>

    <blockquote>

    <blockquote>

    <h2><font face="Arial">Kingfish Return </font></h2>

    <p>

    <img src="boat.jpg" align="left" width="125" height="187"
    alt="Kingfish Return" hspace="10" vspace="10" />

    From all reports this week it seems we are getting a little early
    push of kingfish in the area. Some nice ones were caught close to
    the beach at Redington as well as off St. Pete. Beach near the
    artificial reef. They all ...
    ```

4. Save the changes to skillhr.htm.

5. Refresh the document in your browser and view the result.

6. Close the file in both applications.

CHALLENGE

Challenge exercises expand on, or are somewhat related to, skills presented in the lessons. Each exercise provides a brief introduction, followed by numbered-step instructions that are not as detailed as those in the Skill Drill exercises. You should work through these exercises in the order provided.

1. Add a Background Image

The newsletter you volunteered to create was very successful. Your next assignment is to spice up the document with some graphic elements. The first step is to add a background image.

1. From your WIP_03 folder, open challenge.htm in your Web browser and text editor.

2. If you can log on to the Web, launch your Web browser and go to www.google.com. Conduct a search on background images that would complement the news.htm Web page.

    If you are unable to access the Web, you can use the image called back.gif in the WIP_03 folder.

3. Download the background image to your WIP_03 folder.

4. Add the **`background="back.gif"`** attribute-value pair to the **`<body>`** tag. If you selected your own background image, use that image instead.

5. Save the changes to the text file and refresh the document in the browser.

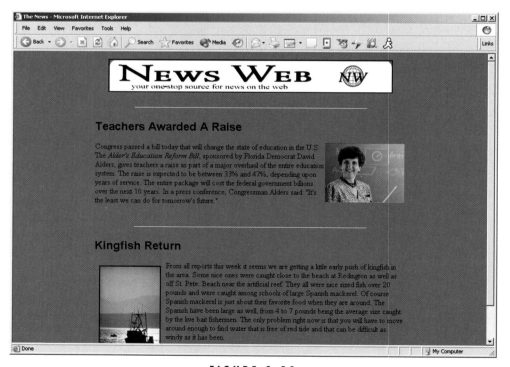

FIGURE 3.23

6. Leave the file open in both applications.

2. Add Borders and Find Dimensions

The newsletter looks better with a background image. You decide, however, that the existing images on the page are incompatible with the background. These are photographic images, so it would be unwise to convert them to transparent GIFs. Instead, you decide to add a border around the images to separate them from the new background image.

1. In the open document, add the **border="2"** attribute-value pair to the two primary **<img>** tags on the Web page (you do not have to add these to the header.gif or footer.gif files).

2. Remove the top horizontal line.

3. From your WIP_03 folder, insert topstory.gif above the text and image content (beneath the banner).

4. Right-click the image.

   You can see the image's dimensions in the Properties dialog box.

5. Insert the image's dimensions in the **<img />** tag.

6. Provide alternate text for the new image. Center-align the image on the Web page.

7. Apply an image border to the image.

8. Save the changes to the text file. Refresh the document in the browser and view the result.

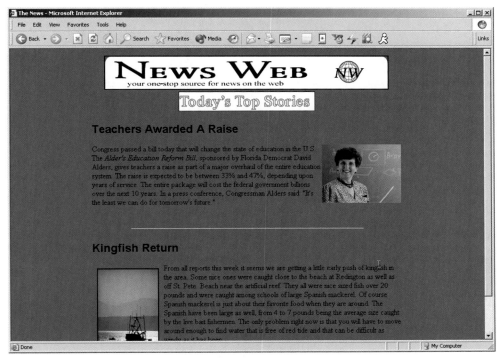

FIGURE 3.24

9. Keep the file open in both applications.

3. Add Navigation

You can use images to create hyperlink navigation so your viewers can access other pages on your site. Even though you have not yet learned how to create hyperlinks, you can build the layout of your navigation and add the links later.

1. In the open file, position your cursor beneath topstory.gif. Insert bullet.gif.

    Bullet.gif should be in your WIP_03 folder.

2. Type "About Us" next to the first bullet image.

3. Insert a space after "About Us". Insert bullet.gif. Type "Archives" next to the second bullet image.

4. Insert a space after "Archives". Insert bullet.gif. Type "Contact Us" next to the third bullet image.

5. Align each text link in the middle of bullet.gif.

6. Find and insert bullet.gif's dimensions in each `<img />` tag.

7. Provide alternate text for each bullet.

    Ideally, this would be the name of the actual link. For now, you can simply add the descriptive text of your choice.

8. Apply the bold style to each text link.

9. Save the changes to the text file. Refresh the document in the browser and view the result.

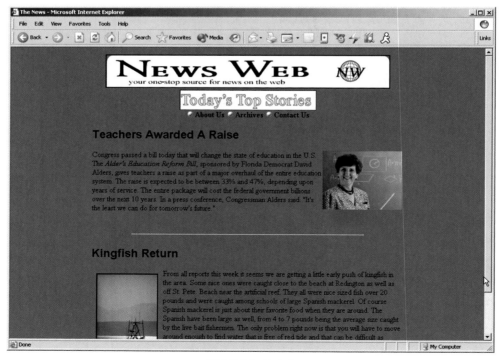

FIGURE 3.25

10. Leave the file open in both applications.

4. Create Different Page Layouts

The Web page is complete. You decide it would be best to offer your client several design choices to promote ideas and discussion. You create several versions of the Web page to show your client.

1. Save the open document as "news02.htm" to your WIP_03 folder.

2. Download another background image to change the color scheme of the page.

3. Move the images in the text areas to the opposite side of the layout.

4. Change the font to a different color, style, and size.

5. Create at least three versions of the page, each with a different background, layout, color, and font.

6. Close all of the files when you are done.

Add Graphics to an Existing Document

The local theater that hired you to create a Web page about the play *To Kill a Mockingbird* wants you to add a few images. Use the Web page you created in the Portfolio Builder from Chapter 2 as your base, and then add appropriate images to support the theme of the play. If you did not complete the Portfolio Builder in Chapter 2, do so now. Then, complete this Portfolio Builder.

To complete this exercise, you should do the following:

■ Open the document you created in the Portfolio Builder in Chapter 2. Save it under a new file name. This gives you two versions of the Web page for your portfolio.

■ Part of becoming a Web page author is finding appropriate images for your pages; you can create images yourself, purchase images from a graphic artist, or use royalty-free art you find on the Web that you have permission to use. Conduct a Web search to locate images that support your theme.

■ Insert the image/s on the Web page. Align them with the text. Make sure you provide the proper size information and alternative text.

■ You can also provide other graphical features, such as horizontal rules (graphic horizontal rules are sometimes called "dividers"). Place the dividers between the sections of text on your page.

CHAPTER 4

Creating Hyperlinks

OBJECTIVES

In this chapter, you learn how to:

- Work with text hyperlinks

- Add links to a page

- Create image hyperlinks

- Add titles to hyperlinks

- Remove borders from images

- Apply absolute and relative links

- Create a base link

- Include e-mail links on Web pages

Why Would I Do This?

Every Web surfer has experienced *hyperlinks*, which are the clickable areas on a Web page that take the viewer to another page or display additional information. In Chapter 3, you learned that when you add an image to a Web page, you actually add a reference to the image; you do not add the image itself. To make image references work correctly, the browser must know exactly where that image is located. So far, that's been an easy task to accomplish because the image has been in the same folder as the Web page itself. When it comes to linking to other pages, however, references become a bit more complicated.

Organizing information in a Web page is one thing; providing an easy way to access that information is another. Hyperlinks are designed to provide viewers with an easy method of accessing unlimited content. So far, we have considered Web pages as individual documents. The beauty of a Web page, however, is its ability to link pages together with hyperlinks, allowing users to navigate through the online information you provide.

As a Web page designer, you need to provide links to additional information that is located on remote sites. Links to other documents, images, downloads, and e-mail addresses are essential elements of most Web sites. In this chapter, you learn how to create hyperlinks to provide access to a wide range of online resources.

VISUAL SUMMARY

An image or a section of text can be used to hyperlink one Web page to another. It doesn't matter if the linked pages are located on the same site or on different sites. Clicking the link takes the user to another Web page or to another location on the same page. Words or phrases that serve as links are underlined, appear in a different color, or both. Images that serve as links usually display a border; this differentiates linked images from nonlinked images.

A **URL (Uniform Resource Locator)** is the Web address of a particular resource, such as an image or a Web page. The hyperlinks in your Web pages link to **relative URLs** (local files or addresses) or **absolute URLs** (addresses or files in different locations, such as other Web servers). For example, the following is an absolute URL to Web Answer's home page: http://www.web-answers.com, as shown below.

FIGURE 4.1

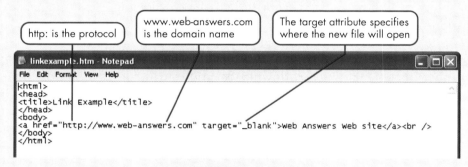

FIGURE 4.2

Let's take a moment to analyze the parts of a sample URL:

```
http://www.web-answers.com/XHTML/contents.htm
```

There are four parts to this URL:

- "http://" is the **hypertext transport protocol**, which is used to transfer hypertext documents (Web pages) across the Internet. A **protocol** is a set of standards for accomplishing a task — in this case, for transferring an HTML page across the Internet.

- "www.web-answers.com" is the domain. A **domain** is the name of the computer on which the file is located. For a Web site, the computer is also known as the **Web server**.

- "XHTML" is the name of a folder.

- "contents.htm" is the file in the XHTML folder.

To construct a complete URL, you combine all of these parts, each of which is separated with a forward slash (/). When you apply a URL to a link or image, the browser interprets (reads) the URL and knows exactly where to search for the particular file that is listed in the Address field.

LESSON 1 Adding Hyperlinks to Text

The concept of hypertext and links originated in the 1940s. They were only ideas back then, however, and were not put into practical use until the dawn of the Internet and the World Wide Web. On the Web, the most common form of link is the ***text link*** (a series of words or a URL). A user can click a text link to access additional information on a topic. This type of link is called an ***anchor tag***, coded with `<a></a>` tags.

The most common anchor tag sends the user to a different page. The new page can be within the same site, or it can be on an entirely different site. The ***destination*** page is called the ***target***; it is listed in the ***hypertext reference attribute (href)***. For instance, if you want to add a link to a page that takes a user to home.htm, you should insert the following code:

```
<a href="home.htm" title="Home Page Link">Click here to go to our home
page!</a>
```

Anything between the opening and closing tags is formatted as a link. If the browser supports it, the ***title attribute*** causes tool-tip-style information to appear when the user points to a link. In the preceding code example, the tool-tip-style information is "Home Page Link," as shown here:

FIGURE 4.3

The URL contained in the link can point to anything — a page on the same server, a page halfway across the world, or even another application. In the following exercise, let's put your knowledge of hyperlinks into action and add a text link to a document.

Create a Text Hyperlink

1 **Copy the contents of your Chapter_04 folder to your WIP_04 folder.**

2 **In your text editor and browser, open recs.htm from your WIP_04 folder. View the document in the browser.**

At the top of the file, we added a reference to our question-and-answer page (faq.htm) and a horizontal rule (**`<hr />`** tag).

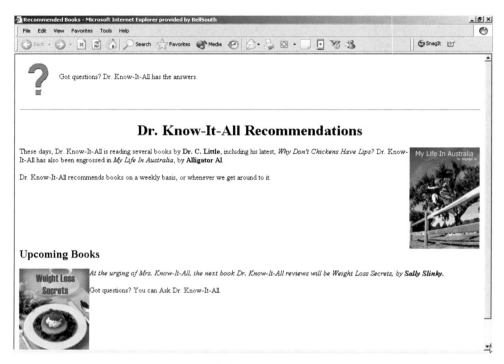

FIGURE 4.4

3   **Use the `<a></a>` tags to create a hyperlink to faq.htm, as follows:**

```
<html>

<head><title> Recommended Books</title></head>

<body>

<p><img src="q.gif" align="middle" alt="?" />Got questions?
Dr. Know-It-All has the

<a href="faq.htm">answers</a></p>

<hr />

<h1 align="center">Dr. Know-It-All Recommendations</h1>

. . .
```

When the user clicks the text link "answers", he advances to faq.htm.

4   **Save the file in the text editor. Refresh the browser and view the result.**

The text "answers", which is contained within the **`<a></a>`** tags, appears blue with an underline. Notice the cursor changes to a hand when it hovers over the link.

5   **Switch to rec.htm in the text editor. Add a title attribute for "Frequently Asked Questions" to the anchor (<a>) tag, as follows:**

```
. . .

<p><img src="q.gif" align="middle" alt="?" />Got questions?
Dr. Know-It-All has the <a href="faq.htm" title="Frequently Asked
Questions" >answers</a>.</p>

<hr />

<h1 align="center">Dr. Know-It-All Recommendations</h1>

. . .
```

When the user hovers the mouse over the link, additional information about the hyperlink displays.

6   **Save the file in the text editor. Refresh the browser. Roll your mouse over the new link, but don't click it.**

When the mouse is placed over the image, a small tool tip displays the text contained in the `title=""` attribute. Not all browsers support this functionality.

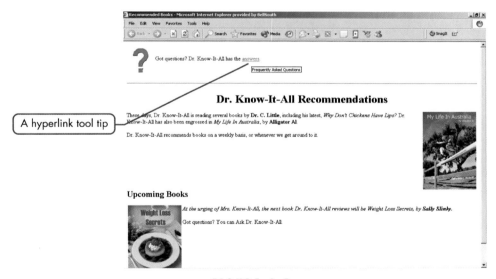

FIGURE 4.5

7   **Click the link.**

We specified faq.htm as the href, so faq.htm displays in the browser window.

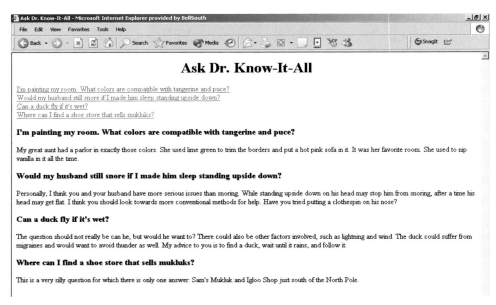

FIGURE 4.6

8   **Save the changes and close the file in your browser and text editor.**

To Extend Your Knowledge . . .

MANY TYPES OF URLs

At last count, there were nearly 100 different protocols used in URLs. You can specify a unique protocol for every type of content available on the Internet. The following are the most commonly used protocols that you will incorporate in your Web pages:

```
http:  ftp:  mailto:
```

LESSON 2 Targets within a Page

In addition to linking to a full page, you can link to a specific location within a page. To do this, use the ***name attribute*** to create an anchor as the target of a link. Targets provide convenient links to specific locations on a page so the user can jump to the desired location quickly and easily. Name attributes are commonly used on longer Web pages, since it can be distracting (and time-consuming) to scroll up and down while you search for a section of information.

The following code is used to create a target using the name attribute:

```
<a name="specific choice">link text</a>
```

In the preceding example, "specific choice" is the name of the target and becomes the destination on the Web page. The user advances to the named destination when she clicks the link.

Developers use ***pseudo-code*** (a plain English translation of an actual code statement) to describe how code works. Using pseudo-code, you can create the link to point to this target:

```
<a href="name of the page#specific choice">link text</a>
```

In this instance, "name of the page" is the HTML page on which the target appears. The word that follows the pound sign (#) is the name we chose for the target. In an instance where both the link and the target refer to the same page, the target would omit the page name and begin with the pound sign and the target's name.

Add an Anchor within a Page

1 **Open WIP_04>faq.htm in your text editor and browser. View the page in your browser.**

Notice the list of links at the top of the page. The list allows viewers to click a link and quickly move to the section of the document they want to read.

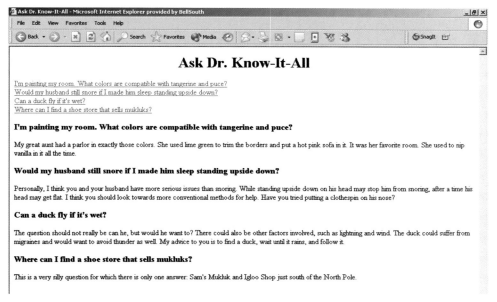

FIGURE 4.7

2 **Add a "Back to Top" link to each of the questions, as follows:**

. . .

```
<h3><a name="room">I'm painting my room. What colors are compatible
with tangerine and puce?</a></h3>

<p>My great aunt had a parlor in exactly those colors. She used
lime green to trim the borders and put a hot pink sofa in it. It
was her favorite room. She used to nip vanilla in it all the
time.</p>

<p><a href="#top">Back To Top</a></p>

<h3><a name="snore">Would my husband still snore if I made him
sleep standing upside down?</a></h3>

<p>Personally, I think you and your husband have more serious
issues than snoring. While standing upside down on his head may
stop him from snoring, after a time his head may get flat. I
think you should look towards more conventional methods for help.
Have you tried putting a clothespin on his nose?</p>

<p><a href="#top">Back To Top</a></p>

<h3><a name="duck">Can a duck fly if it's wet?</a></h3>

<p>The question should not really be can he, but would he want
to? There could also be other factors involved, such as lightning
and wind. The duck could suffer from migraines and would want to
avoid thunder as well. My advice to you is to find a duck, wait
until it rains, and follow it.</p>

<p><a href="#top">Back To Top</a></p>

<h3><a name="mukluk">Where can I find a shoe store that sells
mukluks?</a></h3>

<p>This is a very silly question for which there is only one
answer: Sam's Mukluk and Igloo Shop just south of the North
Pole.</p>

<p><a href="#top">Back To Top</a></p>

</body>

</html>
```

This creates links to the targets within the document.

3 | At the top of the page, add the target for these links.

```
. . .
<body>
<h1 align="center">Ask Dr. Know-It-All</h1>
<a name="top"></a>
<a href="#room">I'm painting my room. What colors are compatible
with tangerine and puce?</a><br />
. . .
```

4 | Save the file in the text editor. Refresh the browser and view the result.

At the bottom of each section of text, note the line of text that reads "Back To Top". Clicking this link allows the user to quickly return to the top of the page without scrolling.

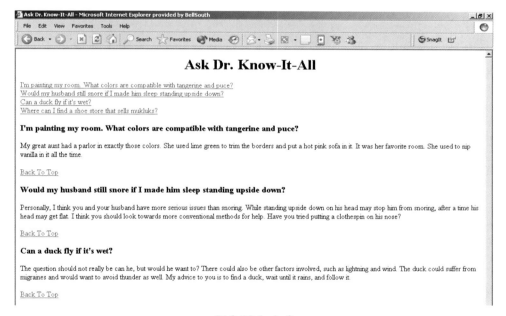

FIGURE 4.8

5 | Click the third question.

The browser immediately jumps to the third question on the page.

6   **Click one of the Back To Top links.**

Even though the link says it will jump to the top of the page, notice that you don't arrive at that location. When you created the Back To Top link, you specified a particular target location that lies below the heading. To fix this, the target at the top of the page could be placed directly below the `<body>` tag.

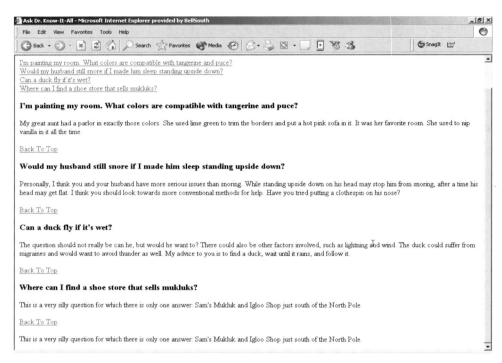

FIGURE 4.9

7   **Save your changes. Close the file in your browser and text editor.**

To Extend Your Knowledge . . .

LINKING CONVENIENCE

One important design concept: if you enable users to jump down the page, you should also enable them to jump back up. Don't forget to add links at the page's bottom to return the visitor to the page's top.

The browser moves to whatever location the target anchor specifies. Make certain that you place your anchors correctly.

LESSON 3   Adding Hyperlinks to Images

When you add a hyperlink to text, you enclose the text in the `<a></a>` tags. Doing so tells the browser that whatever is between the opening and closing tags is clickable, and it will transport the user to the destination specified by the href attribute.

Today, it is common practice to use images and icons instead of words for links. For instance, instead of using the word "Next", you might insert an icon with an arrow. Many times, the link to a home page is an image of a house. Some Web authors create a set of buttons or a graphical navigation menu to serve as their links.

Adding a link to an image works in the same manner as when you add a link to text. The process is the same, except that you enclose the `<img />` tag within the <a></a> tags to make the image a clickable length. For example:

```
<a href="location"><img src="name.gif" /></a>
```

Image links are often used to provide a graphical navigation layout, which many times is more aesthetically pleasing than using a text-based navigation system. Be mindful, however, of the type of images you use for the buttons. Simplicity is often the key to an easy-to-navigate, well-designed Web page.

Create an Image Link

1   **From your WIP_04 folder, open imagelinks.htm in your text editor and browser. View the document in the browser.**

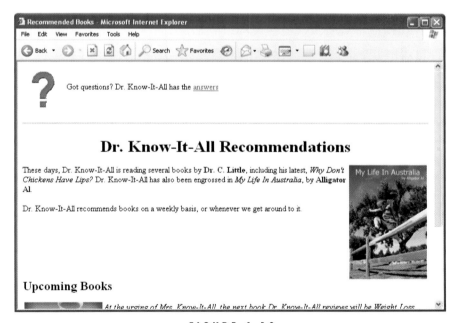

FIGURE 4.10

2   **Add a link to the image, as follows:**

```
<html>
<head><title>Recommended Books</title></head>
<body>
<p>
<a href="faq.htm"><img src="q.gif" align="middle" alt="?" /></a>
Got questions? Dr. Know-It-All has the <a
href="faq.htm">answers</a>.</p>
<hr />

. . .
```

This creates a link to faq.htm that displays when the user clicks the image. Notice how the link works by enclosing the **<img>** tag within the **<a>** tag.

3   **Save the file in the text editor. Refresh the browser and view the result.**

The image is now a link and displays a blue (or purple) border in most browsers. Click the image to verify that you jump to faq.htm.

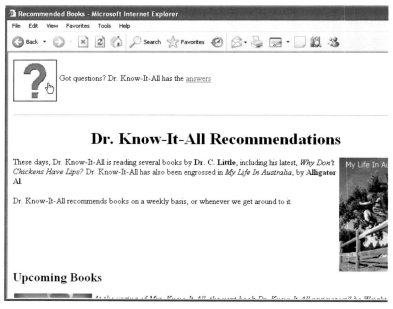

FIGURE 4.11

4   **Click the browser's Back button.**

This returns you to imagelinks.htm.

5   **Close the file in your browser and text editor.**

To Extend Your Knowledge . . .

ORGANIZING YOUR FILES

When you're planning a site, you should include plans for the file structure, including folder and file locations. **Assets** (files), such as images and sounds, should always be stored in their own folders. Each content section should have its own folder. It is important that you (and everyone else involved in the site's development) know where the files and folders are located. When you use a standard location for all of your URLs, you always have a consistent reference point for them.

LESSON 4   Removing Borders

As you noticed in the previous exercise, a linked image displays a blue (or purple) border. In the early days of the Web, designers used this border to indicate that when an image was clicked, it would advance the user to another page, replace a small image with a larger image, or provide additional details about the image. These days, however, designers typically prefer to use an image as a supplemental link or to create a clickable image that doesn't require such an obvious cue as a blue border.

Today's sophisticated users do not need the visual cue of an image border, so designers usually remove them. They do so with the **border attribute**, which controls the border's width. The default border width is 2 pixels. To remove the border on a linked image, you can set the border width to 0 pixels, as follows:

```
<a href="home.htm"><img src="home.gif" border="0" alt="Home" /></a>
```

The border attribute is specified as part of the image tag, but a blue border appears by default if there is a link. As you know, once you click a link, it changes color on your screen — one color is applied to an unclicked link, and a different color is applied to a link after it has been clicked. In essence, the image border is a visual clue that tells the user whether he has clicked the link or not.

You can add attributes to the body tag to change the default color of links. For example, **<body link="green" vlink="yellow" alink="red">**, where:

- **link=""** changes the color of the link, which is blue by default.
- **vlink=""** changes the color of the visited link, which usually defaults to purple.
- **alink=""** is the color of the link at the moment the user clicks it.

You can set the values of the attributes to one of the 16 predetermined colors or to a hexadecimal color. These attributes have been deprecated in XHTML, however, and we recommend that you use CSS to change the default colors of your links.

You can control the presence (or absence) of borders, even if you don't yet know if an image will be linked. This can prevent an unintended border from appearing later.

Remove the Image Border

1   **In your browser and text editor, open removeborder.htm from your WIP_04 folder.**

2   **Set the width of the first image border to 0:**

```
. . .
<title>Recommended Books</title>
</head>
<body>
<p><a href="faq.htm"><img src="q.gif" align="middle" alt="?"
border="0" /></a>Got questions? Dr. Know-It-All has the
<a href="faq.htm">answers</a>.</p>
<hr />

. . .
```

This removes the blue (or purple) border around the image. If the image was not created as an image link, the border displays in black by default. The size of the border can vary, depending on what you require for a particular layout (**border="1"** or **border="5"**, for example).

3   **Save the file in the text editor.**

4   **Refresh the browser.**

The blue border is gone, but the link is still available.

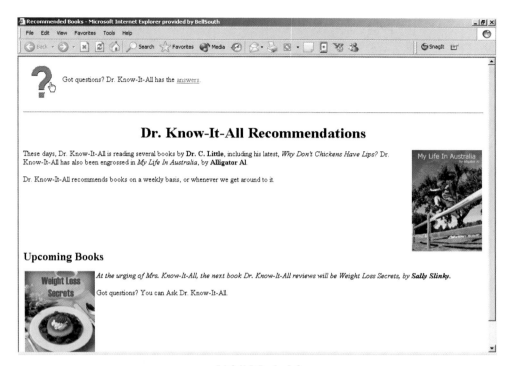

FIGURE 4.12

5   **Close the file in your browser and text editor.**

LESSON 5   Relative vs. Absolute URLs

As we discussed earlier, a browser interprets a URL as absolute or relative. An absolute URL, such as http://www.indhummer.com/index.htm, includes everything from the protocol to the file name. An absolute URL tells the browser everything it needs to know to locate a file. A relative URL includes less information about the location of the file because the file and the Web page are located on the same Web server; they are under the same domain name (the name of a computer on the Internet). When a file and its associated Web page are in the same domain, the browser does not require as much information to locate the file; it assumes that any information missing from the URL is supplied from the current Web page's URL.

Let's consider http://www.web-answers.com. It is an absolute URL, even though it does not include a file name. URLs such as this include default files, usually named "index.htm." When a user enters "http://www.web-answers.com" in the browser Address field, by default the browser loads the file http://www.web-answers.com/index.htm. In this case, http://www.web-answers.com and http://www.web-answers.com/index.htm are the same. You learn more about default files later in this book.

Link to an Absolute URL

1   In your browser and text editor, open absolute.htm from your WIP_04 folder.

2   At the bottom of the page, create a link to an absolute URL, as follows:

```
...
<p>Got questions? You can Ask Dr. Know-It-All.</p>
<br clear="all" />
<p align="center"><a href=http://www.web-answers.com>
Visit Our Sponsor</a></p>
</body>
</html>
```

This creates a text link on the Web page to an absolute URL (a remote location on the Web).

3   Save the changes to the file.

4   Refresh the document in the browser and view the result.

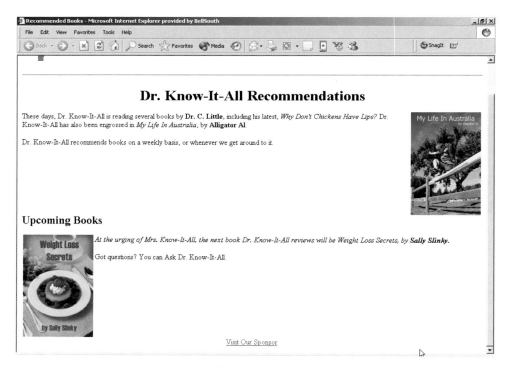

FIGURE 4.13

The link displays in the bottom-center of the page. Scroll down if you can't see the link.

5 | **Click the Visit Our Sponsor link.**

The link takes you to the Web Answers Web site. You must be online to see the www.web-answers.com home page.

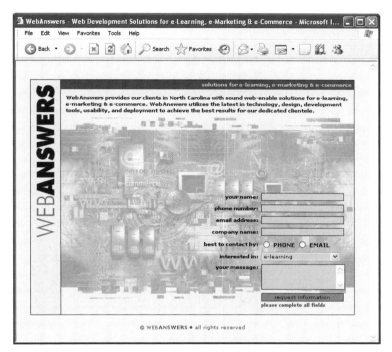

FIGURE 4.14

6 | **Close the file in your browser and text editor.**

To Extend Your Knowledge . . .

TYPES OF URLs

In Web development terms, a protocol is a set of rules for communication; it is a type of common vocabulary used between different computer programs. One protocol is http, which you see at the beginning of many URLs. Five of the most common protocols are:

http: HyperText Transfer Protocol. Web servers and browsers use this protocol to communicate. For example, http://www.yahoo.com.

https: *Secure HyperText Transfer Protocol*. It is similar to http, except that the messages are *encrypted* (scrambled) so they can't be intercepted and read by anyone other than the intended recipient. When you submit your credit card number over the Web, you are (hopefully) using a secure https page. For example, https://www.semortgagesolutions.com/refinance/default.html.

file: A Web browser uses this protocol to access a page on the local hard drive. These URLs start with file:/// — note the extra slash. For example, file:///HardDrive/desktop/WIP/articles/recs.htm.

mailto: This protocol enables the user to send e-mail to a particular person, such as the Webmaster. For example, mailto:webmaster@mysite.com.

ftp: *File Transfer Protocol*. It is primarily used for downloading large files because it is faster than http. Developers and designers use this protocol to upload files to a Web (FTP) site. For example, ftp://ftp10.netscape.com/pub/Netscape6/English/6.01/Mac/MACOS8.5/MacNetscape6Installer.sea.bin.

LESSON 6 Using the <base> Tag

In most cases, you enjoy better results when you use relative URLs rather than absolute URLs. Relative URLs allow you to move an entire site to a new location, such as to a different server. The files do not require renaming, and the site continues to work as it did before the move.

In some situations, however, using relative URLs does not work well. For instance, if a user were to save a Web page to her local hard drive, and that page contained relative URLs, the images and links wouldn't work when she tried to view the page on her computer. The URLs would point to their original location, not to the new location on the user's local hard drive.

Fortunately for Web developers, there is an answer to this dilemma. It's called the **<base />** tag, which acts as a global reference point for a Web page. The browser automatically adds the **<base />** tag to the beginning of each URL it encounters on a page. If you add **<base href="http:// www.nicholaschase.com/" />** to a page, the browser adds that **<base />** tag to every URL on that page. For example, if the browser encounters **<a href="index.htm">Home</a>**, it would automatically look for http://www.nicholaschase.com/index.htm.

Provide a <base> URL

1   In your text editor and browser, open recs.htm from your WIP_04 folder and add a `<base />` tag to the page, as follows:

```
<html>

<head><title>Recommended Books</title></head>

<body>

<base href="http://www.xhtmlclass.com" />

<p>

<a href="faq.htm"><img src="/images/q.gif"
align="middle" alt="? border="0" /></a>

Got questions? Dr. Know-It-All has the
<a href="/faq.htm">answers</a>.</p>

<hr />

. . .
```

This provides a `<base>` URL for all the links within the document. (If you are working on a Web server, use its URL.)

2   Save the file in the text editor.

3   Refresh the browser and view the result.

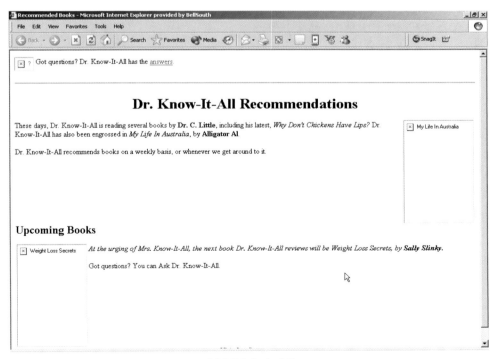

FIGURE 4.15

4 **Close the text editor, but leave the browser open.**

If you are using a Web server, you may see different images than before. If you are not using a Web server, the image disappears because the browser is looking for http://www.xhtmlclass.com/images/q.gif.

5 **Click the image or the text link.**

The Address field should display http://www.xhtmlclass.com/faq.htm. Again, if you are not working on a server, the page does not display, because the browser reads the URL as http://www.xhtmlclass.com/faq.htm. The base URL displays with the faq.htm file attached.

FIGURE 4.16

6 **Close the file in your browser and text editor.**

To Extend Your Knowledge . . .

MORE ON THE <BASE> TAG

The **<base />** **tag** offers the advantages of both relative and absolute links. The page continues to work when downloaded to a local machine. When an entire site is moved from one server to another, it continues to work when the new server's URL is added to the **<base />** tag.

LESSON 7 Linking to an E-mail Address

You already know how to link to files and Web addresses. The next task is to learn how to link to an e-mail address from a Web page. Providing such a link offers site visitors a convenient point of contact to the Webmaster, sales representative, or another individual who is ready and willing to answer visitors' questions.

You use the same tags to create an ***e-mail link*** as you would to create text and image links — with one small difference. The mailto source attribute contains a value command that launches the user's e-mail client when the user clicks an e-mail link. To create a link on your Web site that opens an e-mail window, use a mailto: link, as follows:

```
<a href="mailto:accountName@domainName.com">
send email to the Webmaster</a>
```

Most browsers open a new (blank) e-mail message window when a visitor clicks the e-mail link on a Web page. The recipient's address is automatically placed in the e-mail client's "To:" field. The visitor can then add an appropriate subject line and the content of his choice. It's always best to provide the actual e-mail address as the linked text, such as:

```
<a href="mailto:accountName@domainName.com ">
myaccount@mydomainname.com</a>
```

rather than a descriptive sentence or word.

Problems can occur with this method, however, if the visitor does not have an active e-mail account on the machine he is using to surf the Web. Without an active e-mail account, a message window cannot display, and the message cannot be sent. Developers sometimes avoid using this method in order to keep their e-mail address hidden.

Create an E-mail Link

1   **In your browser and text editor, open emaillink.htm from your WIP_04 folder.**

This is essentially a blank HTML page.

2   **Insert the following code in the body section of your document:**

```
. . .
<title>Email Link</title>
</head>
<body>
<a href="mailto:name@youremail.com">E-mail the Webmaster</a><br />
</body>
</html>
```

Be sure to replace name@youremail.com with a valid e-mail address. This creates a link to an e-mail address and launches the e-mail client installed on the machine.

? If you have problems

If you are in a classroom environment, your computer might not have an installed e-mail client. If an e-mail client is not installed on your machine, the e-mail link will not work properly. Consult with your instructor if this is an issue, or test your Web page on a machine that has an installed e-mail client.

---

3 Save the changes.

4 Refresh the document in your browser and view the result.

FIGURE 4.17

5 If you have a valid e-mail account configured on your current machine, you should be able to click the link and start an e-mail message.

6 Close the file in your text editor and Web browser.

To Extend Your Knowledge . . .

ANYTHING AS A LINK

One of the more interesting aspects of XHTML 2.0 is the idea that virtually anything can act as a link. Rather than write

```
<a href="http://webdesign.about.com/"><h2>Web Design at About</h2></a>,
```

the heading (<h2>) element can act as a link:

```
<h2 href="http://webdesign.about.com/">Web Design at About</h2>
```

CAREERS IN DESIGN

USING ROYALTY-FREE IMAGES

Being a Web designer does not necessarily mean that you have to be a graphic designer as well. If you are working in a team environment, it's likely there is a graphic designer on board, and you can utilize his talents to complete the artistic components of your Web site.

If, however, you are a one-person show who has no interest in graphic design, yet you need images for your sites, you can find virtually any graphic as royalty-free clip art, digital art, or stock images. Many online template sources offer royalty-free pre-made Web interfaces as well.

Before you include any of these resources, make sure that you get the proper permission — if permission is necessary. Some sites include a disclaimer stating that free use of their resources is limited to personal sites.

SUMMARY

In Chapter 4, you learned that a fundamental feature of hypertext is that you can link your documents to many other resources on the Web. You learned how to link to another location in the current document, to other documents on the local Web server, and to remote files on the Internet. You discovered that the target document is related to, and provides more information about, the source document.

You also learned how to use text and images to create links. You learned how to link to a specific point on a page and to an e-mail address. You discovered the distinctions between relative URLs, absolute URLs, and the `<base />` tag, and discovered when to use each of them. You explored file organization, which makes it easier for you and other members of your team to locate files in a timely fashion.

KEY TERMS

Absolute URL

Anchor tag

Assets

Base tag

Border attributes

Destination

Domain

E-mail link

Encryption

File Transfer Protocol (FTP)

Hyperlink

HyperText Reference Attribute (HREF)

HyperText Transfer Protocol (HTTP)

Mailto protocol

Name attributes

Protocol

Pseudo-code

Relative URL

Secure HyperText Transfer Protocol (HTTPS)

Target

Text link

Title attribute

Uniform resource locator (URL)

Web server

CHECKING CONCEPTS AND TERMS

MULTIPLE CHOICE

Circle the letter of the correct answer for each of the following questions.

1. A URL is a _____.
   a. Web site address
   b. hyperlink
   c. protocol used to download e-mails
   d. None of the above

2. What is the default display for a text link?
   a. Black text that is bold
   b. Blue text that is underlined
   c. A blue border is displayed around the text.
   d. Red text with a dotted line

3. You use the _____ tags to create a hyperlink.
   a. <link></link>
   b. <a></a>
   c.
   d.

4. Linking from point to point within a Web page is _____.
   a. convenient for navigation in a long document
   b. not beneficial and should be avoided
   c. isn't available in XHTML
   d. required for government Web sites

5. You can use images as hyperlinks if you place a link attribute within the **<img />** tag.
   a. True
   b. False

6. Why would you use the title attribute in a hyperlink?
   a. To use as default text if the browser does not display the link
   b. To provide the user with more information when he hovers his mouse over a hyperlink

   c. There is no title attribute for the hyperlink.
   d. It creates a subtitle in the top part of the browser window.

7. What is the difference between absolute and relative URLs?
   a. Absolute URLs exist locally, and relative URLs are remote.
   b. Relative URLs exist locally, and absolute URLs are remote.
   c. Absolute URLs point to files in the same directory, and relative URLs point to files in subdirectories.
   d. There is no difference between them.

8. Why would you use the **<base>** tag?
   a. It is required in XHTML.
   b. It provides a base URL for all the links to reference.
   c. It provides a base image for all your links.
   d. It provides a border around a link.

9. How is an e-mail link different from any other link?
   a. An e-mail link uses the href attribute.
   b. An e-mail link uses the mailto: command.
   c. An e-mail link uses the ftp: command.
   d. To create an e-mail link, use the <email></email> tags instead of the <a></a> tags.

10. Why does an image link display with a blue border by default?
    a. To tell the user that the image is a hyperlink
    b. To let users know they can edit the link if they want to
    c. To add color to the image
    d. To indicate the link points to an absolute URL

DISCUSSION QUESTIONS

1. What is the benefit of using hyperlinks? Discuss a possible result of using too many hyperlinks within a document.

2. What are some of the issues regarding publishing Web pages (with hyperlinks) that should be considered during the production phase of the Web site?

3. What are some of the benefits of providing text links in addition to graphical links?

S K I L L   D R I L L

Skill Drill exercises reinforce chapter skills. Each skill that is reinforced is the same as, or nearly the same as, a skill presented in the chapter. We provide detailed instructions in a step-by-step format. You should complete these exercises in the order provided.

1. Create Text Hyperlinks

You are developing a Web site for a golf supply company. Another designer completed the home page, but she forgot to add the navigation buttons that will eventually link to the other pages on the site. In this exercise, you create text links to the other pages and an e-mail link from the main page.

1. From your WIP_04 folder, open golf.htm in a text editor and browser.

    The document displays an image and text that represent the navigation menu you will create.

FIGURE 4.18

2. Create text links to the other pages, as follows:

```
. . .
<body>
<p align="center">
```

```
<img src="golflogo.gif" alt="Golfbusiness Logo"
alt="Logo" width="253" height="84" />

</p>

<h4 align="center" ><font color="#008000">Welcome to
golfbusiness.com. Click the links below to navigate our
Web site.</font></h4>

<p align="center" ><a href="golf.htm">golf carts</a>
-<a href="parts.htm">parts</a>
-<a href="maint.htm">golf
maintenance</a> - contact us</p>

</body>

. . .
```

3. Save golf.htm in your text editor. Refresh the document in the browser and view the changes.

   The links are active in the browser.

FIGURE 4.19

4. Keep the file open in both applications.

2. Create Image Hyperlinks

It is common for logos on a Web site to be linked to the main (home) page. Since the logo image is on the home page, you are going to link to an absolute URL instead.

1. Switch to the open golf.htm in the text editor.

   In the next step, you need an example of a remote URL to use as a link. Use www.web-answers.com, even though it is not a golfing site. It is for illustration purposes only.

2. Link golflogo.gif to http://www.web-answers.com, and remove the image border, as follows:

```
...

<body>

<p align="center">

<a href="http://www.web-answers.com">

<img src="golflogo.gif" alt="Golfbusiness Logo"
alt="Logo" width="253" height="84"
border="0" />

</a>

</p>

<h4 align="center" ><font color="#008000">Welcome to
golfbusiness.com. Click the links below to navigate our
Web site.</font></h4>

<p align="center" ><a href="golf.htm"> golf carts</a> -
<a href="parts.htm">parts</a> -
<a href="maint.htm">golf maintenance</a> - contact us</p>

</body>

...
```

3. Save your file in your text editor and refresh in the browser.

4. Hover your mouse over the image to test the link.

    The cursor changes to a hand.

FIGURE 4.20

5. Leave the file open in both applications.

3. Create a Base URL and Provide Link Titles

In this exercise, you provide a base URL for all the links in the Web page. You then add titles to your links so tool tips display when the user hovers his mouse over the links.

1. In the open document, add the base URL for the Web page in the head portion of the document.

    ```
    <html>

    <head>

    <title>Golfbusiness.com</title>

    <base href="http://www.web-answers.com" />

    </head>

    <body>

    . . .
    ```

2. Add descriptive title attributes to the hyperlinks.

    ```
    <html>

    <head>

    <title>Golfbusiness.com</title>

    <base href="http://www.web-answers.com" />

    </head>

    <body>

    <p align="center">

    <a href="http://www.web-answers.com" title="Golfbusiness.com">

    <img src="golflogo.gif" alt="Golfbusiness Logo" alt="Logo"
    width="253" height="84" border="0" />

    </a>

    </p>

    <h4 align="center" ><font color="#008000">Welcome to
    golfbusiness.com. Click the links below to navigate our
    Web site.</font></h4>

    <p align="center" ><a href="golf.htm" title="Golf Carts" >
    golf carts</a> - <a href="parts.htm" title="Golf Parts" >
    parts</a> - <a href="maint.htm" title="Golf Maintenance" >
    golf maintenance</a> - contact us</p>

    </body>

    . . .
    ```

3. Save golf.htm in your text editor. Refresh the document in the browser and view the changes.

    The logo does not display because of the base URL that you added. Remember, you are working off your hard disk and not the Web server www.web-answers.com.

    The browser shows that a descriptive tool tip displays when the mouse hovers over a link.

4. Remove the base URL by deleting the line of code you inserted in Step 1.

5. Leave the file open in both applications.

4. Link to an E-mail Address

In this exercise, you add a link to an e-mail address to provide a point of contact for the user.

1. Create an e-mail link, as follows:

    ```
    . . .

    <p align="center" ><a href="golf.htm">golf
    carts</a> - <a href="parts.htm">parts</a> - <a
    href="maint.htm">golf maintenance</a> -

    <a href="mailto:info@golfbusiness.com">contact us</a></p>

    . . .
    ```

2. Save the changes to golf.htm in your text editor.

3. Refresh the document in your browser.

    The hyperlink "contact us" has been created.

FIGURE 4.21

4. Close the file in both applications.

CHALLENGE

Challenge exercises expand on, or are somewhat related to, skills presented in the lessons. Each exercise provides a brief introduction, followed by numbered-step instructions that are not as detailed as those in the Skill Drill exercises. You should complete these exercises in the order provided.

1. Open a New Window for a Destination

The home page of your golf supply Web site is complete; but you linked to a remote location from the home page, which is not exactly what the client expected. The client does not want the remote location to display in the original golfbusiness.com window. He wants to ensure that golfbusiness.com remains open in the original window. The client asks you to structure the site so a new window opens for this remote location.

1. From your WIP_04 folder, open golf.htm in a Web browser and text editor.

2. Add the **target="_blank"** attribute to the image link, as follows:

   ```
   . . .

   <a href=http://www.web-answers.com
   title="Golfbusiness.com"
   target="_blank" >

   <img src="golflogo.gif" alt="Golfbusiness Logo"
   alt="Logo" width="253" height="84" border="0" />

   </a>

   . . .
   ```

3. Save the changes to the text file. Refresh the document in the browser and view the result.

4. Click the image link.

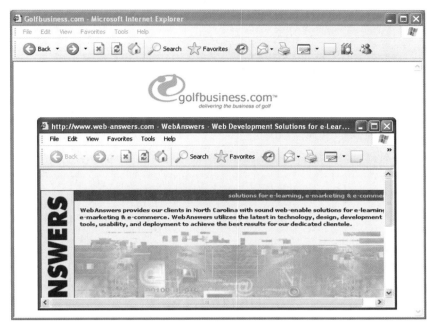

FIGURE 4.22

5. Leave the file open in both applications.

2. Send E-mail to Multiple Addresses

The owner of golfbusiness.com wants all e-mails to be sent to both the Webmaster and the Info mailbox. Your task is to update the e-mail links accordingly. Please note, your computer must have an e-mail client configured for this exercise to work correctly.

1. In the open file, add another e-mail address to the e-mail link.

    ```
    . . .
    <a href="mailto:info@golfbusiness.com,
    webmaster@golfbusiness.com">contact
    us</a>

    . . .
    ```

2. Save the changes to the text file. Refresh the document in the browser and view the result.

3. Click the Contact link to display both e-mail addresses in the To: field of your e-mail application.

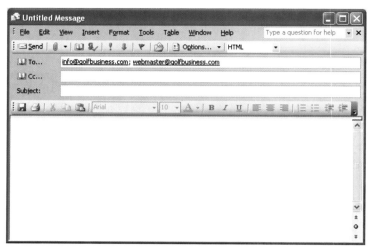

FIGURE 4.23

Your computer must have an e-mail client configured for this step to work correctly; otherwise, your operating system will generate an error or start dialog boxes asking you to set up an e-mail account.

4. Leave the file open in both applications.

3. Add Images for Navigation

The text links are sufficient, but you feel that graphics would add to the overall effectiveness of the site. You decide to add graphical button links to the Web site.

1. Insert the following code to create an image to be used as a button on your page.

```
. . .
<a href="http://www.web-answers.com"
title="Goldbusiness.com" target="_blank">

<img src="golflogo.gif" alt="Golfbusiness Logo"
alt="Logo" width="253" height="84" border="0" />

</a>

</p>
```

```
<img src="golfmaintbutton.gif" border="0" />

<h4 align="center" ><font color="#008000">Welcome to
golfbusiness.com. Click the links below to navigate our
Web site.</font></h4>

<p align="center" ><a href="golf.htm">golf carts</a> -
<a href="parts.htm">parts</a>

- <a href="maint.htm">golf maintenance</a> - <a
href="mailto:info@golfbusiness.com,webmaster@golfbusiness.com">
contact us</a>

</p>
```

2. Save your file in your text editor and refresh the file in your browser.

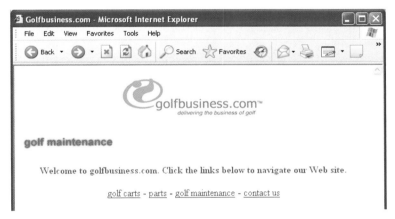

FIGURE 4.24

3. In your WIP_04 folder, locate partsbutton.gif, contactusbutton.gif, and golfcartbutton.gif.

4. Insert the button images on the Web page beside the graphic you inserted in Step 2.

5. Keep the file open in your browser and text editor for use in the next challenge.

4. Create Image Hyperlinks

In this challenge, you create links for the navigation images.

1. Using the images you inserted in the previous exercise, set the images so they do not display borders.

2. Add the proper width and height information to each image.

3. Link each image to the appropriate target. Include a title.

4. Save the changes to the text file and refresh the document in the browser. View the result.

FIGURE 4.25

5. Close the file in both applications.

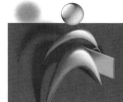

PORTFOLIO BUILDER

Develop a Personal Site

There is no doubt that as a Web site designer, you should publish your own Web site. Now is a good time to start thinking about the content you want to show potential clients. Offering your resume, an "about" page, and examples of your work are essential.

The first step in any Web site project is to create a storyboard. Next, you need to think about what each page on your storyboard should contain. Finally, you need to design the navigation system. To complete this exercise, you should do the following:

- Think about the type of content you want on your Web site. We suggest that you consider a main page that acts as the "about" page, a resume page, and a work page. The work page includes examples of your work.

- Create a storyboard of the pages you want to create for your Web site. Sketch image placement, content ideas, and color schemes.

- Create a flow chart of how you want the navigation of your Web site to flow. Small sites are easy, with each page linking to one another.

- Use images and text creatively. Choose a color scheme and make sure each page is consistent with the overall design of your Web site.

- Link each page on the site to every other page on the site. Make sure you supply some sort of text navigation if you opt to use graphical images. Provide titles for your hyperlinks. If you link off of your site to other online work, think about linking the destination page into a new window. Provide e-mail contact information as well.

CHAPTER 5

Working with Tables

OBJECTIVES

In this chapter, you learn how to:

- Create a data table

- Enter data that spans multiple columns

- Change the dimensions of a table

- Align the data in table cells

- Apply styles to a table

- Add borders and colors to a table

- Change cellspacing and cellpadding

Why Would I Do This?

The ability to include tables in HTML code was one of the first — not to mention important — enhancements that was made to the language. *Tables* are simply rows and columns of cells that can be formatted in various ways. Most Web pages incorporate tables in some form or fashion.

Before tables became available, Web page designers had virtually no way to align text vertically. Their only option was to use the ***<pre> tag*** to set their content to a monospaced font and insert the necessary number of spaces to align content. The characters in a ***monospaced font***, such as Courier, are all the same width. The characters in other fonts, such as Arial or Helvetica, are of variable widths. The `<pre>` tag displayed the content in the browser window exactly as it was placed in the source code. Achieving exact alignment was challenging, and the results were often far from aesthetically pleasing.

Since researchers were the original (and primary) Web users, the ability to format data was a definite advantage. Tables caught on quickly, despite the lack of universal browser support. Today, tables are commonly used in Web page code.

Tables provide more control over the display of your content than any other XHTML element. Besides organizing your content in tabular format, you can design your page using tables as the underlying structure. In this chapter, you learn how to create basic tables to organize your content and Web page layout.

VISUAL SUMMARY

At the most basic level, tables are simply rows and columns of information. You place the information in the proper row and column in your table, and the browser takes care of the display on the Web page.

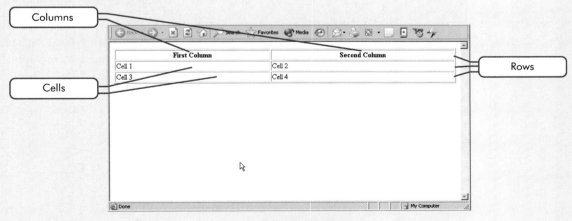

FIGURE 5.1

The table in Figure 5.1 has three rows. Each row has two cells and two columns, and each column has a header. A *row* extends horizontally across the table. A *column* extends vertically through the table. A *cell* is the intersection of a column and a row. A *header* is a cell whose text is often formatted in bold and centered, and always appears at the top of the table. The table in Figure 5.1 displays as wide as the page because the width is set to 100%. You work with heights and widths in more detail later; but for now, understand that the width of a table can be set as a percentage of the available area, or it can be set as a fixed width that is measured in pixels.

Although tables were designed to organize data in a *tabular format* (data displayed in a table or grid), many designers use tables to control the layout of their Web pages. Consider the Web page in Figure 5.2. A table was used to position the images and text in the interface.

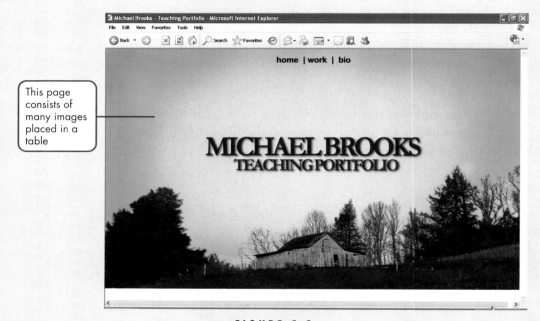

This page consists of many images placed in a table

FIGURE 5.2

Figure 5.2 illustrates an image that was sliced into many smaller sections, and then pieced back together in a table. The smaller image slices are easy to work with, and they download faster than one large image. Tables allow you to create advanced layouts that would otherwise be impossible to design.

LESSON 1   Creating a Basic Data Table

To build a table, you create rows and columns, which in turn produces cells. Table rows are designated by **<tr></tr>**, the *table row tags*. Each row contains data cells, which are designated by **<td></td>**, the *table data tags*. The entire set of rows and cells is enclosed in the **<table></table>** tags. The *table tags* allow you to complete the basic setup for a data table.

To add a column, you add **<td></td>** to each row. To add a row, you add **<tr></tr>** and its associated **<td></td>** tags to the table. To remove a column or row, simply remove these tags and their content.

The following code creates a two-column, two-row, four-cell table that extends the entire width of the page.

```
<table border="1" width="100%">
<tr>
    <td>Cell 1</td>
    <td>Cell 2</td>
</tr>
<tr>
    <td>Cell 3</td>
    <td>Cell 4</td>
</tr>
</table>
```

The example code creates the following table.

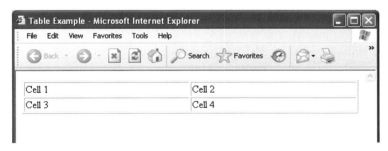

FIGURE 5.3

In the XHTML code for this example, all the text for each row is on a single line. While this may make it easier to see the individual rows, it is usually easier to read the XHTML when the data is divided into smaller chunks.

Notice in the code that a **width=""** attribute is provided for the **<table>** tag. Later in this chapter, you learn how to adjust the width of a table. For now, however, know that the width of a table can be set to a percentage of the screen — in this case, 100%.

Create a Basic Table

1   Copy the contents of your RF_XHTML_L1>Chapter_05 folder to your Work_In_Progress>WIP_05 folder.

2   In your text editor and browser, open tables.htm from your WIP_05 folder.

FIGURE 5.4

This simple Web page contains the basic document tags.

3   In the text editor, establish the table by inserting the table tags, as follows:

```
. . .
<title>Tables</title>
</head>
<body>
<table>
</table>
</body>
</html>
```

The table tags tell the browser where to start and end a table.

4   Add three rows with three cells each, as follows:

```
<html>
<head><title>Tables</title></head>
<body>
<table>
    <tr> <td></td> <td></td> <td></td> </tr>
    <tr> <td></td> <td></td> <td></td> </tr>
    <tr> <td></td> <td></td> <td></td> </tr>
</table>
```

```
</body>
</html>
```

Three rows are created (**`<tr>`** tags), each containing three cells (**`<td>`** tags). This also creates three columns.

5 **Add data to the cells. In the first cell on the first row, enter "1". Enter "2" in the second cell on the first row. In sequence, continue to add data to the cells until you reach the third cell in the third row, and enter "9".**

```
<html>
<head><title>Tables</title></head>
<body>
<table>
    <tr> <td>1</td> <td>2</td> <td>3</td> </tr>
    <tr> <td>4</td> <td>5</td> <td>6</td> </tr>
    <tr> <td>7</td> <td>8</td> <td>9</td> </tr>
</table>
</body>
</html>
```

The numbers you inserted between the **`<td>`** tags become the content of the table cells. You can use anything as content, including images, large amounts of text, and other tables.

6 **Save the file in the text editor and refresh the browser.**

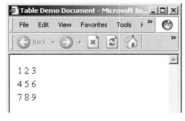

FIGURE 5.5

Notice how the browser displays this code. It shows your table of information, but it doesn't distinguish between the individual cells. You can expand the width of the table to separate the data and/or use borders to clearly define each cell.

7 **Leave the file open in your text editor and browser for use in the next exercise.**

Change the Table's Width

1 **With table.htm active in the text editor window, make the table a little more spacious by setting the width to 75% of the page, as follows:**

```
<html>
<head><title>Tables</title></head>
<body>
<table width="75%">
    <tr> <td>1</td> <td>2</td> <td>3</td> </tr>
    <tr> <td>4</td> <td>5</td> <td>6</td> </tr>
    <tr> <td>7</td> <td>8</td> <td>9</td> </tr>
</table>
</body>
</html>
```

This adds some space between the data in the cells. Although you change the table's width and height later in this chapter, adding the attribute now allows you to create a data table that is easier to read.

2 **Save the changes in the text file and refresh the document in the browser.**

FIGURE 5.6

3 **To see the actual cells of the table, include a border for the table, as follows:**

```
<html>
<head><title>Tables</title></head>
<body>
<table border="1" width="75%">
    <tr> <td>1</td> <td>2</td> <td>3</td> </tr>
    <tr> <td>4</td> <td>5</td> <td>6</td> </tr>
    <tr> <td>7</td> <td>8</td> <td>9</td> </tr>
</table>
```

```
</body>
</html>
```

4   **Save the file in the text editor and refresh the browser.**

Adding a border creates lines between the columns and rows. This viewable grid allows you to see the individual cells more clearly. You can change the border's thickness by increasing the number of pixels in the border attribute.

FIGURE 5.7

5   **Leave the file open in your browser and text editor for use in the next exercise.**

Add Table Headers

As you can see, the table consists of three rows, `<tr>`s, each of which contains three data cells, `<td>`s. You can use the `<th>` tag to create table headers for your columns of data.

1   **In the open file, add headers to the table using the `<th>` tags, as follows:**

```
<html>
<head><title>Tables</title></head>
<body>
<table border="1" width="75%">
    <tr>
        <th>First Column ...</th>
        <th>Second ... </th>
        <th>And Third</th>
    </tr>
    <tr> <td>1</td> <td>2</td> <td>3</td> </tr>
    <tr> <td>4</td> <td>5</td> <td>6</td> </tr>
    <tr> <td>7</td> <td>8</td> <td>9</td> </tr>
</table>
```

```
</body>
</html>
```

Headers are useful when you want to supply information for a column of data. Although you could have created the first row of text using the **<td>** tags and then applied formatting to differentiate the headings from the other text, using the **<th>** tags is faster and more convenient.

2   **Save the file in the text editor and refresh the browser.**

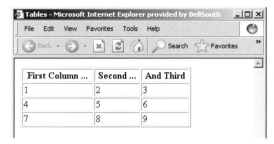

FIGURE 5.8

3   **Close the file in your text editor and browser.**

To Extend Your Knowledge . . .

CELL HEADERS

In the previous exercise, even though you didn't set any style information, the headers were automatically bolded and centered within their cells. Other than these simple formatting differences, header cells are the same as data cells. Originally, all three columns were the same width; now, however, the first column is slightly wider than the rest, allowing for the larger amount of text it contains. Remember, unless you specify otherwise, a table automatically adjusts to its widest and longest cells.

LESSON 2   Spanning Columns and Rows

Even if laying out grids of information were all you could do with tables, they would still be useful elements to include on Web pages. Luckily, you can do much more with tables: you can mix and match rows and columns, you can merge one table into another, and you can adjust alignments. For example, if you want to include a table header that applies to multiple columns in the table, you can add the **colspan=""** (*column span*) attribute to the header tag. The value contained within the quotes determines exactly how many columns the cell spans. If necessary, the **colspan=""** attribute can cause the cell to span the width of the entire table.

```
<table border="1" width="100%">

<tr>

    <th colspan="2">Title of the Table</th>

</tr>

<tr>

    <td>Cell 1<br />Cell 1<br />Cell 1<br />Cell 1</td>

    <td>Cell2Cell2Cell2Cell2Cell2Cell2Cell2Cell2</td>

</tr>

<tr>

    <td>Cell 3</td>

    <td>Cell 4</td>

</tr>

</table>
```

FIGURE 5.9

In Figure 5.9, notice that there is only one cell in the first row. That cell is set to span both columns of the table (**colspan="2"**). This single cell has the equivalent width of two cells, even though it appears to be one continuous cell. If another cell were added to this first row, it wouldn't make the first cell narrower. The additional cell would expand the width of the table and take the position of a new third column.

You can achieve a similar effect of expanding cells using the **rowspan=""** (*row span*) attribute, which vertically extends the cell along a row.

```
<table border="1" width="100%">

<tr>

    <th colspan="2">Title of the Table</th>

</tr>

<tr>
```

```
<td rowspan="2">Cell 1<br />Cell 1<br />Cell 1<br />Cell 1</td>
<td>Cell2Cell2Cell2Cell2Cell2Cell2Cell2Cell2</td>
</tr>
<tr>
<td>Cell 4</td>
</tr>
</table>
```

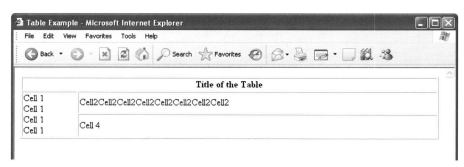

FIGURE 5.10

In Figure 5.10, Cell 1 occupies the first column of the second row, so the second row contains only one additional cell, eliminating Cell 3. The reason for this change lies in the way that browsers construct tables. Each cell is placed in the first available position; although Cell 4 appears to occupy the first position in its row, it is actually placed in the second column.

Span the Row of a Table

1   In your text editor and browser, open span.htm from your WIP_05 folder.

2   Add a row and use the `colspan=" "` attribute to cause a single cell to span three rows, as follows:

```
<html>
<head><title>Tables</title></head>
<body>
<table border="1" width="75%">
<tr><td colspan="3"> </td></tr>
    <tr>
        <th>First Column ...</th>
        <th>Second ... </th>
```

```
            <th>And Third</th>
    </tr>
. . .
```

This creates a single cell that spans all three columns in the table.

3 **Add the header for the table — "Today's Objectives" — in the row that spans across the table, as follows:**

```
<html>
<head><title>Tables</title></head>
<body>
<table border="1" width="75%">
<tr><td colspan="3">Today's Objectives</td></tr>
    <tr>
        <th>First Column ...</th>
        <th>Second ... </th>
        <th>And Third</th>
    </tr>
. . .
```

"Today's Objectives" appears in the top expanded row. As you can see, however, the text displays at the default settings and offers no formatting, because you did not use the **<th>** tag. If you choose not to use the **<th>** tag for a table header, you can apply other formatting tags to emphasize the text (bold, italic, size).

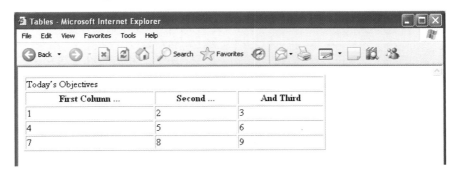

FIGURE 5.11

4 **Format the table header using the Level 3 heading tag (<h3>) and center-align the text in the cell, as follows:**

```
. . .
</head>
<body>
<table border="1" width="75%">
<tr><td colspan="3"><h3 align="center">Today's
Objectives</h3></td></tr>
    <tr>
        <th>First Column ...</th>
        <th>Second ... </th>
        <th>And Third</th>
    </tr>
. . .
```

The text displays in the center of the expanded cell as a Level 3 heading.

5   **Save the changes to the text file and refresh the document in the browser.** 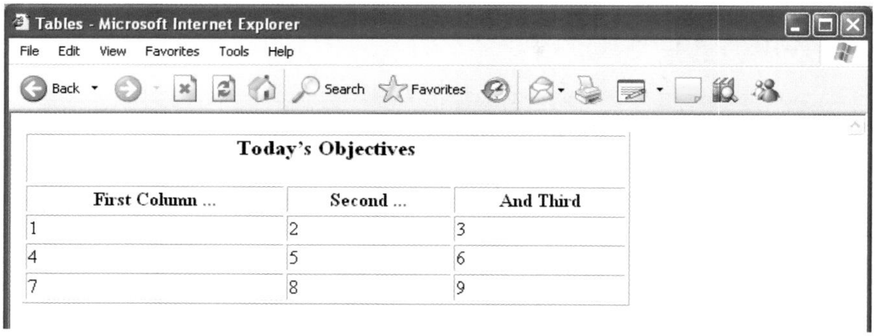

FIGURE 5.12

Notice that there is a space beneath "Today's Objectives". This is due to the **<h3>** tag, which automatically places a space beneath any contained text.

6   **Leave the file open in your text editor and browser for use in the next exercise.**

Span the Column of a Table

1   **In the open span.htm document in the text editor, add a column to the table using the rowspan="" attribute, and change the colspan="3" to colspan="4", as follows:**

```
...

</head>

<body>

<table border="1" width="75%">

<tr><td colspan="4"><h3 align="center">Today's
Objectives</h3></td></tr>

<tr><td rowspan="5"> </td></tr>

    <tr>

        <th>First Column ...</th>

        <th>Second ... </th>

        <th>And Third</th>

    </tr>

...
```

This adds an empty column to the left of the table. The column now spans five rows: it spans the four existing rows and one self-contained row.

2 **Add descriptive text for the content of the expanded column, as follows:**

```
...

<table border="1" width="75%">

<tr><td colspan="4"><h3 align="center">Today's
Objectives</h3></td></tr>

<tr><td rowspan="5">Notes:</td></tr>

    <tr>

        <th>First Column ...</th>

        <th>Second ... </th>

        <th>And Third</th>

    </tr>

...
```

"Notes:" displays in the cell.

3   Save the changes to the file, and refresh the document in the browser.

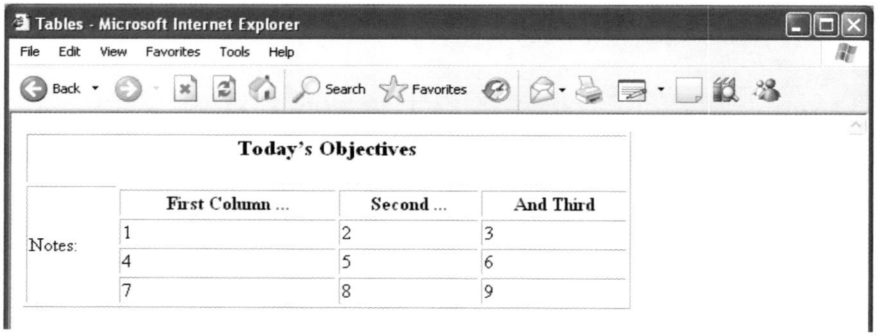

FIGURE 5.13

The table displays a column with the descriptive text "Notes:" in the middle of the cell. It would be better to have "Notes:" display at the top of the cell, so any notes added to the table can fall beneath that text. Later in this chapter, you learn how to align text vertically and horizontally within cells.

4   Close the file in your text editor and browser.

To Extend Your Knowledge . . .

USING TABLES

You know how to create header rows using the `<th>` tag. You could have rendered the same effect by creating table rows and bolding the text within the table definitions, as follows:

```
<tr><td><b>Some Text Heading Here</b></td></tr></table>
```

LESSON 3   Height and Width

The most common reason to create a table is to fit content within a predefined area. In such cases, it's important to have as much control over sizing (height and width) as possible. In tables, height and width can apply to any of four items: cells, rows, columns, and/or the table itself.

You can use various methods to control height and width in tables. The first technique is using percentages, as you did earlier — you instruct the browser to use a particular percentage of the available area. This method enables you to set the height and width of a table based on the size of the area in which it resides. This technique is generally more useful for text than for images. Sometimes, however, a layout requires you to precisely set the size of the table (to an absolute number). In such a situation, you can use pixel measurements. For example:

```
<table width="300" height="200">

. . .

</table>
```

This code produces a table that is 300 pixels wide and 200 pixels high, regardless of the size of the browser.

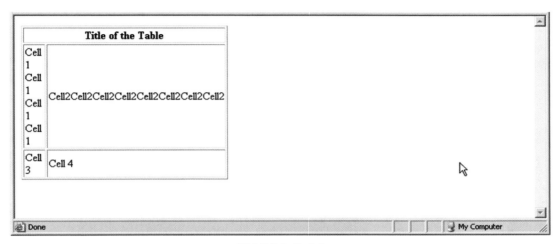

FIGURE 5.14

The table displays at this size only, even without units specified, because the pixel is the only unit of measurement these attributes render. On the other hand,

```
<table width="50%">

. . .

</table>
```

produces a table that adjusts to half the width of the browser window, whatever that width may be, as shown in Figure 5.15.

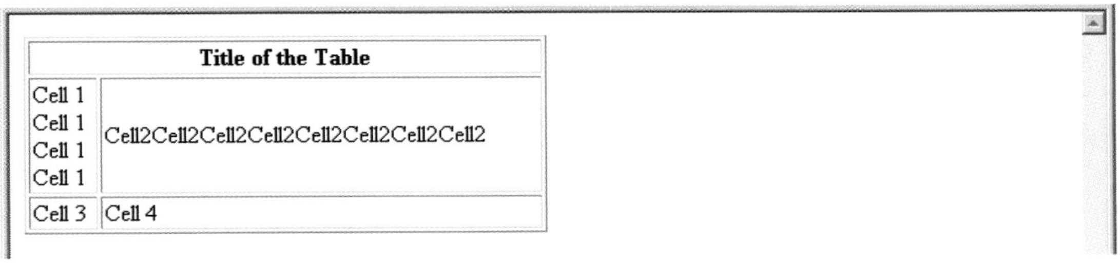

FIGURE 5.15

One exception to this rule is when the content of the table, such as an image, is larger than the specified table size. In that case, the browser displays the table as small as possible without compromising the content.

The height and width attributes are being deprecated in XHTML. For many browsers, however, these attributes provide the only way to control the height and width of a table; so, for now, they remain in use.

Controlling Column and Row Sizes

In addition to setting the size of the entire table, you can control the size of individual rows and columns. You do this by setting the size of the rows, or setting the size of the individual cells. In the sample table, you could set the height of the second row of data, as follows:

```
<table border="1" width="100%">
<tr>
   <th colspan="2">Title of the Table</th>
</tr>
<tr>
   <td width="100" height="150">Cell 1<br />Cell 1<br />Cell 1<br />
Cell 1</td>
   <td>Cell2Cell2Cell2Cell2Cell2Cell2Cell2Cell2</td>
</tr>
<tr height="100">
   <td>Cell 3</td>
   <td>Cell 4</td>
</tr>
</table>
```

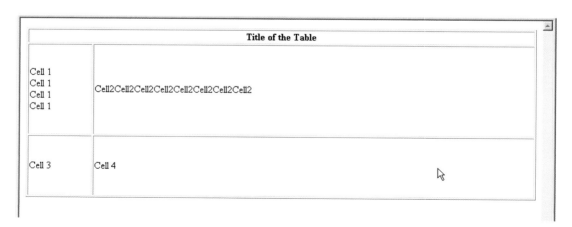

FIGURE 5.16

First, you set the width of the first cell (100 pixels). The width of the widest cell dictates the width of the column, so the width of the column is 100 pixels. Similarly, you set the height of the cell to 150 pixels, so the entire row expands to that height. You can also directly control the height of a row by setting the height attribute in the **<tr></tr>** tags.

You can also set the size of rows and columns based on percentages. If the size of the table is larger than necessary to display the content, the browser tries to render the table so the rows and columns are approximately the same size. For instance:

```
<table border="1" width="100%" height="100%">
<tr>
    <th colspan="2">Title of the Table</th>
</tr>
<tr>
    <td>Cell 1</td>
    <td>Cell 2</td>
</tr>
<tr>
    <td>Cell 3</td>
    <td>Cell 4</td>
</tr>
</table>
```

Here, all height and width attributes were removed, except those for the table itself.

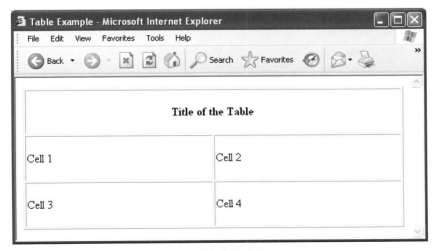

FIGURE 5.17

When you set height and width attributes using percentages, you can control the relative size of columns and rows and still allow them to adjust as the table is modified. For example:

```
<table border="1" width="100%" height="100%">
<tr>
   <th colspan="2">Title of the Table</th>
</tr>
<tr>
   <td width="25%">Cell 1</td>
   <td>Cell 2</td>
</tr>
<tr height="50%">
   <td>Cell 3</td>
   <td>Cell 4</td>
</tr>
</table>
```

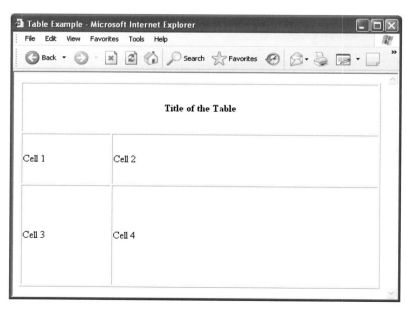

FIGURE 5.18

Another factor that can affect the size of columns and rows is the amount of content in a particular cell. While the browser normally tries to keep items evenly spaced in the absence of other instructions, a cell with more data requires more room in the table.

Change the Size of the Table

1   **In your text editor and browser, open size.htm from your WIP_05 folder.**

2   **Add code to set the table's width to 300 pixels, as follows:**

```
. . .
</head>
<body>
<table border="1" width="300">
<tr><td colspan="4"><h3 align="center">Today's
Objectives</h3></td></tr>
<tr><td rowspan="5">Notes:</td></tr>
    <tr>
. . .
```

This sets the table's width to 300 pixels.

3   **Save the changes to the file and refresh the document in the browser.**

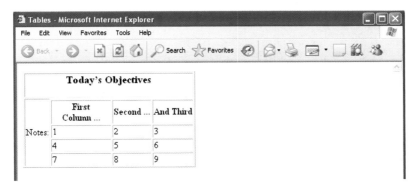

FIGURE 5.19

4   **Return to the text file and change the table's width to 600 pixels, as follows:**

```
. . .
<title>Tables</title>
</head>
<body>
<table border="1" width="600">
<tr><td colspan="4"><h3 align="center">Today's
Objectives</h3></td></tr>
```

```
<tr><td rowspan="5">Notes:</td></tr>
    <tr>
. . .
```

This sets the table's width to 600 pixels.

5   Save the changes to the text file and refresh the document in the browser.

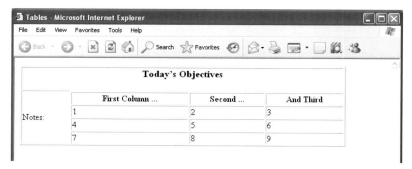

FIGURE 5.20

6   Leave the file open in your text editor and browser. Continue to the next exercise.

Change the Size of Cells

1   In the open size.htm in the text editor, change the height of the header row to 100 pixels, as follows:

```
<html>
<head><title>Tables</title></head>
<body>
<table border="1" width="600">
<tr><td colspan="4"><h3 align="center">Today's
Objectives</h3></td></tr>
<tr><td rowspan="5">Notes:</td></tr>
    <tr>
        <th height="100">First Column ...</th>
        <th>Second ... </th>
        <th>And Third</th>
    </tr>
. . .
```

Changing any cell (or header) in a row forces the other cells in that row to display that height also.

2 Save the changes in the text file and refresh the document in your browser.

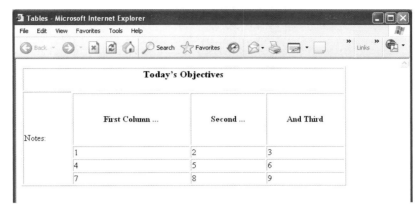

FIGURE 5.21

3 Return to the text editor and change the height of the header row to 75 pixels, as follows:

```
<html>
<head><title>Tables</title></head>
<body>
<table border="1" width="600">
<tr><td colspan="4"><h3 align="center">Today's
Objectives</h3></td></tr>
<tr><td rowspan="5">Notes:</td></tr>
    <tr>
        <th height="75">First Column ...</th>
        <th>Second ... </th>
        <th>And Third</th>
    </tr>
  . . .
```

The header displays 75 pixels in height.

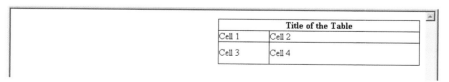

FIGURE 5.22

4   **Close the file in your text editor and browser.**

LESSON 4   Alignment

A significant part of the work involved in laying out a Web page is aligning the content. You can position the content to the right, left, or center; sometimes you must ensure that content is at the top or bottom of a page section.

Similar to images, you can set text to flow around tables; the code for the table must be placed ahead of the coded text you want to flow around the table. In addition, entire tables can be aligned to the center, left, and right. For example:

```
<table border="1" align="right">

...

</table>
```

aligns the table on the right side of the browser window.

FIGURE 5.23

Aligning the Data

Just as the table can be aligned, each individual cell can have its own alignment attributes, both horizontal and vertical. Content can be aligned horizontally to the left (**align="left"**), right, or center, and can be aligned vertically to the top (**valign="top"**), bottom, or middle. With no instructions, a cell defaults to align horizontally to the left and vertically in the center.

Consider the following example, which results in a wide variety of alignments.

```
<table border="1" width="100%" height="100%">
<tr>
   <th colspan="3">Title of the Table</th>
</tr>
<tr>
   <td align="right">Cell 1</td>
   <td align="left">Cell 2</td>
   <td align="center">Cell 3</td>
</tr>
<tr>
   <td valign="top">Cell 4</td>
   <td valign="bottom">Cell 5</td>
   <td valign="middle">Cell 6</td>
</tr>
</tr>
</table>
```

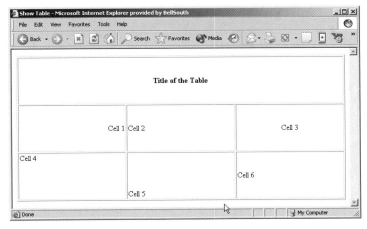

FIGURE 5.24

Notice that the alignments of Cell 1 and Cell 2 force the content to come together, no matter how much content is in either cell. This right/left alignment method can be useful when aligning different types of content, such as recipe ingredients and their associated amounts. Let's use "1/4 cup molasses" as an example: right-align "1/4 cup", and in the adjacent cell, left-align "molasses" to create two perfectly aligned columns of measurements and ingredients.

Align the Table

1   **In your text editor and browser, open alignment.htm from your WIP_05 folder.**

2   **Center-align the table, as follows:**

```
. . .
<title>Tables</title>
</head>
<body>
<table border="1" width="600" align="center">
<tr><td colspan="4"><h3 align="center">Today's
Objectives</h3></td></tr>
<tr><td rowspan="5">Notes:</td></tr>
    <tr>
. . .
```

This center-aligns the table on the Web page.

3   **Save the changes to the text file and refresh the document in the browser.**

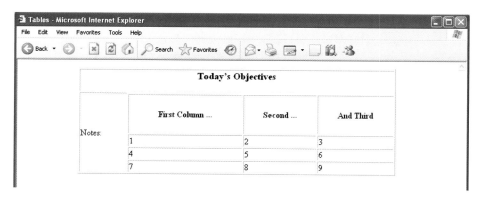

FIGURE 5.25

4   **Return to the text editor and right-align the table on the Web page, as follows:**

```
<html>
<head><title>Tables</title></head>
```

```
<body>

<table border="1" width="600" align="right">

<tr><td colspan="4"><h3 align="center">Today's
Objectives</h3></td></tr>

<tr><td rowspan="5">Notes:</td></tr>

    <tr>
```
. . .

The table displays on the right side of the Web page.

5   **Save the changes to the text file and refresh the document in the browser.**

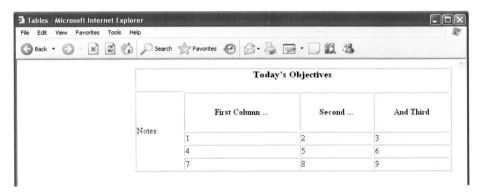

FIGURE 5.26

6   **Leave the file open in both applications for use in the next exercise.**

Align Data in a Table

1   **With alignment.htm active in the text editor, center-align the table, as follows:**

```
<html>

<head><title>Tables</title></head>

<body>

<table border="1" width="600" align="center">

<tr><td colspan="4"><h3 align="center">Today's
Objectives</h3></td></tr>

<tr><td rowspan="5">Notes:</td></tr>
```
. . .

The table displays in the center of the Web page.

2   **Vertically align "Notes:" at the top of the page, as follows:**

```
. . .
<table border="1" width="600" align="center">
<tr><td colspan="4"><h3 align="center">Today's
Objectives</h3></td></tr>
<tr><td rowspan="5" valign="top">Notes:</td></tr>
    <tr>
        <th height="75">First Column ...</th>
        <th>Second ... </th>
        <th>And Third</th>
. . .
```

The text displays at the top of the cell, instead of the default center alignment.

3   **Save the changes in the text file and refresh the document in the browser.**

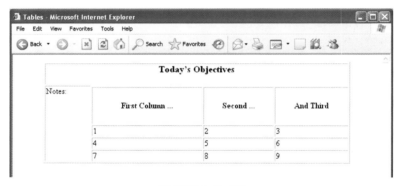

FIGURE 5.27

4   **Close the file in your browser and text editor.**

To Extend Your Knowledge . . .

THE IMPORTANCE OF TEMPLATES

For several reasons, the template is one of the most important concepts in Web site design. A template allows you to create a common look and feel for a site, which enhances the user's experience. You can include all the elements of the user interface in a template, so you can place more emphasis on creating content, rather than maintaining individual pages.

LESSON 5 Styling a Table

You can divide tables into three main sections: header, footer, and body. These parts are used in the same way as their counterparts in a word-processing program, with the header and footer appearing along the top and bottom of each printed page of a multipage table.

You can set the header and footer to display before the body of the table has finished loading. To control the loading order (header, footer, and then body), you can place the footer code in front of the body code so the browser doesn't have to wait for the entire body to load before you can see the footer. To isolate the sections of a table, use the **<thead></thead>, <tbody></tbody>,** and **<tfoot></tfoot>** tags.

A table that loads the header, footer, and then body is constructed as follows:

```
<table border="1" width="100%" height="100%">
<thead>
    <tr>
        <th colspan="3">Title of the Table</th>
    </tr>
</thead>
<tfoot>
    <tr>
        <td colspan="3">The footer appears at the bottom, even though it
seems like it should be at the top.</td>
    </tr>
</tfoot>
<tbody>
    <tr>
        <td align="right">Cell 1</td>
        <td align="left">Cell 2</td>
        <td align="center">Cell 3</td>
    </tr>
    <tr>
        <td valign="top">Cell 4</td>
        <td valign="bottom">Cell 5</td>
        <td valign="middle">Cell 6</td>
    </tr>
```

```
</tbody>
</table>
```

Figure 5.28 shows you how the table looks in the browser.

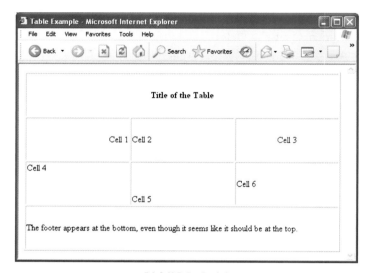

FIGURE 5.28

As of this writing, not all browsers fully support this function. In browsers that do not support header/footer control, the footer might appear at the top of the table, directly below the header.

Style the Table

1 In your text editor and browser, open style.htm from your WIP_05 folder.

2 Add the table header, as follows:

```
<html>
<head><title>Tables</title></head>
<body>
<table border="1" width="600" align="center">
<thead>
<tr><td colspan="4"><h3 align="center">Today's
Objectives</h3></td></tr>
</thead>
<tr><td rowspan="5" valign="top">Notes:</td></tr>
    <tr>
```

```
        <th height="75">First Column ...</th>
        <th>Second ... </th>
        <th>And Third</th>
...
```

3   **Add descriptive column headers.**

```
...
</thead>
<tr><td rowspan="5" valign="top">Notes:</td></tr>
    <tr>
        <th height="75">Call List</th>
        <th>To Do</th>
        <th>Groceries</th>
    </tr>
    <tr> <td>1</td> <td>2</td> <td>3</td> </tr>
    <tr> <td>4</td> <td>5</td> <td>6</td> </tr>
    <tr> <td>7</td> <td>8</td> <td>9</td> </tr>
</table>
...
```

These are the descriptive column headers for your Today's Objectives list.

4   **Add the table body section.**

```
...
<thead>
<tr><td colspan="4"><h3 align="center">Today's
Objectives</h3></td></tr>
</thead>
<tbody>
<tr><td rowspan="5" valign="top">Notes:</td></tr>
    <tr>
        <th height="75">Call List</th>
        <th>To Do </th>
        <th>Groceries</th>
    </tr>
```

```
        <tr> <td>1</td> <td>2</td> <td>3</td> </tr>
        <tr> <td>4</td> <td>5</td> <td>6</td> </tr>
        <tr> <td>7</td> <td>8</td> <td>9</td> </tr>
    </tbody>
    </table>
    . . .
```

These tags identify the body of the table. We chose not to add an expanded row along the bottom of this table as a footer, so we excluded the **<tfoot>** tag. If you were to add a footer to the bottom of the table, it would be beneficial to contain it within the **<tfoot>** tags.

5   **Save the changes to the text file and refresh the document in the browser.**

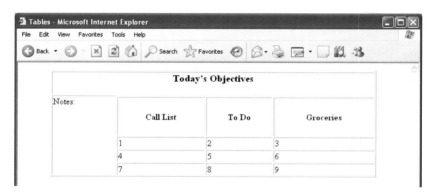

FIGURE 5.29

6   **Close the file in your text editor and browser.**

To Extend Your Knowledge . . .

PLANNING A TABLE

The easiest way to create a table (considering all of the coding involved) is to plan your idea on paper before you begin coding. This method works best for tables you are designing for page layout, rather than for structuring data, but it's useful for both.

If you are working in a tabular format to align data into columns and rows, creating a paper version ensures that you remember to include all the necessary data, such as headers. If you need to use tables to achieve a particular visual result, sketching the layout of the page helps you know how to structure the tables, where to place the tables, how many tables you need, where to place supporting images, and other design elements.

LESSON 6   Borders and Colors

You can change the ***border color*** of a table, which is, by default, the black border around the rows and columns of the table. You can use the **bordercolor=""** attribute to change the color of the table border to a flat uniform color. Internet Explorer (the only browser that supports this feature) allows you to specify the attributes **bordercolorlight** and **bordercolordark** to set the color of the light and dark sides to create a chiseled 3-D effect.

The **bordercolor=""** attribute has been deprecated in XHTML and will be removed altogether from XHTML 2.0. An alternative is to use CSS to control the color and effects of table borders. The following code shows how to change the border color of the table using the **bordercolor** attribute:

```
<table border="1" bordercolor="green">
```

This produces the following border in a browser.

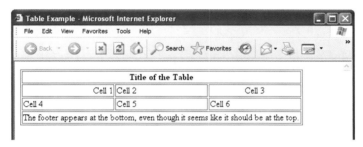

FIGURE 5.30

You can use any of the 16 predefined colors or hexadecimal colors when changing the color of your table border.

Changing the Background Color

You can change the ***background color*** of the entire table, a row, or an individual cell. The **bgcolor=""** attribute works with the **<table>, <tr>,** and **<td>** tags. This method of changing the background color has been deprecated in XHTML 1.0 and completely removed from XHTML 2.0. Nonetheless, you can use CSS to change the background color in a table, row, or individual cell.

To change the background color in a table to red, you would enter the following code:

```
<table bgcolor="red">
```

To change the background color in a row to blue, you would enter

```
<tr bgcolor="blue">
```

To change the background color in a cell to green, you would enter

```
<td bgcolor="green">
```

Change the Table Colors

1   In your text editor and browser, open color.htm from your WIP_05 folder.

2   Change the background color of the table to yellow.

```
. . .
<title>Tables</title>
</head>
<body>
<table border="1" width="600" align="center" bgcolor="yellow">
<thead>
<tr><td colspan="4"><h3 align="center">Today's
Objectives</h3></td></tr>
</thead>
. . .
```

You can use the predefined color yellow, or you can choose any shade of yellow from the hexadecimal color system.

3   Change the background color of the heading row to green.

```
. . .
<body>
<table border="1" width="600" align="center" bgcolor="yellow">
<thead>
<tr><td colspan="4" bgcolor="green"<>h3 align="center">Today's
Objectives</h3></td></tr>
</thead>
. . .
```

The entire row changes to green.

4   Change the cell color that contains "Notes:" to gray.

```
. . .
</thead>
<tbody>
<tr><td rowspan="5" valign="top" bgcolor="gray">Notes:</td></tr>
    <tr>
```

```
<th height="75">Call List</th>
<th>To Do </th>
```

. . .

The cell's background color changes to gray. Even if an entire table is set to a particular color, the modified cell color takes precedence over the table's background color.

5 **Change the border color to gray.**

```
<html>
<head><title>Tables</title></head>
<body>
<table border="1" width="600" align="center" bgcolor="yellow"
bordercolor="gray">
<thead>
<tr><td colspan="4" bgcolor="green"><h3 align="center">Today's
Objectives</h3></td></tr>
```

. . .

The border changes to gray.

6 **Save the changes to the text file and refresh the document in the browser.**

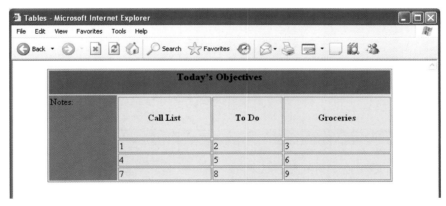

FIGURE 5.31

7 **Close the file in your text editor and browser.**

LESSON 7   Cellspacing and Cellpadding

Cellspacing is the gap between the cells in a table. *Cellpadding* is the space between the content of a cell and its borders. Both are used to fine-tune the appearance and alignment of content in a table. These attributes are both set on the table itself and can be used independently or together. For example:

```
<table cellpadding="15" border="1">
```

creates a space around the content of a cell.

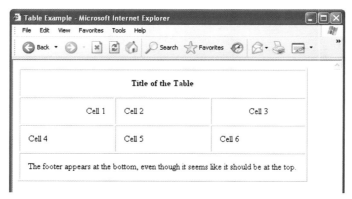

FIGURE 5.32

Cellspacing works in a similar manner but actually controls the width of the interior borders themselves. For example:

```
<table cellspacing="15" border="2">
```

produces the following table.

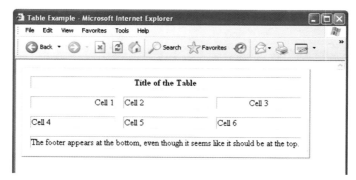

FIGURE 5.33

In many cases, the positioning is the same whether you use cellpadding or cellspacing; the difference lies in whether you can see what is behind the table.

Change Cellspacing and Cellpadding

1 **In your text editor and browser, open cellspacing.htm from your WIP_05 folder.**

2 **Change the cellspacing of the table.**

. . .

```
<title>Tables</title>

</head>

<body>

<table border="1" width="600" align="center" bgcolor="yellow"
bordercolor="gray" cellspacing="10">

<thead>

<tr><td colspan="4" bgcolor="green"><h3 align="center">Today's
Objectives</h3></td></tr>

</thead>
```

. . .

This places 10 pixels between each cell.

3 **Change the cellpadding of the table.**

```
<html>

<head><title>Tables</title></head>

<body>

<table border="1" width="600" align="center" bgcolor="yellow"
bordercolor="gray" cellspacing="10" cellpadding="10">

<thead>

<tr><td colspan="4" bgcolor="green"><h3 align="center">Today's
Objectives</h3></td></tr>

</thead>
```

. . .

This places 10 pixels between the content of the cell and the cell wall.

4   Save the changes to the text file and refresh the document in the browser.

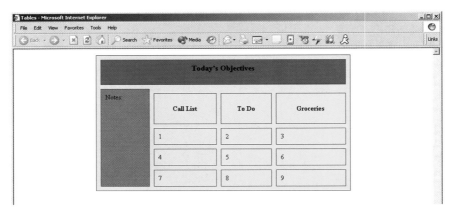

FIGURE 5.34

5   Close the file in your text editor and browser.

To Extend Your Knowledge . . .

ADDING SPACERS

Some designers use transparent images called ***spacers*** to expand cells to a specific size. Spacers are transparent, so the viewer cannot see them on the Web page. Spacers are usually 1 pixel in width, so they separate cells by 1 pixel; they are often much longer in height than width.

Some older browsers would collapse the cells that did not have content. Using spacers allowed the table to appear as intended. Designers could also choose to use a nonbreaking space (` `) to prevent cell collapse. Both techniques are slowly being phased out by most designers since browsers no longer collapse empty cells.

LESSON 8   Nested Tables

Although using tables for advanced layout techniques (such as mortised Web pages) is not within the scope of this book, it is necessary to discuss ***nested tables*** (one table contained within another). Nesting one or two tables within a larger table is rather simple; but the idea behind ***mortised Web pages*** is to use many tables to piece together images and other elements that would be impossible using other XHTML features. Mortised Web pages are usually created in a Web editor; simple nested tables, however, can be hand-coded in XHTML.

Consider the following example of a simple nested table:

```
<table>
 <tr>
  <td>
    <table>
     <tr>
       <td>

       </td>
     </tr>
    </table>
  </td>
 </tr>
</table>
```

Nest a Table

1 In your text editor and browser, open nested.htm from your WIP_05 folder.

2 Add a table to the Notes section.

```
. . .
</thead>
<tbody>
<tr><td rowspan="5" valign="top" bgcolor="gray">
<table>
    <tr><td>Notes:</td></tr>
    <tr><td>1. </td></tr>
    <tr><td>2. </td></tr>
    <tr><td>3. </td></tr>
    <tr><td>4. </td></tr>
    <tr><td>5. </td></tr>
    <tr><td>6. </td></tr>
</table>
```

```
</td></tr>
    <tr>
        <th height="75">Call List</th>
        <th>To Do </th>
        <th>Groceries</th>
    </tr>
. . .
```

3   **Save the changes to the text file and refresh the document in the browser.**

The table displays with the nested table in the Notes section. You can format nested tables in a wide variety of ways. Remember to plan the display of your content prior to coding the table/s to save time and (possible) errors.

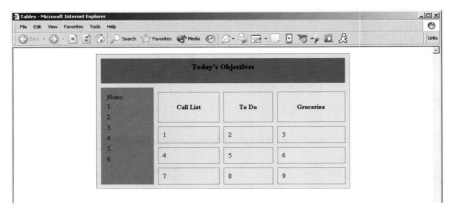

FIGURE 5.35

4   **Close the file in your text editor and browser.**

To Extend Your Knowledge . . .

TABLES AND POSITIONING

Before tables became the norm on the Web, very few page-layout options were available. Tables allow designers to turn a page into a literal grid in which they can puzzle together a professional-looking design and apply precise positioning.

Using mortised design techniques has become a very popular strategy for many Web designers. CSS also offers advanced positioning that will eventually replace the use of tables. When CSS first appeared, it was not well supported in browsers, so many designers opted to use traditional HTML tables. As browsers have become more supportive of CSS, designers have started using CSS layout techniques instead of tables or a combination of both.

SUMMARY

In Chapter 5, you learned that tables allow Web page authors to vertically align content on a Web page. Before the use of tables, authors could place text and images horizontally, but they had little control over vertical placement; at most, authors could control vertical alignment of images using the `valign=""` attribute.

You learned how to create basic data tables to arrange text in easy-to-read tabular format. You also learned to expand rows and columns to create customized tables. You discovered how to format tables using borders, border sizes, background colors, cellspacing, and cellpadding. You found that you can merge two or more tables to create a nested table, which offers increased flexibility and control over the display of the content.

KEY TERMS

Background color	Header	Spacer
Border color	Monospaced font	Table
Cell	Mortised Web page	Table data tag
Cellpadding	Nested table	Table row tag
Cellspacing	<pre> tag	<table> tag
Column	Row	Tabular format
Column span	Row span	

CHECKING CONCEPTS AND TERMS

MULTIPLE CHOICE

Circle the letter that matches the correct answer for each of the following questions.

1. Why are tables useful?

   a. They provide a way to display content vertically.

   b. You can organize data in tabular format.

   c. You can design page layouts that would be impossible with other XHTML elements.

   d. All of the above.

2. What basic tags create a table?

   a. <table> tag only

   b. <table>, <tr>, and <td> tags

   c. <tr> and <td> tags

   d. <row> and <column> tags

3. A table row is defined by the <td> tag.

   a. True

   b. False

4. What tag do you use to create the table header?

   a. <td>

   b. <tr>

   c. <th>

   d. None of the above.

5. The default width of the table is determined by the content of the table.

   a. True

   b. False

6. What element is used to expand a row?

   a. colspan

   b. rowspan

   c. merge

   d. None of the above.

7. You can specify the height and width of a table using exact pixels or percentages.

   a. True

   b. False

8. You can align data in a table, and you can align the table itself.

   a. True

   b. False

9. To change the space between cells, you can use the _____.

   a. cellspacing attribute

   b. cellpadding attribute

   c. nonbreaking space element

   d. You cannot change the spacing

10. Why are footers and headers beneficial?

   a. They make the page load faster.

   b. They load the appropriate information in order.

   c. They provide important information about the table.

   d. None of the above.

DISCUSSION QUESTIONS

1. What are some of the most common uses of tables on Web pages today, and why?

2. Why did tables become so popular?

3. Why is it important to use CSS to format your tables, rather than use XHTML elements?

S K I L L   D R I L L

Skill Drills reinforce chapter skills. Each skill reinforced is the same as, or nearly the same as, a skill presented in the lessons. We provide detailed instructions in a step-by-step format. You should complete these exercises in the order provided.

1. Create a Table

1. In your text editor, open skilltable.htm from your WIP_05 folder.

2. Create a basic table using the **`<table>`** tags.

3. Add a table header row that spans two columns and contains the text "Student Grade".

4. Create a second row with two cells. Add "Name" to the first cell, and add "Pass/Fail" to the second cell.

5. Create five more rows with two cells in each row, as follows:

```
<table>
    <tr>
      <td width="100%" colspan="2">
Student Grade
</td>
    </tr>
    <tr>
      <td>Name</td>
      <td>Pass/Fail</td>
    </tr>
    <tr>
      <td></td>
      <td></td>
    </tr>
    <tr>
      <td></td>
      <td></td>
    </tr>
    <tr>
      <td></td>
      <td</td>
    </tr>
    <tr>
      <td></td>
      <td></td>
    </tr>
    <tr>
      <td></td>
      <td></td>
    </tr>
</table>
```

In this drill, we are temporarily leaving the cells without content. We could have used nonbreaking spaces (** **) or spacer images to prevent browsers from collapsing empty cells.

6. Create a final row that spans across two cells and contains "Spring Semester". Center-align "Spring Semester" and apply bold styling.

7. Add a border to the table. Set the size to 1.

8. Set the table's width to 75% of the screen size.

9. Save the changes to the text file and refresh the document in your browser and view the result.

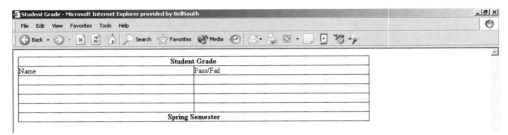

FIGURE 5.36

Older browsers may collapse these cells and change the appearance of the table since we do not have spacer images or content in the cells.

10. Leave the file open for the next exercise.

2. Change the Table Display and Alignment

1. In the open document, align the table in the center of the browser window.

2. Center-align the cells that contain "Name" and "Pass/Fail".

3. Center-align the content in the empty cells beneath the table headers.

4. Save the changes to the text file. Refresh the document in the browser and view the result.

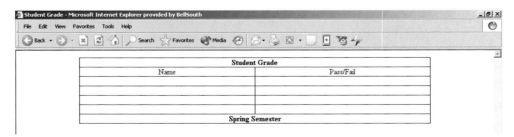

FIGURE 5.37

5. Leave the file open for the next exercise.

3. Add Headers, Footers, and Body

1. In the open document, contain the header cell within the **`<thead>`** tags.

2. Contain the body of the table within the **`<tbody>`** tags.

3. Contain the footer of the table within the **`<tfoot>`** tags.

4. Save the changes to the text file. Refresh the document in the browser.

5. Leave the file open for the next exercise.

4. Format the Table's Color

1. In the open file, change the background color of the entire table to gray.

2. Change the table header's background color to black.

3. Format the font inside the header cell to white.

4. Change the border color of the table to dark gray.

5. Save the changes to the text file. Refresh the document in the browser and view the result.

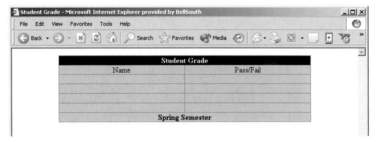

FIGURE 5.38

6. Close the file in both applications.

CHALLENGE

Challenge exercises expand on, or are somewhat related to, skills presented in the lessons. Each exercise provides a brief introduction, followed by numbered-step instructions that are not as detailed as those in the Skill Drill exercises. You should complete these Challenge exercises in the order provided.

1. Create a Simple Page Layout

You know how to create a basic table. You want to use your knowledge to create a page layout that includes tables. You decide to create an ad about an online XHTML course that includes tables, formatted text, and images.

1. In your text editor, open course.htm from your WIP_05 folder.

2. Create a table that displays three rows.

3. Set the table to center-align, with no borders, and at 80% of the screen width.

4. Expand the top and bottom rows by adding a table data tag to each row.

5. Open the text file named chapter5content.txt.

6. Copy the text beneath the Top Row section of the text file into the first row of the table.

7. Copy the text beneath the Bottom Row section of the text file into the last row of the table.

8. Save the changes to the file. Open the document in your browser and view the result.

9. Leave the file open for the next exercise.

FIGURE 5.39

2. Nest Tables

Your next task is to add additional course information in tabular format. Create a nested table in the left cell, and position the data into columns and rows. (In the next exercise, you add an image that aligns to the right of the text; positioning the table to the left will not affect the location of the image.)

1. In the open document, position your cursor in the first cell of the second row. At this point, you should only have one cell in each row.

2. Create a table within this cell that has three rows and three columns.

3. In the first row of the table you created in the previous step, add a header that spans across the table.

4. Add "Take the Online Course and Learn:" in the header row.

5. In the second row, add the following items (one item per cell): "XHTML", "Browser Support", and "Web Server".

6. In the third row, add the following items (one item per cell): "CSS Basics", "Intro to Images", and "and More!"

7. Center-align the table within the cell. Make sure no border displays.

8. Leave the file open for the next exercise.

FIGURE 5.40

3. Create an Image Layout

An image will liven up this rather lackluster Web page. Positioning an image to the right of the text will fill in a lot of the extra white space and create a more balanced design.

1. In the open document, position your cursor in the second row of the main table before the table header.

2. Create a second nested table with two rows and two columns.

3. Set the cellpadding and cellspacing of your nested table to 0.

4. Align the table to the right side of the browser window.

5. In the first cell of the nested table, insert ad1.gif.

6. Insert ad2.gif in the cell next to ad1.gif.

7. Move down to the first cell in the third row and insert ad3.gif.

8. Insert ad4.gif in the cell next to ad3.gif.

9. Leave the document open for the next exercise.

FIGURE 5.41

4. Format Table Data

The final step is to format the text. You can change the default text and add some background color to parts of the table. You can also format other elements in the table by containing the content within format tags.

1. In the open document, change the heading of the table to a suitable color, font, and text size.

2. Add your e-mail address in the last row.

3. Format the background color of the header row. Use any color you prefer.

4. Change the font style throughout the document to any font you prefer.

5. In the main table, second row, second cell (the one that contains the image table), change the cell's width to 210 pixels.

6. Change the alignment of all the cells' contents however you prefer.

7. Save the changes in your text editor. Refresh the document in your browser and view the result.

8. Close the file in both applications.

FIGURE 5.42

PORTFOLIO BUILDER

Create a Sports Schedule

A local sports club hired you as a Web design consultant. The club's manager wants an online sports schedule that features the next season of professional football games. The club hired you to create a Web page that offers next season's schedule in tabular format. They want you to maintain the scoring of each game. To complete this exercise, you should do the following:

- Log on to the National Football League's Web site at http://www.nfl.com/.

- View their schedule and scoring information. Decide how you can create a Web page layout (using tables) that will allow you to display this information in an easy-to-read format. Consider future updates while you design the site.

- Identify which teams are playing, and where and when. In addition, you might want to include empty cells for future scoring information for a particular game.

- When you create the Web page, consider the table's formatting. Think of creative ways to format, such as using team colors when supplying information about a particular team. You can also link to a team's official Web site.

CHAPTER 6

Creating XHTML Forms

OBJECTIVES

In this chapter, you learn how to:

- Create a basic form

- Work with form data

- Submit forms

- Create text and password fields

- Insert radio buttons and check boxes

- Include selection menus

- Generate multiline text areas

- Incorporate hidden fields

- Produce form buttons

Why Would I Do This?

Site designers willingly spend considerable time and effort on the presentation of information to their viewers; but they often overlook the benefits of acquiring information from viewers. As the Web is an interactive medium, it can be used as a tool to collect significant amounts of data, on a variety of topics, from all types of users.

Forms can help Web designers gather information from users for any number of important reasons including:

- Asking users for their preferences to customize the information they enter.

- Using online surveys about users' tastes and interests.

- Processing information for e-commerce transactions. When processing an e-commerce transaction, we need a variety of information such as item numbers, quantity, and shipping address.

- Allowing users to search using simple text boxes where keywords can be entered.

In this chapter, you learn how to create forms for your Web pages, which allow you to collect useful information from your viewers, and ultimately use that information to enhance the content on your sites.

VISUAL SUMMARY

The purpose of an online form is to acquire information from the user and send it to the server. HTML is a *client-side language*, which means the user's computer or browser interprets the code and does the work. For many practical purposes, it is necessary to send information from a Web page to a server. A computer language used by a Web server is called a *server-side language*. A server is simply a computer that performs a specific management function, such as making Web sites available to users, processing e-mails, or storing files.

Once HTML passes the information to the server, the server can then perform a variety of actions with the information (or store it in a database for retrieval later). The information is then processed using server-side applications or scripts. A server-side script is a piece of code processed by a remote computer.

Server-scripts are usually written in languages such as ASP.net, PHP, or ColdFusion and are outside the scope of this book. Some languages, such as the Java programming language, can be used as either a client-side or server-side language. A wealth of information on these languages is available on the Web.

Forms can contain many different types of input fields, including text boxes and drop-down menus. In Figure 6.1, you see a basic form with input fields that collect and submit user data. Certain types of input fields are more appropriate in one situation than another. You explore a number of these input options in this chapter.

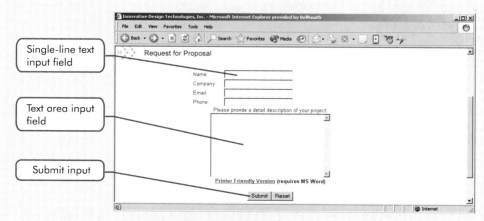

FIGURE 6.1

Standard forms, similar to the one shown above, are created using XHTML or HTML. CSS, however, provides additional control over the presentation of forms because it allows you to change the field colors, background colors, and so forth.

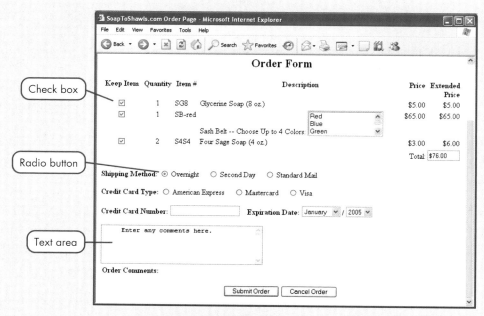

FIGURE 6.2

LESSON 1   Creating a Basic Form

A form consists of a **<form>** tag with one or more input tags. The **<form>** tags tell the browser where a form begins and ends. The **<form>** tag also contains useful information, such as where the *form data* will be sent, how the form data is submitted, and the name of the form.

The *input fields* (also called "input types") can be designed as text boxes ("text") or *submit buttons* ("submit"). An input tag can also have a name attribute, which helps the server identify the information when it is submitted by the browser. For example, if you were building a form that asked for a user's telephone number, you might use **name="phone"** to tell the server exactly what it is receiving.

The following code is the basic format for a form that includes a text field:

```
<form>
Enter your information here:
<input type="text" name="myTextField" />
</form>
```

This code would produce a simple Web page, as shown in Figure 6.3.

FIGURE 6.3

Unlike a typical Web form, there is no submit button in this example; because there is only one text box, the user can press Enter/Return to submit this form. Many viewers would not realize that they could press the Enter/Return key to submit their input, so it's best to include a submit button on every form you create. You learn more about buttons throughout this chapter.

The example form in the previous illustration does not include any other instructions; so submitting the form simply returns the browser to the same page. When you submit the form, the information in the text field is added to the URL (the Address or Location field of the browser).

In this case, the text "blah" was entered in the text field, and then the Enter/Return key was pressed. This placed "blah" in the Address field, as shown in Figure 6.4.

The text entered is appended to the URL

FIGURE 6.4

Information added to a URL is referred to as *URL parameters*. Web developers use this method to pass information to the server. In a real-world scenario, you would use a Web server combined with other scripting technologies to perform some sort of action with the form data. We cannot provide a server for you to work with, but we provide a script that allows you to see the form in action.

Create the Form

1   **Copy the content of your Chapter_06 folder to your WIP_06 folder.**

2   **Open forms.htm in a text editor and in a Web browser.**

The source code shows the basic document tags.

3   **In the text editor, position your cursor beneath the `<body>` tag, and enter the `<form>` tags, as follows:**

```
<html>
<head><title>Form Test Page</title></head>
<body>
<form>
    <input />
</form>
</body>
</html>
```

The `<form>` tags tell the browser where to expect the form to start and end. The input fields for each form you include on a Web page must be placed within the `<form>` tags. Note that the input field is an empty tag.

4   **Save the change to the text file and refresh the document in the browser.**

FIGURE 6.5

The form displays a single input field in the browser. The input's type is not yet defined; you have not described the input field as a text field or *check box*. You learn more about defining the types of inputs you can use with forms later in the chapter.

5   **Return to the text file. Include a name for the input field, as follows:**

```
<html>
<head><title>Form Test Page</title></head>
<body>
<form>
    <input name="welcome" />
</form>
</body>
</html>
```

6   **Save the change to the text file and refresh the document in the browser.**

There are no changes to the input field; the document looks the same as before. The idea behind including the **name=" "** attribute is to identify the field so you can easily transfer its content later.

7   **Click your cursor in the input field. Type "Hello World".**

FIGURE 6.6

8   **Press the Enter/Return key.**

Nothing happens to the page; however, "Hello World" displays in the Address field.

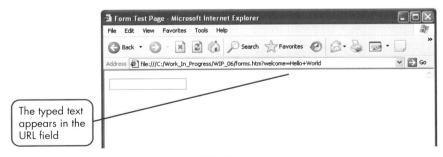

The typed text appears in the URL field

FIGURE 6.7

9   **Close the file in your browser and text editor.**

To Extend Your Knowledge . . .

THE NEXT GENERATION OF WEB FORMS

The W3C recommends the new ***XForms*** model as an XML application and a replacement for standard HTML/XHTML forms. XForms offer everything that HTML/XHTML forms offer — plus a lot more. Currently, XForms is at version 1.0. Although XForms is not within the scope of this book, we recommend that you visit www.w3c.org to find out more about this new technology.

LESSON 2 Form Data

Form data is the information that the user types into the form fields. Once the user types information into a simple form (that does not contain submission instructions) and presses Enter/Return, the information in the Address/Location field in the browser changes; it displays the file path and the information that was submitted with the form.

For example, in the preceding exercise, the URL in the Address/Location field includes a question mark toward the end of the line. The question mark tells the server that what follows is data. The data could be one piece of information or multiple pieces. In either case, the data is sent as a ***name-value pair*** to a specified location, such as a database on a server. A name-value pair is a single piece of information to be transmitted to a server consisting of two elements: a name, which identifies the information; and a value, which is the information itself.

All form information is submitted in name-value pair format. The browser strips the data from the name-value pair and attaches it to the URL. If our sample form were on an actual Web server, the URL might be

```
http://www.web-answers.com/login.htm?username=Nick
```

This data could be extracted from the URL and used in some way, such as displaying the form results to the user. To retrieve the data, however, you need to use a script. In addition, if you want to send the user to another location, you must specify that as well. As you work through this chapter, you learn how to accomplish all of these operations.

The Form Action

Our sample page isn't very useful yet, since it doesn't actually do anything. What you need to do next is create a page to receive your information, once it has been sent by the browser. The receiving page is called the ***form action***, because sending the information to the receiving page is the "act" the browser performs with the information.

The action is used with a relative or absolute URL in the `action=""` attribute of the form element, such as in the following form:

```
<form action="myFormAction.asp">
   Enter your information here:
   <input type="text" name="myTextField" />
</form>
```

In this case, when you submit the form, the browser would try to open the URL

```
file:///<yourpathhere>/myFormAction.asp?myTextField=myinfo
```

In almost every case, this URL represents some sort of program, such as an Active Server Page (which uses the file extension .asp) or a CGI script. The Web server executes the program and usually performs an action, such as processing an order or adding user information to a database, and then returns an HTML page to the browser.

Creating Active Server Pages and CGI scripts are separate disciplines; entire books are dedicated to the subjects. Some ISPs provide their own CGI scripts to serve these functions, and require that you use their scripts. You can talk with your ISP about their policies and what scripts they provide, if any. Other service providers allow you to add scripts that you create yourself, or download from resources such as

www.cgiforme.com

www.cgiscripts.net

www.scriptarchive.com

Since we don't have the luxury of using a Web server with this book, the script we provide executes and displays the values you type in the form. The script shows you these values in the URL in the Address/Location field. Any URL can be used as the action of a form, and the browser takes over from there.

Add the Action Attribute

1   **From the WIP_06 folder, open login.htm in a text editor and browser.**

The code displays with a script tag and the necessary attribute to call an outside script for the form processing. Working with advanced scripts is outside the scope of this book. We use this particular script to illustrate form action.

2   **Add an action to the form that calls on a script to process the data.**

```
<html>
<head><title>Form Test Page</title></head>
<body>
<script src="scriptvalues.js" language="JavaScript"
type="text/javascript"></script>
```

```
<h2>Please Log In</h2>
<form action="login_action.htm">
    <input name="username" />
</form>
</body>
</html>
```

The form will send the information to the login_action.htm page for processing. *JavaScript*, another client-side language will be used to simulate a server-side language. JavaScript is often used to make sure users enter form information correctly before the form data is sent to the server for processing.

3   **Save the file in the text editor and refresh your browser.**

FIGURE 6.8

You don't see a change, but the new code will be loaded into the browser.

4   **In the browser window, type any text into the text field, and then press Enter/Return.**

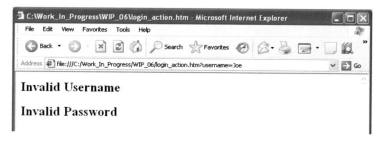

FIGURE 6.9

Notice that the browser goes to login_action.htm, which you specified as the form's action in Step 2. While you did receive messages telling you that the username and password were incorrect, that's not important right now. The important point is the URL; notice that it's not login.htm anymore — it's login_action.htm. The script processed the data it obtained from the form's input field, and then displayed the result on the next page.

5   **Close the file in your browser and text editor.**

To Extend Your Knowledge . . .

A PLETHORA OF METHODS FOR PROCESSING FORMS

The examples provided in this chapter for data collection and form processing are just a few of the many ways you can work with forms. A number of technologies are available to you, from advanced programming languages to the mail protocol.

As you continue to increase your abilities in creating forms, keep in mind the myriad options available to you.

LESSON 3   Text Inputs

As you now know, you can create a form that submits information to a URL that is designated as the form action. You also know that you must use name-value pairs because only inputs that have names are submitted to the form action. Next, let's examine the variety of input types that allow you to create powerful forms.

Text input is the most familiar type of form input. You used a text input form — a text box — in the previous exercise. A text input is a single-line option that allows users to enter alphanumeric text (letters and numbers).

You have some control over these text fields. Using attributes, you can control the size of the field, the number of characters the user can type into it, and the values that you want the field to contain when the page first loads. For example, you can make our sample form load with an initial value that includes explanatory text. You can also set the size of the field (**size=""**) to 15 characters and the maximum number of characters that the user can type (**maxlength=""**) to 30, as shown here.

```
<form action="myFormAction.asp">
   Enter your information here:
 <input type="text" name="myTextField" value="your name here"
 size="15" maxlength="30" />
</form>
```

The preceding code results in the following page:

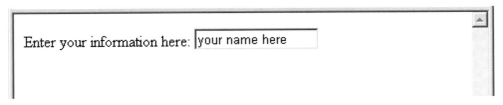

Enter your information here: your name here

FIGURE 6.10

You can provide an initial value by adding the **value=""** attribute to your input tag. The copy between the quote marks displays when the page is loaded, as shown in the previous illustration.

As its name suggests, this copy is only the initial value. When the user types his information into the box, the new copy replaces the original (initial value) text.

Assume you are maintaining a Web site for a company that sells everything from soap to shawls. Before you can change anything on the site, you must log in using your username and password. An HTML form is used to gather the username and password information.

Add Text Fields

1   **In your text editor and browser, open soaptoshawls.htm from your WIP_06 folder.**

2   **Insert the following code:**

```
. . .
<center>
<h2>Please Log In</h2>
<form action="login_action.htm">
    Please enter your username: <input type="text"
size="20"name="username" />
</form>
</center>
</body>
. . .
```

This text field will be used to gather the username from the user. Notice that the size of the text box has been set to be 20 characters.

3   **Save the file in the text editor and refresh your browser.**

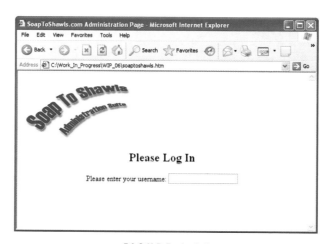

FIGURE 6.11

4 Type some words in the box.

If you type more than 20 characters, the text scrolls to the left but allows you to continue to type.

5 Press Enter/Return to submit the form.

6 Look at the URL in the Address/Location field. All of your text was submitted.

FIGURE 6.12

The page tells you that this information is invalid. This happened because the script that is processing your data is looking for a specific username and password — which you have not yet supplied.

7 Choose the Back button to return to the soaptoshawls.htm file.

8 Leave the file open in your text editor and browser for use in the next exercise.

Limit the Number of Characters

Although you can set the number of characters that display in a text field, it doesn't control the amount of text that can be submitted. While this is not generally a problem, programmers often need to limit the amount of text that is returned. For instance, the text may be destined for a database that allows only a certain number of characters. You can use the **maxlength=""** attribute to control the number of characters entered.

1 Insert the following code:

```
. . .

<form action="login_action.htm">

    Please enter your username: <input type="text" size="20"
name="username" maxlength="10" />

</form>

. . .
```

This will set the maximum number of characters in the text box to 10.

2 Save the file in the text editor and refresh your browser. Try to type more than 10 characters in the text box in the browser.

While there appears to be room in the box, the browser allows you to type only 10 characters.

FIGURE 6.13

You cannot go beyond the limit defined in the **maxlength=" "** attribute. In addition to assigning a maximum number of characters to text fields, you can also establish an initial value.

3   **Use the `value=" "` attribute to add explanatory text to the text box. Change the maximum length to allow for all of the text, which in this case is 20.**

```
. . .
<center>
<h2>Please Log In</h2>
<form action="login_action.htm">
    Please enter your username: <input type="text" size="20"
name="username" maxlength="20" value="Enter Your Userid" />
</form>
</center>
</body>
</html>
```

4   **Save the file and refresh the browser.**

The text you typed as the value appears in the text box.

FIGURE 6.14

You specified this initial value by adding the **value=""** attribute to your input tag. The copy between the quote marks displays when the page is loaded, as shown in the previous example.

5   **Close the file in your text editor and browser.**

To Extend Your Knowledge . . .

FORM SUBMISSION OPTIONS

Before scripting languages became popular, there were very few options for form submission. If you used a scripting language such as CGI, it could have been costly, too, depending on your hosting account.

One option that was often used to submit forms without an advanced script (and is still used today) is the mailto: command. The mailto: command was used with the `action=""` attribute with an e-mail address as the value. For example:

```
<form action="mailto:name@domain.com">
```

When the user submitted the form, the result from the name-value pair was sent to the address via the mail protocol. This method was not perfect — the data was sent unsecured, and it was difficult to read once retrieved. In addition, the mailto method offered less flexibility to perform other actions on the data.

LESSON 4   Passwords

In addition to taking log-in information, online forms can also take the user's password. The difficulty in acquiring a user's password is the need to hide the information from onlookers to ensure the security of the user's account. For example, ATM machines do not display password text; instead, the text is replaced with placeholder characters. You can do the same with ***password input*** on an ***online form***.

Password input is similar to text input, with one exception: the characters that the user types display as asterisks or bullets (depending on the user's browser and operating system), rather than actual text characters. For example, you can change the sample form to use password input instead of text input, as follows:

```
<form action="myFormAction.asp">

Enter your information here:

<input type="password" name="myTextField" value="your name here"
size="20" maxlength="30" />

</form>
```

When you use this code, the browser obscures the initial value, as well as anything that the user types, as shown in Figure 6.15.

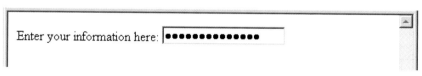

FIGURE 6.15

If you submit this form, however, the URL parameter shows the flaw in this plan.

```
file:///<your path here>/myFormAction.asp?myTextField=mysecretinfo
```

As you can see, password boxes don't really encrypt the information — they just hide it from someone who may be watching the user as he types. If the preceding sample form were submitted, the password would be visible to anyone who knew where to look (in the URL field). Later in this chapter, you learn how to resolve this particular problem. For now, however, remember that information is not necessarily secure just because it's in a password box.

Adding a Submit Button

A second complication that arises when adding a password box to the log-in form is unrelated to security: How do you submit information when you have multiple information fields on your form? Up to now, you pressed the Enter/Return key to submit the sample form. This method worked perfectly because there was only one text box in the form. Now that you have multiple information fields on your form, however, that method no longer works properly. You need another way to submit the form — you need to add a submit button.

A submit button is just another type of input, which is coded as follows:

```
<input type="submit" />
```

The submit button displays on your Web page with the words "Submit Query", as shown in Figure 6.16.

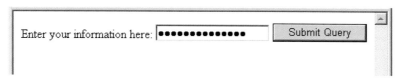

FIGURE 6.16

The browser interprets this as a form button that, when clicked, submits the form. You work with submit buttons in detail later in the chapter.

Create a Password Field

1   In your text editor and browser, open passwords.htm from your WIP_06 folder.

2   Insert the following code:

```
. . .
Please enter your username: <input type="text" size="20"
name="username" maxlength="20" value="Enter Your Userid" />

<br />

    Please enter your password: <input type="password" size="20"
name="password" />

<br />

</form>

. . .
```

This will add a password input box that is 20 characters wide.

3   Insert the following code:

```
. . .
Please enter your username: <input type="text" size="20"
name="username" maxlength="20" value="Enter Your Userid" />

<br />

    Please enter your password: <input type="password" size="20"
name="password" />

<br />
```

```
<input type="submit" />
</form>
...
```

This will add a submit button, just below the password field.

4   **Save the changes to the text file and refresh the document in the browser.**

FIGURE 6.17

The form displays what seems to be a basic text field and a submit button. Notice that you used the line-break tag to force the button down to the next line. Similar to any other XHTML element, you can control the display of form elements on the page.

5   **Type random letters in the password box in the browser window.**

FIGURE 6.18

Rather than the actual characters you type, bullets or asterisks display in the text field. This leads you to believe the information is secure — but don't be fooled.

6   **Type the username "sandra" and password "bunnies", and then click the Submit Query button to submit the form.**

In this case, you must submit the name and password completely in lowercase letters.

7   **Look at the URL in the Address/Location field.**

FIGURE 6.19

The username and password display in the browser's Address field.

8   **Save your changes in your text editor.**

9   **Close the file in your browser and text editor.**

LESSON 5   Radio Buttons and Check Boxes

If you listen to the radio on a car stereo, you may have six or more buttons that are programmed to go to preset radio stations. If you select a button on the radio to go to a station, the last button is deselected and the station changes. Radio buttons are ***mutually exclusive***, meaning that only one button can be selected at a time.

Radio buttons in HTML forms work in the same fashion. Radio buttons are used to allow users to pick a single answer among multiple choices. If your professor gives an online test using multiple-choice questions, radio buttons can be used to allow users to pick the single answer they think is correct.

Radio buttons are also known as ***radio groups*** because, in most cases, they're only useful when there's more than one option from which to choose. Use radio buttons when you want to allow users to choose from several options, but make only one selection at any given time.

For example, we can use a radio group ("radio") on our sample form, as follows:

```
<form action="myFormAction.asp">
   What is your choice?
   <br />
  <input type="radio" name="choice" value="Y" checked="checked" />Yes
  <input type="radio" name="choice" value="N" />No
  <input type="radio" name="choice" value="M" />Maybe
  <br />
  <input type="submit" />
</form>
```

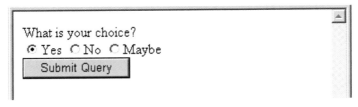

FIGURE 6.20

There are a couple of points to notice about radio groups. Contrary to what you might think, radio buttons are not grouped according to where they are located on the page. Radio buttons in different areas of the page can be grouped together by assigning the same name to each of the buttons. Notice that all three of the buttons in the sample code have the same name — which is what defines a radio group. Buttons in a different group have a different name.

In a button group, one button is denoted as "checked." The reason for the strange notation (**checked="checked"**) is because in older versions of HTML, you simply included the word "checked" to designate which button was selected by default. With the advent of XHTML, however, all attributes must have an assigned value.

Clicking another button selects it and deselects the previous button. This means that you must make a selection in a radio group — the default button remains selected if you don't select another button. You can be certain that a value will be submitted — as long as you make sure that a value is selected initially. (If not, the user may submit the form without making a choice, which defeats the purpose of a radio group.)

The last point to remember about radio groups is that the value submitted is the data in the value attribute, not the text next to the radio button. For example, if the user were to submit our sample form as is, the value passed would be "Y", not "Yes".

Check Boxes

Check boxes appear on printed forms whenever users must check all answers that apply to the question. For example, when you visit a new doctor for the first time, you might be given a form asking about your medical history. The form could ask you to check all medications you are currently taking and a list of medications could be listed. You would check the box beside every medication that you are currently taking.

In a similar fashion, HTML forms use check boxes to indicate something to which the user must agree, or a group of items from which the user must choose. Check boxes ("checkbox") are similar to radio groups — if they aren't clicked, their values are not submitted. The difference is that check boxes can provide several different values for the same name; the user can select more than one choice without removing the check from the previous choice.

You can change your sample radio buttons to check boxes, as follows:

```
<form action="myFormAction.asp">
   What is your choice?
   <br />
  <input type="checkbox" name="choice" value="Y" checked="checked" />Yes
  <input type="checkbox" name="choice" value="N" />No
  <input type="checkbox" name="choice" value="M" />Maybe
  <br />
  <input type="submit" />
</form>
```

This changes your form slightly, as shown in Figure 6.21.

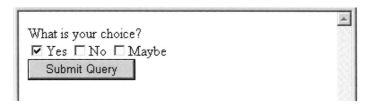

FIGURE 6.21

The primary differences between check boxes and radio buttons are that check boxes can be left completely unselected, and more than one check box can be selected at one time.

Create Radio Buttons

1 | **In your text editor and browser, open order.htm from your WIP_06 folder.**

2   **Add the following code:**

```
...
<b>Shipping Method:</b>
<input type="radio" value="1" name="shipping" checked="checked" />
Overnight    
<input type="radio" value="2" name="shipping" />
Second Day    
<input type="radio" value="3" name="shipping" />
Standard Mail
<br /><br />
<b>Credit Card Type:  </b>
<input type="radio" value="1" name="card_type" />
American Express    
<input type="radio" value="2" name="card_type" />
Mastercard    
<input type="radio" value="3" name="card_type" />
Visa    
<br /><br />
...
```

This will add three radio buttons named "shipping" to the Shipping Methods section, add three radio buttons named "card_type" to the Credit Card Type section, and add appropriate values for each radio button that is selected.

3 **Save the file and refresh the browser.**

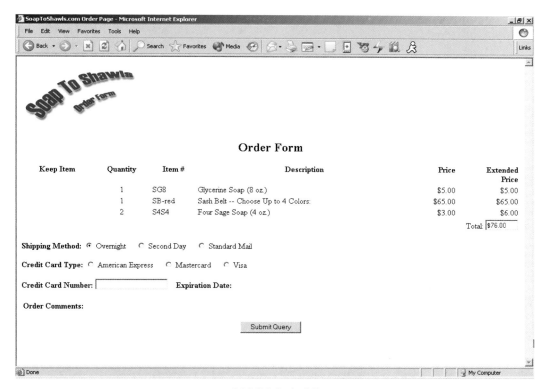

FIGURE 6.22

You have two groups of buttons, but only one of them has values.

4 **Submit the form exactly as it is, and look at the values that are passed.**

While the value for the selected button was passed, no value was passed for card_type, because none was selected.

Remember that radio buttons are grouped according to their name, not where they are located on the page. Radio buttons in different areas of the page can be grouped together by assigning the same name to each of the buttons.

5 **Choose the Back button in your browser and leave the file open in both windows.**

Check the Radio Groups

1   In the open order.htm file, swap the names of one of the shipping buttons and one of the card_type buttons.

```
. . .
<br />
<b>Shipping Method:</b>
<input type="radio" value="1" name="shipping" checked="checked" />
Overnight    
<input type="radio" value="2" name="card_type" />
Second Day    
<input type="radio" value="3" name="shipping" />
Standard Mail
<br /><br />
<b>Credit Card Type:  </b>
<input type="radio" value="1" name="card_type" />
American Express    
<input type="radio" value="2" name="shipping" />
Mastercard    
<input type="radio" value="3" name="card_type" />
Visa    
<br /><br />
<b>Credit Card Number: </b> <input type="text" name="ccnumber" />
   

. . .
```

2 Save the file in the text editor and refresh your browser. Experiment with the two groups of buttons.

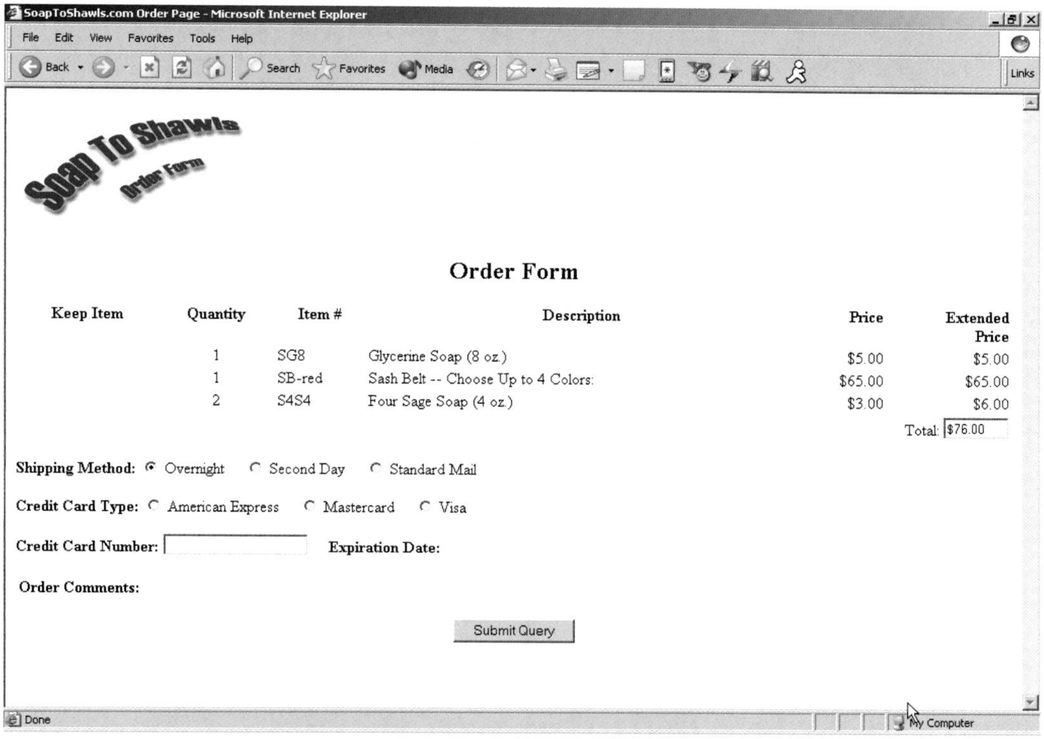

FIGURE 6.23

At one moment, one button may be selected in each of the two rows; at the next moment, two buttons may be selected in one row and none in the other row. This is due to the changes you made to the button groups.

3 Undo the last change in the text editor so each button belongs to the proper group.

4 Leave the file open in both windows.

To Extend Your Knowledge . . .

TABBING THROUGH FORMS

You can enable your visitors to tab through your form fields simply by adding `tabindex=""` to your input tags, as follows:

```
<input type="text" name="name" size="20" maxlength="30" tabindex="1" />
```

This example shows that the user tabs to a text box the first time he presses the Tab key.

The `tabindex=""` value determines the order you tab through text boxes and other fields on the Web page. If you want the tab order to skip a field, use a negative value beginning with "–1", then "–2", and so on. Each negative value is bypassed when the user tabs through your form.

Add Check Boxes

1   **In the open order.htm file, insert the following code:**

```
. . .
<tr>
      <th>Keep Item</th><th>Quantity</th>
      <th>Item #</th><th>Description</th><th>Price</th>
      <th>Extended<br />Price</th>
</tr>
<tr>
      <td><input type="checkbox" name="item" value="SG8"
checked="checked" /></td><td>1</td><td>SG8</td>
      <td>Glycerine Soap (8 oz.)</td><td>$5.00</td><td>$5.00</td>
</tr>
<tr>
      <td><input type="checkbox" name="item" value="SB"
checked="checked" /></td><td>1</td><td>SB-red</td>
      <td valign="top" >Sash Belt — Choose Up to 4 Colors</td>
      <td>$65.00</td><td>$65.00</td>
</tr>
<tr>
      <td><input type="checkbox" name="item" value="S4S4"
checked="checked" /></td><td>2</td><td>S4S4</td>
      <td>Four Sage Soap (4 oz.)</td><td>$3.00</td><td>$6.00</td>
</tr>
. . .
```

This will add a check box name item for each of the three products in the table at the top of the page.

2 Save the file and refresh the page in your browser.

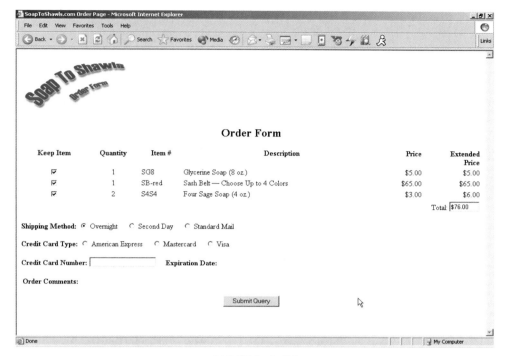

FIGURE 6.24

The check boxes appear at the start of each line, and all of them are checked.

3 | Uncheck one of the boxes and submit the page.

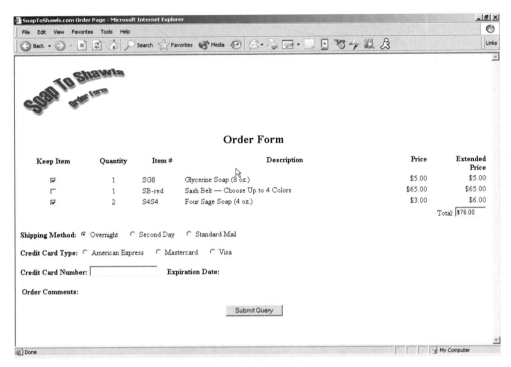

FIGURE 6.25

The items that were checked were submitted, but the item that was unchecked was not submitted.

4 | Close the file in your browser and text editor.

LESSON 6 Select Boxes

Select boxes (also known as pull-down menus, drop-down boxes, drag-down menus, or drop lists) are radio-button-and-check-box hybrids. One type of select box acts as a radio button, and the other type behaves as a check box.

A select box is not simply another type of input. Instead, it is a select element that contains one or more option elements. The traditional select box shows only one value at a time and allows the user to select only one option (through the selected attribute or through user action). For example:

```
<form action="myFormAction.asp">
    What is your choice?
    <br />
```

```
<select name="choice">

    <option value="Y" selected="selected">Yes</option>

    <option value="N">No</option>

    <option value="M">Maybe</option>

</select>

<br />

<input type="submit" />

</form>
```

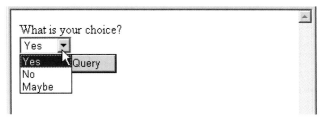

FIGURE 6.26

What you see in Figure 6.26 is a select box that consists of a **<select></select>** element that contains one or more **<option></option>** elements. The select box is the overall object, so that's where the name of the form belongs. The values, on the other hand, are contained in the **<option>** elements. A select box can have any number of options; but remember, users scroll only so far before giving up and moving to another page, so you should attempt to restrict your options to a reasonable number.

As with check boxes and radio buttons, the browser doesn't care about the label (the description of the field) for a particular option; the browser is only concerned with the value assigned to the option. To avoid potential problems, however, it is best to specify a value on each option, even if the value is the same as the label.

You can also set a size on the select box, which displays the number of options by default. For example:

```
<select name="choice" size="3">

  </select>
```

To make the select box act as a set of check boxes, you can add the **multiple=""** attribute; otherwise, only one value can be submitted at a time, similar to a radio group. Similar to **checked** and **selected** attributes, the **multiple=""** attribute used to be written without a value in HTML; but now, XHTML requires that a value is included.

```
<form action="myFormAction.asp">

    What is your choice?

    <br />

<select name="choice" size="3" multiple="multiple">
```

```
    <option value="Y" selected="selected">Yes</option>

    <option value="N">No</option>

    <option value="M">Maybe</option>

  </select>

  <br />

  <input type="submit" />

</form>
```

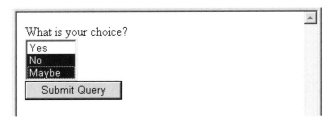

FIGURE 6.27

The page looks the same in the browser, but now users can hold down the Shift key to choose more than one option, and hold down the Control key to select multiple adjacent options.

Add a Select Box

1   In your text editor and browser, open select.htm from your WIP_06 folder.

2   Insert the following code:

```
. . .

<input type="radio" value="3" name="card_type" />

Visa    

<br /> <br />

<b>Credit Card Number: </b> <input type="text"

name="ccnumber" />   

<b>Expiration Date: </b>

<select name="exp_month">

<option value="1">January</option>

<option value="2">February</option>

<option value="3">March</option>

<option value="4">April</option>
```

```
</select>

/

<select name="exp_year">

<option value="2005">2005</option>

<option value="2006">2006</option>

<option value="2007">2007</option>

</select>

<br /><br />

<table><tr><td valign="top"><b>Order Comments:
</b></td><td></td></tr></table>

. . .
```

This will add select boxes for the credit card expiration month and year. To reduce the amount of code you must type, only the first few months of the year have been included.

? If you have problems

In HTML, it was very common to leave the `<option>` tag open and to omit the value. Early browsers used the label in this case, but some newer browsers use the "index" of the choice. For instance, if the second choice is selected, it might pass the value "1." (Lists are **zero-based**, meaning that the first choice is "0.") To avoid potential misunderstandings and problems, you must specify a value on each option, even if it is the same as the label.

---

3 Save the file and refresh the browser.

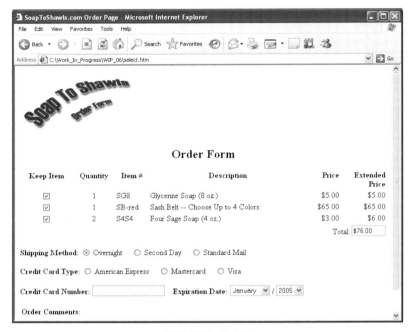

FIGURE 6.28

The select boxes appear. Without a value designated as selected, the first value in the list is selected by default.

4 Leave the file open in both windows.

Add a Multiple-Choice Select List

A second type of select element is more of a list than a menu. This list, which looks the same as the preceding select boxes, allows users to select multiple values.

1 In the open select.htm file, insert the following code:

```
. . .
<tr>
    <td><input type="checkbox" name="item" value="SB"
checked="checked" /></td><td>1</td><td>SB-red</td>
    <td valign="top" >Sash Belt — Choose Up to 4 Colors
    <br />
    <select name="colors" size="3" multiple="multiple">
    <option value="red">Red</option>
```

```
<option value="blue">Blue</option>

<option value="green">Green</option>

<option value="black">Black</option>

<option value="yellow">Yellow</option>

<option value="purple">Purple</option>

<option value="other">Other (add comments)</option>

</select>

</td><td>$65.00</td><td>$65.00</td>

</tr>

. . .
```

This will add the color select list to the Sash Belt item.

2   **Save the file and refresh the browser.**

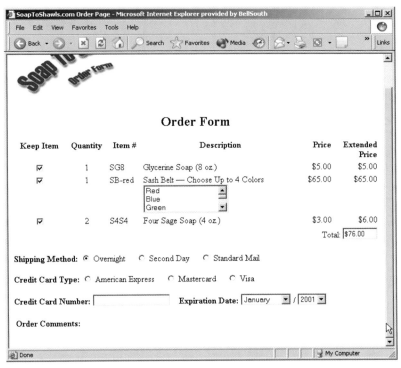

FIGURE 6.29

Notice the select list. You created a select box, but by giving it a size attribute — even if you set the size to 1 — you tell the browser to render it as a list (with a scroll bar, if necessary), as shown here.

3   **Scroll through the values in the list and choose a few of them.**

You may need to hold down the CTRL or Shift key as you click to select multiple items. Notice the multiple values for colors.

4   **Close the file in your text editor and browser.**

LESSON 7 Text Areas

Now that you have explored text inputs, you can work with a second type of text box: the ***text area*** ("textarea"), which is a multiline text box. A text area is an excellent choice when you want to provide an area for free-form comments from users.

A text area allows users much more latitude in what they input. Instead of being limited to writing in a single one-line window, users can see all (or most) of what they type, depending on the size that the Web page author sets for the text area. The `<textarea>` tag includes attributes that indicate how many columns and rows it should take up on the page, but this doesn't limit the number of characters it can hold.

For example, you can add a `<textarea>` tag to your sample form, as follows:

```
<form action="myFormAction.asp">
    What is your choice?
    <br />
    <textarea cols="60" rows="5">
    The initial text for a textarea goes into the textarea element.
    </textarea>
    <br />
   <input type="submit" />
</form>
```

The following results are displayed in the Web browser.

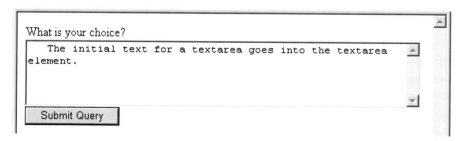

FIGURE 6.30

Not only did you retain the initial text, you retained the spaces at the beginning of the text as well. Spaces and line feeds are preserved with this input option.

One issue with using text areas is that you cannot easily limit the number of characters that a user inputs. If the application executed by the form action has a size limitation, the data must be checked against that limit before being used. When too much data (a very large file) is passed to a Web server, the server may crash. You should discuss this issue with the system administrator for your Web server and plan accordingly. He may tell you there is a size limit on the data that can be safely sent to your server.

Add a Text Area

1   **In your text editor and browser, open textarea.htm from your WIP_06 folder.**

2   **Insert the following code:**

```
. . .
<table><tr><td valign="top"><b>Order Comments:   </b></td><td>
<textarea name="comments" rows="5" cols="40">
     Enter any comments here.
</textarea>
</td></tr></table>
. . .
```

This will add a text area for order comments, including some text to explain how to use the text area.

3   **Save the file in your text editor and refresh the browser.**

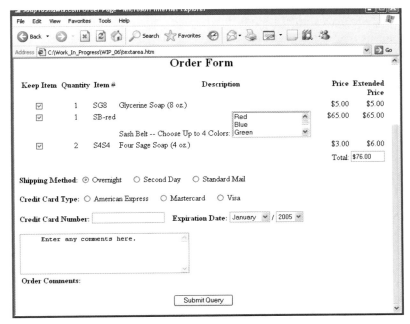

FIGURE 6.31

Notice the text area and its initial text.

4   **Close the file in your text editor and browser.**

To Extend Your Knowledge . . .

ASP

Active Server Pages (ASP or ASP.net) is another scripting language that programmers use to create Web pages. Similar to ColdFusion MX, ASP is a server-side language that integrates with XHTML code and affects a Web page in one way or another — such as sending data to a server for processing. Newer versions of ASP are branded as ASP.net. ASP is based on the Visual Basic programming language and is a bit more difficult to learn than ColdFusion, which mimics the tag structure of XHTML. Both languages were designed for the same purpose — to create Web pages/sites.

LESSON 8   Hidden Elements

We already discussed most of the visible elements on the page; but what if you want to include information on the form that the user doesn't need to see? It's not that the user shouldn't know this information — it's just that the information may not be relevant at that moment, and displaying it would only confuse the user and clutter the page. For example, you might want to:

- Include a session number that identifies this particular user, which you need on the script that processes the form.

- Include information about which pages this user already visited.

- Include information on which page the user visited immediately before coming to the form.

- Provide additional information about a product that would be required for packaging.

None of this information should be shown to the user, but it must be submitted with the rest of the information on the form. In these situations, you should use *hidden fields*. A hidden field ("hidden") is a type of input that doesn't actually appear on the page but is submitted to the server with the form. For example:

```
<input type="hidden" name="myFieldName" value="myFieldValue" />
```

Hidden input fields allow you to include hidden data in a form for submission.

Add a Hidden Field

1 In your text editor and browser, open hidden.htm from your WIP_06 folder.

2 Insert the following code:

```
. . .
<h2 align="center">Order Form</h2>
<form action="order.htm">
<input type="hidden" name="order_id" value="1234" />
<table width="100%" border="0">
. . .
```

This will add the order number to a hidden field on the page.

3 Save the file in the text editor and refresh your browser.

There should be no change in how the page appears in the browser.

4 Submit the page.

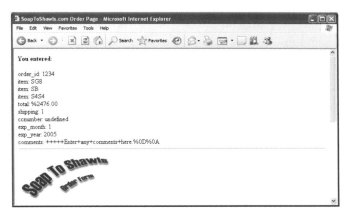

FIGURE 6.32

Notice that the hidden field was also submitted.

5 Close the file in your text editor and browser.

To Extend Your Knowledge . . .

HIDDEN FIELDS

Not only is the so-called hidden field submitted with the page, but it is also in plain view in the URL. As with passwords, hidden fields are a convenience, but they are not substitutes for security.

One of the most common security errors made on the Web today is leaving sensitive or important information in hidden fields. Information in hidden fields is visible to anyone who chooses "View Source" on the page. It would be a simple matter for an experienced programmer to change hidden information. In the case of an e-commerce site, he could lower the price on an item he wants to purchase.

LESSON 9   Buttons

Now that the rest of your sample page is in place, you can focus on submit buttons. You had a brief introduction to the submit button when you created password fields. Now let's take a closer look.

Submit buttons allow the user to click a button to submit a form. Order forms often include a pair of submit buttons — click one button to submit the order, click the other button to cancel it. If you include two buttons on the page, however, how will your users distinguish one from the other if they both are labeled "Submit Query"? (And what do queries have to do with orders anyway?)

Fortunately, you can set the value on a submit button, just as you can with reset and other buttons. You can also name buttons. Naming buttons causes the name value to be passed to the server, where the program can decide what action to take based on which button was clicked.

If you were to name the submit button in your sample form, as follows,

```
<input type="submit" name="submitButton" value="Submit Form" />
```

the name and value would be added to the URL and submitted to the server.

FIGURE 6.33

As you see, the submit button changed from the default text "Submit Query" to the text that is specified in the **value=""** attribute.

Reset Buttons

Reset buttons ("reset") are similar to submit buttons, but they have a completely different purpose. Rather than submitting the form, a reset button returns the form to its original state. Notice that we didn't say a reset button clears the form — it doesn't, unless the form was empty originally. Instead, a reset button restores the initial values that you set in the form.

A reset button looks very similar to a submit button, and the two are coded in a similar fashion. For example:

```
<input type="reset" value="Undo Changes To Form" />
```

displays as follows.

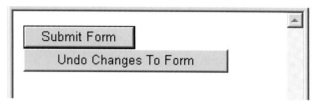

FIGURE 6.34

Add Form Buttons

1   In your text editor and browser, open buttons.htm from your WIP_06 folder.

2   Insert the following code:

```
. . .
<center>
<input type="submit" name="submitorder" value="Submit Order" />
</center>
. . .
```

This code will name the existing submit button and change the default text that displays on the button.

3   Add a reset button next to the submit button.

```
. . .
<center>
<input type="submit" name="submitorder" value="Submit Order" />
<input type="reset" name="cancelorder" value="Cancel Order" />
</center>
. . .
```

This provides the user with the option of clearing the form.

4   Save the changes in the text file and refresh the document in the browser.

5   Scroll to the bottom of the page.

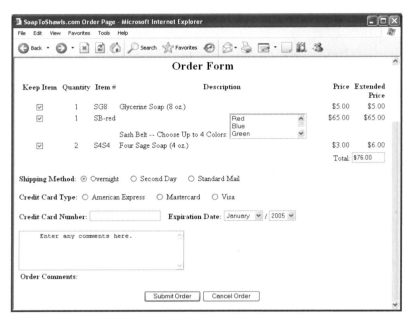

FIGURE 6.35

The buttons display next to each other at the bottom of the Web page.

6   Clear the form, and then enter random information into the fields.

7   **Submit the form by clicking the Submit Order button.**

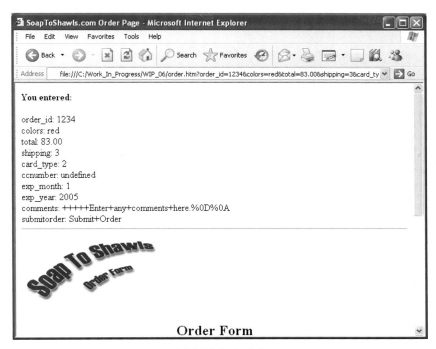

FIGURE 6.36

All the values display on the next page, even the hidden values. This form is processed with a client-side script written in JavaScript; to achieve the same results on an Internet published Web site, you must use a special server-side script or program, such as ASP or ColdFusion.

8   **Save your changes.**

9   **Close the file in your browser and text editor.**

CAREERS IN DESIGN

CERTIFICATION

The nature of your project determines whether you should consider any sort of Web certification. If you are simply dabbling in Web design or using it for personal use, then certification is probably not important to you — although learning the principles could prove useful later.

A variety of popular certifications is available to you. The CIW (Certified Internet Webmaster) certification series offers different types of Web development certification. You can choose one or several paths of study to obtain certification. Some of the certifications offered include CIW Associate, CIW Security Analyst, Master CIW Designer, and Master CIW Enterprise Developer. To learn more about the CIW series, log on to www.ciwcertified.com.

SUMMARY

In Chapter 6, you learned that forms allow you to collect information from your viewers. You can create simple forms that collect a few lines of text data, or you can create elaborate forms that gather a wide variety of data — as well as provide users with selection options.

As you worked with forms, you discovered that many attributes are provided for the form itself and the elements it contains. These attributes allow developers to control the kind of form data they collect, including text fields, password fields, selection fields, and text areas. You also learned that "hidden" data is not always well hidden, especially from an experienced hacker who knows where to look.

Although basic XHTML forms are very useful, forms that include advanced scripts to collect and manipulate data are much more powerful. A number of technologies are available to perform these advanced actions, including the new XForms standard, CGI scripts, and ASP scripts.

KEY TERMS

Check box	Mutually exclusive	Server-side language
Client-side language	Name-value pair	Submit button
Form	Online form	Text area
Form action	Password input	Text input
Form data	Radio button	URL parameters
Hidden field	Radio group	XForms
Input field	Reset button	Zero-based
JavaScript	Select box	

CHECKING CONCEPTS AND TERMS

MULTIPLE CHOICE

Circle the letter that matches the correct answer for each of the following questions.

1. Which tag creates a form?
   a. <form>
   b. <input>
   c. <newform>
   d. <submitform>
   e. None of the above

2. Why is it important to name your form and form fields?
   a. To identify the field when you are looking at the source code
   b. Naming the fields identifies the input.
   c. You can transfer the value of a field through a URL.
   d. Both b and c

3. Why would you limit the number of characters allowed in a text field?
   a. To save space on the page
   b. Because the information is being placed in a database
   c. You can enter as many characters as you want.
   d. None of the above

4. Using password fields automatically secures the data.
   a. True
   b. False

5. Radio buttons are used for _____.
   a. single-option choices
   b. multiple choices
   c. collecting text
   d. All of the above

6. Radio groups allow the user to _____.
   a. make only one choice at any given time
   b. make as many choices as he wants
   c. choose nothing from the list of options
   d. None of the above

7. Check boxes allow the user to _____.
   a. make multiple choices at a given time
   b. make only one choice at a give time
   c. choose nothing from the list of options
   d. All of the above

8. Selection fields are excellent when you need to choose from a long list of options.
   a. True
   b. False

9. Hidden fields allow you to transfer values without the user's knowledge.
   a. True
   b. False

10. What form button should always be available to the user?
    a. Submit button
    b. Go button
    c. Reset button
    d. Radio button

DISCUSSION QUESTIONS

1. What are some of the benefits of using forms?

2. Why would you want to collect form data in a database?

3. When would you want to require a user to input data?

4. Discuss how tables might be useful when creating forms.

SKILL DRILL

Skill Drills reinforce chapter skills. Each skill reinforced is the same as, or nearly the same as, a skill presented in the lessons. We provide detailed instructions in a step-by-step format. You should complete these exercises in the order provided.

1. Create a Basic Form

1. Open the file named teaform.htm from your WIP_06 folder.

2. Add the basic form tags to the file, after the image tags.

3. Name the form "teaorder".

4. In the form, include descriptive text in a paragraph, as follows: "We will process your order in 48 hours or less."

5. Save the changes to the file. Load the Web page in a browser.

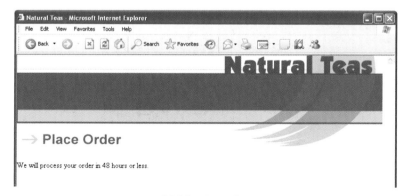

FIGURE 6.37

6. Keep the file open for the next exercise.

2. Add Text Inputs

1. In the open file, beneath "We will process your order in 48 hours or less," type "Account Information". Insert two line breaks after the text.

2. On the next line after the two line breaks, type "Full Name:".

3. Next to "Full Name:" create a text box that is 30 characters in length. Name the text box "full_name".

4. Add the value "Enter full name here" to the full_name field. Include a line break after the input.

5. After the line break, type "Email".

6. Add another text box that is 30 characters in length. Name the new field "email". Include a line break after the input.

7. Add the descriptive text "Password" after the line break.

8. Add a password input field that is 30 characters in length. Name the field "password". Include two line breaks after the input.

9. Save the changes and load the Web page in a browser.

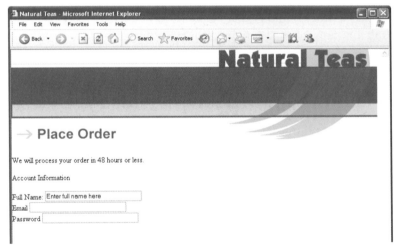

FIGURE 6.38

10. Keep the file open in your browser and text editor for use in the next exercise.

3. Create Select Options

1. In the open file, beneath the code for the password field, type "Select Tea(s)". Insert two line breaks after this text.

2. After the line breaks, create a check box named "raspberry". Press the spacebar. Next to the check box, type the text "Raspberry Tea – 6.00". Include a line break after the text.

3. After the line break, create a check box named "lemonbalm". Press the spacebar. Next to the check box, type the text "Lemon Balm – 6.00". Include a line break after the text.

4. Repeat Steps 2 and 3 for the following flavors, naming each input accordingly: Anise, Peppermint, and Green Tea. After the last line of text, include two line breaks.

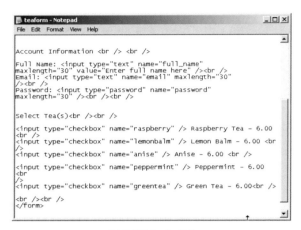

FIGURE 6.39

5. After the line breaks, type "Payment", and then include two line breaks.

6. After the line breaks, create a radio group. Name it "pay". Include three payment options: COD, Credit Card, and Check Card. Label each option accordingly. Include two line breaks.

7. After the line breaks, type "Shipping". Include two line breaks.

8. After the line breaks, create a pull-down menu named "ship" with the following options: Standard, 2nd Day, and Overnight. Include two line breaks.

9. Save the changes and refresh the document in the browser.

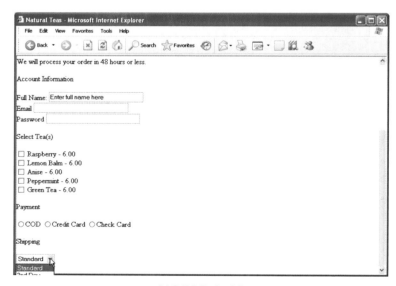

FIGURE 6.40

10. Keep the file open for the next exercise.

4. Provide a Comment Section and Create Form Buttons

1. After the last entry in the open file, type "Comments and Suggestions". Include two line breaks.

2. Create a text area that is 10 columns in length and includes 20 rows.

3. Include the initial text, "Please provide any comments, suggestions, or instructions for your order."

4. After the text area, include two line breaks.

5. Include a submit button with the value "Send Order".

6. Next to the submit button, create a reset button with the value "Clear Form".

7. Save the changes in the file and refresh the document in your browser.

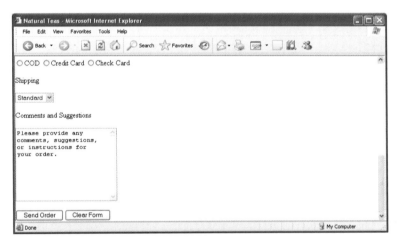

FIGURE 6.41

8. Close the file in both applications.

CHALLENGE

Challenge exercises expand on, or are somewhat related to, skills presented in the lessons. Each exercise provides a brief introduction, followed by numbered-step instructions that are not as detailed as those in the Skill Drill exercises. You should complete the exercises in the order provided.

1. Create a Form Action

In the Skill Drills, you created a simple order form for Natural Teas. In this exercise, you include form information, such as where to submit the form when the user clicks the submit button.

1. Open teaform.htm from your WIP_06 folder.

2. In another text editor window, open login.htm.

3. Copy the script code (the **`<script>`** tags and content) from login.htm and paste it beneath the **`<body>`** tag in teaform.htm.

4. Close login.htm.

5. In the **`<form>`** tag in teaform.htm, add an action to submit the form to teaform.htm (**`action="teaform.htm"`**).

6. Save the changes to the file and refresh the document in the browser.

7. If you want, fill in the fields and submit the form.

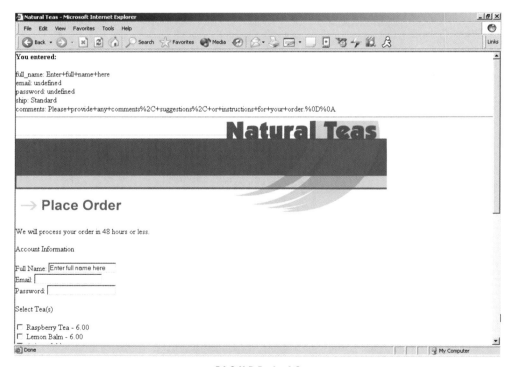

FIGURE 6.42

8. Reload (do not click the Back button) teaform.htm in the browser.

9. Leave the file open for the next exercise.

2. Put the Form into a Table

1. In the open file, beneath Account Information, create a table that is 300 pixels wide, with two columns, three rows, and no borders.

2. Cut and paste "Full Name" and place it in the first cell on the top row.

3. Cut and paste the text input "fullname" into the second cell on the top row.

4. Repeat Steps 2 and 3 for the "Email" text input and the "Password" input.

5. Bold the descriptive text for the text inputs and the password inputs.

6. Save the changes in the file and refresh the document in the browser.

7. Leave the file open for the next exercise.

3. Format the Form Content

1. In the open file, bold the tea flavor options next to the check boxes.

2. Bold the payment options next to the radio buttons.

3. Bold the sentence "We will process your order in 48 hours or less."

4. In the section headings (e.g., Payment), increase the font size, change the font color, and bold the text.

5. Format the document however you prefer. Place elements into tables, change colors, and change font attributes.

6. Save the changes to the file and refresh the document in the browser.

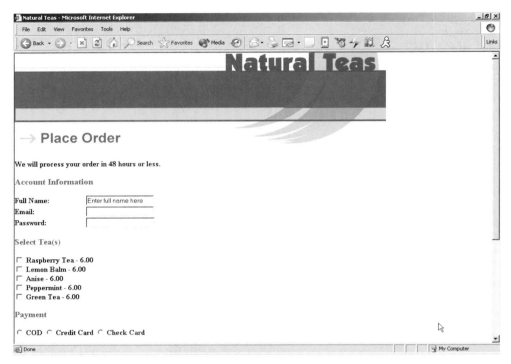

FIGURE 6.43

7. Leave the file open for the next exercise.

4. Reset the Document and Print

1. In the open file, click the reset button on the form.

2. In the Full Name field, type your full name.

3. Complete the rest of the form as if you were placing an order.

4. Choose Print>Print Preview to preview the document.

5.   If you have access to a printer, print the document.

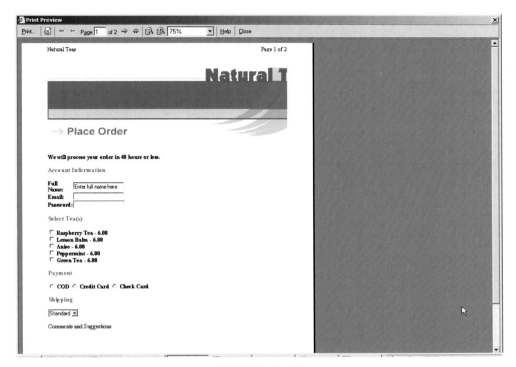

FIGURE 6.44

6.   Close the file in both applications.

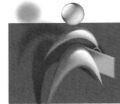

PORTFOLIO BUILDER

Create a Survey Form

The owners of a local ice cream store, JiJi's Ice Cream, want to collect information from their customers. They decided to publish an online survey so they can save on printing costs. As an incentive, they will give a free ice cream sundae to any customer who submits an online survey. JiJi's hired you to create the online form and set it up so the information is sent to their e-mail address. To complete this exercise, you should do the following:

- Think about what type of important information could be collected from ice cream store customers. Obvious information would be name and contact information. Other information would be favorite ice cream flavors, favorite frozen yogurt flavors, how often they buy ice cream, and what other types of frozen treats they enjoy. It would be helpful to know if they purchase ice cream from other locations, as well as what kind of ice cream they have at home.

- Create a storyboard for your Web page. The heading for the page should be "JiJi's Ice Cream Give-Away".

- Knowing what type of information you need to collect, consider the type of form elements you should use to accomplish your task. Make notes on these elements next to the sections in the storyboard.

- Create the form using a variety of form elements. If necessary, use a table for alignment. Consider other formatting methods and what graphical elements you can use to enhance the form. Research other methods of submitting this form, such as CGI scripts.

CHAPTER **7**

Working with Frames

OBJECTIVES

In this chapter, you learn how to:

- Create a frameset page

- Include nested frames

- Work with individual frames

- Control content location and borders

- Create targets

- Work with parent frames

- Provide an alternative page for browsers that do not support frames

Why Would I Do This?

Frame documents can be very useful. They allow different HTML pages to be displayed in a single browser window. Consider a car dealership that sells new and used vehicles from manufacturers such as Hummer, BMW, or Porsche. Many buyers go to well-known car-selling sites on the Internet and search through hundreds of vehicles to find their ideal automobile. Other buyers may go directly to the dealership's primary Web site and search for vehicles.

In this scenario, the dealership needs to display the automobiles on many different Web sites. Since the inventory is large and changes often, it is impractical to enter the information more than once. The simplest solution is to have Web pages that show just the inventory of the dealership and to allow each site to separately display the site name, branding, navigation, and other information needed for that site.

Frames allow us to solve this type of problem by enabling designers to create separate pages that can be displayed together in the same window. The idea behind frames was to subdivide a Web page into logical sections. Certain sections of a page, such as the navigational elements and menus, would be fixed; every page on a site would display those elements in exactly the same place. The user would know where to find those elements, regardless of what page she was on. Other sections of the window would be scrollable and would contain content that changed dynamically (based upon user choices) or was updated on a regular basis.

This structure served more than one purpose. First, the user could view a long page and always keep sight of the navigational elements. Second, only the parts of the page that change need to be loaded by the browser; this, of course, allows the page to load faster than if every element on the page were unique. At the height of their popularity, frames were most commonly used to add a logo and navigational elements to the top of the page and a menu along the left side.

Frames are slowly disappearing from Web pages due to the inherent disadvantages of using them and may eventually be replaced with newer technologies. However, they are useful in many situations, and most Web designers are likely to encounter a site design that requires their use. In this chapter, you learn all about the benefits, as well as the drawbacks, of using frames when designing a Web page.

VISUAL SUMMARY

Frames allow you to divide the browser window into parts (sections), with each part displaying a different document. Dividing a browser window into sections allows designers to create navigational systems quickly and easily. It also provides more control over the organization and display of the content, much the same as tables.

The following illustration shows a Web site's navigational system that was set up using frames.

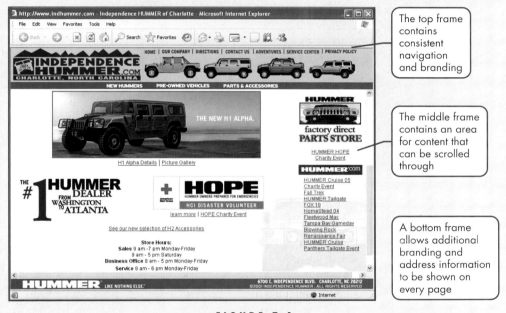

The top frame contains consistent navigation and branding

The middle frame contains an area for content that can be scrolled through

A bottom frame allows additional branding and address information to be shown on every page

FIGURE 7.1

This interface is used for the Independence Hummer Web site to allow easy inclusion of pages from external Web sites. For example, when a user chooses an inventory button, a page is loaded into the content frame from another Web site.

FIGURE 7.2

Tables also allow us to separate the elements of the page into areas such as navigation and content. The following illustration shows a similar design using tables.

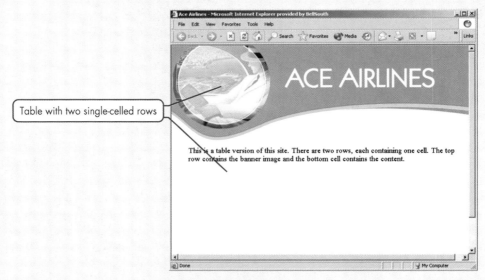

FIGURE 7.3

If we use tables to logically organize the areas of the page, we need to make sure the tables are configured in an identical fashion on every page. It is often difficult to be consistent on sites that contain many pages. In addition, tables do not give us an easily incorporated mechanism for pulling content from external sources such as other Web sites.

Frames sound like a great idea but come with their own disadvantages. For example, if the user prints the page, the browser could print a single frame (such as the navigation frame) and not print the content area. This can be very frustrating for users who may not realize they should click within a specific area before choosing to print the document.

Search engines also create problems for framed Web sites. Search engines index pages based on the importance of the content. If we have a frame design, it is likely we have a content frame with the primary content. The search engine will be most interested in the page that contains this content, since it contains the keywords the user is most likely attempting to locate.

When the user goes to the page from a search engine listing, the content page appears, but not within the *frameset*. This means the user could see the page without any navigation or branding information. The user can literally get stuck on a single page of a Web site. Advanced techniques (beyond the scope of this book) can be used to partially get around these problems.

LESSON 1   The Frameset

When building a frame-based site, you work with two kinds of pages: the frameset and the frames. A frameset is very similar to the layout of a printed document; it tells the browser how to lay out the page and what frames to include in each section. A frameset is never seen by the end user; it is simply an HTML file that displays other HTML files (the frames).

The frameset tells the browser what content to put into its particular area on the page. The frameset must be the first file loaded into the browser. The code in the frameset file tells the browser which files to display, where on the page to display the files, and how much space on the page to allocate to each file.

Consider the following framed site. Look closely at its structure.

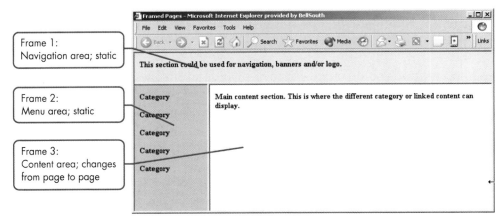

FIGURE 7.4

To build this page, you would create a frameset that divides the window into three sections: the navigation at the top, the featured categories on the left side (the menu), and the content on the right side. There are several ways to achieve this result, all of which involve dividing the page into rows and columns. Some sites take this concept a step further and subdivide the rows and columns into smaller units.

The following example is a simple page with two columns, each of which displays a different page.

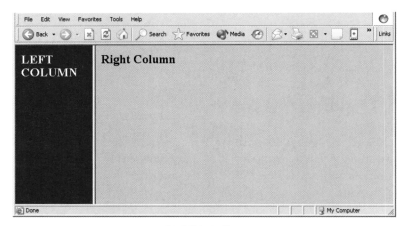

FIGURE 7.5

This page was created by building a frameset using the **<frameset>** tag, which split the page into two columns. Then, a frame with content (a page) was assigned to each of those columns. In the following code, notice the column attribute, **cols=""**. In this case, it divides the page into two sections — one 20% of the page and the other 80% of the page. The frameset page is used strictly for dividing the screen, so multiple Web pages can display at the same time.

```
<html>
<head>
<title>Frames</title>
</head>
<frameset cols="20%, 80%">
     <frame src="left.htm" />
     <frame src="right.htm" />
</frameset>
</html>
```

The files "left.htm" and "right.htm" are regular XHTML files — there is nothing special about them. The content assigned to a row or column can be the XHTML file of your choice.

As you learned earlier, you can divide framesets into columns or rows, each of which can be further subdivided into columns or rows. You can specify the width of columns and the height of rows in percentages or pixels. You can also use the asterisk (*) character to indicate that you want a particular row or column to take up the balance of the page.

For instance, to create a page with two rows, the first of which is 100 pixels high and the second of which occupies the rest of the page, you would write the following code:

```
<html>
<head>
<title>The Winter and the Summer</title>
</head>
<frameset rows="100, *">
     <frame src="winter.htm" />
     <frame src="summer.htm" />
```

```
</frameset>
</html>
```

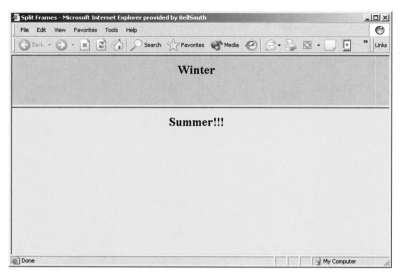

FIGURE 7.6

Measurements in percentages are relative sizes — they represent a percentage of the page or of the frame in which the column or row resides. Measurements in pixels are fixed sizes. If you want a frame to be a specific size to match the height or width of an image, you should use pixels as the units of measurement for the rows or columns. The result of the type of measurement applied is most apparent when you resize a window. A frame size specified as a percentage (***relative size***) adjusts to match the new window size, whereas a frame size specified as pixels (***fixed size***) remains the same size.

Create the Frameset

1   **Copy the contents of your Chapter_07 folder to the Work_In_Progress>WIP_07 folder.**

? If you have problems

This chapter uses some nonstandard XHTML Transitional attributes associated with frames. To achieve the desired effect without using CSS, the pages you create in this chapter will not produce a valid XHTML Strict document. We note which attributes have been deprecated.

2   **In your text editor, open frameset.htm from your WIP_07 folder.**

This document acts as a canvas upon which you build framed pages. You divide the page into sections, and within those sections, indicate what content to display.

3   **Insert the following code:**

```
<html>
<head>
<title>Frameset Page</title>
</head>
<frameset rows="25%,75%">
</frameset>
<body>
</body>
</html>
```

This creates the shell of the frameset (the empty frameset) by making two rows and allotting a portion of the window to each (25% to one and 75% to the other).

Later, you can subdivide the second row into two columns.

4   **Add frames of content, menu.htm and listing.htm, as follows:**

```
<html>
<head>
<title>Frameset Page</title>
</head>
<frameset rows="25%,75%">
    <frame src="menu.htm" />
    <frame src="listing.htm" />
</frameset>
<body>
</body>
</html>
```

This content page displays in the sections you allotted on your frameset page. In standard HTML, the end **</frame>** tag is not required; to be a valid XHTML element, however, you must close the **<frame>** tag.

5   Save the page.

6   Open frameset.htm in your browser.

FIGURE 7.7

You created two rows and assigned a relative size to each. In fact, the size of the screen (not the frames you added) determined the actual size of the rows.

7   Resize the window and watch the row sizes change.

This is acceptable in some situations, but not here. The top frame needs to remain the same size as the menu elements, which means a fixed size should be applied to the top row.

8   Change the height of the top row to 125 pixels, and set the second row to take up the balance of the space, as follows:

```html
<html>
<head>
<title>Frameset Page</title>
</head>
<frameset rows="125, *">
    <frame src="menu.htm" />
    <frame src="listing.htm" />
</frameset>
```

```
<body>
</body>
</html>
```

9 Save the file, and refresh the browser.

FIGURE 7.8

Some browsers have difficulty refreshing frames. If you don't see a difference in your browser, you may need to open a new browser window and reopen the page. In the refreshed/new browser window, notice that the top frame matches the size of the menu, even when you resize the window.

Later in the chapter, you remove the borders of the frames to create a seamless design. Setting the height any higher than 125 pixels would create too much white space on the page.

10 Close the file in your browser and text editor.

To Extend Your Knowledge . . .

FRAME CONTENT

Some Web-based content systems use frames to incorporate content from various Web sites into a single interface. For instance, many eLearning software systems, such as the Docent Learning Management System, present Web-based courses in the bottom frame while displaying a standard logo and navigation in the top frame. This allows developers to concentrate on building content, while the software uses a frame design to automatically control the navigation.

LESSON 2 Nested Framesets

When creating a frameset, you must choose between rows and columns; both cannot reside in the same frameset. You can, however, replace a row with a frameset that defines columns (or vice versa). Adding one frameset to another is called "nesting the framesets." Any number of framesets can be nested within another.

You can use two methods to add a **_nested frameset_**: you can add it directly or through a separate framed document that contains a frameset. The direct method adds a second frameset within the code where one frame would normally be placed, as follows:

```
<html>
<head>
<title>The Winter and the Summer</title>
</head>
<frameset cols="50%, 50%">
          <frame src="winter.htm" />
          <frameset rows="25%, *">
               <frame src="summer.htm" />
               <frame src="spring.htm" />
          </frameset>
</frameset>
</html>
```

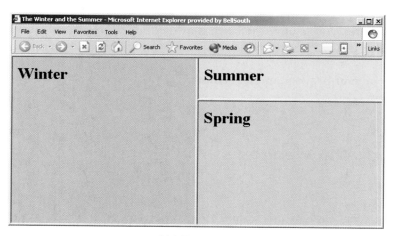

FIGURE 7.9

As an alternative, you can retain your original frameset but make the content of one of its frames another frameset. For instance, the original frameset is

```
<html>
<head>
<title>The Winter and the Summer</title>
</head>
<frameset cols="50%, 50%">
          <frame src="winter.htm" />
          <frame src="warm.htm" />
</frameset>
</html>
```

where the content of warm.htm is

```
<html>
<head>
<title>The Warm Months of the Year</title>
</head>
<frameset rows="50%, 50%">
          <frame src="summer.htm" />
          <frame src="spring.htm" />
</frameset>
</html>
```

This code creates the same result as the previous example.

Create a Frameset Using Columns

1   In your text editor, open subframe.htm from your WIP_07 folder.

2   Create a frameset in subframe.htm. This time, instead of specifying rows, specify columns, as follows:

```
<html>
<head>
<title>Subframe Page</title>
</head>
  <frameset cols="25%, 75%">
        <frame src="featurecat.htm" />
        <frame src="listing.htm" />
```

```
        </frameset>
<body>
</body>
</html>
```

3   **Save subframe.htm and open the file in your browser.**

FIGURE 7.10

4   **Close the file in your text editor and browser.**

You will nest this file into another frameset in the following exercise.

Nest a Frameset within a Frameset

1   **In your text editor, open frameset2.htm and make the following change:**

```
. . .
<title>Frameset Page</title>
</head>
<frameset rows="125, *">
    <frame src="menu.htm" />
    <frame src="subframe.htm" />
</frameset>
</html>
```

This will allow a second frameset (subframe.htm) to open in the second row of the first frameset.

2   Save the file.

3   Open frameset2.htm in the browser.

FIGURE 7.11

The bottom frame was replaced with a document that defined its own frameset.

4   Leave the windows open for the next exercise.

Nest the Framesets

1   In the open frameset2.htm file in the text editor, replace the second frame with the same frameset that is in subframe.htm.

```
<html>
<head>
<title>Frameset Page</title>
</head>
<frameset rows="125, *">
    <frame src="menu.htm" />
        <frameset cols="25%, 75%">
        <frame src="featurecat.htm" />
        <frame src="listing.htm" />
    </frameset>
```

```
</frameset>
<body>
</body>
</html>
```

2 Save the file in your text editor.

3 Refresh the browser.

FIGURE 7.12

You shouldn't see any change. The page now uses the second frameset tag to create the nested frameset instead of using the code in a separate document.

4 Close the file in your browser and text editor.

To Extend Your Knowledge . . .

CSS VS FRAMES

Even though tables and frames can be used for horizontal and vertical content display, there are many unresolved issues regarding frames (which you discover at the end of this chapter).

CSS offers powerful positioning features that allow finer control over page layout than tables or frames. With the promise of XHTML 2.0 on the horizon, it's important that you begin to consider using CSS.

LESSON 3   Controlling Individual Frames

The frameset is only half the story. You also need to work with individual frames. You can control the appearance of frames, such as their size and scrolling, with the addition of attributes.

Attributes don't affect the content of a frame; they only affect the presentation of a frame. For instance, you can control the size of a frame (with the height and width attributes), whether the user can change the size (using the *noresize attribute*), and whether a scroll bar is available (using the *scrolling attribute*). To create a fixed-size frame that cannot be resized by the user and has a scroll bar, you would write the following tag:

```
<frame src="mypage.htm" height="200" scrolling="yes"
noresize="noresize" />
```

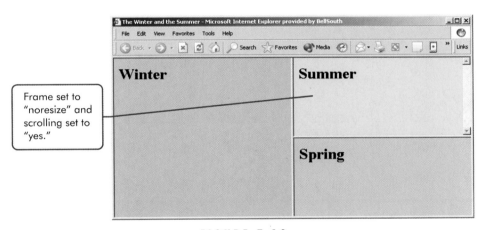

FIGURE 7.13

The `scrolling=""` attribute has three permissible values: yes, no, and auto (auto adds a scroll bar only if it's needed). These values apply to both vertical and horizontal scroll bars.

The `noresize=""` attribute, similar to the `checked=""` attribute you learned about in Chapter 6, is normally written without a value. To create a well-formed XHTML page, however, you must assign a value to the `noresize=""` attribute. This accounts for the seemingly redundant appearance of `noresize="noresize"`.

Control the Size of a Frame

1   **In your text editor and browser, open frameset3.htm from your WIP_07 folder.**

2   **In the browser, position the cursor over the horizontal line separating the top frame from the rest of the page.**

FIGURE 7.14

The cursor changes to a two-sided vertical arrow.

❓ If you have problems

It's important to remember that your users will use monitors of various sizes, many of which could be quite different from yours. If you were to create a frame using a percentage, and your users turned off scrolling and prohibited resizing, you could inadvertently create a frame that did not display all of its content.

---

3   **Hold down the mouse button and drag the frame border to resize the frame.**

If a user resized a page this way, it would ruin your layout. Let's add the **`noresize=""`** attribute to prevent the user from being able to do so.

4   **In the text editor, add the `noresize=""` attribute to the first frame.**

```
...
<title>Frameset Page</title>
</head>
<frameset rows="125, *">
    <frame src="menu.htm" noresize="noresize" />
```

```
<frameset cols="25%, 75%">
    <frame src="featurecat.htm" />
    <frame src="listing.htm" />
```

...

5 **Save the file and refresh the browser.**

6 **Try to resize the frame.**

The two-sided arrow doesn't appear. This solves one problem but creates another. At this size, you see a scroll bar on the window, even though it's not necessary.

7 **Eliminate the scroll bar with the `scrolling=""` attribute.**

```
<html>
<head><title>Frameset Page</title></head>
<frameset rows="125, *">
    <frame src="menu.htm" noresize="noresize" scrolling="no" />
    <frameset cols="25%, 75%">
        <frame src="featurecat.htm" />
        <frame src="listing.htm" />
```

...

The noresize and scrolling attributes are optional and are not a part of the XHTML Transitional standard. A document that contains these attributes is not considered a valid XHTML document. You can control these elements using CSS in combination with the XHTML Transitional frameset.

3 **Save the file and refresh the browser.**

FIGURE 7.15

The scroll bar disappears from the top row.

9   **Close the file in your text editor and browser.**

To Extend Your Knowledge . . .

FORMATTING FRAMES

Some of the formatting features used in frames (such as the border attributes) are supported in some browsers, but not all. As an alternative, you should consider other methods of page layout than standard HTML frames. If you choose to use frames, you should comply with the XHTML Transitional standard and use CSS as a presentational tool. Another alternative is to explore using XFrames, which we discuss in greater detail at the end of this chapter.

LESSON 4 Controlling Content Location and Borders

In addition to controlling the size of a frame, you can also control the location of the content within the frame and whether the frame has a border by using the `marginheight=""`, `marginwidth=""`, and `border=""` attributes.

For instance, you could add a 5-pixel margin around the top and bottom of a frame, as well as a 10-pixel margin on the left and right, by writing

```
<frame src="mypage.htm" marginheight="5" marginwidth="10" border="0" />
```

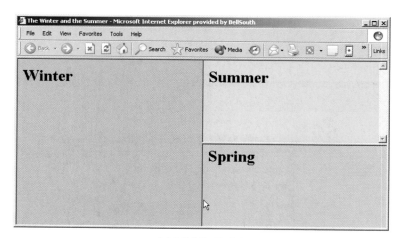

FIGURE 7.16

In Figure 7.16, the border was removed from the particular frame (`border="0"`). All the other frames in the frameset still have borders. Be careful when you use this process, since it can sometimes result in a "half" border if one neighboring frame has a border, but the other doesn't.

Neither the **marginheight=""** nor the **marginwidth=""** attribute is supported in the XHTML Transitional standard. These attributes have been replaced with features from CSS.

Set the Margins and Border

1   In your text editor, open frameset4.htm from your WIP_07 folder.

2   Set the marginheight="" attribute on the top frame.

```
. . .
<title>Frameset Page</title>
</head>
<frameset rows="125, *">
    <frame src="menu.htm" noresize="noresize" scrolling="no"
marginheight="4" />
    <frameset cols="25%, 75%">
        <frame src="featurecat.htm" />
        <frame src="listing.htm" />
. . .
```

3   Save the file and open it in your browser.

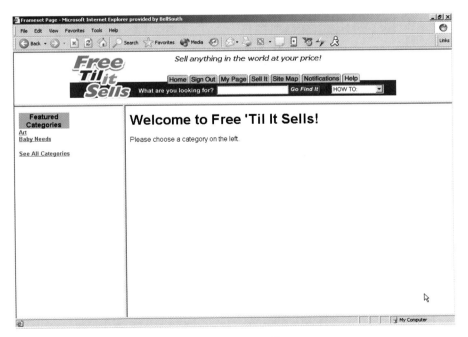

FIGURE 7.17

This adds a 4-pixel separation between the content of the top frame (menu.htm) and the frame border.

4   Next, let's remove the borders from the top and left frames.

```
. . .
<title>Frameset Page</title>
</head>
<frameset rows="125, *" >
    <frame src="menu.htm" noresize="noresize" scrolling="no"
marginheight="4" frameborder="0" />
    <frameset cols="25%, 75%">
        <frame src="featurecat.htm" frameborder="0" />
        <frame src="listing.htm" />
    </frameset>
</frameset>
</html>
```

5   Save the file and refresh the browser.

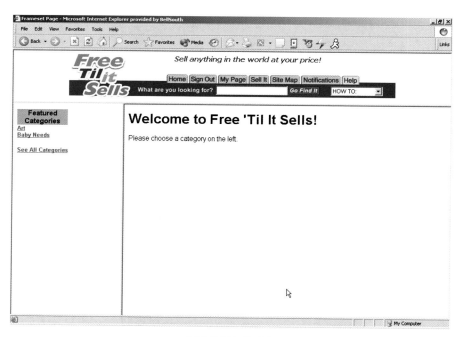

FIGURE 7.18

The frame border is removed from only one frame; the other frame border is still intact. The border attribute isn't actually specified for the frameset element, but browsers currently support it. Remember, this attribute is not included in the XHTML Transitional standard.

6   **Remove the borders completely.**

```
. . .
<title>Frameset Page</title>
</head>
<frameset rows="125, *" border="0">
        <frame  src="menu.htm"  noresize="noresize"  scrolling="no"
marginheight="4" frameborder="0" />
    <frameset cols="25%, 75%">
        <frame src="featurecat.htm" frameborder="0" />
. . .
```

7   **Save the file and refresh the browser.**

FIGURE 7.19

All frames are now border-free. The page display is unified and seamless. The user is unaware that the "page" is actually several pages framed together. This method of framing is used specifically for navigation. The menus at the top and left remain in the same positions as the user navigates through the pages of the site.

8   **Close the file in your browser and text editor.**

LESSON 5   Targets

In the first four lessons in this chapter, you used frames to determine the appearance of a Web page, as well as its layout; but the real power of frames is its ability to let you click a link in one frame, which causes new content to display in another frame, leaving the overall layout intact.

You can create this structure by adding a target to a link. The ***target attribute*** tells the browser where to display the new content. There are several ways to add a target; the most common is to name your frames. Once named, you can target the frames directly. You can name a frame anything you want, but the name can't start with an underscore — that character is used for special purposes, as we discuss later.

Let's see how ***named frames*** work. You can, for instance, structure your familiar seasonal frameset with named frames, as follows:

```
<html>
<head>
<title>The Winter and the Summer</title>
</head>
<frameset cols="50%, 50%">
        <frame src="winter.htm" name="winterframe" />
        <frameset rows="25%, *">
            <frame src="summer.htm" name="summerframe" />
            <frame src="spring.htm" name="springframe" />
        </frameset>
</frameset>
</html>
```

If you then add a target to the link in spring.htm that references the winter frame, such as

```
<a href="spring.htm" target="winterframe">winter</a>!
```

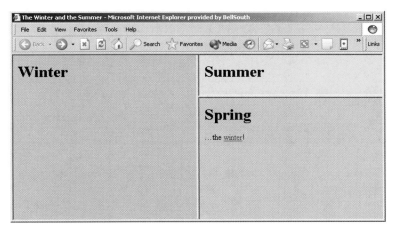

FIGURE 7.20

you can change the content of the winter frame. The **target=" "** attribute tells the browser where to send the content.

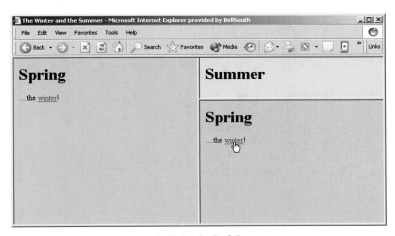

FIGURE 7.21

If you click the new link, the browser displays spring.htm as the content in the frame called winterframe.

Set a Target

| 1 | In your browser and text editor, open **frameset5.htm** from your **WIP_07** folder. |

2   Under Featured Categories, choose the Sports and Recreation link.

FIGURE 7.22

The content displays in the same frame as the link because a target frame was not specified.

3   Close the file in your browser.

4   In frameset5.htm, assign names to all frames.

```
. . .
<title>Frameset Page</title>
</head>
<frameset rows="125, *" border="0">
    <frame src="menu.htm" noresize="noresize" scrolling="no"
marginheight="4" frameborder="0" name="menu" />
    <frameset cols="25%, 75%">
        <frame src="featurecat.htm" frameborder="0"
name="categories" />
        <frame src="listing.htm" name="content" />
    </frameset>
</frameset>
</html>
```

5   Save the file in the text editor.

6   Close the file in your text editor.

7   In your text editor, open featurecat.htm from your WIP_07 folder.

8   Add a target to the Sports and Recreation link, as follows:

. . .

```
    <tr><td class = "basefont"><b><a href = "art.htm">Art
</a></b></td></tr>

    <tr><td class="basefont"><b><a href = "baby.htm">Baby
Needs</a></b></td></tr>

    <tr><td class="basefont"><b><a href = "playground.htm"
target="content">Sports and Recreation</a></b></td></tr>

    <tr><td> </td></tr>

    <tr><td class="basefont"><b><a href="allcat.htm">See All
Categories</a></b></td></tr>

    </tbody>

  </table>
```

. . .

9   Save the file and refresh the browser.

10   **Click the Sports and Recreation link.**

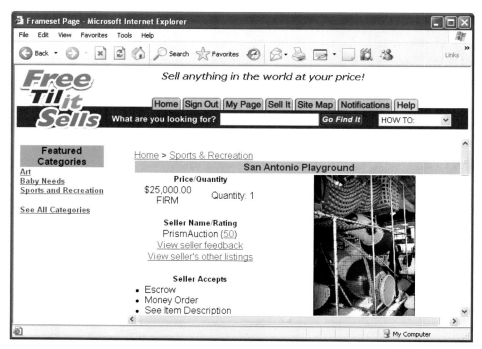

FIGURE 7.23

The new page opens in the frame on the right. The most common method for adding a target is to name the frames and then add the **target=""** attribute that references the named frames.

11   **Close both applications.**

LESSON 6   Using a Base Target

Using named targets enables you to send content to the frame of your choice. If every link on a page had the same target, however, such as a list of links that all send their information to the "content" frame, setting the targets on the links could become quite tedious. The sample page you are using in this chapter has only four links, which is certainly not a burden. Consider, however, a page with hundreds of links, all of which have the same target. Retyping the same target hundreds of times would take up a considerable amount of your valuable development time.

To avoid this problem, you can utilize the **\<base\>** tag that you used in the beginning of this book to specify a base URL; you can use the same **\<base\>** tag to specify a base target. If you want to direct all links without a target to the frame called "main," you can add a **\<base\>** tag, as follows:

```
<base target="main" />
```

Add a Base Target

1	**Open WIP_07>featurecat.htm in the text editor.**

2	**Remove the target from the Sports and Recreation link that you added in Step 8 in the last exercise.**

3	**Add a \<base\> tag to the list of featured categories by inserting the following code.**

```
<html>
<head>
<title>Free 'Til It Sells!</title>
<link href="images/SearchFourm.css" type="text/css"
rel="stylesheet" />
<link href="images/Style1.css" type="text/css" rel="stylesheet" />
    <base target="content" />
</head>
<body>
  <table cellspacing="0" cellpadding="0">
    <tbody>
    <tr>
. . .
```

4	**Save the file.**

5	**Open frameset6.htm in the browser.**

If your browser was already open before Step 3, refresh the left frame so the changes in featurecat.htm take effect. You should see no change.

6	**Click the Sports and Recreation link.**

The new page still takes you to the content frame.

7	**Close the file in your browser and text editor.**

To Extend Your Knowledge . . .

REFRESHING FRAMES

Refreshing the overall page doesn't always refresh individual frames. To refresh an individual frame on the Macintosh, hold down the mouse button in the particular frame, and then choose the Refresh Page (or Refresh Frame) option. On a Windows system, right-click the frame you want to refresh, and then choose the Refresh Frame option from the pop-up menu.

LESSON 7 Using Targets for Special Cases

Using a base target can save you the time and effort of adding a target to each link individually. Doing so can, however, raise a new problem: What do you do when you want one or two links to replace the content in the same frame? Fortunately, there are special targets that you can use for this and other special cases:

- The _self target replaces the content in the same frame.

- The _parent target sends the content to the parent document of the frame. (You'll learn about parents in a moment.)

- The _blank target opens a new window for the content.

- The _top target replaces the main frameset.

Add the _self Target

In our sample Free 'Til It Sells page, if you click the See All Categories link, the linked document moves to the content frame; but that's not what you want to happen. You want the original page that displays the text link, "See All Categories," to stay where it is. You also want the page to remain in place no matter where the original page starts. Let's add a _self target to solve this problem.

1 **Open featurecat.htm in the text editor.**

2   **Add the _self target to the See All Categories link.**

. . .

```
    <tr><td class="basefont"><b><a href="playground.htm">Sports
and Recreation<a></b></td></tr>

    <tr><td> </td></tr>

    <tr><td class="basefont"><b><a href="allcat.htm"
target="_self">

See All Categories</a></b></td></tr>

    </tbody>

  </table>
```

. . .

3   **Save the file.**

4   **Open frameset7.htm in your browser.**

A scroll bar does not separate the left and right panels — which happens when the long list of category links displays — because there is not enough content in these sections to automatically generate a scroll bar.

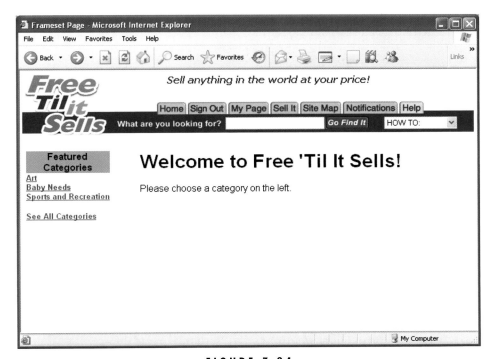

FIGURE 7.24

5   Click the Sports and Recreation link to verify that the new content still goes to the content frame.

6   Click the See All Categories link.

FIGURE 7.25

The list appears in the left frame, even though the base target indicates that it should go to the content frame.

7   Leave your file open in your text editor and browser for use in the next exercise.

Open a New Window

Another option for creating targets is to open an entirely new window. This can be useful if the content to which you're linking is not directly related to what's on the current page, or if you want to display content from another site. When you open a new window, you avoid sending users away from your site. When they finish looking at the other page, your original page remains open and in view.

1   Double-check that featurecat.htm is open in the text editor and that frameset7.htm is open in the browser.

If necessary, click the browser's Back button to return to the Featured Categories page.

2   Change the `<base>` tag to a _blank target.

```
. . .
<base target="_blank" />
</head>
<body>
  <table cellspacing="0" cellpadding="0">
. . .
```

3   Save the file. Refresh the category frame in your browser.

4   Click the Sports and Recreation link to open a new window.

FIGURE 7.26

You might also choose to open a new window if you have an extensive list of items, such as the results of a search. With a new window, the user would not have to continually click the Back button to reload the list page.

5   Close the new Sports and Recreation window.

6   Leave the original browser window and the featurecat.htm (text editor) open.

Link the Logo to the Main Window

Rather than opening a new window, you can replace the current window (as opposed to the current frame) with new content. You can do so by targeting the top window. This is normally done to "break a user out" of frames — that is, take the user from a subdivided page back to a single page with no frames.

1   **Open WIP_07>menu.htm in the text editor, and open frameset7.htm in the browser.**

2   **Target the link on the logo to the _top frame.**

```
. . .
<tbody>
 <tr>
  <td valign="top" width="144" rowspan="4">
    <a href="home.htm" target="_top">
     <img height="112" src="images/FTIS_logo.gif" width="144"
border="0" />
    </a>
  </td>
. . .
```

3   **Save the file. Refresh the _top frame in the browser.**

4   **Click the logo.**

FIGURE 7.27

The page no longer includes any framed sections.

5   Close the file in your text editor and browser.

To Extend Your Knowledge . . .

WEB SITE FLOWCHARTS

As if linking a large Web site isn't cumbersome enough, linking and targeting frames can be a nightmare without proper planning. Before beginning any Web project that consists of three or more pages, you should consider creating a flowchart to help guide you through the process. A **flowchart** is a diagram that shows the navigational flow of a Web site. It identifies the pages that will be linked together and in what manner. It also identifies the external links that will be provided, as well as the areas of the site that will be limited to specific viewers. Consider this flowchart for a small Web site.

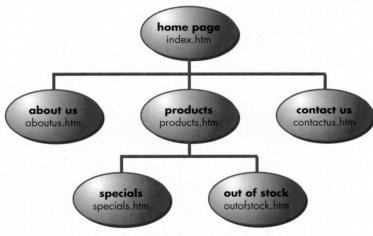

FIGURE 7.28

Flowcharts can be elaborate computer-generated diagrams or simple sketches on paper. To prevent broken links and incorrect targeting, we recommend that you create a flowchart of your Web site before actually creating and linking the site's pages.

LESSON 8 Parents

Another common way to manage content in a frameset is to send content to the ***parent***, which is the actual frameset document. Identifying a frameset as a parent allows you to target that frameset instead of a specific frame. For instance, when you sent the Sports and Recreation page to its own window in the previous exercise, it didn't look very good because the top interface disappeared.

Instead, you could have sent the Sports and Recreation page to the bottom two frames. These two frames are part of a single frameset that can be considered the "parent" of each frame. To replace these bottom frames with linked content (and keep the top frame), you can send the content to the parent of the link page. For instance, let's look at the frameset

```
<html>
<head>
<title>Frameset Page</title>
</head>
<frameset rows="125, *" border="0">
    <frame src="menu.htm" noresize="noresize" scrolling="no"
marginheight="4" frameborder="0" name="menu" />
    <frameset cols="25%, 75%">
        <frame src="featurecat.htm" frameborder="0" name="categories" />
        <frame src="listing.htm" name="content" />
    </frameset>
</frameset>
</html>
```

You are working with a link in featurecat.htm in the categories frame; logically, the "parent" would be the frameset enclosing that frame, represented by **`<frameset cols="25%, 75%">`** in the preceding code.

Check the Parent

1   **Open featurecat.htm in the text editor.**

2   **Set the base target as _parent.**

```
. . .
<link href="images/SearchFourm.css" type="text/css"
rel="stylesheet" />
<link href="images/Style1.css" type="text/css" rel="stylesheet" />
  <base target="_parent" />
```

```
</head>
<body>
. . .
```

3 | Remove the `target="_self"` attribute from the See All Categories link.

```
<tr><td class="basefont"><b><a href="allcat.htm">See All
Categories</a></b></td></tr>
```

4 | Save the file.

5 | Open frameset8.htm in your browser.

6 | Click the See All Categories link.

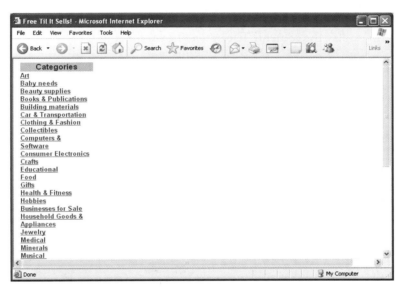

FIGURE 7.29

The entire window was replaced. Think about why this occurred.

7 | Close featurecat.htm in the text editor. Close frameset8.htm in your browser.

LESSON 9 The "Future" of Frames

With all that you now know about frames, you probably think that Web designers must find them indispensable. You may also wonder why you don't see them used more often — even FreeTilItSells.com, the site we used as the example in this chapter, doesn't use frames on the actual site.

Why Frames Have a Bad Reputation

When frames were first used on Web pages, browsers were (fairly) primitive, and Web page authoring tools even more so. There were few WYSIWYG (what you see is what you get) editors, and the features they provided were quite basic. Even Netscape, the innovative company that created frames, didn't support them in the original Netscape Navigator Gold — their own authoring tool.

As a result, authors learned how to work with frames in the same way they learned to do everything else in HTML — they copied existing code. At that time, the accepted method for learning HTML was to examine sites that you liked, study the source code, and then do the best you could to develop code of your own. Without any formal education in HTML coding, and without knowing any better, many Web authors inadvertently developed nonstandard code that caused problems for viewers. (The strict XHTML guidelines were put in place to rectify this problem.)

The majority of the early frame-based sites could only be viewed with the Netscape browsers; all other browsers (and there were quite a few of them) were unable to display frames — or the content they contained. While it makes sense that frames wouldn't appear in the browsers that did not support the frame's technology, why did those browsers also fail to display the content? The answer lies in the source code.

Take a moment to examine the source code of frameset.htm. You can see that there is no actual content in the code, only instructions that a nonframes browser doesn't understand, and therefore, ignores. A nonframes browser would "see" a blank window instead of the planned page, and that is exactly what it would display to the viewer.

Over the past couple of years, this problem has become much less of an issue, as virtually every modern browser supports frames. Now that we're moving toward designing pages for PDAs and cell phones, however, the issue of successfully displaying framed pages is being examined once again.

Additional problems can arise when you index search engines, as well as when external sites link to your pages. Sometimes a search engine indexes one of the pages within a frame but does not index the actual frameset page. When this happens, the page displays outside the frameset and the rest of the pages and their content are not indexed.

Accommodating the Frameless: the <noframes> Tag

Fortunately, you can use the **<noframes>** tag to provide content to browsers that don't recognize frames. For instance, you could add some explanatory text to frameset.htm, as follows:

```
<noframes>

  <body>

     Thank you for visiting our Web site. We are currently working on a
frameless version of this site.
```

```
</body>
</noframes>
```

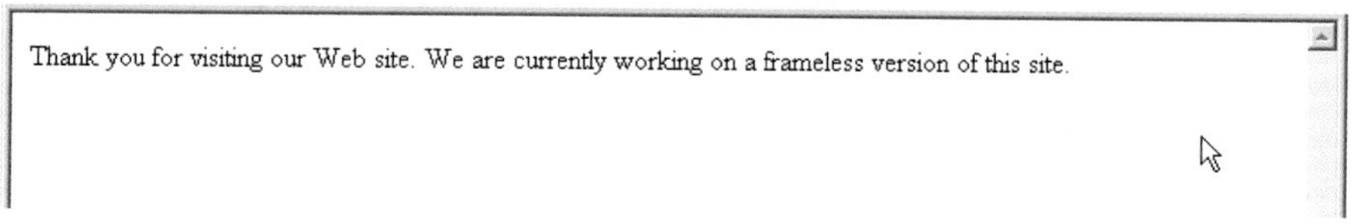

Thank you for visiting our Web site. We are currently working on a frameless version of this site.

FIGURE 7.30

We omitted the **<body>** tag from the sample code used earlier in the chapter, since it would have prevented the frames from working. Now you can restore it.

Any browser that understands frames also understands the **<noframes>** tag and knows to ignore the content within it. Any browser that doesn't understand frames doesn't understand **<noframes>**, either; such a browser ignores the **<frameset>**, **<frame>**, and **<noframes>** tags, displaying only (in this case) the body content.

Add <noframes> Tags

1   **In your text editor, open frameset9.htm from your WIP_07 folder.**

2   **Add the <noframes> tags beneath the frameset code.**

```
...
<frameset rows="125, *" border="0">
    <frame src="menu.htm" noresize="noresize" scrolling="no"
marginheight="4" frameborder="0" name="menu" />
    <frame src="listing.htm" name="content"/>
</frameset>
</frameset>
<noframes>
  <body>
    Thank you for visiting our Web site. We are currently working
on a frameless version of this site.
  </body>
</noframes>
<body>
</body>
</html>
```

| **3** | **Save the changes and refresh the document in the browser.** |

The page displays as a framed site because the browser supports frames. If you were using a browser that did not support frames, the content between the `<noframes>` tags would display.

| **4** | **Close the file in both applications.** |

To Extend Your Knowledge . . .

THE ELIMINATION OF FRAMES

All of our discussion on frames will become a moot point when XHTML 2.0 becomes the standard. In their effort to separate content from presentation, the authors of XHTML 2.0 removed frames from their recommendation (as of this writing). Frames are relegated, instead, to a separate module that may (or may not) be supported by browsers.

Removing frames from the standard is not necessarily a loss. Many of the features of frames, such as creating multiple independent sections on a page, and being able to change content in only one section, can be duplicated using other features. XHTML 2.0 offers one solution, **XFrames**, which promises to answer the frames problems. For more information on XFrames, visit www.w3.org/TR/xframes/.

SUMMARY

In this chapter, you learned how to create framed pages. You discovered how to create a frameset and create a framed page. You became familiar with manipulating the appearance of individual frames. You also learned to direct content to a specific frame, to the entire window, or to a new window. You became familiar with some of the issues regarding frames and the alternatives for non-frames-savvy browsers, including the XFrames solution.

KEY TERMS

Fixed size	Nested frameset	Scrolling attribute
Flowchart	Noframes tag	Subframe
Frames	Noresize attribute	Target attribute
Frameset	Parent	XFrames
Name frame	Relative size	

CHECKING CONCEPTS AND TERMS

MULTIPLE CHOICE

Circle the letter that matches the correct answer for each of the following questions.

1. What tag creates a "canvas" where you can build framed pages?
   a. <frame>
   b. <frame target="">
   c. <frameset>
   d. <noframes>
   e. None of the above

2. Which of the following is a relative size?
   a. 50
   b. 50%
   c. Both a and b
   d. None of the above

3. How is the asterisk (*) symbol used when creating a frameset?
   a. It represents the "rest of the screen" when sizing a frame.
   b. It represents the entire screen when sizing a frame.
   c. It means "start at the end of the screen."
   d. It means "start at the beginning of the screen."

4. Nested frames allow you to specify both rows and columns for framed content.
   a. True
   b. False

5. Why would you remove a frame border?
   a. To make the page appear seamless
   b. To allow the Web designer to add content that stretched from one margin all the way to the other
   c. To ensure that all browsers could correctly display the content
   d. All of the above

6. What attribute prevents a framed page from scrolling?
   a. scrolling="no"
   b. scrolling="auto"
   c. scrolling="yes"
   d. You cannot control the scrolling.

7. What target method would you use to place a destination page in a new window?
   a. target="_newwindow"
   b. target="_self"
   c. target="_blank"
   d. target="_parent"

8. What is the purpose of the base target?
   a. It saves you the work of adding the target to each link individually.
   b. No matter where you are on the page, you can return to the base target.
   c. When you click the home page icon, it accesses the base target.
   d. All of the above

9. Why are frames being eliminated in XHTML 2.0?
   a. Some browsers do not support frames.
   b. Framed pages can display differently than the author intended, depending on the computer used to view the page.
   c. You can have legal problems linking to outside Web sites when these sites display within the framed pages.
   d. All of the above

10. To prevent problems with browsers that do not support frames, you can _____.
    a. use a base target
    b. use the <noframes> tag
    c. create pages without frames
    d. use the _self target

DISCUSSION QUESTIONS

1. What are some of the benefits of using frames?

2. What are some of the problems associated with using frames?

3. What other alternatives to frames can you foresee, besides the up-and-coming XFrames?

4. Why do mainstream sites use frames? Do you agree with their method? Why or why not?

S K I L L   D R I L L

Skill Drills reinforce chapter skills. Each skill that is reinforced is the same as, or nearly the same as, a skill presented in the lessons. We provide detailed instructions in a step-by-step format. You should work through the exercises in the order provided.

1. Create a Frameset Page

You want to create a Web site that displays some of your favorite poetry from various poets. You opt to create a framed site so your visitors can easily navigate the content. Start by creating the frameset page.

1. In your text editor, open index.htm from your WIP_07>skilldrill folder.

2. In index.htm, create a frameset that creates two framed columns.

3. Set the left frame to 150 pixels. Set the right column to fill up the rest of the screen.

4. Use WIP_07>skilldrill>links.htm as the content of the left frame.

5. Use WIP_07>skilldrill>main.htm as the content of the right frame.

6. Save your changes. Load index.htm in a browser.

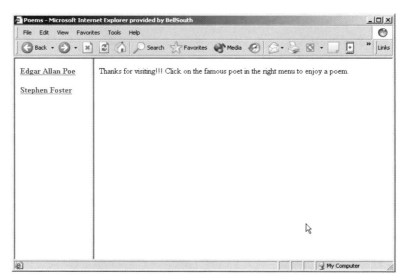

FIGURE 7.31

7.   Keep the file open for use in the next exercise.

2. Define Frame Attributes

In order for the browser to display your pages correctly, you must define the frames in the frameset. In this exercise, you name each frame and define margins and borders.

1.   In the open file, name the links.htm frame "links", and name the main.htm frame "main".

2.   Set the links frame to have no margins.

3.   Make sure the links.htm frame does not scroll.

4.   Remove the frame borders from links.htm.

5.   Change the background color of links.htm to a light gray.

6.   Save the changes to the file. Refresh the document in the browser.

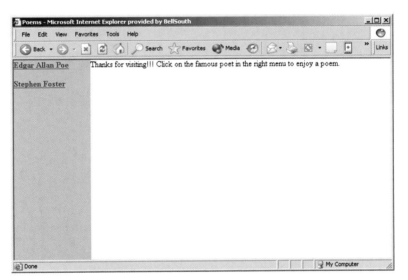

FIGURE 7.32

7.   Keep the file open for the next exercise.

3. Create Targets

In addition to naming the individual frames, you need to provide targets for the links; when the link is clicked, the page is sent to the proper target — which is the named frame.

1.   In the open file, add a base target to index.htm that links to itself.

2.   Target the link to Edgar Allan Poe to display in the main frame.

3.   Target the link to Stephen Foster to display in the main frame.

4. Add a link to poe.htm and foster.htm that links back to main.htm.

5. Provide a target for the links to main.htm to display in the main frame.

6. Save the changes to the file. Refresh the document in the browser.

7. Test the links.

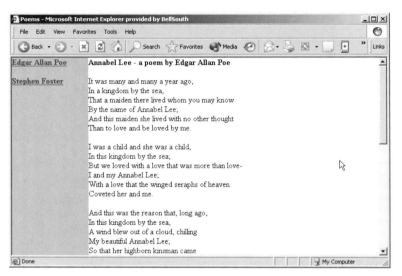

FIGURE 7.33

8. Keep the file open for the next exercise.

4. Provide a Browser Alternative

To make sure all visitors can access your Web pages, you need to provide an alternative for browsers that do not support frames.

1. In the open index.htm file, create a noframes section.

2. Include a paragraph that explains why the content of the page does not display (because the user's browser does not support frames).

3. Change the target of the links in the frameset page to open in a new window.

4. Save the changes. Test the links in the browser.

5. Switch back to index.htm in the text editor. Change the links back to targeting the main frame.

6. Save the changes. Test the links in the browser.

7.   Close the file in both applications.

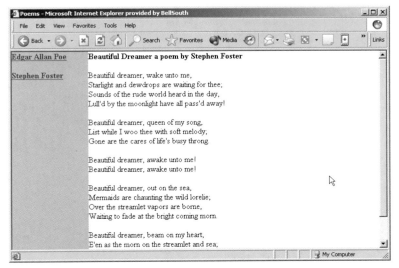

FIGURE 7.34

CHALLENGE

Challenge exercises expand on, or are somewhat related to, skills presented in the lessons. Each exercise provides a brief introduction, followed by numbered-step instructions that are not as detailed as those in the Skill Drill exercises. You should work through the exercises in the order provided.

1. Create an Alternative Page

In this Challenge, you create an alternative page for the poem page you worked with in the Skill Drill exercises.

1.   Create a new XHTML document named "alter.htm". Save it in the WIP_07>skilldrill folder.

2.   Create a table that displays the links in a column on the left and displays the main content on the right side of the screen.

3.   Create two links, "Edgar Allan Poe" and "Stephen Foster". Link them to the corresponding pages.

4.   Place the content from main.htm in the section of the table on the right.

5. Save the changes to the file. Open the file in a browser.

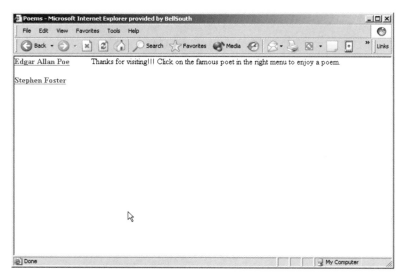

FIGURE 7.35

6. Leave the file open for the next exercise.

2. Create Content for Nonsupported Browsers

In this exercise, you add the content for the **<noframes>** tag.

1. Open the index.htm frameset page in a new text editor window.

2. Remove the content in the **<noframes>** section.

3. In the alter.htm file, copy the code between the opening **<body>** tag and the ending **</body>** tag.

4. Paste the code in index.htm. Save your changes.

5. Open index.htm in your browser. The content between the **<noframes>** tags should not display.

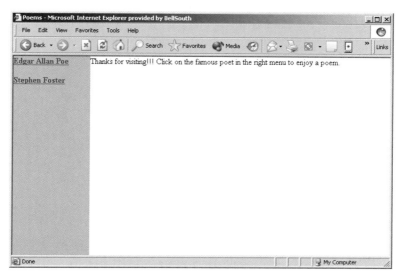

FIGURE 7.36

6. Leave the file open for the next exercise.

3. Create a Banner

Next, you add a banner section to the frameset.

1. In the open index.htm, create another frame across the top of the page.

2. Set that frame size to 100 pixels.

3. Create an XHTML document named "banner.htm". Save it in the skilldrill folder.

4. Insert WIP_07>skilldrill>banner.gif into the banner.htm file.

5. Remove all borders, and make sure the banner frame does not scroll.

6. Save the changes to the file. Refresh the document in the browser.

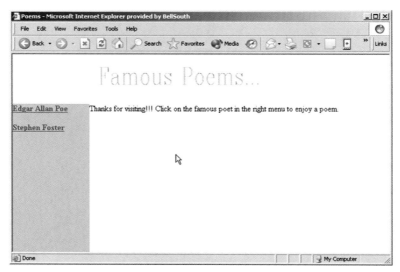

FIGURE 7.37

7. Leave the file open for the next exercise.

4. Provide a Linked Logo

In this exercise, you modify the design and add more content.

1. Create three additional pages of content in the main frame of index.htm.

    You link to this content later. This content does not have to be poems. The idea is simply to get used to adding content to a framed site.

2. Add the links to the links.htm page. Target the links to the main frame.

3. Create a link on links.htm that links to a remote URL. It can be any site of interest, such as www.web-answers.com.

4. Link to an e-mail address.

5. Change the format and layout of the site to appear more aesthetically appealing.

6. Add more content to the main page.

7. Refresh index.htm in your browser. Test the links.

8. Close the file in both applications.

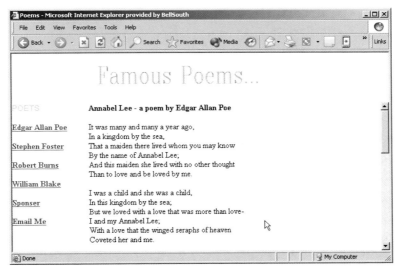

FIGURE 7.38

PORTFOLIO BUILDER

Create an Image Catalog

A stock photo company hired you to create an online image catalog. They specialize in three categories of images. They want an intuitive navigation system, a simple home page, and three additional pages to display their images. You decide that using frames is the best choice for the layout of the Web site.

To complete this exercise, you should do the following:

- Find a Web site that allows you to use free stock images, such as www.sxc.hu. Pick three categories of images and download four images for each category.

- Consider how you want to create the framed layout of the site. You need to create one page for each category, a main page, and a menu page.

- Build the Web site. Include a main page as the original load page, and provide a menu page so visitors can navigate through the site.

- Consider what kind of menu page you want to use. Will you offer text navigation, or will you provide buttons? On each category page, place four images that relate to that category.

- Consider how to link all the pages within the site. Be sure to test the links to ensure they display in the correct frame.

CHAPTER 8

Prepping and Publishing a Web Site

OBJECTIVES

In this chapter, you learn how to:

- Add comments to content and code
- Work with special character entities
- Add meta data to your pages
- Include a document type definition

- Validate a Web site
- Register a domain name
- Work with hosting companies
- Submit a page to search engines

Why Would I Do This?

As you completed the lessons and exercises in the first seven chapters in this book, you learned the essentials of creating Web documents. Now that you understand how to create basic XHTML files, you can focus on the final stages of building and publishing a Web site. Part of this work involves adding comments to your code. Comments make it easier to update the code and provide useful information about the content of the code to members of your team or others who might want to reuse your code.

Another important aspect of finalizing a site is adding keywords and descriptions to the pages. *Keywords* are the subject words used by online databases and *search engines* that help Web surfers locate your site quickly and easily.

You also need to register your own domain, validate your XHTML documents, and upload your site to a Web server. You concentrate on all of these key subjects in this chapter as you learn how to successfully create a fully functional Web site.

VISUAL SUMMARY

The diagram in Figure 8.1 shows the step-by-step process of publishing a Web site. In general, you should have a good idea of the type of site you want to build, as well as the content you want to include, before you begin the site-creation process.

We recommend that you sketch a site layout (storyboard) and flowchart as the first step in the design process. A *storyboard* is a series of sketches that illustrate your site on a page-by-page or section-by-section basis. In your storyboard, you can include notes about navigation, content, types of graphics, audio, and any other information that would be helpful to you and your team during development. Storyboards can be invaluable in keeping you on track during every stage of development.

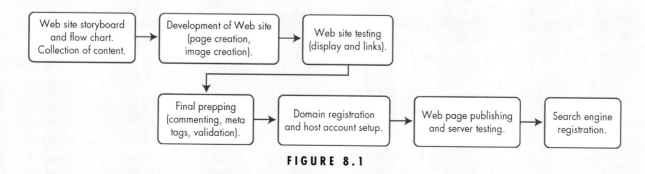

FIGURE 8.1

After the storyboard is complete, you develop and test the site. Then, you add comments and **<meta>** tags, followed by site *validation*. After you decide on whether to purchase Web space on someone else's domain or register your own domain name, the final step is to upload your site to the Web. Once posted (*uploaded*), you should consider how best to promote your Web site so the viewing public knows that it is available for access and use.

LESSON 1 The Comment Tag

Some Web chapters are so large that several developers are needed to complete the scripting. Often, developers are located in different cities (or countries) and work on the same chapter simultaneously. You must not overlook those occasions when a developer starts a chapter, goes on vacation, and turns over the coding to someone else while he is away from the office. How can you ensure that all these disparate individuals who are involved in your chapter understand what has already been scripted, and why?

The answer is to write *comments* (notes) within the code. Commenting allows you to write anything about the code or chapter that you think is important or that you might forget when you resume coding later. You can use comments to "comment out" sections of the document that you don't want to display in the browser but that you don't want to delete (people can look at these sections if they view the source code). You do not have to remove your comments from the code before uploading the site to the Web; comments do not change the code in any way, nor do they display in the browser.

Commenting is the perfect communication mechanism for teams of developers. The group leader can specify the goals of the script within the coding environment itself. Everyone on the team sees the same comments and can follow the same directions.

The **<comment>** tag doesn't look the same as other XHTML tags. For example:

```
<!-- this is a comment -->
```

The exclamation point followed by two dashes indicates the beginning of a comment. Another set of two dashes indicates the end of the comment. The HTML/XHTML parser ignores the content between the dashes and hides the content from the Web page display.

Add a Comment Line

1	Copy the files from the Chapter_08 folder into your WIP_08 folder.

2   **Open PoetrySite>index.htm in your text editor and Web browser.**

The main page displays a complete Web site.

FIGURE 8.2

3   **In the source file, add a comment at the top of the page to identify the author's contact information.**

```
<html>
<head>
<title>My Favorite Poems</title>
<!--Contact author of site: Joe Smith - joesmith@joesmith.com. -->
</head>
<body topmargin="0" bgcolor="#ffffff">
. . .
```

You can provide your contact information for those who view your source code.

4   **Add a comment to the bottom of the file indicating copyright information.**

```
. . .
<!-- The design of this Web site is copyrighted by Joe Smith.
Please contact me at joesmith@joesmith.com if you wish to
use any of the content. -->
</body>
</html>
```

Providing important copyright information can warn viewers about your policy for copying content or code from your Web pages.

5   Save the changes to the file. Refresh the document in your browser.

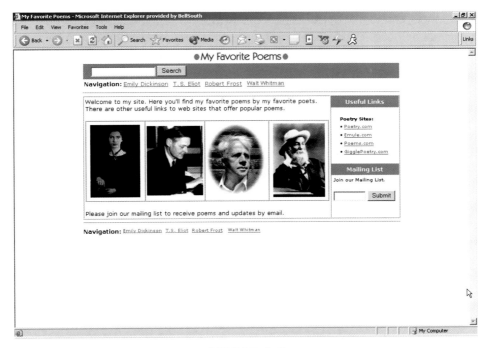

FIGURE 8.3

The content placed within the **<comment>** tags does not display in the body of the Web page.

6   Leave the file open in both applications for the next exercise.

To Extend Your Knowledge . . .

COMMENTING TECHNIQUES

You can use comments as reminders of when and where to place content updates. When you edit XHTML code, comments allow you to identify where a particular section of content begins and ends.

LESSON 2 Adding Character Codes

At times, the Web browser does not display standard characters because the browser assumes that they are part of a command. For example, under normal circumstances, the browser would not display an actual XHTML tag on a Web page (such as `<p>`). Instead, the browser would insert a paragraph break at that point in the document. Assume you are creating a Web page to explain how to write XHTML code. You will need a way to allow the code to display on the Web page without being interpreted by the browser.

The way around this problem is to use special character references. You encode the actual ASCII value of the character in the document by prefixing the character with an ampersand (`&`) and a hash mark (`#`), and following it with a semicolon (`;`).

- The ampersand tells XHTML that what follows is a special character definition.

- The hash mark says that the character is being represented by its ***ASCII value***, which is the numeric representation of a character on a computer system. If you omit the hash mark, the browser expects a special character name, called a ***character entity***, not its ASCII value.

- Special character references end with semicolons; when the browser reaches a semicolon, it knows it has reached the end of the character.

The following illustration shows some of the character references and how they display on a Web page.

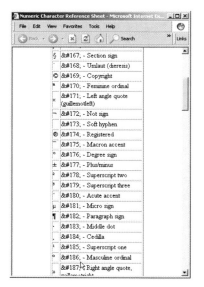

FIGURE 8.4

Some characters also have entity names that allow you to specify that character entity instead of the ASCII value. For instance, the left and right brackets around an HTML command have the ASCII values of **060** and **062**, respectively; but they are also called "**lt**" and "**gt**." Therefore, the character "**<**" can be represented as either **<<** or **<**, and the character "**>**" can be represented as either **>** or **>**.

A list of ASCII values and character entity names is included at the back of this book.

Using the numeric ASCII values is preferred to using the entity names because not all browsers support all entity names. Browsers must, by definition, support all ASCII values, since ASCII is how the computer interprets the characters. It is safe to include commonly used entity names for characters such as **<**, **>**, and **"** (for quotes). These names are easier to recognize in the code than their numeric equivalents.

XHTML Strict only recognizes the following special character names:

- **&** Ampersand (&)
- **<** Less than, open bracket (<)
- **>** Greater than, close bracket (>)
- **"** Double quote (")
- ** ** Nonbreaking space (hard space) ( )

Add Copyright Information

| **1** | **In the open file, switch to the text editor window.** |

| **2** | **Add copyright information to the bottom of the page.** |

```
. . .
<p><font size="2" face="verdana">
Please join our mailing list to receive poems and updates by email.
</font></p>
<p align="center"><font face="verdana" size="2">Copyright &#169;
2004. Joe Smith.</font></p>
</td>
</tr>
</table>
. . .
```

This provides the character code for a copyright symbol.

3   **Save the changes to the file. Refresh the document in the browser.**

FIGURE 8.5

The copyright symbol displays in the string of text along the bottom of the screen. The copyright symbol is not available on your keyboard. You can create the copyright symbol using the entity name "**©**". The entity name is not supported in XHTML, however, so the numeric value should be used instead.

4   **Switch to the text editor window. Add the following quoted material.**

```
. . .
<p><font size="2" face="verdana">

Welcome to my site. Here you'll find my favorite poems by my
favorite poets. There are other useful links to web sites that
offer popular poems.</font></p>

<p><font size="2" face="verdana">&quot;Success is counted
sweetest by those who ne&rsquo;er succeed.&quot; -
Emily Dickinson</font></p>

<table border="1" cellpadding="0" cellspacing="0" width="100%">
. . .
```

The character references use entity names to create double quotes and a single quote.

? If you have problems

The character entity only displays if the font you selected is also loaded on the viewer's machine. The viewer might experience problems if the browser does not interpret the encoding correctly.

5 | Save the changes to the file. Refresh the document in the browser.

FIGURE 8.6

The paragraph is placed within quotes. Although you could have used the actual quote characters from your keyboard, using the character entity ensures the quotes display properly.

6 | Leave the file open in both applications for the next exercise.

LESSON 3   Working with Meta Information

Meta information is literally information about information; *<meta> tags* provide useful information about the content of your Web site. **<Meta>** tags allow you to boost your site's ranking in some search engines and online directory listings by providing additional keywords and descriptions of the site. You can assign many attributes to **<meta>** tags. The most important attributes for search engine submission are **name="description"** and **name="keywords"**.

Normally, a search engine displays the first sentence of a page that it finds during a search. While this is certainly accurate, you might prefer that something more meaningful displays when a search engine returns a hit on your page. The ***description value*** tells the search engine precisely what to return as the description of the page, rather than the first sentence of the page.

As you know, keywords are words or phrases that a user is likely to type into a search engine when looking for information on the Web. The best way to develop a list of keywords for your site is to think about what you would type into a search engine if you were looking for information on your particular topic. When accurate keyword values are assigned to a site, the site receives a much higher ranking than one with poor keyword assignment. Below is some sample code that illustrates description and keyword values:

```
<html>

<head>

<title>Example of a Web page using Meta tags.</title>

<meta name="description" content="Learn how to use meta tags to increase
your chances of high rankings in search engine results pages." />

<meta name="keywords" content="example, Meta, tags" />

</head>
```

Add <meta> Tags to the Home Page

1 In the open document, switch to the text editor window.

2 Add keywords to the document using the `meta name=""` attribute.

```
<html>

<head>

<title>My Favorite Poems</title>

<meta http-equiv="keywords" content="famous poets, Emily Dickinson,
Robert Frost, T.S. Eliot, Walt Whitman, favorite poems">

<!--Contact author of site: Joe Smith - joesmith@joesmith.com.-->

</head>

...
```

3 Add a description to the document.

```
<html>

<head>

<title>My Favorite Poems</title>

<meta http-equiv="description" content="The My Favorite Poems Web
site is a collection of favorite famous poems. Join the mailing
list to receive site updates.">
```

```
<meta http-equiv="keywords" content="famous poets, Emily Dickinson,
Robert Frost, T.S. Eliot, Walt Whitman, favorite poems">
<!--Contact author of site: Joe Smith - joesmith@joesmith.com.-->
</head>
```

. . .

The description provides a detailed overview of the content of a site. The description displays in the search engine results page.

For now, do not add the closing slash to the **<meta>** tags. Later in the chapter, you validate the tags and correct this error.

4 **Modify the page title so it's more descriptive.**

. . .

```
<title>My Favorite Poems - a collection of popular poems by famous
poets.</title>
```

. . .

The new title provides a more descriptive explanation of the Web site. This is important for viewers scanning several links to similar sites.

5 **Save the changes to the file. Refresh the document in the browser.**

FIGURE 8.7

The document display remains unchanged. The Title bar reflects the modification.

6 **Leave the file open for the next exercise.**

To Extend Your Knowledge . . .

RANKING HIGH IN A SEARCH ENGINE RESULT

A search engine query often returns hundreds (sometimes thousands) of matching Web pages. In most cases, the 10 most likely matches are displayed first. These matches are called the "top 10." Of the hundreds of listings provided, most viewers look at about 30 listings. If your Web site is not included in the first 30 listings, it will probably be overlooked. Here are some techniques you can use to improve your chances of a higher ranking.

1. Pick Strategic Keywords. Decide what words you predict users will type into the Search field when looking for a site such as yours. Those are your strategic keywords, which should accurately reflect the content of your Web page. Your keywords should be two or more words long. Too many sites will be relevant for a single word, such as "dogs." Such stiff competition reduces your chances of success.

2. Position Your Keywords Carefully. Make sure your keywords appear in strategic locations on your Web pages — the most important of which is the page title. Failure to put important keywords in the page title is one reason relevant Web pages receive poor rankings.

3. Produce good content. Search engines are becoming increasingly able to ignore meta information that simply attempts to grab every user who searches on a keyword. Google, for example, ranks your page based on how many popular Web sites your site links to and how many other Web sites refer (or link) to your site. For instance, if you have a Web site on dog training, your site would rank well if it linked to popular dog training sites and if popular dog training sites also linked to your site. Producing good information for your site and providing good links to other information is the best way to ensure you get the attention of modern search engines.

Use keywords for your page headlines, if possible. They should also appear in the first paragraph of a page. Search engines read Web pages from top to bottom, assigning lesser importance to information as it moves down the page. Keep in mind that tables can push your text farther down the page (because tables break apart when search engines read them), assigning less relevance to keywords in the lower sections of the page.

LESSON 4   Validating a Web Site

Web page validation is an essential final step in Web page development, particularly when you use XHTML to code your documents. Web page validation checks your XHTML source code against a particular document type definition to ensure you properly coded your Web pages.

Although validation is not required when using HTML (it is advised), XHTML documents must be validated before they can be defined as XML applications. Since XHTML is the new standard for the Web, you should become familiar with the three document types.

Document Type Definitions

Applications such as browsers use ***document type definitions (DTD)*** to specify the "rules" that apply to a document's source code. DTD tags are required in XHTML and will be increasingly needed as developers transition to XML. The tags tell the browser what kind of XHTML source code it can expect to render.

XHTML specifies three primary document types: Strict, Transitional, and Frameset. You had a brief introduction to these document types in Chapter 1. Let's take a moment to review them.

Use the XHTML Strict DTD tag when you do not include any of the deprecated tags from previous versions (namely presentational tags such as **<b>** and **<font>**) in your document. You can use XHTML Strict with Cascading Style Sheets (CSS). This code should be typed as a single line of code (without hitting the Enter or Return key to insert a line break). The XHTML Strict DTD tag is

```
<!DOCTYPE html PUBLIC "-//W3C//DTD XHTML 1.0 Strict//EN"
"http://www.w3.org/TR/xhtml1/DTD/xhtml1-strict.dtd">
```

Most developers currently use the transitional standard for XHTML, which requires the transitional DTD. The XHTML Transitional DTD tag is needed when you include some of the HTML presentational features, either with or without CSS. The XHTML Transitional DTD tag is

```
<!DOCTYPE html PUBLIC "-//W3C//DTD XHTML 1.0 Transitional//EN"
"http://www.w3.org/TR/xhtml1/DTD/xhtml1-transitional.dtd">
```

Use the XHTML Frameset DTD tag when you want to use HTML frames. The XHTML Frameset DTD tag is

```
<!DOCTYPE html PUBLIC "-//W3C//DTD XHTML 1.0 Frameset//EN"
"http://www.w3.org/TR/xhtml1/DTD/xhtml1-frameset.dtd">
```

Let's look at the first example of a DTD tag — the XHTML Strict DTD.

- The first part, <!DOCTYPE html, specifies the document element of an XML (XHTML) document (i.e., it specifies the element that surrounds all other elements of the document). <!DOCTYPE html therefore means the document must start with <html> and end with </html>.

- The second part, PUBLIC "-//W3C//DTD XHTML 1.0 Strict//EN", indicates the type of XHTML you used, which in this example is Strict. Remember, in XHTML Strict, you cannot include presentational tags in the code.

- The third and final part, "http://www.w3.org/TR/xhtml1/DTD/xhtml1-frameset.dtd", is the URL for the DTD. Here, the code in your page is compared against the actual DTD.

The DTD tag is placed above all the other tags in your document. It indicates which type of XHTML is used, as well as the location of the actual DTD, so the document can be compared to that language reference. Eventually, the use of the DTD will allow developers to use new types of document definitions. For example, two companies could create a new set of definitions that would allow them to easily exchange data between different computer systems. This is the intent of XML, to easily allow different computer systems to exchange information.

You can use the W3C's validators to validate HTML, XHTML, CSS, and XML files. To do so, include a link to http://validator.w3.org/ in your document, and then simply click the link to validate the document.

Validate the Home Page

1   **In the text editor of the open document, define index.htm as an XHTML Transitional document by providing the proper DTD at the top of the document, before the `<html>` tag.**

```
<!DOCTYPE html PUBLIC "-//W3C//DTD XHTML 1.0 Transitional//EN"
"http://www.w3.org/TR/xhtml1/DTD/xhtml1-transitional.dtd">

<html>
```

. . .

Your document includes presentational elements, including the `<font>` tag, which is why you must define index.htm as an XHTML Transitional document. This text must be typed as a single line of text without clicking the Enter or Return button until the end of the line is reached.

2   **Save the changes to file. Refresh the Web browser.**

The display remains the same, since you only added information about the XHTML DTD.

3   **If you have an active Internet connection, log on to http://www.htmlhelp.com/tools/validator/ upload.html.**

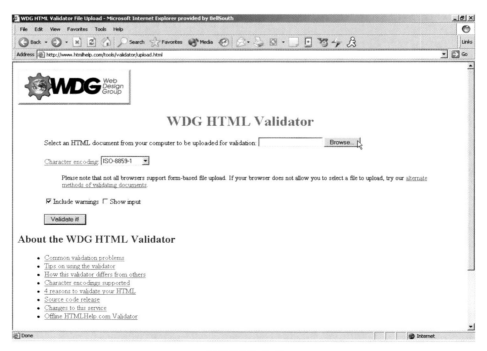

FIGURE 8.8

Htmlhelp.com offers an excellent XHTML validation service. You can upload documents from your machine, or provide a URL.

4 Click the Browse button to display the Choose File dialog box.

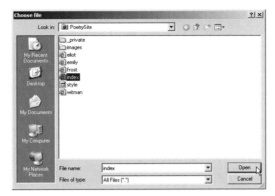

FIGURE 8.9

5 Choose index.htm from the list of files in the PoetrySite folder. Click the Open button.

The file uploads and displays in the text field on the Web page.

6 Click the "Validate it!" button on the Validation page.

FIGURE 8.10

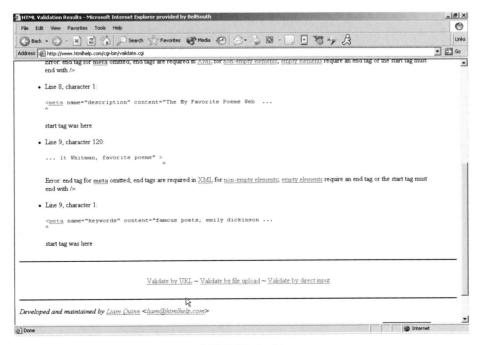

FIGURE 8.11

The results page returns some errors. We intentionally included errors in the code so you would have the opportunity to correct them and revalidate.

7   **Leave the file open in both applications.**

Correct Validation Errors

1   **In the text editor of the open file, make the following minor corrections at the ends of the `<meta name="">` lines in index.htm.**

```
. . .

<head>

<title>My Favorite Poems - a collection of popular poems by famous
poets.</title>

<meta name="description" content="The My Favorite Poems Web site
is a collection of favorite famous poems. Join the mailing list to
receive site updates." />

<meta name="keywords" content="famous poets, Emily Dickinson,
Robert Frost, T.S. Eliot, Walt Whitman, favorite poems" />

<!--Contact author of site: Joe Smith - joesmith@joesmith.com. -->

</head>

<body bgcolor="#ffffff">

. . .
```

The lack of the closing "/" at the end of each **`<meta>`** tag resulted in the **`<meta>`** tags remaining open. With the added "/" on each **`<meta>`** tag, the tags are now properly closed and the code complies with the XHTML standards. Keep in mind that sometimes one error might cause the validation program to report another error. More often than not, correcting an obvious error prevents other errors from showing.

2   **Save the changes to index.htm in the text editor.**

3   **Click the Back button in the Web browser to return to the original validation page.**

4   **Reupload the document.**

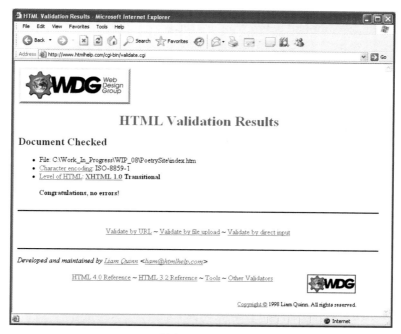

FIGURE 8.12

These minor corrections resolved the errors.

5   **Close the file in the text editor.**

To Extend Your Knowledge . . .

MORE ON <META> TAGS

As you know, meta keywords and descriptions are the most popular meta information used today. You should include them on every Web page. Search engines, such as AltaVista, use these `<meta>` tags to help identify and catalog your pages (as you learn later in this chapter). These are not the only `<meta>` tags available to you. Here are some other tags you can use:

`<meta name="revisit" content="15days" />` This tag tells the search engine how often it should revisit your page. This is especially helpful if you update your pages on a regular basis. Every time the search engine visits your site, it updates its index with your new content.

`<meta name="robots" content="nofollow" />` This is useful if you have a "linear" Web site—you want visitors to see the main page first, and then navigate the site in a specific manner, rather than find your site through one of the other individual pages. The content values include all, index, nofollow, and noindex.

For more information on `<meta>` tags, visit http://www.searchenginewatch.com/webmasters/article.php/2167931.

LESSON 5 Publishing a Web Site

There are still many tasks to complete before you are ready to publish your Web site, one of which is to decide if you are going to register your own ***domain name***. Domain names are not required, but they are certainly very beneficial, especially if you are building a commercial site (.com). Domain names are used in URLs to identify specific Web sites. For example, in the URL http://www.web-answers.com, the domain name is web-answers.com.

Every domain name has a suffix (usually three letters) that indicates which top-level domain it belongs to. The most commonly used suffixes and the associated top-level domains are:

- .com for commercial business
- .edu for educational institutions
- .gov for government agencies
- .mil for the military
- .net for network organizations
- .org for nonprofit organizations

The Importance of a Domain Name

The primary reason to own a domain name is that it always stays with you, regardless of where the site is hosted. For example, if you change your Web hosting service, you don't need to worry that your regular visitors will no longer be able to find your site. If they know your site name as www.mywebsite.com on one Web host, that is exactly how it remains on every other Web host — as long as you own your domain name. Users simply enter your Web address as usual, and they are directed to your new site.

Registering a Domain Name

Securing a domain name involves searching for an available name, and then registering that name with InterNIC through a domain registrar. A ***domain registrar*** is a company that allows you to register domain names through them, and then they update ***InterNIC***, which is the organization that indexes domain names.

After you choose a domain name, such as mygreatwebsite.com, you must go to a registrar and pay a registration fee that ranges from $15 to $35 (annually). Once registered, you have rights to the name for a year, or however long you registered the name. Renewals are optional.

When you register your domain name, be prepared to pay your fee with a credit card (it's a requirement). Two popular places to register your domain name are NetworkSolutions.com and Register.com.

Your Hosting Service Provider

Selecting a Web site hosting provider that best suits your needs can be a confusing (and sometimes frustrating) task. As you sift through the multitude of hosting options, you will find that hosting prices vary significantly, as do the supplied technologies. You must decide if you need a simple account, database support, FrontPage extensions, and much more.

While all Web hosts experience downtime, it is important to identify the extent of these lapses in service. Your host's downtime greatly affects your site. When your host is down, your Web site is down, too. You should expect your host to have at least 95% uptime (or better). Don't fall for the 100% uptime that some providers boast. It doesn't exist. A good host alerts you about problems before your viewers have a chance to notice them.

Your host should have a strong customer-care and technical-support team. Be sure to ask about the availability of commercial technical support. Often, if you are paying an unbelievably low hosting price, your host is cutting corners somewhere. In addition, beware of the hosting provider that does not offer a telephone number for technical support.

It is important to question both high- and low-cost hosting packages. When evaluating prices, be sure to find out exactly what is (and is not) included in the price. Look at other factors driving the price. Are you paying for a package that you don't really need? Does the package provide all the technologies you require? If you don't need the technologies in one package, find another package.

Check Domain Name Availability

1   If you have an active Internet connection, log on to www.register.com.

FIGURE 8.13

2   Look for the text box that allows you to search for a domain name.

It's located below the Start arrow.

3   Type in your preferred domain name. Choose the domain name extension, such as .com or .edu.

4   Click the Go button to submit the search.

Register.com searches for this domain name. If it is available, you have the option to reserve it; if it is not available, alternate domain names and extensions are provided.

5   Leave the Web browser window open for the next exercise.

To Extend Your Knowledge . . .

UPLOADING YOUR SITE AND GOING LIVE

When development is complete and your Web site is ready, all your files are stored only on your computer. To make your Web site available to the public, you need to transfer your files to a computer (your Web host's server) that has a special connection to the Internet — which is, of course, a Web server.

Once you have established a hosting account and your hosting provider has given you the necessary information about the Web server so you can transfer your domain name, you can upload your pages to the Web server and "go live." (Remember, you don't have to register your domain name to publish your site.) If you are not comfortable transferring your domain name, most hosting providers will transfer the domain for you.

The most common method of copying/moving files from your computer to the Web server is to use **File Transfer Protocol (FTP)**. To access an FTP server, you need an FTP address, a username, and a password, all of which your hosting service or server administrator should provide to you. Many hosting services provide FTP instructions and/or software for you to use.

LESSON 6   Search Engine Registration

At one time or another, you have probably used a search engine (such as yahoo.com, google.com, altavista.com, or ask.com) to locate specific information on the Web or to locate a particular Web site. A search engine is actually an online URL database or index. When you log on to a search engine, you enter specific keywords, click the Search button, and the search engine looks through its index to locate Web pages that match your keywords. The pages the search engine returns are ordered according to how relevant they are to your *search criteria* (your keywords); the most relevant sites are placed at the top of the list, and sites of lesser relevance are placed lower in the list.

Submitting to a Search Engine

Getting your page to display in the top 10 on a search return isn't easy. Don't be discouraged if you have trouble locating your Web page in a search return after you register your site. Most likely, many other sites pertain to the same subject as yours, especially if yours is a commercial Web site. Even though `<meta>` tags are supposed to bring your Web site to the top of every search list, there are no guarantees.

An excellent source of information for search engine submission is www.searchenginewatch.com. The site includes information on how search engines work, alternative ways to register your sites, as well as online marketing resources.

Registering Your Web Site

In order for a search engine to return a site in its list of results, the site must first be registered with the search engine. You can register your site with each individual search engine, or you can register your site with a submission service that, in turn, registers your site with multiple search engines. Keep in mind that each search engine is different. Some require information about the site, others allow you to resubmit or edit your site, and some ask you to place a reciprocal link to their search engine. To ensure correct registration, be certain you understand the requirements of each search engine before you register your site.

The actual registration process is quite simple. After you upload your site to a Web server, log on to various search engines and follow the instructions to register your Web page. Each search engine provides a link that says, "Add Your URL" or "Register Your Site." Clicking this link takes you to the registration page. Once on the registration page, you complete an online form with your site's URL, and then submit the form to the search engine's database. Within a few weeks, your site should be active on the search engine.

It's a good idea to test each search engine to ensure your site is properly registered. Go to each of the search engines where you registered your site, enter the appropriate keywords, and check to see that your site is included on the list of returns.

Register a Web Page

1   **Log on to www.altavista.com, a popular search engine.**

2   **Click the Submit a Site link.**

FIGURE 8.14

? **If you have problems**

The instructions to register a site with AltaVista were accurate at the time of this writing. It is possible the registration process may have changed. To ensure a successful registration, be sure you follow the on-screen instructions on AltaVista.

---

3   Follow the on-screen instructions for submitting a Web site.

You can submit individual Web pages. For instance, you can submit the home page, www.mysite.com, and each individual page's URL, such as www.mysite.com/about.htm. We recommend that you provide unique **\<meta\>** tags for each page within your Web site, and then register each page's URL with the search engines of your choice.

4   Repeat Steps 2 and 3 to register each page within your Web site.

5   Close the browser window.

To Extend Your Knowledge . . .

CASE SENSITIVITY

Depending on the Web server, HTML file names may be case sensitive. Knowing how to name files correctly minimizes the possibility of links being broken due to incorrect file-naming conventions. We recommend that you use only lowercase file names.

Usernames and passwords are usually case sensitive. Check with your hosting provider to ensure that you understand their case requirements.

S U M M A R Y

In this chapter, you learned that Web site creation includes much more than writing XHTML code. You learned before you publish a Web site, you must prepare it in various ways. You discovered how to add comments to your code, which allow you to insert information and content throughout your Web site that does not display in the browser window. Comments allow you to provide additional information for those who view your source code, including contact information and copyright policies.

You learned that **\<meta\>** tags allow you to insert keywords and descriptions about your site and that **\<meta\>** tags allows search engines to return your site in their search results. You learned that you must carefully consider the description you include on your page, since this description is what is returned to the user on the search results page.

You discovered that you must validate a Web page as an XHTML file before you can publish the document on the Web. Online validation services make it easy to check your code — and then correct any errors — before you publish your documents. You learned that you can register a domain name, and then upload your site to a reputable hosting service to "go live" on the Web. Finally, you discovered how to register your pages with search engines to ensure that the Web-viewing audience notices your site.

CAREERS IN DESIGN

THE DIFFERENT FACES OF WEB DEVELOPERS

Anyone reading this book who has had experience in the print industry understands the vast difference between the roles of creative personnel and production professionals. In that arena, designers are responsible for developing the look and feel that shapes the perceptions and experiences of the audience. Once the designer has finalized the layout of the piece, the production phase of the workflow begins. Print production professionals are responsible for ensuring the quality of the images, the clarity of the typography, and the other processes required to reproduce the design in quantity.

In the world of Web design, the same situation exists. Web designers are responsible for the look, feel, and effectiveness of the visitor's experience; their responsibility ends there. The next step in the process lies in the hands of Web developers — the programmers, database experts, and site maintenance professionals responsible for the "wiring" of the site.

The skills required for these two types of positions, while equally important, are dramatically different. This holds true in all aspects of professional communication. Creative talent ensures the quality of the user experience, while technical expertise ensures proper preparation and delivery of the content to the end user. As your career matures, it will become apparent on which side of the fence your talents lie — creative or technical.

KEY TERMS

ASCII value

Character entity

Comments

Description value

Document Type Definition (DTD)

Domain name

Domain registrar

File Transfer Protocol (FTP)

InterNIC

Keyword

Meta tags

Search criteria

Search engine

Storyboard

Upload

Validation

CHECKING CONCEPTS AND TERMS

MULTIPLE CHOICE
Circle the letter that matches the correct answer for each of the following questions.

1. How is the comment tag different than other tags?
  a. There are no opening and closing tag commands.
  b. Comment tags begin with an exclamation point and two dashes.
  c. The comment tag displays content in the Title bar.
  d. None of the above

2. What is the character entity for a nonbreaking space?
  a. ©
  b.
  c. "
  d. None of the above

3. Meta tags are container tags.
  a. True
  b. False

4. What meta value allows you to provide a description in a search engine results page?
  a. Keywords
  b. Description
  c. Title
  d. Author

5. Why should you assign descriptive titles to your documents?
  a. Sometimes search engines display the title as the actual link to the Web page.
  b. So readers know the exact page they are on.
  c. The title is one of the basic document tags.
  d. All of the above

6. Why is it so important to validate your Web pages?
  a. You must ensure your XHTML source code meets the DTD requirements.
  b. You must ensure your XHTML source code meets the FTP requirements.
  c. You must ensure your XHTML source code meets the FCC requirements.
  d. None of the above

7. What DTD is used for nonpresentational code?
  a. Transitional
  b. Strict
  c. Frameset
  d. Nonpresentational

8. What protocol uploads documents to a Web server?
  a. http
  b. mailto:
  c. smtp
  d. ftp

9. You are required to register every Web page.
  a. True
  b. False

10. Why is it best to use only lowercase file names?
  a. In case the server is case sensitive, this helps prevent broken links.
  b. To ensure everything is in the same format.
  c. Adhering to one file-naming convention helps keep your files better organized.
  d. All of the above

DISCUSSION QUESTIONS

1. List at least three ways to take advantage of commenting code and content.

2. When would you want to avoid using **<meta>** tags, and why?

3. Discuss other ways to promote a Web site besides search engine registration.

S K I L L   D R I L L

Skill Drills reinforce chapter skills. Each skill reinforced is the same as, or nearly the same as, a skill presented in the lessons. We provide detailed instructions in a step-by-step format. You should work through these exercises in the order provided.

1. Comment a Web Page

In this exercise, you provide comment lines for those who view your source code. You explain that other users are allowed to use the poems in their own collections.

1. Open index.htm from the WIP_08>PoetrySite folder.

2. Create the following comment beneath the **<body>** tag.

   ```
   <!--This is a collection of my favorite poems. Please feel free
   to link to my Web page or use the poems for your own favorite
   collection. -->
   ```

3. Save the changes to index.htm.

4. Open the other documents within the PoetrySite folder. Add comment lines beneath the **<body>** tags to describe the documents. The comments can be brief descriptions about the poet featured on the page, or they can be copyright information.

5. Save your changes.

6. Open index.htm in a browser. Navigate through the site to ensure that the comments do not display on the pages.

7. Save your changes. Keep the file open for the next exercise.

2. Add <meta> Tags

You decide to include **<meta>** tags to increase the chances that your Web pages gain a high ranking on search engine results pages, as well as to provide a description of your pages to viewers.

1. From the PoetrySite folder, open emily.htm in the text editor and the browser.

2. Use **<meta>** tags to add keywords in the head of the document, such as "Emily Dickinson, famous poet, poetry, There is a Word."

3. Add the following description (using the **`description=""`** attribute) beneath the keyword **`<meta>`** tag in the head of the document.

   `"Emily Dickinson was born in Amherst, Massachusetts, on December 10, 1830."`

4. Provide the following descriptive title to the **`<title>`** tag: "Emily Dickinson, famous poetess."

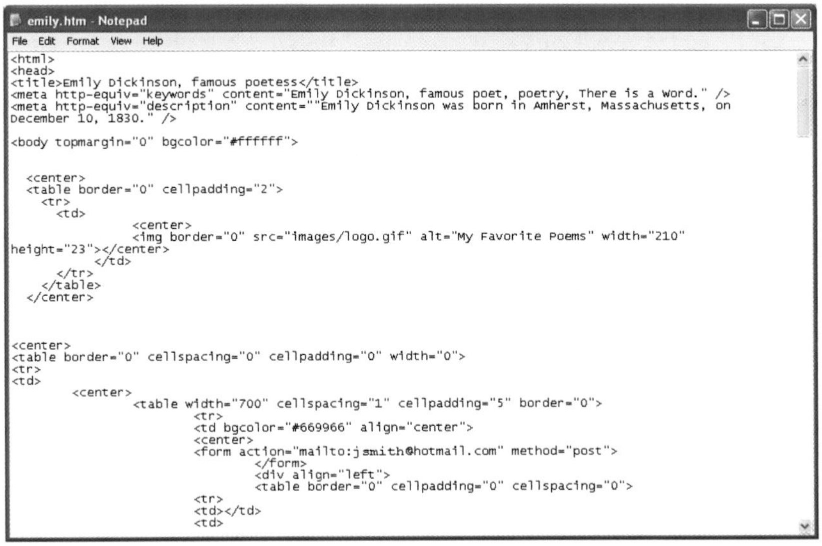

```
emily.htm - Notepad
File Edit Format View Help
<html>
<head>
<title>Emily Dickinson, famous poetess</title>
<meta http-equiv="keywords" content="Emily Dickinson, famous poet, poetry, There is a word." />
<meta http-equiv="description" content=""Emily Dickinson was born in Amherst, Massachusetts, on
December 10, 1830." />

<body topmargin="0" bgcolor="#ffffff">


  <center>
  <table border="0" cellpadding="2">
    <tr>
      <td>
                <center>
                <img border="0" src="images/logo.gif" alt="My Favorite Poems" width="210"
height="23"></center>
            </td>
      </tr>
    </table>
  </center>



<center>
<table border="0" cellspacing="0" cellpadding="0" width="0">
<tr>
<td>
        <center>
                <table width="700" cellspacing="1" cellpadding="5" border="0">
                        <tr>
                        <td bgcolor="#669966" align="center">
                        <center>
                        <form action="mailto:jsmith@hotmail.com" method="post">
                                </form>
                                <div align="left">
                                <table border="0" cellpadding="0" cellspacing="0">
                        <tr>
                        <td></td>
                        <td>
```

FIGURE 8.15

5. Save the changes to the file. Refresh the document in the browser.
6. Close all open windows.

3. Add Character Entities

In this exercise, you provide the year for copyright and the author of the Web page.

1. Open emily.htm in the text editor.
2. Add quotes around the actual body of the poem (excluding the title).
3. There is no copyright symbol on the keyboard. Use the character entity or code for the copyright symbol to add the text "Copyright © 2004. Joe Smith." beneath the poem.
4. Save the changes to the file. Open the document in a browser.
5. Modify the rest of the poet pages by adding quotes around the poems and adding the copyright information at the bottom of the page, directly beneath the poem.

6. Save the changes to the file. Test the Web site in your browser.

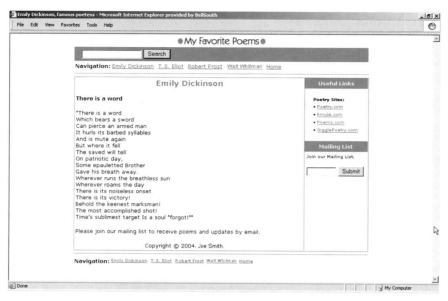

FIGURE 8.16

7. Close all open windows.

4. Validate the Web Site

The final step is to ensure your pages conform to the XHTML standard. You decide to use the Web site validator at www.htmlhelp.com.

1. Open index.htm in the text editor.

    The file is located in the PoetrySite folder.

2. Remove the alt name-value pair from all the image tags.

3. Save the changes to the file. Launch your browser.

4. Navigate to http://www.htmlhelp.com/tools/validator/. Validate the page by following the instructions for uploading a document from your hard drive.

    Errors display on the results page because image tags require the `<alt>` tag.

5. Return to the text editor that contains index.htm. Add the `alt=""` attributes (with values) to all the images.

6.   Save the changes to the file. Reupload the document to http://www.htmlhelp.com/tools/validator/.

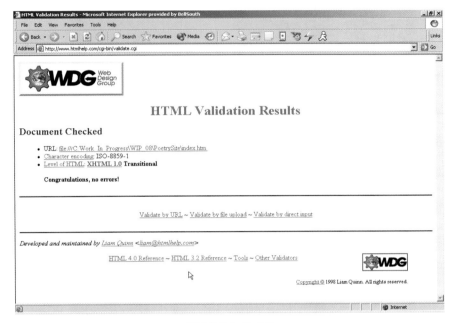

FIGURE 8.17

7.   Close the file in both applications.

CHALLENGE

Challenge exercises expand on, or are somewhat related to, skills presented in the lessons. Each exercise provides a brief introduction, followed by numbered-step instructions that are not as detailed as those in the Skill Drill exercises. You should work through these exercises in the order provided.

1. Comment Out Sections of Body Content

Now that you've prepped the poetry site for final publication, complete the chapter by adding content, obtaining a hosting account, and validating the rest of the Web site.

1.   From the WIP_08>PoetrySite folder, open emily.htm in the text editor.

2.   Beneath the poem, add the following poem:

```
The Forgotten Grave
After a hundred years

Nobody knows the place, --
Agony that enacted there,
Motionless as peace.
```

```
Weeds triumphant ranged,
Strangers strolled and spelled
At the lone orthography
Of the elder dead.

Winds of summer fields
Recollect the way, --
Instinct picking up the key
Dropped by memory.
```

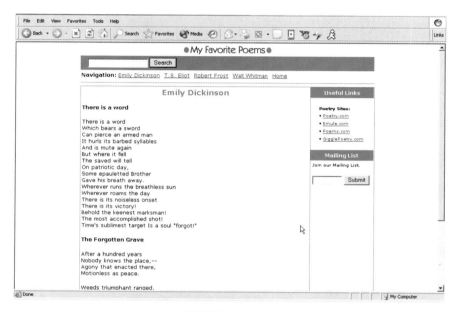

FIGURE 8.18

3. Save the changes. Open the file in a browser to display the new poem.

4. Comment out the poem you just inserted on the page.

5. Above the commented poem, add another **`<comment>`** tag and include the following: "Next poem to be featured."

6.   Save the changes to index.htm. Refresh the document in the browser.

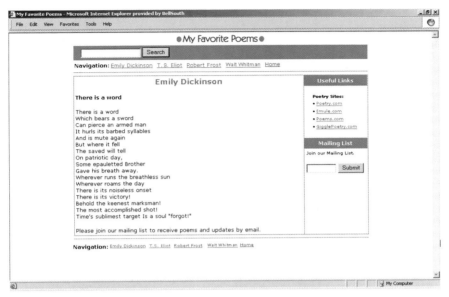

FIGURE 8.19

7.   Save the file and leave it open for the next exercise.

2. Prepare for Search Engines

Before you publish your documents on the Web, you should provide additional information for search engine indexing. In this exercise, you use **<meta>** tags to add keywords and a description.

1.   From the WIP_08>PoetrySite folder, open each poet's XHTML document in a text editor.

2.   Provide 10 meta keywords for each page.

3.   Provide a meta description for each page.

4.   Change each title to one that is more descriptive.

5. Think of other ways to provide content for the site to increase search engine ranking, such as descriptive headings.

FIGURE 8.20

6. Save your changes. Test the document in the browser.

7. Close all files in your browser and text editor.

3. Find Free Hosting

In this exercise, you search the Web for free hosting service providers and set up an account so you can publish your documents.

1. Launch a browser and go to www.google.com.

2. Type in "free Web hosting" in the Search field.

    You should receive a long list of free Web hosting services.

3. Find a service that suits your needs, such as the one found at http://free.prohosting.com (shown here). Create an account with the hosting provider.

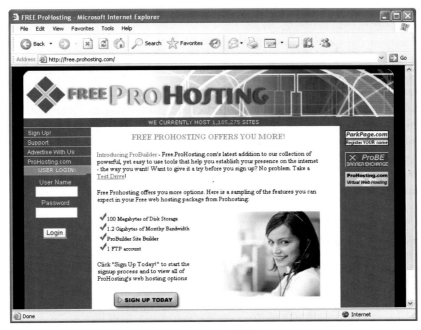

FIGURE 8.21

4. To test the service, upload the entire content of the PoetrySite folder to their server.

5. Navigate through the Web site to ensure all the links work.

4. Validate an Entire Site

Even though you can validate documents on the Web by providing a URL, in this exercise you upload your document to the online validator, and then correct any errors that are returned.

1. Log on to the free online validation service.

2. Upload WIP_08>PoetrySite>emily.htm. Validate the document.

   You should receive a long list of errors that includes capital commands, missing quotes, and missing ending tags.

3. Using the error results page, navigate through the source file and make the necessary corrections.

4. Save the changes to the file. Reupload the file to the validation service. Correct any errors that remain.

5. Repeat this process with the rest of the documents in the PoetrySite folder.

6. Close all open files and applications.

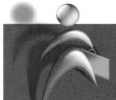

PORTFOLIO BUILDER

Publish a Portfolio Web Site

A published Web portfolio provides a very effective way to show your work to potential clients — all they need is an Internet connection to view your entire collection of pieces. Before you can publish an online portfolio of your work, however, you need to create the files, which should have been done in Chapter 4. If you did not complete the Portfolio Builder in Chapter 4, please do so now, and then you can complete this exercise.

To publish your portfolio site:

- Examine your source code to determine which document type definition is best for your pages. Validate your documents against that DTD.

- Depending on your specific needs, you can decide if you need to purchase a domain name of your own, or if you can use the domain name of your Web hosting service.

- After you decide whether to host your site with a free service or pay for a service, create a hosting account.

- If you choose to use a free Web hosting service, find out if the service will place any kind of advertisement on your page. You must consider how advertisements will affect your site's design.

- Upload your pages using whatever FTP method your hosting provider suggests.

- Make sure you include **<meta>** tags for each of your Web pages, regardless of whether you manually index your pages or you use a service that indexes the pages for you.

- Register each of your pages with the search engines of your choice.

CHAPTER

Using Cascading Style Sheets (CSS)

OBJECTIVES

In this chapter, you learn how to:

- Use inline style sheets

- Redefine HTML tags

- Apply custom classes and ID selectors

- Add pseudo-classes

- Link to external CSS files

- Apply "the box" analogy and positioning

- Control invisibility and layering

Why Would I Do This?

HTML was never well suited to control the formatting of a Web page. XHTML deals with this problem by removing most formatting options from the language and using other technologies to control the formatting of the page. Cascading Style Sheets (CSS) is the most popular technology for Web page formatting. CSS is tightly integrated into XHTML; therefore, no modern XHTML textbook is complete without a basic discussion of CSS.

Cascading Style Sheets were designed to separate the style of a Web page from its content. When you use CSS, HTML still describes the content, so the context of the data remains intact. With the content in place, Cascading Style Sheets allow you to define the appearance of page elements in a single block of code. For instance, you can define the font for an entire document in one style sheet, without placing multiple **<font>** tags throughout the document. This method ensures greater consistency using simpler code that downloads faster.

CSS has capabilities that go beyond the scope of this book. The examples concerning CSS are meant to serve as an introduction for aspiring Web designers. After completing this book, you may want to consult a reference manual that offers a more in-depth exploration of CSS.

Similar to other new technologies, CSS was originally implemented inconsistently in different Web browsers. This led to compatibility problems when developing Web pages, which stopped many Web designers and developers from using the technology. As CSS has grown more standardized over the last few years, it has become a mainstream technology designated to play an important role in the future of Web design.

CSS offers several advantages over traditional HTML formatting:

- A single style sheet can control the appearance of an entire Web site. By changing a single style sheet, you can change the appearance of the entire site.

- CSS allows greater control over the positioning of elements. Items can be precisely positioned on the page, even overlapped. Anyone who has used HTML tables to lay out a complex Web page understands the need for enhanced precision when positioning items.

- CSS allows greater control over formatting. For instance, you can specify the exact number of pixels or points to use for your font sizes, instead of choosing generic sizes in HTML.

- CSS allows designers to customize HTML for a Web page. For instance, you can modify the **<p>** tag to always display text in 10-point Arial.

- HTML is slowly being replaced by XHTML and XML. Most Web designers and developers will be required to use CSS for both of those languages. Additionally, many HTML presentation tags (such as the **<font>** tag) will be eliminated from the standard.

- You can combine CSS, XHTML, and JavaScript to create striking effects.

XHTML, CSS, and JavaScript were designed to work together as a virtual unit. ***DHTML (Dynamic HTML)*** is a term used to describe the combination of CSS, JavaScript, and XHTML. DHTML allows designers to create animations and other special effects. Designers and developers are expected to increase their understanding of DHTML and discover the advantages of using CSS, JavaScript, and HTML in unison.

This chapter and the one that follows offer an introductory guide to CSS. In this chapter, you consider the basics of CSS.

VISUAL SUMMARY

You can use CSS to enhance and improve Web sites in several different ways. For example, the EyeCareCenter.com site (shown below) uses CSS to position a background image in the upper-right corner of the browser window. No matter how the screen is resized, the image always remains in position in this area.

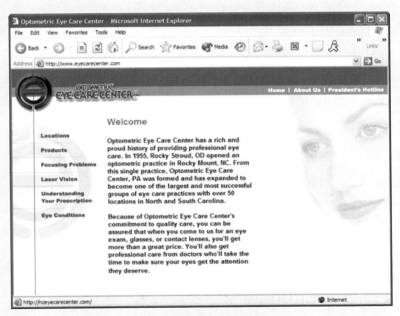

FIGURE 9.1

This is very different than a background image in HTML, which tiles at high resolutions and can't be placed in a specific area of the screen. Using the CSS code in the following figure, you can position the background image in the top-right corner of the page and know that it will remain there regardless of whether the user scrolls down or resizes the browser window.

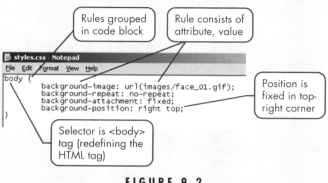

FIGURE 9.2

CSS code consists of *declarations*, which are chunks of CSS that consist of selectors and rules. The *selector* is the class to which the rule is applied. The selector can be an HTML tag, such as all `<table>` tags. When HTML tag names are used as selectors, the rule applied overwrites the default display styles of the tag. This process is known as *redefining HTML tags*. Let's use pseudo-code to explain the structure of CSS statements, which always follow this syntax:

```
selector { property: value; }
```

CSS commands establish rules for selectors. A *rule* is a guideline for how the selector will display on the page. A rule consists of a *property*, such as `background-color` or `font`, followed by a colon, and then the *value* assigned to the property. Depending on the property, the value can take on a number of values, such as `hidden, visible,` or `blue`.

CSS statements end with a semicolon, and multiple CSS statements can be grouped together using brackets (`{}`). You can establish more than one rule within brackets in the same way that multiple statements can be included in most programming languages. Take a moment to examine the following CSS statement:

```
body {
background-color: red;
font-family: Arial, Helvetica, sans-serif;
font-size: 10px;
}
```

In this example, three rules are created for the body selector. In this example, we are redefining the `<body>` tag to override the default display properties. Using this code on a Web page would create a page that has text that is 10 pixels tall, in Arial, Helvetica, or a similar font with a red background color. CSS ignores whitespace in a similar manner to XHTML, so this block of code could also be written this way.

```
body {
background-color: red;
font-family: Arial, Helvetica, sans-serif;
font-size: 10px;
}
```

Or the code could be written in this fashion:

```
body { background-color: red; font-family: Arial, Helvetica,
sans-serif; font-size: 10px; }
```

Developers are likely to see CSS code written all three ways. As an aspiring developer, you should develop your own style that is easy to read and use it consistently.

You can incorporate the CSS shown above into a Web page in three ways:

- As an ***inline style sheet***, which works as an attribute within an HTML tag.

- As an ***embedded style sheet***. Using this method, CSS rules are defined in the HTML document using the **<style>** tag.

- As a ***linked (external) style sheet***. Using this method, the style sheets are saved as external documents, using the ".css" extension. The **<link>** tag links the HTML document to the external file. This is the most powerful way to use style sheets because a single file can control the appearance of an entire Web site or even multiple Web sites.

Selectors can also be custom classes that you can apply to any tag in the document. A ***custom class*** is a rule (or rules) that tells the browser how to display any item to which the selector is applied. In other words, any member assigned to the class takes on the characteristics of the class.

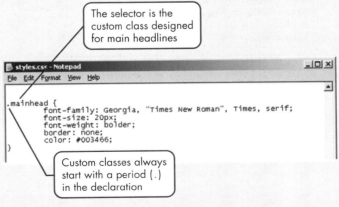

The selector is the custom class designed for main headlines

```
styles.css - Notepad
File  Edit  Format  View  Help

.mainhead {
        font-family: Georgia, "Times New Roman", Times, serif;
        font-size: 20px;
        font-weight: bolder;
        border: none;
        color: #003466;
}
```

Custom classes always start with a period (.) in the declaration

FIGURE 9.3

Inline styles are created with the **style** attribute of HTML tags. The **style** attribute is an extension to HTML that allows you to directly apply styles to a single HTML tag. You create inline styles as follows:

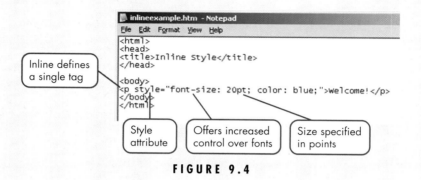

Inline defines a single tag

Style attribute

Offers increased control over fonts

Size specified in points

FIGURE 9.4

You can also create CSS styles to accommodate special situations. These styles are known as *pseudo-classes* because they represent situations that do not exist in HTML. Consider the following code that creates a rollover effect when the user moves the mouse pointer over a hyperlink.

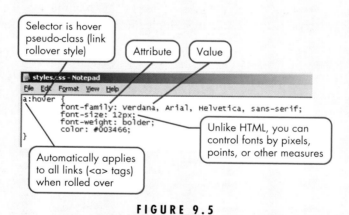

Selector is hover pseudo-class (link rollover style)

Attribute

Value

Unlike HTML, you can control fonts by pixels, points, or other measures

Automatically applies to all links (<a> tags) when rolled over

FIGURE 9.5

One of the most interesting aspects of CSS is its ability to control the placement of an object. In HTML, most positioning is static, meaning items appear in a position according to when they appear in the HTML code. CSS allows greater control over positioning in a number of ways. For instance, you can specify an absolute position, which means that you specify the exact pixel position of an object on the page.

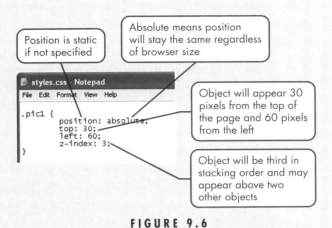

FIGURE 9.6

LESSON 1   Using Inline Style Sheets and Redefining HTML Tags

Inline style sheets appear within HTML tags and are also part of the HTML language. Using this method, CSS rules are established using the **style** attribute of an HTML element, as shown in the following example:

```
<p style="font-size: 12pt; color: blue;">This sentence will display in
12-point blue text.</p>
```

Notice how the rules stated in the **style** attribute are enclosed within quotes. This statement establishes multiple rules that are separated by semicolons (**;**). The rules established in the inline style sheet are written exactly the same as other rules.

Using inline style sheets isn't very different than using tags (such as **<font>**) because you are setting the formatting for each individual tag. This method allows you to use the powerful formatting control of CSS. For instance, you can set the font size to exactly 12 point, as shown in the previous example. This level of control cannot be accomplished with traditional HTML.

Inline style sheets are probably the least powerful way to use CSS because they do not allow you to set the styles for an entire Web page or Web site—which is, as you know, one of the primary benefits of using CSS. When you use CSS to apply styles globally, you reduce file size and ensure a consistent visual representation from section to section and from page to page. In addition, this method makes updating the page/site much simpler. Using inline styles doesn't take advantage of these benefits; for this reason, most developers rarely use inline styles.

Redefining HTML Tags

One of the most interesting aspects of CSS is its ability to customize existing HTML commands. This is also one of the easiest facets of CSS to use and understand. In this context, HTML commands are "redefined" to override the default style of the tag. When you redefine HTML tags, the tag formatting is overridden and replaced by the new rules you create with CSS. For example, consider the following HTML page:

```
<html>
<head>
<title>style1.htm-demonstrates basic CSS</title>
<!-- define a CSS rule for the body tag -->
<style type="text/css">
body {background-color: red;}
</style>
</head>
<body>
My Web page.
</body>
</html>
```

Notice the syntax of the CSS code. The **type="text/css"** tells the browser that you are using a CSS style. The term **background-color** represents the **bgcolor** property of the **<body>** tag. In CSS, properties with more than one word are always hyphenated, such as **background-color** instead of **background color**.

The **<style>** tag creates a style sheet. You are creating a rule that states that the **<body>** tag will always have a red background. You established the rule in the **<head>** section of the document. (This isn't absolutely necessary but seems reasonable because you want the rule applied to the entire page.)

You can also change the **<body>** tag in other ways. For example, consider the EyeCareCenter.com Web site shown in the Visual Summary. No matter how the window is resized, the image always appears in the top-right corner.

As another type of example, consider that you can also use this type of command to redefine the **<table>** tag. Assume that you create a basic HTML page and use the following code to insert a table:

```
<table width="500" height="277" border="3" cellpadding="0"
cellspacing="0">
</table>
table {  background-image: url(images/face_01.gif);
background-repeat: no-repeat;
```

```
background-attachment: fixed;
background-position: right top
}
```

These statements place the image in a fixed position relative to the element that contains it. In the first example, the placement of the image is relative to the body (entire document) that contains it. In the second example, the placement of the image is relative to the table that contains it.

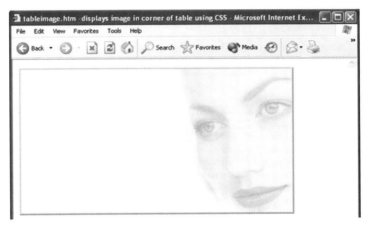

FIGURE 9.7

Redefining HTML tags often involves the use of specific fonts. For instance, the following command eliminates the need of the **<font>** tag in the document:

```
body {  font-family: Arial, Helvetica, sans-serif; font-size: 9px}
```

Because most text appears within the **<p>** tag, you can arrive at the same result by redefining the **<p>** tag:

```
p {  font-family: Arial, Helvetica, sans-serif; font-size: 9px}
```

Lastly, you can define rules for special situations that involve multiple HTML tags. For instance, you could define a rule that sets bold items in a list to the color blue. To do so, you must define a rule that says, "the content between the **** and **** tags should be blue if these tags are contained within the **<li>** and **</li>** tags." You establish this type of rule as follows:

```
li b {color: blue;}
```

Remember, this rule only affects bold type that appears within a list item.

Redefine HTML Tags

1   **Copy the content of the Chapter_09 folder into your Work_In_Progress>WIP_09 folder.**

2	**In your Web browser, open finish.htm from the WIP_09>eyecare folder.**

This is the finished version of the file you work on throughout this chapter.

FIGURE 9.8

3	**After you inspect the file, close it in your Web browser.**

4	**In your Web browser and text editor, open start.htm from the WIP_09>eyecare folder.**

This is your starting point for the page.

FIGURE 9.9

5 | Insert the following code directly before the `</head>` tag.

```html
<html>
<head>
<title>Eye Care Center</title>
<style type="text/css">
h1 {
        font-family: Arial, Helvetica, sans-serif;
        font-size: 18px;
        color: #333333;
        font-weight: bold;
}
</style>
</head>
<body>
<table width="599" border="0" cellspacing="0" cellpadding="0">
. . .
```

This code creates a style for the main headline by redefining the **`<h1>`** tag.

6 | Save the file in your text editor and refresh your browser.

The text of the headline changes.

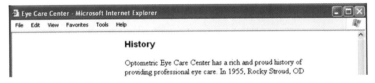

FIGURE 9.10

7 | Insert the following commands directly before the `</style>` tag you just created.

```css
. . .
        color: #333333;
        font-weight: bold;
}
```

```
body {

        font-family: Arial, Helvetica, sans-serif;

        font-size: 10pt;

}
</style>
</head>
<body>

. . .
```

This code creates the style for the content text on the page. Since you want to use this style for most of the text, you can define it as part of the `<body>` tag.

8 | **Save the file in your text editor and refresh your browser.**

The text style changes.

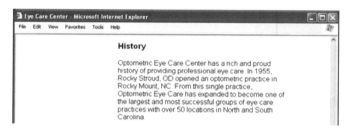

FIGURE 9.11

9 | **Close the file in your browser and text editor.**

To Extend Your Knowledge . . .

RULE INHERITANCE

The term "cascading" refers to the rules of applying style sheets. For instance, a rule that establishes a text style for the `<body>` tag automatically applies to any `<p>` tags unless you override a specific `<p>` tag with a different rule.

DEFAULT STYLES

When defining a rule that you want to serve as a default style throughout a document (such as the style of your content text), it is usually best to redefine the `<body>` tag.

LESSON 2   Using Custom Classes and ID Selectors

Classes can be defined and shared among multiple tags. Instead of assigning a CSS rule to an HTML tag, you can create a custom class and assign the rule to the class. A class name always starts with a period. Consider the following style that turns certain text bold and red:

```
.boldred { font-weight: bold; color: red; }
```

You can assign the **.boldred** class to text by including it in the HTML tag using the **class** attribute.

```
<p class="boldred">This text will display bold and red.</p>
```

The **<span>** tag allows you to apply a style to text that exists within another tag, as shown in the following example:

```
<p>To get your refund <span class="boldred">you must mail in the
enclosed card</span> with the proper information.</p>
```

The **<span>** or **<div>** tag is often used to apply a style to elements that may not otherwise be logically grouped within a single tag. As an example, we may want to create a span or div that contains an explanatory picture and quote. We could apply a border and change the background color and text to set this section apart from the rest of the page.

ID Selectors

ID selectors are very similar to custom classes. Since ID selectors are so similar to custom classes, you may wonder why they are used at all. The reason is that *ID selectors* are designed for one-time usage; you create an ID selector for a single element. The primary reason for ID selectors is to create a single element that can be referenced in JavaScript or other scripting languages.

A period starts the name of a class, but a hash symbol (**#**) marks the beginning of an ID selector. For instance, if you want to create an ID selector named **blue**, you would write

```
#blue {color:blue}
```

To define a table that will be used as a quote, you would write

```
table#quote { font-size: 10 pt }
```

The previous statement requires you to use the **ID** attribute in the HTML tag that represents this selector, as shown here:

```
<table ID="quote">
```

Create and Use a Custom Class

1 **In your text editor and browser, open customclasses.htm from your WIP_09>eyecare folder.**

This is essentially the same file you used in the previous lesson.

2 **In your text editor, insert the following code directly before the `</style>` tag.**

```
. . .
        font-family: Arial, Helvetica, sans-serif;
        font-size: 10pt;
}
.quote {
        font-family: Arial, Helvetica, sans-serif;
        font-size: 9pt;
        font-weight: bold;
}
</style>
</head>
<body>
. . .
```

This code creates a custom class for quotes. In CSS code, a period is always the first character in the name of a custom class.

3 **Find the following code in your document.**

```
<p>&quot;My family has gone to Optometric Eye Care Center
```

This marks the beginning of the quote.

4 **Change the statement to the following:**

```
<p class="quote">&quot;My family has gone to Optometric Eye Care
Center
```

This code applies the custom class to the quote in the document.

5 **Save the file in your text editor and refresh your browser.**

The quote text becomes slightly smaller and bold.

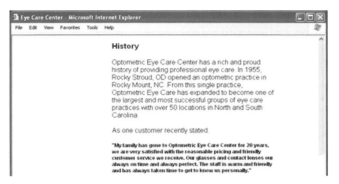

FIGURE 9.12

6 **Keep the file open in your text editor and browser for the next exercise.**

Create and Use an ID Selector

1 **In the open customclasses.htm, insert the following code directly before `</style>` tag.**

```
. . .
font-size: 9pt;
        font-weight: bold;
}
#menu {
        font-family: Verdana, Arial, Helvetica, sans-serif;
        font-size: 12px;
}
</style>
</head>
<body>
. . .
```

This code creates an ID selector for the menu of hyperlinks at the bottom of the page.

2 **Scroll to the bottom of the page and find the following code:**

```
<p><a href="locations.htm">Locations</a>
```

3   **Change the code to the following:**

```
<p id="menu"><a href="locations.htm">Locations</a>
```

This code applies the ID selector to the **<a>** tag.

4   **Save the file in your text editor and refresh your browser.**

5   **Scroll to the bottom of the page to see the text style applied to the links.**

FIGURE 9.13

Users who have their default font set to Arial may not see a significant change.

6   **Close the file in your browser and text editor.**

To Extend Your Knowledge . . .

INHERITANCE

In the previous exercise, you applied an ID selector to the **<p>** tag that enclosed the hyperlinks. In this instance, the text in the **<a>** tags inherits the properties of the parent **<p>** tag. You can override the parent properties by assigning properties to the **<a>** tag.

LESSON 3   Using Pseudo-Classes

The word "pseudo" means fake, pretend, or artificial. The term pseudo-class represents situations that don't actually occur in HTML. For instance, the **a:hover** class doesn't exist in HTML but allows us to create a rollover effect for hyperlinks—without using images.

Pseudo-classes were designed to cover special situations. For instance, the **<a>** tag in HTML establishes a hyperlink. You can set up HTML code to change the color of a hyperlink, change the color of a selected link, or change the color of a previously visited link. Consider the following example, where the link color is set to a dark gray (**#666666**), the visited link color to a light gray (**#CCCCCC**), and the active link color to white (**#FFFFFF**).

```
<a href="#" link="#666666" vlink="#CCCCCC" alink="#FFFFFF">Link</a>
```

Using CSS, you can set the same properties in the following fashion:

```
a:link {
      color: #666666;
}
a:visited {
      color: #CCCCCC;
}
a:active {
      color: #FFFFFF;
}
```

The most useful pseudo-class in CSS is probably **a:hover**, which allows you to define a rule that specifies what happens when a user rolls the mouse over a hyperlink. Consider the following CSS statement, which changes a link color to green when a user moves the mouse over the link:

```
a:hover {
      color: #009966;
}
```

As an alternative, you could have used **onmouseover** events in the **<a>** tags, but the **a:hover** pseudo-class provides the added advantage of allowing you to set up one simple rollover that affects all of the links on the page.

Use Pseudo-Classes in an HTML Document

1   **In your text editor and browser, open pseudoclasses.htm from your WIP_09 folder.**

This is essentially the same file you used in the previous lesson.

2   **Insert the following code directly before the </style> tag in the head section of the document.**

```
...
font-family: Verdana, Arial, Helvetica, sans-serif;
      font-size: 12px;

}
a:link {
      color: #330066;

}
a:visited {
      color: #CCCCCC;

}
a:active {
```

```
        color: #666666;
    }
    a:hover {
        color: #993333;
    }
    </style>
    </head>
    <body>
    . . .
```

3   **Save the file in your text editor and refresh your browser.**

Links now display in dark blue, visited links display in light gray, and active links display in dark gray. The links should change to burgundy when you move the mouse over them.

FIGURE 9.14

4   **Close the file in your text editor and browser.**

To Extend Your Knowledge . . .

WHEN TO USE ID SELECTORS

Use ID selectors when you want to apply a style to a single element on the page and when you want to access the element in JavaScript or another scripting language.

LESSON 4   Linking to External CSS Files

An *external style sheet* is CSS code placed in a separate (external) file. This is the most powerful way to use CSS since a single text file can control the formatting of an entire site. As a matter of convention, an external CSS file is a text file saved with a ".css" extension.

The text file contains only the CSS code you need in the site. For instance, let's assume that you want to create three CSS rules. One rule is for the primary headline of each page, which is used with the **<h1>** tag. Another rule is for the secondary headline of each page, which is used with the **<h2>** tag. A third rule is for the content text on each page, which displays between each **<p>** and **</p>** tag. Let's start by creating a text file with the following code:

```
P {font-family: sans-serif; font-size: small; color:gray}
H1 {font-family: serif; font-size: x-large; color: blue}
H2 {font-family: serif; font-size: large; color: blue}
```

To apply the external style sheet to an HTML file, you use the **<link>** tag. For instance, if you name the file stylesheet.css, you can include the following code in the head section of the HTML document:

```
<link rel="stylesheet" href="stylesheet.css" type="text/css">
```

Link an External Style Sheet to an Existing File

1   **In your text editor and browser, open external.htm from your WIP_09>eyecare folder.**

This is essentially the same file you used in the previous lesson.

2   **Select all the text between the <style> and </style> tags. (Do not select the <style> tag or the </style> tag as part of your selection area.)**

FIGURE 9.15

3   **Choose Edit>Cut to remove the text from the document.**

4   **Save the file in your text editor.**

5 Create a new text file. Choose Edit>Paste to paste the CSS code you cut in Step 2 into the new text file.

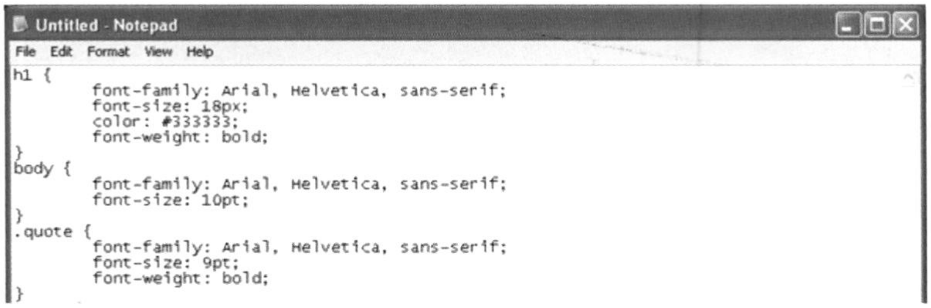

```
Untitled - Notepad
File  Edit  Format  View  Help
h1 {
        font-family: Arial, Helvetica, sans-serif;
        font-size: 18px;
        color: #333333;
        font-weight: bold;
}
body {
        font-family: Arial, Helvetica, sans-serif;
        font-size: 10pt;
}
.quote {
        font-family: Arial, Helvetica, sans-serif;
        font-size: 9pt;
        font-weight: bold;
}
```

FIGURE 9.16

6 Save the file as "mystyles.css" in the WIP_09>eyecenter folder.

7 If it is not already open, reopen external.htm in your text editor from the WIP_09>eyecenter folder.

8 Find the following code in the head of the document:

```
<style type="text/css">
</style>
```

9 Delete the code you found in Step 8 and replace it with the following:

```
<html>
<head>
<title>Eye Care Center</title>
<link rel="stylesheet" href="mystyles.css" type="text/css">
</head>
<body>
<table width="599" border="0" cellspacing="0" cellpadding="0">
. . .
```

10 Save the file in your text editor and refresh your browser.

The styles are integrated from the external file you created.

11 Close the file in your text editor and browser.

To Extend Your Knowledge . . .

CUSTOM HOVER CLASSES

The `a:hover` pseudo-class allows you to create a uniform rollover effect for a page. You can also create custom classes, such as `a.top:hover` and `a.left:hover`, when you want to create different rollover effects for multiple navigation structures. You apply pseudo-classes to individual tags just as you apply other custom classes, such as `<a href="#" class="top">`.

LESSON 5   Understanding "the Box" Analogy and Positioning

CSS allows much greater control over the positioning of elements than allowed by traditional HTML. For the most part in HTML, the browser positions elements on the Web page in the order they appear in the source code, which is referred to as *static positioning*. Using CSS, you specify precise coordinates to position any element in an exact position on the screen, which is referred to as *absolute positioning*. Using absolute positioning, you can place elements in specific areas of the screen, such as the top, left, bottom, or right, or at an exact distance from the top, left, bottom, or right edges.

Relative positioning allows you to offset an element relative to where it would normally appear in the document. For example, you could specify that an image should appear 50 pixels to the left of where it would appear by default. When an element appears inside another element, such as when you use the `<span></span>` tags within the `<p></p>` tags, you can set the position of the element relative to the parent element. For instance, if an image resides within a table, you can specify that the image should appear on the right side of the table. If you prefer, you can place the image a specific number of pixels from the right side of the table.

Sometimes, images must remain unaffected when the page on which they reside scrolls up or down. To control an image in this way, you can place an image in a particular place on the screen, and then specify that the image should remain in that position when a user scrolls down the page; this is referred to as *fixed positioning*.

You can also specify whether an image should be visible or invisible. The `visibility` property determines whether you can see the element on the page. If you use the `visibility` property to make an element invisible (assign a value of `hidden`), space is still reserved for the element in the document's layout (in case you want to see the element later). As an alternative, you can use the `display` property to make an element invisible, but this property removes the element from the layout and does not reserve room for it.

The ability to specify the exact position of an element creates the possibility that elements might overlap one another. In this case, you can use the *z-index property* to specify the stacking order of positioned elements. You can stack elements above or below other elements. By default, elements are stacked from back to front in the order in which they appear in the HTML document.

The "Box" Analogy

CSS treats every element as if it were contained within an invisible box. The box contains (1) the element, (2) a padding area around the object, (3) a border around the padding area, and (4) an invisible margin around the border. You can control the padding, margin, and border through various CSS properties.

CSS was designed to give designers increased control over various aspects of each element. The "box" analogy is important because it affects the positioning of objects on the page. In addition, you can turn the visibility of the boxes on and off.

Positioning

With HTML, you have one positioning choice: the static model, which means the elements appear on the page in the order they appear in the code. CSS, on the other hand, supports many ways to position elements, including static positioning, absolute positioning, and relative positioning.

Absolute positioning allows you to move and position elements anywhere on the page. By specifying *X,Y* coordinates, you can place elements anywhere within the content area of the browser. The content area is where HTML pages display; in other words, the main part of the browser window, not including the title bar, location bar, status bar, and other browser controls. Absolute positioning also allows you to stack objects on top of one another.

Relative positioning starts with the place the element would normally appear if static positioning were applied and allows you to move the element relative to that position. In other words, you can move an element relative to the parent element that contains it (such as the browser window or a table).

You can use the **position** property to set the position of any element. The **position** property can be set to a value of **static, absolute, relative**, or **fixed**. The default value is **static**, which will be applied if no value is specified.

You can apply the **background-attachment** property to set the absolute position of an element with attributes such as **left, top, right**, or **bottom**. This property usually takes two attributes, such as **bottom** and **left** or **top** and **right**. The **background-attachment** property also has the added benefit of placing the element in the background, so the element doesn't affect the placement of other elements on the page.

Use Absolute Positioning

In this exercise, you use absolute positioning and the **background-attachment** property to place an image.

1   **In your text editor, open mystyles.css from the WIP_09>eyecare folder.**

This is the external CSS file that you created in the previous exercise.

2   **Find the following CSS code that redefines the <body> tag.**

```
. . .

body {
        font-family: Arial, Helvetica, sans-serif;
        font-size: 10pt;
}

. . .
```

3   **Insert the following code:**

```
. . .

body {
        font-family: Arial, Helvetica, sans-serif;
        font-size: 10pt;
        background-image: url(images/face.jpg);
        background-repeat: no-repeat;
        background-position: left top;
}
.quote {
        font-family: Arial, Helvetica, sans-serif;

. . .
```

This code inserts the background image on the page.

4   **Save the file in your text editor.**

5   **In your browser, open external.htm from the WIP_09>eyecare folder.**

This is the file that you modified in the previous lesson. Notice the background image in the top-left corner of the document.

FIGURE 9.17

6   **Make sure your Web browser is sized small enough for the scroll bars to appear. Scroll to the bottom of the page.**

The image scrolls with the rest of the page because the default position is `static`.

FIGURE 9.18

7   **Return to the mystyles.css file in your text editor. Find the code for the body selector and insert the following line:**

. . .

```
background-image: url(images/face.jpg);
background-repeat: no-repeat;
background-position: left top;
background-attachment: fixed;
}
```

```
.quote {

     font-family: Arial, Helvetica, sans-serif;

...
```

This code changes the background image to a fixed position.

8   **Save your changes to mystyles.css and refresh external.htm in your Web browser.**

If you do not currently see a scroll bar, resize your window to force the scroll bars to appear. The image remains in a fixed position on the screen, even though the text scrolls.

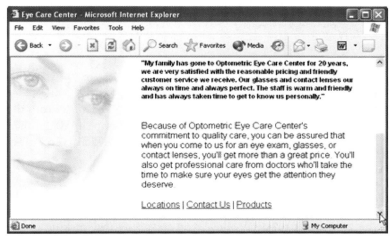

FIGURE 9.19

9   **Close the file in your browser and text editor.**

To Extend Your Knowledge . . .

PROPERTIES AS PERCENTAGES

The `left` and `top` properties may be expressed as percentages. Other properties, such as right or bottom, may not be expressed as percentages.

POSITIONING AND BROWSER COMPATIBILITY

Use the `<div>` or `<span>` tags around elements that you want to position. Doing so helps to avoid compatibility issues in older browsers.

LESSON 6   Controlling Invisibility and Layering

You can use the **visibility** or **display** properties to control the visibility of elements on a page. If you use the **visibility** property to make an element invisible, the page layout reserves space for the element, even though you can't see it.

```
.hidden {
     visibility: hidden;
}
```

The **display** property is similar to the **visibility** property, but the **display** property removes the element from the layout, as well as removes the space the element occupied. To use the **display** property to remove an element, you would write

```
display:none;
```

At this point, you may wonder about the usefulness of the **visibility** and **display** properties. To illustrate their importance, imagine that you want a menu to appear when a user rolls the mouse pointer over a button. When the user rolls off the button, you want the menu to disappear. When the user rolls over another button, you want the menu to change. Using the **visibility** and **display** properties with JavaScript allows you to create these (and other) advanced effects.

The Z-Index Property

As you learned earlier, the **z-index** property allows you to specify the stacking order for the elements on a page. This feature allows you to layer various elements, which can exist on top of or below other elements. You assign a number as the **z-index** property, which represents the element's position in the stack.

The **z-index** attribute can also be set to a value of **auto**. Elements with a value of **auto** take the default value that would normally be assigned by the browser. The **auto** attribute is only used in rare situations.

Elements with a low **z-index** value appear below elements with a higher **z-index** value. For example, if the highest-numbered element in a stack has a **z-index** of **9**, elements with **z-index** **1–8** would appear below this element in the stack. To apply the **z-index** property to elements, you must first set their positioning.

A *layer* is a term many Web designers use to describe the use of CSS elements with absolute positioning and **z-index** values. When creating a layer (which can be any HTML element), designers typically add **<div>** and **</div>** or **** and **** tags around the items they want to move and stack, but doing so is not required. In the recent past, most designers avoided using layers due to compatibility issues with Netscape version 4 browsers. Most positioning incompatibilities have been resolved in current browsers, and the use of layers is quickly becoming commonplace.

Make Items Invisible

1   **In your text editor, open mystyles.css from the WIP_09>eyecare folder.**

This is the external CSS file you created earlier.

2   **Insert the following CSS code at the end of the document to create a new custom class.**

```
. . .
a:hover {
      color: #993333;
}
.hidden {
      visibility: hidden;
}
```

3   **Save your changes to the file.**

4   **In your text editor and browser, open invisible.htm from the WIP_09>eyecare folder.**

This is essentially the same page you used in the previous lessons.

5   **Find the following code in the document:**

```
<p class="quote">&quot;My family
```

This **<p>** tag uses a custom class that you created earlier.

6   **Change the class by changing the code to read as follows:**

```
<p class="hidden">&quot;My family
```

7   **Save the file in your text editor and refresh your browser.**

The paragraph referenced by the custom class is now invisible. Notice the browser still leaves room for the element even though it is no longer visible.

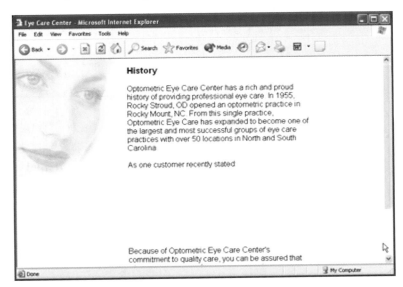

FIGURE 9.20

8   **Return to mystyles.css in your text editor. Find the following code at the bottom of the document:**

```
.hidden {
     visibility: hidden;
}
```

You created this code in Step 2.

9   **Change the code to the following:**

```
.hidden {
     display: none;
}
```

10   **Save the file in your text editor and refresh your Web browser.**

The **display** property removes the area reserved for the invisible element.

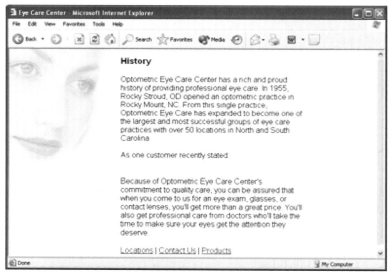

FIGURE 9.21

11   **Close the file in your Web browser and text editor.**

Use Absolute Positioning

1   **In your Web browser and text editor, open absolute.htm from the WIP_09>absolute folder.**

This simple HTML file includes three **<img>** tags and displays three pictures.

FIGURE 9.22

2   **In your text editor, insert the following code directly before the </head> tag:**

```
<html>
<head>
<title>absolute.htm - shows absolute positioning</title>
<style type="text/css">
.pic1 { position: absolute;
     top: 50;
     left: 60;
}
</style>
</head>
<body>
<img src="smallpic1.jpg" width="90" height="90" />
. . .
```

3   **Find the following code that establishes the first image.**

```
<img src="smallpic1.jpg" width="90" height="90" />
```

4   **Change the statement to apply the class you created in Step 2.**

```
<img src="smallpic1.jpg" width="90" height="90" class="pic1" />
```

5 **Save the page in your text editor and refresh your browser.**

The position of the image changes from its original static location to the absolute position you specified in the code.

FIGURE 9.23

6 **Return to your text editor and add the following code directly before the `</style>` tag to create a second custom class:**

```
. . .
      top: 50;
      left: 60;
}
.pic2 { position: absolute;
      top: 50;
      right: 60;
}
</style>
</head>
<body>
. . .
```

This code specifies a location of 50 pixels from the top margin and 60 pixels from the right margin.

7 **Find the second `<img>` tag in your document and change the code to apply the second custom class.**

```
. . .
</head>
<body>
```

```
<img src="smallpic1.jpg" width="90" height="90" class="pic1" />
<img src="smallpic2.jpg" width="90" height="90" class="pic2" />
<img src="smallpic3.jpg" width="90" height="90" />
</body>
</html>
```

8 **Save the file in your text editor and refresh your browser.**

FIGURE 9.24

9 **Change the size of the browser window.**

The image should remain 60 pixels from the left margin no matter how you resize the window.

10 **Return to your text editor and find the custom class for the second image, as shown in the following code:**

```
. . .
.pic2 { position: absolute;
      top: 50;
      right: 60;
}
. . .
```

11 **Change the code to replace the word "top" with the word "bottom".**

```
. . .
.pic2 { position: absolute;
      bottom: 50;
      right: 60;
}
. . .
```

12 **Save the file in your text editor and refresh your browser.**

13 **Change the size of the browser window.**

The image should stay 50 pixels from the bottom of the window no matter how you resize the window.

14 **Close the file in your text editor and browser.**

Use the Z-Index Property to Layer Elements

1 **In your text editor and browser, open zindex.htm from your WIP_09>absolute folder.**

This file is similar to the one you created in the previous exercise.

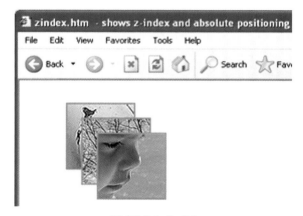

FIGURE 9.25

The page uses absolute positioning to "layer" each image on top of the other ones. The images are layered according to the order in which they appear in the HTML document — the first image appears on the bottom because it appears first in the code.

2 **Find the following code in the head of the document. It establishes the position of the first image.**

```
. . .

.pic1 { position: absolute;
     top: 30;
     left: 60;
}

. . .
```

3   Change this code to the following to establish a z-index of 3.

```
...
.pic1 { position: absolute;
    top: 30;
    left: 60;
    z-index: 3;
}
.pic2 { position: absolute;
    top: 50;
    left: 80;
...
```

4   Save the file in your text editor and refresh your browser.

The first picture moves to the top of the stacking order.

FIGURE 9.26

The images always appear with the lowest z-index value on the bottom and the highest on the top of the stacking order.

5   Close the file in your text editor and browser.

To Extend Your Knowledge . . .

USING CUSTOM CLASSES

Remember, custom classes use a period in the selector when the rule is created. The period is not used in the HTML. For example, the rule `.quote { color:blue; }` could be applied by a statement such as `<p class="quote>`, but not `<p class=".quote">`. This is a common mistake when applying classes.

LAYERING

A `z-index` parameter is not required when elements overlap. The browser automatically assigns a stacking order based on where the elements appear in the code. If you want to change the default stacking order, you must use the `z-index` parameter.

S U M M A R Y

In this chapter, you considered the basic uses of CSS. You received adequate background to use CSS as a formatting tool. Now you are prepared to use CSS and XHTML together to create formatting effects that are impossible with traditional HTML only.

You discovered that CSS was created to separate the content (markup) of a Web page from its formatting. CSS allows designers to override the default styles used by the browser. It also allows developers to create custom styles that they can apply whenever necessary. CSS allows you to remove many formatting tags, including the `<font>` and `<b>` tags. Using CSS, you can write simpler, shorter code, accompanied by smaller file sizes.

You learned that you must use declarations to create CSS statements. Declarations consist of a selector and a rule. A selector is the object assigned to the rule, and a rule consists of an attribute and a value. A selector can be an HTML tag that you are redefining; it can also be a special situation, known as a "pseudo-class," which is a name given to a rule that you can apply to specific HTML elements.

You discovered that the most powerful way to use CSS is through external style sheets. External style sheets can be linked to HTML documents through the `<link>` tag. Using an external style sheet allows a Web designer to control the formatting of an entire Web site from one external file.

As you completed the lessons in this chapter, you found that CSS allows much greater flexibility in the positioning of elements than can be accomplished using traditional HTML. You can position elements relative to where they would normally appear in the document, or you can use absolute positioning to specify exact coordinates for placing the element on the page. Finally, you learned that using the `z-index` attribute allows designers to control the stacking order of elements that may appear above or below other elements on the page.

KEY TERMS

Absolute positioning	Fixed positioning	Redefining HTML tags
Cascading Style Sheets (CSS)	ID selector	Relative positioning
Custom class	Inline style sheet	Rule
Declaration	Layer	Selector
DHTML (Dynamic HTML)	Linked style sheet	Static positioning
Embedded style sheet	Property	Value
External style sheet	Pseudo-class	Z-index property

CHECKING CONCEPTS AND TERMS

MULTIPLE CHOICE

Circle the letter that matches the correct answer for each of the following questions.

1. How can you use CSS in Web pages?
   a. To override the default styles of HTML tags
   b. To create custom classes
   c. To create a style for a single tag by using its ID
   d. As an inline style placed in a single HTML tag
   e. All of the above
   f. None of the above

2. How are inline styles applied to HTML tags?
   a. By creating a custom class of objects
   b. By redefining the <body> tag
   c. By placing the style in an external file
   d. By using the style attribute in the tag

3. Why do developers often avoid using inline styles?
   a. Because they do not apply to the entire Web page
   b. Because they do not redefine the default style of an HTML tag
   c. Because they do not apply to the entire Web site
   d. All of the above
   e. None of the above

4. Why is an external CSS file the most powerful way to use CSS in a Web site?
   a. Custom classes are only allowed in external CSS files.
   b. ID selectors are only allowed in external CSS files.
   c. Flow-of-control loops in external files can be used to format multiple lines of text.
   d. The appearance of the entire site can be controlled by a single file.

5. What is the default value of the **position** property?

   a. Static

   b. Absolute

   c. Relative

   d. Fixed

6. You can use the _____ pseudo-class to create a text rollover effect when the user moves the mouse over a hyperlink.

   a. a:mouseover

   b. a:rollover

   c. a:hover

   d. a:onclick

7. Since ID selectors are similar to custom classes, why are they used?

   a. Because they allow glow properties

   b. To create an entire class of objects

   c. Because they allow the use of the Back button

   d. To create a single element that can be referenced in JavaScript or other scripting languages

8. If an image's **visibility** property is set to **hidden**, space is still reserved for the image in the layout of the page (even though it is invisible).

   a. True

   b. False

9. If an image's **display** property is set to **none**, space is still reserved for the image in the layout of the page (even though it is invisible).

   a. True

   b. False

10. What constitutes a CSS rule?

   a. Attributes and values

   b. Event handlers and element styles

   c. Layers, elements, and properties

   d. HTML and JavaScript

DISCUSSION QUESTIONS

1. When formatting a Web site, why is CSS a better alternative than HTML?

2. How can you position items in CSS?

3. How does CSS address shortcomings in HTML?

4. Why is the use of CSS in an external file the most powerful way to use CSS? How might this technique make Web site development and maintenance more profitable for a designer?

SKILL DRILL

Skill Drill exercises reinforce chapter skills. Each skill that is reinforced is the same as, or nearly the same as, a skill presented in the chapter. We provide detailed instructions in a step-by-step format. You should work through the exercises in order.

1. Redefine HTML Tags

In this exercise, you add a custom class to an existing HTML document. By adding a custom class, you can define new styles and redefine the default styles of the HTML tag created by the browser.

1. Open WIP_09>skillpopulation.htm in your text editor and browser.

2. In your text editor, insert the following lines of code:

```
. . .
<style type="text/css">
<!--
/* add body styles here */
body {
font-family: Verdana, Arial, Helvetica, sans-serif;
margin: 0px;
}
h1 {
font-size: 18px;
color: #FFFFFF;
. . .
```

3. Insert the following lines of code:

```
. . .
      margin-left: 20px;
      border: thin solid #666666;
}
/* add th & td styles here */
th {font-size: 12px; background-color: #CCCCCC; padding: 2px;}
td {font-size: 11px; background-color: #FFFFCC; padding: 5px;}
.population {
      text-align: center;
```

```
border-right-width: thin;.population {text-align: right;
```

. . .

Notice how each declaration was written onto a single line.

4. Save the file in your text editor and refresh your browser.

5. Leave the file open for the next exercise.

2. Add a Custom Class

In the previous exercise, you added three style rules to a page by redefining HTML tags. In this exercise, you further expand the use of CSS by creating custom classes.

1. In the open skillpopulation.htm in your text editor, insert the following lines of code:

    . . .

    ```
            text-align: right;
        }
        /* Add a custom class */
        .country {
            border-right-width: thin;
            border-right-style: solid;
            border-right-color: #666666;
        }
    .rank {
            border-right-width: thin;
            border-right-style: solid;
            border-right-color: #666666;
        }
        -->
        </style>
        </head>
    ```

    . . .

2. Save the file in your text editor and refresh your browser.

    The custom class adds borders to the columns on the Population table.

3. Close the file in your text editor and browser.

3. Style Pseudo-Classes

In this exercise, you create pseudo-class rules for the `<a>` tag. You create the four states of a link (link, visited, hover, and active), as well as give the browser instructions to use these rules in place of HTML default link colors and styles. Now you can create rollover states without creating graphic images or writing JavaScript code.

1. Open WIP_09>skillcoolcompany.htm in your text editor and browser.

    Some CSS style rules were already created.

2. In your text editor, insert the following lines of code:

    ```
    . . .
            color: #333333;
            margin: 0px;
            text-align:center;}
    /* insert link pseudo-classes here */
    a:link { text-decoration: none;  color: #FFFFFF;}
    a:visited {text-decoration: none;     color: #CCCCCC;}
    a:hover {text-decoration: underline;  color: #FFFF99;}
    a:active {text-decoration: none;      color: #FFFF00;}
    /* html headings */
    h1 {font-size: 24px;  color: #99CCFF; text-align: left;}
    h2 {font-size: 14px;  color: #000000;}
    . . .
    ```

3. Save the file in your text editor and refresh your browser.

    The browser renders links to match the design of the page.

4. Leave the file open for the next exercise.

4. Position Elements

In this exercise, you use **text-align, padding**, and **margin** values to position elements in the browser window. With careful planning, these rules allow designers to bypass the limitations of HTML styles and positioning so they can finely control page layout.

1. In the open skillcoolcompany.htm in your text editor, insert the following code:

    ```
    . . .
    /* This style controls the div placement*/
    #pageHeader {
    ```

```
background-color: #333366;

text-align: right;

width: 533px;

height: 400px;

background-image: url(images/blue_keys.jpg);

padding: 25px 0px 15px 25px;

margin: 0px;

}

/* This style controls the actual link placement*/

-->
```

. . .

2. Save the file in your text editor and refresh your browser.

    The rule you created is applied where the ID selector is used (**id="pageHeader"**). In this case, the **<div>** tag has specified **width, height, background-image, padding**, and **margin** values. The **padding** attribute forces text to move inward from the edges of the div. The **margin** value order is top, right, bottom, and left (the **margin** attribute adds space around a **<div>** tag). In this case, **0px** is specified, which ensures all margins are equal.

3. Insert the following lines of code:

    . . .

```
h2 {font-size: 14px;  color: #000000;}
h3 {font-size: 10px;  color: #999999;}
/* This style controls the actual link placement*/
.pageNavigation {
text-align: right;
padding-right: 330px;
}
-->
</style>
</head>
```

    . . .

    This rule aligns the link text to the right side of the div. The **padding** value holds the link 330 pixels from the right edge.

4. Find the following line of code:

```
h3 {font-size: 10px;  color: #999999;}
```

This is a partial style rule. The formatting of the code is compacted to remove white space. You need to reformat the rule to the default style that you have been using in this chapter, and then modify the code by adding an additional property.

5. Change the code you found in the previous step to the following:

```
. . .
/* html headings */
h1 {font-size: 24px;  color: #99CCFF;  text-align: left;}
h2 {font-size: 14px;  color: #000000;}
h3 {
font-size: 10px;
color: #999999;
margin-top: 200px;
margin-right: 15px;
}
/* This style controls the div placement*/
#pageHeader {
     background-color: #333366;
. . .
```

The **<h3>** tag moves 200 pixels down and 15 pixels in from the edge of the div.

6. Save the file in your text editor and refresh the file in your browser.

7. Close all files in your browser and text editor.

CHALLENGE

Challenge exercises expand on, or are somewhat related to, skills presented in the lessons. Each exercise provides a brief introduction, followed by numbered-step instructions that are not as detailed as those in the Skill Drill exercises. You should work through these exercises in order.

1. Redefine Nested HTML Tags

In this exercise, you use nested tags as selectors to create style rules to format the U.S. Bill of Rights. Creating precise rules allows you to attain a level of visual control that was formerly reserved for print design. Consider the following lines of code that appear in the HTML document.

```
<p><strong>articles</strong>...</p>

<p><strong class="rights">Amendment I:</strong>...</p>
```

Both lines show the **<strong>** tag nested within a **<p>** tag. In this exercise, you create a CSS style rule to apply only to a **<strong>** tag nested within a **<p>** tag.

1. From your WIP_09 folder, open challengecustom.htm in your browser and styles.css in your text editor.

2. Insert the following lines of code in styles.css:

```
...

/* custom selectors.*/

/* controls text when strong tag nested inside paragraph tag

example: "<p><strong>TEXT</strong></p>"  */

p strong {

        font-size: 14px;

        text-transform: uppercase;

        color: #000000;

        margin-right: 5px;

        font-style: italic;

}

/* controls text when strong tag with a class of rights is nested
inside paragraph tag

example: "<p><strong class="rights">TEXT</strong></p>" */

...
```

3. Save the file in your text editor and refresh your browser.

All instances of the **<strong>** tag nested inside a **<p>** tag are styled. Next, you apply a different style to the amendment headings.

4. Insert the following lines of code:

```
...

/* controls text when strong tag with a class of rights is nested
inside paragraph tag

example: "<p><strong class="rights">TEXT</strong></p>"  */

p strong.rights {

        font-size: 12px;
```

```
        text-transform: capitalize;

        color: #000066;

        margin-right: 5px;

        font-style: normal;

}

/* controls text when strong tag nested inside paragraph tag

example: "<td class="header"> <h1>TEXT</h1> </td>"  */

. . .
```

5. Save the file in your text editor and refresh your browser.

6. Keep these files open for the next exercise.

2. Create Custom Pseudo-Classes

In the file you just created, main navigation links exist on the left, and named anchor links exist below each amendment. The way the pseudo-classes for the `<a>` tag are written, both links look the same. Combining the power of pseudo-classes and custom classes allows you to change the appearance of one of the navigation structures to improve the usability of the site.

1. Review the open challengecustom.htm in your browser.

2. In your text editor, insert the following code in styles.css:

```
. . .

a:hover {text-decoration: underline;}

a:active {text-decoration: none;}

/* mainNav html links */

a.mainNav:link {text-decoration: none; color: #000033;}

a.mainNav:visited {text-decoration: none; color: #006699;}

a.mainNav:hover {text-decoration: underline; color: #990000;
background-color: #FFFFFF;}

a.mainNav:active {text-decoration: none; color: #FF0000;}

/* custom classes */

.navigation {

        font-size: 12px;

. . .
```

3.   Save the file in your text editor and refresh challengecustom.htm in your browser.

Links in the main navigation structure and text anchor links display differently.

4.   Close the file in your text editor and browser.

3. Add a Temporary Style for Positioning

CSS displays an element using the box analogy to determine the boundaries of the element. Positioning is affected by the various properties used in the box analogy. This can make positioning difficult, since many of the boundaries of an object are invisible by default. In this exercise, you create a temporary style to resolve this problem.

1.   In your browser, open challengeposition.htm from your WIP_09 folder.

You see two images of Mount Rushmore and the text "Mount Rushmore." With default settings and no styles applied, the document appears rather simplistic.

2.   Open positionstyles.css and challengeposition.htm in your text editor.

3.   In challengeposition.htm, use the `<link>` tag to attach the positionstyles.css file to the HTML page.

4.   Refresh challengeposition.htm in your browser.

The document should now have styles applied. In the next step, you create a temporary style to better see `<div>` tags as you position elements.

5.   Insert the temporary style into the head of the page.

```
. . .
<title>positioning</title>
<!-- create link here -->
<link href="positionStyles.css" rel="stylesheet" type="text/css">
<style type="text/css">
div {
border: thin solid red;
}
</style>
</head>
<body>
<div id="parent">
. . .
```

6. Refresh challengeposition.htm in your browser.

   All **<div>** tags display on-screen with a thin red line around them. This aids in seeing the effect of the **margin** and **padding** values, as well as the effect positioning has on the **<div>** tag.

7. Leave both files open for the next exercise.

4. Use Absolute and Relative Positioning

In the previous exercise, you created a temporary style to make it easier to see the outer boundaries of elements placed on the page. In this exercise, you position the objects and then remove the temporary style you created in the previous exercise.

1. In positionstyles.css, insert the following positioning properties:

   ```
   . . .
          background-color: #999966;

   }

   #parent{

   position:absolute;

   width:800px;

   height:600px;

   z-index:1;

   background-image: url(images/rushmore_bg.jpg);

   border: medium solid #FFFFCC; left: 25px; top: 25px;

   }

   . . .
   ```

   The position is set to **absolute** to make **<div id="parent">...</div>** inherit positioning from the browser window. The **width** and **height** properties are set to make the div the same size as the background image.

2. Insert the following rule for the **<div>** tag with the **child ID**:

   ```
   . . .
   border: medium solid #FFFFCC; left: 25px; top: 25px;

   }
   /* Insert rule for child 1 here */
   ```

```
#child1{
    position:relative;
    width:179px;
    height:121px;
    z-index:4;
    left: 25px;
    top: 38px;
}
/* Insert rule for child 2 here */
#child2{
    #text{
...
```

The **position** is set to **relative** to make **<div id="child1">...</div>** inherit positioning from **<div id="parent">...</div>**. The **width** and **height** properties are set to make the div the same size as the nested image. Finally, the **z-index** is set to **4** to layer the image above the background.

3. Insert a rule for **<div id="child2">...<.div>**.

```
...
    top: 38px;
}
/* Insert rule for child 2 here */
#child2{
    position:relative;
    width:121px;
    height:179px;
    z-index:4;
    top: 180px;
    left: 625px;
}
```

```
#text{

        background-color: #FFFFFF;

}

. . .
```

4. Save positionstyles.css in your text editor and refresh challengeposition.htm in your browser.

    The images reposition in the browser. The banner with "Mount Rushmore" is the last item to reposition.

5. Insert the following lines of code in the **#text** rule:

```
. . .

        left: 625px;

}

#text{

        position:absolute;

        width:100%;

        height:40px;

        z-index:2;

        left: 0px;

        top: 460px;

        background-color: #FFFFFF;

}

. . .
```

6. Remove the temporary div rule you created in the previous challenge from challengeposition.htm.

7. Save positionstyles.css in your text editor and refresh challengeposition.htm in your browser to see the results of your changes.

8. Close both files in your text editor and browser.

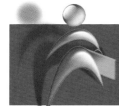

PORTFOLIO BUILDER

Create CSS Rules

In this chapter, you found that utilizing CSS allows you to achieve a level of visual sophistication unavailable with simple HTML. When you construct CSS rules (which are easy to write), you follow simple rules of syntax. How you apply style rules determines their success.

As you learned in the lessons, rules are inherited from parent rules and in turn inherit the styles of nested rules (children). By creating a style rule to apply a font to the **<body>** tag contents, (**<body>...</body>**), you force nested tags to inherit your choice of font. Any **<h1>...</h1>** content will appear in the same font face unless you create a rule that applies specifically to **<h1>** tags.

To complete this Portfolio Builder, follow these steps:

1.   Open cssinheritance.htm from your WIP_09 folder in your Web browser. The document contains default HTML heading, anchor, and paragraph styles.

2.   Attach the style sheet inheritthestyle.css.

3.   Preview cssinheritance.htm again in your browser. The page shows which heading (**h1, h2, h3, h4, h5, h6**) controls which content. This structure creates "content hierarchy," which allows for easier data surfing by individuals with disabilities. Creating style rules for body pages and heading tags allows you to control the visual hierarchy of your content.

4.   Modify the body style rule to add a **font-family** of **Verdana, Arial, Helvetica, sans-serif**, and a **font-size** of **11px**. This expanded rule allows you to control the use of font, as well as set a base font size of 11 pixels. Any tag in the body without a specific style rule will inherit these font values.

5.   Next, add heading styles to control the visual balance of elements. We recommend using the following values:

Redefine	Font size (pixels)	Color (hexadecimal)	Style
h1	36	#E8FDFF	bold
h2	22	#666666	bold
h3	14	#990000	bold
h4	14	#FFFFFF	bold
h5	10	#666666	bold
h6	10	#999999	bold

6.   When creating the rules for headings, consider that each heading has a **style** value of **bold**. You could easily write each rule to contain the **bold** value. Remember, however, that you can combine CSS rules. To simplify your styles, you can create a companion style for your headings. Any heading rule will inherit this rule, as well as use its individual style rule. Any heading style could in turn ignore the **bold** value by specifying its own style. By specifying **normal**, you can ignore this inheritance.

```
h1, h2, h3, h4, h6, h6 {

    font-style: bold;

}
```

CHAPTER **10**

Working with Advanced Layouts

OBJECTIVES

In this chapter, you learn how to:

- Nest tables in an advanced layout
- Apply headers and footers to tables
- Work with column groups

- Style table content
- Add table background information
- Format table borders

Why Would I Do This?

Tables have been used as a Web page layout tool for quite some time; tables were not designed for that purpose, but rather to display tabular content. In Chapter 9, you discovered that CSS offers a far more appropriate method for page layout (called *divs*), which were specifically designed for the task.

At the time of this writing, HTML and XHTML Transitional tables are still widely used in Web page layouts. This being said, tables combined with Cascading Style Sheets offer an advanced technique for Web page layout and design. As a Web page author, you must determine which methods are the most effective choices for your unique requirements.

In this chapter, you take a closer look at using tables, CSS, and divs to format the pages of a Web site. The advanced formatting techniques covered include nesting tables, setting sizes, and using Cascading Style Sheets to control the appearance of tables.

VISUAL SUMMARY

A *template* is one of the most important components in the design of a Web site. Templates define the general layout of a document, allowing you to provide a common look and feel that is so important in creating a positive user experience. In addition, templates provide all the elements in the user interface. Using templates to develop Web pages, you can concentrate on creating effective content, rather than focus on site maintenance.

It's likely that your pages will conform to one or two template styles — usually to a main page style and a secondary page style. When you set up a new Web page template, place ease of maintenance at the top of your list of concerns. Choose styles that lend themselves to easy editing. There is little sense in implementing a complicated, multilevel style when it is not necessary to do so. Using templates will save countless hours of development time, not to mention frustration.

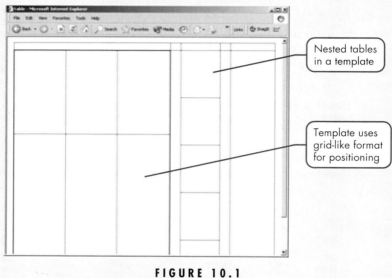

FIGURE 10.1

Figure 10.1 illustrates a layout (template) that uses only tables. As the illustration shows, you can use nested tables to achieve the desired visual effect. When you use this method of design, however, you are faced with compatibility and editing issues. In the upcoming XHTML standard, using tables for Web page layout will be deprecated in favor of using XHTML for structure and CSS for presentational design.

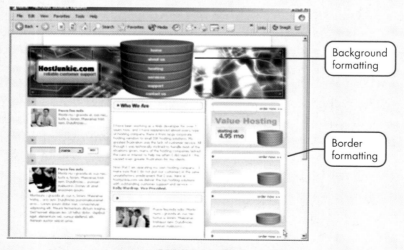

FIGURE 10.2

Figure 10.2 shows how you can use CSS to change a table display. Even though choosing CSS to change the table display is better than using some of the formatting attributes in the HTML/XHTML Transitional standard, the table is still being misused in this example.

Content positioning using CSS

FIGURE 10.3

Figure 10.3 illustrates elements on a Web page positioned with CSS. Even though it is sometimes challenging to find the correct coordinates, it is likely the best option for positioning content on a page. Nonetheless, you should analyze your specific needs for each new Web page to determine which method is most appropriate.

LESSON 1   Working with Advanced Table Layouts

Before you begin any Web site project, you should create a storyboard that illustrates where the main content of the page will display. Completing this important initial step saves significant time during the production stage of the chapter. As you design your storyboard, it becomes readily apparent if you need to work with tables, nested tables, or other block elements to create the layout and flow of your site.

Working with nested tables can prove difficult, especially if you created the tables in a Web-editing program such as Macromedia Dreamweaver. When you work with Web-editing programs, the direct hands-on time you spend with the source code is usually quite limited. If a problem arises with an intricate table design, you might find it difficult to edit the source code and find the answer to the problem because you are unfamiliar with the code.

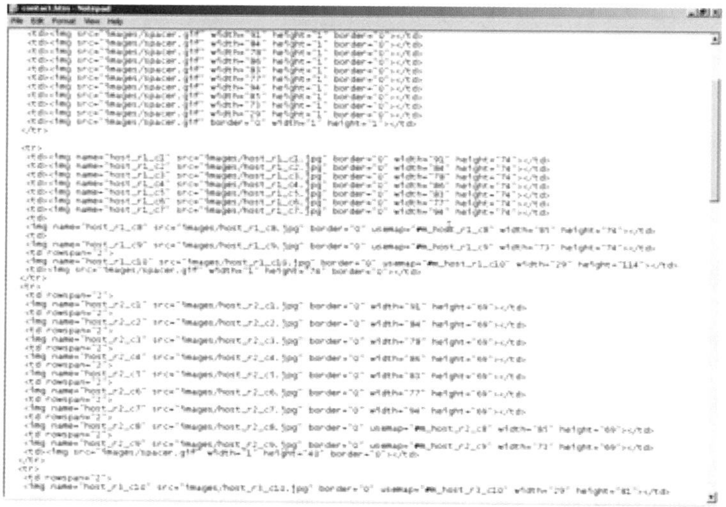

FIGURE 10.4

Figure 10.4 shows source code created in a Web-editing program. As you can see, following the code that defines the table is quite challenging. When you use a Web editor to develop templates that contain multiple nested tables, work hands-on with the code as much as possible to achieve better results. Another suggestion is to use <comment> tags to identify where one table ends and another begins.

Create a Multinested Table

1   **Copy the contents of your Chapter_10 folder to the Work_In_Progress>WIP_10 folder.**

2   **Open WIP_10>HangRight>index.htm in your browser and text editor.**

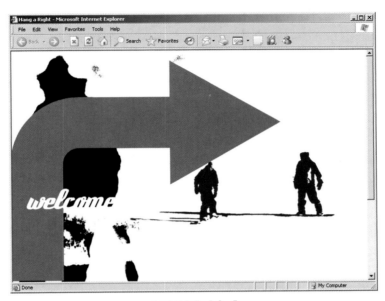

FIGURE 10.5

The Web page displays what appears to be a single image. When you view the document in the text editor, however, you see that the design is actually multiple images pieced together within a table.

3   **In the open index.htm file, create a nested table that displays text content on the page.**

```
. . .
<html><head><title>Hang a Right</title></head>
<body bgcolor="ffffff" topmargin="0" leftmargin="0"
marginheight="0" marginwidth="0">

<table border="0" cellpadding="0" cellspacing="0" width="750"
align="left">

     <tr>

     <td width="50%"><img src="images/topleft.gif" border="0"
width="353" height="406" /></td>

     <td width="50%"><img src="images/topright.gif"
border="0" width="397" height="406" /></td>

     </tr>
```

```
<tr>
     <td width="50%">
<img src="images/left.gif" border="0" width="353"
height="267"><p>
<img border="0" src="images/space.gif" width="1"
height="1"></p>
<p><img border="0" src="images/space.gif" width="1"
height="1"></p>
<p><img border="0" src="images/space.gif" width="1"
height="1"></p>
<p><img border="0" src="images/space.gif" width="1"
height="1"></p>
<p> </p>
</td>
     <td width="50%" valign="top">
<!--CONTENT TABLE-->
     <table border="0" cellpadding="0" cellspacing="0"
width="390"  align="center">
     <tr>
     <td>

     </td>
     <td>

</td>
<td>

</td>
</tr>

<tr>
<td colspan="3">

</td>
```

```
</tr>
<tr>
<td>

</td>
<td>

</td>
<td>

</td>
</tr>
<tr>
<td colspan="3">

</td>
</tr>
</table>
<!--END OF CONTENT TABLE-->
</td>
</tr>
</table>
</body>
```

? If you have problems

As you complete the exercises in this chapter, pay careful attention to changes in the code. In many of the steps, you replace existing code and add new code. If you experience unexpected results, check the steps and make sure you didn't miss any new or replaced code.

4   **Save the file in your text editor and refresh your browser.**

No changes appear because you have not yet added content to the new table.

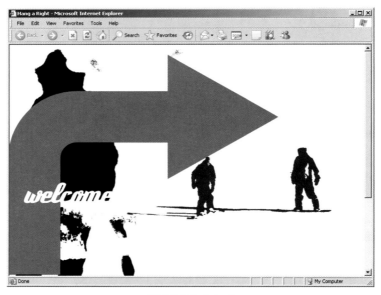

FIGURE 10.6

?   **If you have problems**

Even though the code you enter in these exercises is standard, you nest a number of tables and perform other tasks that are extremely sensitive to minor errors. Be certain to copy changes exactly from the text and to check your work for typographical errors.

---

5   **In index.htm in your text editor, add content to the nested table.**

```
. . .
<!--CONTENT TABLE-->
    <table border="0" cellpadding="0" cellspacing="0"
width="390"  align="center">
    <tr>
    <td>
    <p>
    A section of content goes here. This is enough space to add
a paragraph or more of text, even images.
<br />
```

```
<img src="images/button.gif" border="0" width="37" height="40" />
</p>
</td>
<td>
<img src="images/space.gif" border="0" width="20" height="1" />
</td>
<td>
<p>
A section of content goes here. This is enough space to add a
paragraph or more of text, even images.
<br />
<img src="images/button.gif" border="0" width="37" height="40" />
</p>
</td>
</tr>
<tr>
<td colspan="3">
<img src="images/space.gif" border="0" width="1" height="20" />
</td>
</tr>
<tr>
<td>
<p>
A section of content goes here. This is enough space to add a
paragraph or more of text, even images.
<br />
<img src="images/button.gif" border="0" width="37" height="40" />
</p>
</td>
<td>
<img src="images/space.gif" border="0" width="20" height="1" />
</td>
<td>
```

```
<p>

A section of content goes here. This is enough space to add a
paragraph or more of text, even images.

<br />

<img src="images/button.gif" border="0" width="37" height="40" />

</p>

</td>

</tr>

<tr>

<td colspan="3">

<img src="images/space.gif" border="0" width="1"height="20" />

</td>

</tr>

</table>

<!--END OF CONTENT TABLE-->

...
```

6   **Save the file in your text editor and refresh your browser. Scroll down to see the changes.**

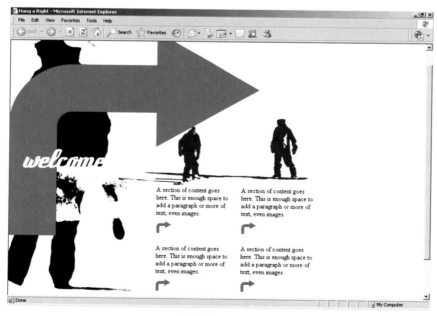

FIGURE 10.7

The text displays in a nested table within the main table.

7   **In index.htm in your text editor, create a new row at the beginning of the content table that spans three columns.**

```
. . .
<!--CONTENT TABLE-->
<table border="0" cellpadding="0" cellspacing="0" width="390"
align="center">
<tr>
<td colspan="3">


</td>
</tr>
<tr>
<td>
. . .
```

8   **Add a table to the new row that contains the text menu links.**

```
. . .
<!--CONTENT TABLE-->
<table border="0" cellpadding=0 cellspacing=0 width="390"
align="center">
<tr>
<td colspan="3">
<!--MENU-->
     <table border="0" cellpadding="0" cellspacing="0"
width="390" align="left">
     <tr>
     <td>
     <a href="index.html">home</a>    
     <a href="page.htm">about</a>    
     <a href="page.htm">news</a>    
     <a href="page.htm">services</a>    
     <a href="page.htm">store</a>    
     <a href="page.htm">contact</a>    
     </td>
```

```
      </tr>
      </table>
<!-- END OF MENU -->
</td>
</tr>
<tr>
. . .
```

9   Save the file in your text editor and refresh your browser.

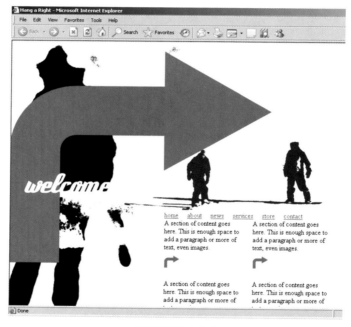

FIGURE 10.8

The link menu displays directly above the content you inserted earlier. You now have two nested tables in one main table.

10   Close the file in both windows.

To Extend Your Knowledge . . .

FINDING TEMPLATES

As a professional designer, you will sometimes need fresh ideas or concepts for new Web site projects. There is a plethora of Web templates, graphics, and code available on the Web, and many of them are available at no cost.

One excellent resource for Web page templates, kits, and resources is www.elated.com. The designers at Elated.com were kind enough to allow us to use some of their templates for the exercises and examples used throughout this book. You can download free templates and purchase templates at their Web site.

LESSON 2 Working with Column Groups

In Chapter 5 you learned how to apply alignment attributes to particular table cells and to entire rows. You also discovered how to apply an attribute to an entire column without coding each cell individually.

While changing the alignment on one column of a table is relatively simple, it's not such an easy task when you need to modify the alignment of hundreds of columns. To make the job of modifying a large number of columns significantly easier, you can place the *<colgroup> tag* at the top of the table, and then list individual columns and their attributes within the `colgroup`. You can place an attribute on an individual `<col>` tag, indicating that the attribute applies to every cell in that particular column. You do not need to individually modify each cell in the column.

The following code illustrates how to align individual columns using the `<col align="">` attribute.

```
<table border="1" width="100%" height="100%">

<colgroup>

      <col align="left" />
      <col />
      <col align="right" />
</colgroup>
<thead>
```

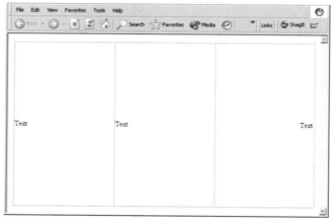

FIGURE 10.9

The example code aligns the first column to the left and the last column to the right. We included an empty `<col>` tag as a placeholder for the middle column, even though we did not include an alignment instruction. This placeholder ensures that the browser knows where to apply the alignment instructions — to the first, second, or third column.

The `<colgroup>` tag sets alignment attributes for entire columns; if necessary, you can override the values on individual cells. Using the `<colgroup>` tag, you apply generic controls to a large number of cells, and then refine the effects on specific cells.

Add to a Multinested Table

1   **Open WIP_10>HangRight>page.htm in your text editor and browser.**

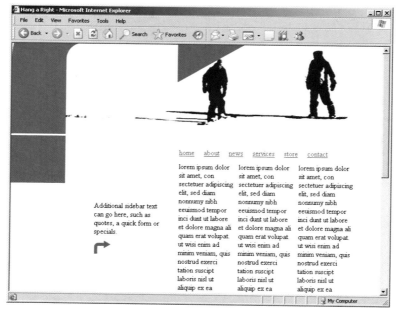

FIGURE 10.10

The text in the Web page is called "filler" text or "Greeked" text. You use Greeked text for design/layout purposes when the actual content of a site is not yet complete.

2 **Add column information to the table, including three columns of text content.**

```
...
</td>
</tr>
</table>


<table border="0" cellpadding="3" cellspacing="3" width="390"
align="center">
<colgroup>
     <col align="left" />
     <col />
     <col align="right" />
</colgroup>
<tr>
<td>
<p>
lorem ipsum dolor sit amet, con sectetuer adipiscing elit, sed
diam nonnumy nibh eeuismod tempor inci dunt ut labore et dolore
magna ali quam erat volupat. ut wisi enim ad minim veniam, quis
nostrud exerci tation suscipt laboris nisl ut aliquip ex ea
commodo consequat. duis autem vel eum irure dolor in henderit
in vulputate velit esse consequat.</p>

<p>vel illum dolore eu feugiat nulla facilise at vero eos et
accusam et ius to odio dignissim qui blandit prae sent luptatum
zzril delenit aigue dous dolore et molestias exceptur sint
occaecat cupidiata non simil pro vident tempor sunt in clulpa
qui officia deserunt mollit anium ib est abor um et dolor fuga.

...
```

3 Save the file in your text editor and refresh your browser.

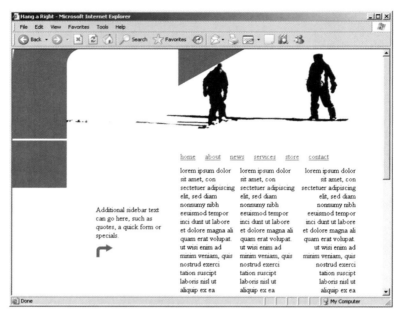

FIGURE 10.11

The right column aligns to the right of the table.

4 Close the file in your text editor and browser.

To Extend Your Knowledge . . .

COLUMN GROUP AND CSS

You can use `<col>` and `<colgroup>` tags to attach CSS class designations to a particular column.

For example, if you created a class called "measurements" that styled all text as italic, adding class="measurements" to a `<col>` tag would tell the browser to apply that style to the entire column.

LESSON 3   Applying Text Styles to a Table

Similar to other XHTML elements, you can attach CSS styling information to tables, rows, and columns. This information can be in the form of a style attribute or a class. In most cases, you will enjoy better success if you use a class, and then assign style attributes to the class. The most obvious reason for this preference is because classes are easy to maintain. If the elements on the page have the proper class designations, changing the style information becomes a straightforward activity.

You can realize another advantage of using classes during the planning process. When you think through your design in terms of classes and determine which elements belong to each class, you will present your material in an efficient and consistent manner — without suffering from the pitfalls of coding first and asking questions later. When you follow the simple rules of site planning, you create better designs, develop cohesive content, and establish an effective flow from one section to the next — as well as save precious development time.

Add Style to the Content of a Table

1   **From your WIP_10>HangRight folder, open page2.htm in your text editor and browser.**

This is essentially the same file you created in the previous lesson.

2   **Launch a new text editor window. Open WIP_10>HangRight>default.css in the new text editor window.**

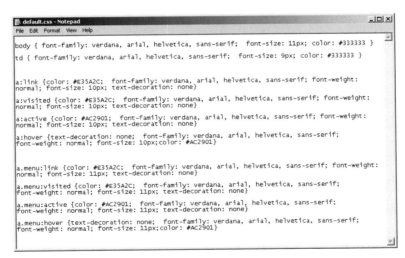

FIGURE 10.12

We already defined the style properties for page.htm. We applied styles to the **<body>**, and **<td>** (table definition) tags. In addition, we created classes for the menu links. (The menu links are styled differently than body links, which is why we created the class.) In this exercise, you use default.css to change the content in the entire local site.

3   Switch to the text editor window that contains page2.htm. Use the `<link>` tag to assign default.css as the style sheet for the Web page.

```
<html>

<head>

    <title>Hang a Right</title>

<link rel="stylesheet" type="text/css" href="default.css">

</head>
```

4   Save the changes to page2.htm in the text editor and refresh your browser.

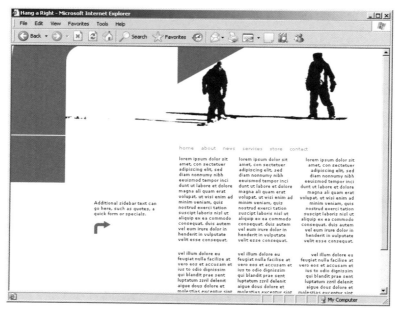

FIGURE 10.13

The body text changes, and future links in the body (not the Link menu at the top) take on the CSS information from the "a" selector. The menu links take on the CUSTOM class information.

5   Add the custom class information to the menu links (to set them apart from the regular body links you add later).

```
<td colspan="3">

<!-- menu -->

<table border="0" cellpadding="3" cellspacing="3" width="390"
align="left">

<tr>

<td>
```

```
<a class="menu" href="index.html">home</a>    

<a class="menu" href="page.html">about</a>    

<a class="menu" href="page.html">news</a>    

<a class="menu" href="page.html">services</a>
    

<a class="menu" href="page.html">store</a>
    

<a class="menu" href="page.html">contact</a>
    

</table>

</td>

</tr>

</table>
```

6   **Save the changes to page2.htm in your text editor and refresh your browser.**

FIGURE 10.14

The links display a slight change in size.

7   **Close both open files in your text editor and your browser.**

To Extend Your Knowledge . . .

CSS GENERATORS

Creating CSS styles is not a complicated task, but sometimes you might need a little help developing a design concept. Online generators can aid you in creating CSS styles. The Web page http://www.csscreator.com/version2/pagelayout.php contains one such CSS generator.

Simply log on to the site, select the HTML/XHTML standard you want to use, and then choose from the various properties listed. The generator creates a page, and then you can copy that code directly to your file.

LESSON 4   Adding a Background Style to a Table

In Chapter 3, you discovered how to add a background image to a Web page. Using similar techniques, you can add a background to a table. For example, the following code adds a background image to our sample table:

```
<table style="background-image: url('images/berries.jpg')">
```

As another alternative, you can add the background information to a CSS class that, in turn, applies the information to the table. This method is often a better choice than applying the information directly to the table and allows more powerful options for the background image.

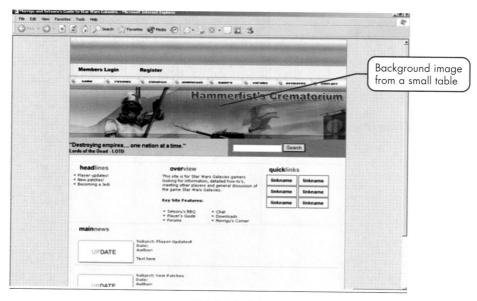

FIGURE 10.15

You can add background images to tables, rows, or individual cells, but browser differences can present definite problems when you do so. For instance, Netscape tends to render the background image of a table for every cell. To prevent this from happening, you can specifically assign the background on a cell as an empty string (`<td background="">`), which allows the overall table background to show through. (The `<td background="">` code is not CSS. The bug is a leftover from pre-CSS days and so is the fix.)

You are not restricted to applying images as backgrounds. Many table designs call for background colors, which you can apply directly from a style sheet:

```
<style>

        .myClass { background-color: #FFFFFF }

</style>
```

Add Background Information to a Table

1   **From the HangRight folder, open page3.htm in your text editor and browser.**

This is essentially the same file you created in the previous exercise.

2   **Add background information to the left table.**

```
<!-- LEFT TABLE -->

<table cellpadding="10" cellspacing="0" width="163" align="left"
style="background-color: #DCDCDC">

<tr>

<td>

Additional sidebar text can go here, such as a quick form
or specials.

<br />

<img src="images/button.gif" border="0" width="37" height="40"
border="0">

</td>

</tr>

</table>

<!--END LEFT TABLE-->
```

3   **Find and remove the following code from the left table.**

```
<img src="images/button.gif" border="0" width="37" height="40"
border="0" />
```

This will remove the button image from the left table.

4 ⎢ **Save the file in your text editor and refresh your browser.**

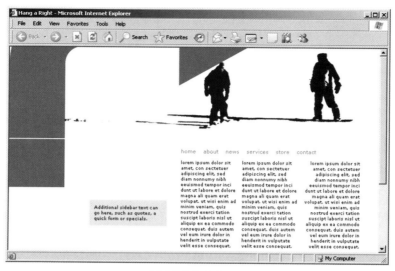

FIGURE 10.16

The left table now has a gray background.

5 ⎢ **Close the file in your text editor and browser.**

To Extend Your Knowledge . . .

STYLE GUIDES

Many larger organizations conform to corporate *style guides* that include standard selected styles used for all documentation, whether printed or for the Web. Style guides include important information on font, size, hierarchy, and much more.

You can use CSS to create standard style sheets to share within an organization. Organizations with large intranet and/or Internet sites usually have several departments that generate content. When all of the various departments use standard style sheets to create and update content, they remain in conformance with the organization's standard style guides.

LESSON 5   Formatting Table Borders

The sample table you have seen throughout this chapter displays a simple border that was not set with CSS. When you use CSS to set the border property of a table, you refer only to the exterior border of the entire table, not to the borders of the cells. This CSS feature allows you to create a border around the "box" of the table.

You can apply several different properties to table borders, just as you can apply various properties to backgrounds and fonts. These properties include the border width, style, and color, all of which are noted in the following code:

```
border: 2px dotted blue;
```

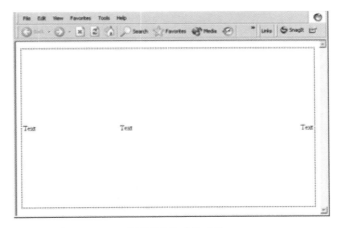

FIGURE 10.17

Figure 10.17 shows the result of the sample code. The border around the individual cells was removed because CSS can only render the exterior table border.

Format a Table Border

1   **In your text editor and browser, open page4.htm from your WIP_10>HangRight folder.**

This is essentially the same file you created in the previous exercise.

2   **Add border information to the left table.**

```
<!-- LEFT TABLE -->

<table style="border: 2px dotted black;" cellpadding="10"
cellspacing="0" width="163" align="left" style="background-color:
#DCDCDC">


<tr>

<td>
```

```
Additional sidebar text can go here, such as quotes, a quick form
or specials.<br />
```

3 | Save the file in your text editor and refresh your browser.

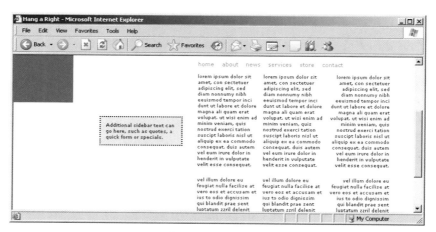

FIGURE 10.18

A border displays around the left table.

4 | Experiment with the table border. Use different border widths, colors, and types.

5 | Save the file in your text editor and refresh your browser.

6 | Change the border back to a 2-pixel dotted black line.

7 | Close both applications.

To Extend Your Knowledge . . .

SLICING

Professional Web designers often rely on a graphic design program such as Macromedia Fireworks or Adobe Photoshop to create Web interfaces. The interface is created as a single image, using the advanced tools in these programs to easily make visual changes, depending on feedback from the client or internal feedback from other designers. Once the interface is approved, designers use a technique called **slicing** to turn the single image into several smaller images that can be assembled into a complete HTML page using a combination of tables and CSS formatting.

SUMMARY

In this chapter, you learned how to manipulate tables by adding styles to a style sheet. You analyzed the three primary methods of page layout: tables, CSS divs, and CSS-formatted tables. To determine which of these technologies is most compatible and best suits your needs, consider your viewing audience. Software applications such as Macromedia Fireworks and Adobe Photoshop can write this code for you, but a complete understanding of the source code is required to create professional-level Web sites.

You also learned that you must consider maintenance issues when you make design decisions. A site that is easy to manage is a far better choice than one that requires significant time to update. You found that using CSS divs resolves most maintenance issues, while it offers you enhanced control over the display of your content.

Finally, you learned how to add background color and images to a table, as well as how to add a border around the exterior of a table. Using these advanced features allows you to create increasingly complex tables that enhance your professional-looking Web pages.

KEY TERMS

Colgroup tag   Style guide   Template
Slicing

CHECKING CONCEPTS AND TERMS

MULTIPLE CHOICE

Circle the letter that matches the correct answer for each of the following questions.

1. Why would you use tables for a Web page layout rather than use CSS?

   a. You know that the audience will not use browsers that support CSS.

   b. You are going to use tables for tabular display.

   c. Both a and b

   d. None of the above

2. What is the primary reason to refrain from using tables for page layout?

   a. Tables were not designed for page layout.

   b. Tables are not well supported by browsers.

   c. Tables create a large amount of code that can increase download time and be confusing to work with.

   d. Both a and c

3. What is the purpose of the `<colgroup>` tag?

 a. To create columns in a table

 b. To set the alignment of columns in a table

 c. To merge two columns

 d. To merge two rows

4. Nested tables are only used in page layout.

 a. True

 b. False

5. What is the specific purpose of tables?

 a. To arrange images and text on a Web page

 b. To display tabular data

 c. To create borders around content

 d. None of the above

6. You can use the CSS `background-image` property to place an image in a table.

 a. True

 b. False

7. You can use CSS to create a border around each cell in a table.

 a. True

 b. False

8. How can you remove the background color from a cell when the background color was already applied to an entire table?

 a. Use an empty string in the `<td>` tag.

 b. Use `bgcolor="#FFFFFF"` in the `<td>` tag.

 c. You cannot change the background color of a cell when a background color was already applied to the table.

 d. None of the above

9. You can use external style sheets to create div styles for Web pages.

 a. True

 b. False

10. Using divs, you can achieve the same layout as with a table, but you have increased control over positioning and styling.

 a. True

 b. False

DISCUSSION QUESTIONS

1. Provide a good example for each page-layout method you learned in Chapters 2, 3, and 4 of this book.

2. Why is CSS a better alternative for formatting tables than XHTML?

3. List two good reasons for using divs (rather than tables) to lay out a Web page.

4. What other Web site design alternatives offer positioning control? What are the benefits of each alternative?

SKILL DRILL

Skill Drill exercises reinforce chapter skills. Each skill that is reinforced is the same as, or nearly the same as, a skill presented in the chapter. We provide detailed instructions in a step-by-step format. You should work through these exercises in order.

1. Add a Nested Table

You were asked to apply advanced layout techniques to an existing Web page to better organize the content and improve the appearance of the pages. To do so, insert a nested table and align the content of the table.

1. Open doctorit.htm from the WIP_10 folder in your text editor and browser.

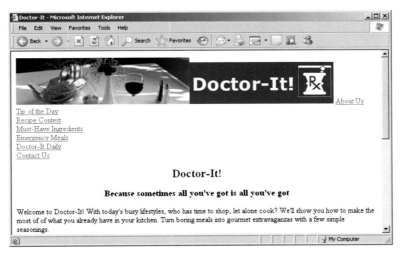

FIGURE 10.19

2. Nest a table by creating a new cell.

```
...
<h3 align="center">Because sometimes all you've got is all you've
got</h3>

<p>Welcome to Doctor-It! With today's busy lifestyles, who has
time to shop, let alone cook? We'll show you how to make the most
of what you already have in your kitchen. Turn boring meals into
gourmet extravaganzas with a few simple seasonings.</p>

<p>You'll never be afraid to hear the words "What's for dinner?"
again.</p>

</td>

<td width="70%">

<table width="100%">

<tr>

<td valign="top">

<b>Recipe of the Day: Tuna Noodle Casserole</b>

<br />

<i>Ingredients:</i>
...
```

3. Create a new cell in the nested table.

    ```
    . . .
    <p>Serves up to 6 people.</p>

    <p>You can get the recipe of the day sent right to your mailbox
    by subscribing to <a href="daily.html">Doctor-It! Daily</a>. It's
    free!</p>

    </td>

    <td>

    </td>

    </tr>

    </table>

    </body>

    . . .
    ```

4. Find the following code in your document. Select this code and choose Edit>Cut in your text editor.

    ```
    <h2 align="center">Doctor-It!</h2>

    <h3 align="center">Because sometimes all you've got is all you've
    got</h3>

    <p>Welcome to Doctor-It! With today's busy lifestyles, who has
    time to shop, let alone cook? We'll show you how to make the most
    of what you already have in your kitchen. Turn boring meals into
    gourmet extravaganzas with a few simple seasonings.  </p>

    <p>You'll never be afraid to hear the words "What's for dinner?"
    again.</p>
    ```

5. Paste this code into the new cell by clicking between the **<td>** and **</td>** tags and choosing Edit>Paste in your text editor.

    ```
    . . .
    <p>Serves up to 6 people.</p>

    <p>You can get the recipe of the day sent right to your mailbox
    by subscribing to <a href="daily.html">Doctor-It! Daily</a>. It's
    free!</p>

    </td>

    <td>

    <h2 align="center">Doctor-It!</h2>

    <h3 align="center">Because sometimes all you've got is all you've
    got</h3>
    ```

```
<p>Welcome to Doctor-It! With today's busy lifestyles, who has
time to shop, let alone cook? We'll show you how to make the most
of what you already have in your kitchen. Turn boring meals into
gourmet extravaganzas with a few simple seasonings.  </p>

<p>You'll never be afraid to hear the words "What's for dinner?"
again.</p>

</td>

</tr>

</table>

</body>

. . .
```

6. Cut and paste the **<p align="center"><img src="images/drlogo.jpg"
   alt="Logo" width="300" height="90"/>** code from the top of the document to the
   top of the cell content and add the **valign** attribute.

```
. . .

<p>You can get the recipe of the day sent right to your mailbox
by subscribing to <a href="daily.html">Doctor-It! Daily</a>.
It's free!</p>

</td>

<td valign="top">

<p align="center><img src="images/drlogo.jpg" alt="Logo"
width="300" height="90" /></p>

<h2 align="center">Doctor-It!</h2>

<h3 align="center">Because sometimes all you've got is all you've
got</h3>

. . .
```

7. Cut and paste **<img src="images/table.jpg" alt="Table Imagine"
   width="361" height="100" />** into the following cell.

```
. . .

<td>

<table width="100%">

<tr><td valign="top">

<img src="images/table.jpg" alt="Table Imagine" width="361"
height="100" />

<b>Recipe of the Day: Tuna Noodle Casserole</b>

. . .
```

8.   Save the file in your text editor and refresh your browser.

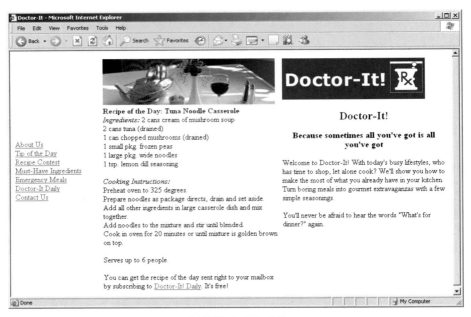

FIGURE 10.20

9.   Close the file in your text editor and browser.

2. Provide Style Information

Now that you've positioned the content in a table, you need to format the content. As this is the only page you will work on, apply an internal style sheet to the document.

1.   In your text editor and browser, open doctorit2.htm from your WIP_10 folder. This is essentially the same file you created in the previous drill.

2.   Add an internal style sheet to format the elements on the page.

```
<html>

<head><title>Doctor-It</title>

<style>

*{font-family: Arial}

h2 {font-size: 14pt; color: blue}

h3 {font-size: 12pt; color: gray}

.link {font-size: 10pt}

</style>
```

```
</head>

<body>

. . .
```

3. Apply the link custom class to the seven links in the document.

4. Save the file in your text editor and refresh your browser.

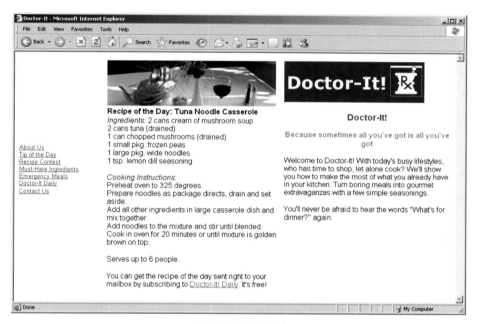

FIGURE 10.21

5. Close the file in your browser and text editor.

3. Format the Table Background

In this exercise, you add background color to the main document, main table, and nested table to add a little bit of color to the document.

1. In your text editor and browser, open doctorit3.htm from your WIP_10 folder.

2. In the open document in your text editor, add style information to format the body background and main table background.

```
<html>

<head><title>Doctor-It</title>

<style>

*{font-family: Arial}

h2 {font-size: 14pt; color: blue}
```

```
h3 {font-size: 12pt; color: gray}

.link {font-size: 10pt}

.recipe {background-image: url("images/berries.jpg")}

.maintable {background-color: #F0F8FF}

body {background-color: #6495ED}

</style>

</head>

<body>

...
```

3. Apply class information to the main table to change the background color and to change the **<td>** width from 20% to 150 pixels.

```
...
body {background-color: #6495ED}

</style>

</head>

<body>

<table class="maintable">

<tr><td width="150">

...
```

4. Apply class information to the nested table to add a background image.

```
...
<a class="link" href="mailto:webmaster@doctor-it.net">Contact Us</a></p>

</td>

<td width="70%">

<table width="100%" class="recipe">

<tr><td valign="top">

<img src="images/table.jpg" alt="Table Imagine" width="361" height="100" />

<b>Recipe of the Day: Tuna Noodle Casserole</b>

...
```

5.   Save the file in your text editor and refresh your browser.

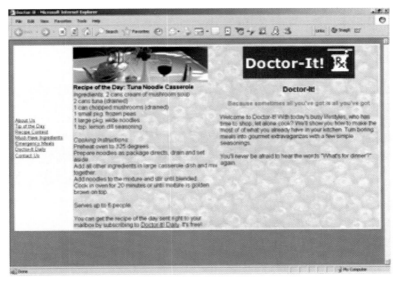

FIGURE 10.22

6.   Close the file in your text editor and browser.

4. Format the Table Borders

As a final step, you decide to add a border around the content of the document. This border creates necessary contrast between the background and the content.

1.   In your text editor and browser, open doctorit4.htm from your WIP_10 folder.

2.   Change the border information for the main table.

```
</style>
<body>
<table class="maintable" style="border: 3px dashed #000000">
<tr><td width="150">
<a class="link" href="about.html">About Us</a><br />
```

3.   Save the file in your text editor and refresh your browser. You should see a dotted line around the main table.

4.   In the text editor, change the border of the table to a 2-pixel solid line.

```
</style>
<body>
```

```
<table class="maintable" style="border: 2px solid #000000">

<tr><td width="150">

<a class="link" href="about.html">About Us</a><br />
```

5. Save the file in your text editor and refresh your browser.

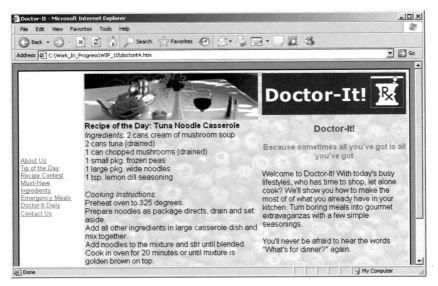

FIGURE 10.23

6. Close the file in your text editor and browser.

CHALLENGE

Challenge exercises expand on (or are somewhat related to) skills presented in the lessons. Each exercise provides a brief introduction, followed by numbered-step instructions that are not as detailed as those in the Skill Drill exercises. You should work through these exercises in order.

1. Replace a Table with Divs

The Doctor-It site shows vast improvement from when you started the chapter, but there is still additional work to do. You decide to remove all the tables and display the content in divs. There is no need to follow the original layout; use your creative talents to place the content in multiple divs.

1. Open WIP_10>challenge.htm in your text editor and browser.

2. Create a div that contains the link information. Position the div appropriately.

3. Create a div that contains the following image and content. Position the div appropriately.

```
. . .
<img src="images/table.jpg" alt="Table Imagine" width="361"
height="100" />

<b>Recipe of the Day: Tuna Noodle Casserole</b>

<br />

<i>Ingredients:</i>

2 cans cream of mushroom soup<br /> 2 cans tuna (drained)<br />

1 can chopped mushrooms (drained)<br />

1 small pkg. frozen peas<br />

1 large pkg. wide noodles <br /> 1 tsp. lemon dill seasoning<br />

<br />

<i>Cooking Instructions:</i>

<br />

Preheat oven to 325 degrees.<br />

Prepare noodles as package directs, drain and set aside.<br />

Add all other ingredients in large casserole dish and mix
together.<br />

Add noodles to the mixture and stir until blended.<br />

Cook in oven for 20 minutes or until mixture is golden brown on
top.<br />

<p>Serves up to 6 people.</p>

<p>You can get the recipe of the day sent right to your mailbox
by subscribing to <a href="daily.html">Doctor-It! Daily</a>. It's
free!</p>

. . .
```

4. Create another div that contains the following image and content. Position the div appropriately.

```
. . .
<p align="center"><img src="images/drlogo.jpg" alt="Logo"/></p>

<h2 align="center">Doctor-It!</h2>

<h3 align="center">Because sometimes all you've got is all you've
got</h3>
```

```
<p>Welcome to Doctor-It! With today's busy lifestyles, who has
time to shop, let alone cook? We'll show you how to make the most
of what you already have in your kitchen. Turn boring meals into
gourmet extravaganzas with a few simple seasonings.</p>

<p>You'll never be afraid to hear the words "What's for dinner?"
again.</p>

...
```

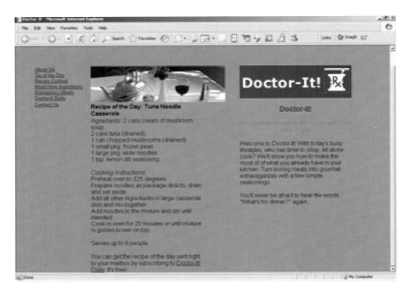

FIGURE 10.24

5. Save your changes and leave the file open for the next exercise.

2. Apply Span Styles

Now that the content is in the correct position, use the **<span>** tag to format the content.

1. In the open challenge.htm in your text editor, add a class to the internal style sheet that applies bold formatting to the text.

2. Create a style in the internal style sheet that applies a hover pseudo-class to all links in the document.

3. Apply bold formatting to various sections of text, including the current bolded information that uses the **<b></b>** tags.

4. Save the file in your text editor and refresh your browser.

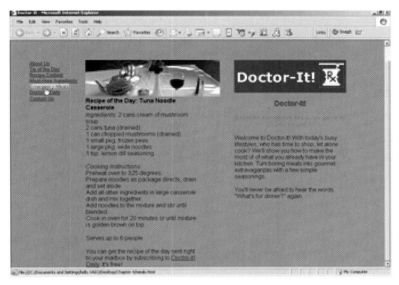

FIGURE 10.25

FIGURE 10.25

5. Leave the file open for the next exercise.

3. Format the Divs

In this exercise, you format the div boxes by changing their borders and background properties.

1. In the open challenge.htm in your text editor, change the background of all the divs to the color or image of your choice.

2. Apply different border information to each div.

3. Arrange the divs in different positions to render a variety of layouts. Position the divs on the page so the content is similar to the layout the table provided.

4. Save the file in your text editor and refresh your browser.

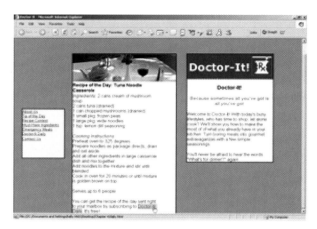

FIGURE 10.26

5. Leave the file open for the next exercise.

4. Create External Styles

The final step in the development of the Doctor-It site is to create an external style sheet that you can use to quickly change the properties in the document, if necessary.

1. Launch a new text editor window. Save the file as "docstyle.css" in the WIP_10 folder.

2. Copy and paste the internal style sheet properties to docstyle.css. Delete the style tags in challenge.htm.

3. Link the external style sheet (docstyle.css) to challenge.htm.

4. Create a class for each div (.div1, .div2, and .div3), and then cut and paste the property information from the **<div>** tag into the class information, keeping the **<div>** tag in challenge.htm.

5. Add the class information to the appropriate div (`div class="div1"`).

6. Save the changes to docstyle.css and challenge.htm. Refresh your browser.

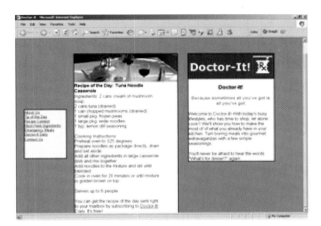

FIGURE 10.27

7. Close the files in your text editor and browser.

PORTFOLIO BUILDER

Create Web Page Templates

Using different layouts and designs, you can show potential clients numerous ways to create Web pages. You can use tables and divs to position content: divs offer far more control over the style used in the div blocks, whereas tables are the best choice for positioning sliced images.

Now that you have a solid understanding of how to use tables and divs to create Web pages, use your skills to design and develop a variety of layouts for your portfolio.

■ Think about several different types of pages you'd like to design using tables and divs. Pick one topic and create several variations of the layout. Choose a variety of styles, fonts, and images to showcase the flexibility of your design skills.

■ Create several different versions of the page using tables to position the content. If you prefer, create a "style" version of each to demonstrate the different technologies you can use to render the same effect.

■ Add the pages to your portfolio. Link to each page and provide a description. Explain what element/s you used in each layout.

CHAPTER **11**

Integrating Other Technologies

OBJECTIVES

In this chapter, you learn how to:

- Create client-side scripts

- Use inline JavaScript

- Understand functions

- Recognize case-sensitivity issues

- Embed a Flash file into an HTML document

Why Would I Do This?

HTML is the basis for all Web pages. Other technologies can be used for more complex purposes, but HTML must be used as a starting point for every Web page. In this chapter, we'll consider how other technologies, including client-side scripts and embedded objects, are added to Web pages and can interact with HTML. The bulk of this chapter will focus on JavaScript as a client-side language. We will also consider Flash as an example of an embedded object.

HTML was designed with a limited purpose: to describe the content of a document to a Web browser, which could then present the information to the viewer. Interactivity was limited; any interactive elements were managed by the server, not the browser. Typically, early users clicked links, entered search terms in their browsers, and servers provided the requested information. This simple procedure was usually successful, even though oftentimes quite slow — which quickly became an inconvenience for most Internet users.

Since HTML was very limited, presentation tags were created, and eventually technologies such as JavaScript, CSS, and Flash were created to extend HTML and integrate into the existing framework for creating Web pages. Today's Web sites, however, are information resources that offer text, still images, animations, slide shows, catalogs, audio, and much more. Contemporary users expect a customized online experience and presume that most sites will respond to their choices interactively — as well as instantaneously.

JavaScript allows users to interact with Web pages without using a server or waiting for new pages to load. It also allows developers to create content based on user choices and to take greater control over the Web browser. You can use JavaScript in a number of common applications:

- Creating a rollover, such as a button graphic, that changes when the user rolls the mouse over it.

- Validating the content of a field in a form, such as ensuring the user entered his e-mail address correctly.

- Computing a calculation, such as the amount of tax on a purchase order.

- Creating a pop-up window to display an advertisement. The ad displays in a separate window from the Web page that triggered it.

- Creating animation using a combination of JavaScript and other technologies, such as Cascading Style Sheets (CSS).

These applications include many of the most common uses of JavaScript. Since JavaScript contains much of the same functionality as traditional programming languages, many additional possibilities also exist. Multiple scripts can be included in the same page and can exist in the head or body sections of the document or even in external files.

With each new release, browsers continue to become increasingly powerful, which creates additional options for client-side scripting. The client in "client-side" is, of course, the browser. In ***client-side scripting***, the browser directly manipulates content, rather than sending the content to the server for manipulation (***server-side scripting***). With advanced client-side scripts, you can instruct the browser to perform sophisticated functions, such as display form data on a results page or change images when a mouse hovers over them.

Using client-side scripting, you can force an image to change when the user rolls his mouse over the image; you can create content dynamically; in some cases, you can even replace traditional applications with client-side scripts. In this chapter, you learn how to perform all of these functions as you explore how to create and apply client-side scripts.

Like JavaScript, Macromedia Flash also offers new options for interactivity. Flash files are known as ***Flash movies*** that can be inserted into Web pages to create interfaces, animation, video, sound, or any combination of these items. Flash movies require the use of a browser plug-in and have a ".swf" file extension.

This chapter also explains the code that is needed to embed an object within an HTML page. Please note: The Flash plug-in must be downloaded and installed for the exercises in this book to work correctly. Code examples will prompt users to install the plug-in, if it is not currently installed. The plug-in can also be downloaded from www.adobe.com/downloads.

VISUAL SUMMARY

One of the primary benefits of client-side scripting is enabling the user to interact with content on a Web page. For instance, a Web page may provide information on a specific topic. As the user rolls her mouse over different objects on the page, client-side scripts tell the browser to display related information — a different item displays as the user moves from one object to the next.

Other client-side scripts ensure users complete online forms correctly; the script instructs the browser to validate the form before sending the form to the server for processing. This feature is an excellent time-saver — rather than wait for the forms to travel back and forth between browser and server during validation, the process takes place at the browser level, which removes much of the inconvenience of completing online forms. The browser immediately detects errors in a form (such as a birth date of February 31) and prompts the user to make the necessary corrections.

Consider a simple script inserted into a transitional XHTML document. The **`<script>`** tag allows JavaScript code to be inserted into the HTML code.

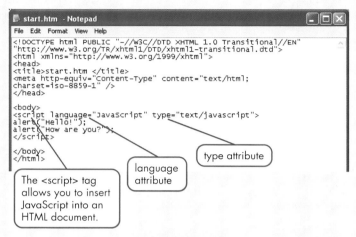

FIGURE 11.1

- The **`<script>`** tag allows you to insert JavaScript into an HTML document.
- The ***language attribute*** specifies the scripting language that appears within the HTML. Browsers often support a variety of scripting languages, with JavaScript being the most popular.
- The ***type attribute*** specifies the type of information included in the script.

The following image shows how the HTML code in Figure 11.1 (with JavaScript) displays in a browser window.

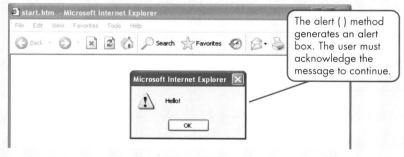

FIGURE 11.2

Web designers are likely to interact with Flash movies, or another similar technology, at some point in their career. The Flash authoring software, or Web design software such as Macromedia Dreamweaver, will create the necessary code for you to insert a Flash file into an HTML file. However, studying the code needed is a necessary step for the development of Web designers and developers.

Flash was originally designed as Web animation software that could produce impressive animation with small file sizes. Later editions of Flash have included ActionScript, a built-in scripting language based on the same standards as JavaScript. This means that JavaScript developers find ActionScript easy to learn and use. Consider the following code example, which displays a Flash movie within an XHTML page.

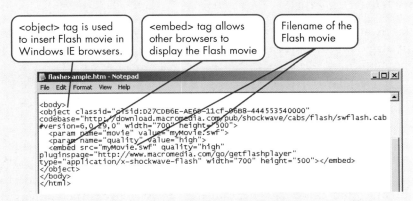

FIGURE 11.3

A Flash movie is inserted into a Web page in a similar way that an image is inserted into HTML. Like an image, the Flash movie is not a part of the HTML file but is referenced in the source code of the page. Flash movies require a plug-in (or additional piece of software that must be installed in the browser. This makes the code to insert the Flash file more complicated than an image tag.

LESSON 1   Creating Client-Side Scripts

The first client-side scripting appeared in Netscape Navigator 2.0 — it was called LiveScript. LiveScript was loosely based on the then-emerging Java programming language and was promptly renamed JavaScript to capitalize on Java's quickly growing popularity. Java and JavaScript are distinctly different languages, however, and should not be confused.

Microsoft released another client-side language, known as **VBScript**, based on the Visual Basic programming language. This language was primarily used on Internet Explorer browsers and proved less popular than JavaScript with most developers. Given the popularity of JavaScript, Microsoft later published their own version, known as **Jscript**. JavaScript and JScript were essentially the same language, with some differences that created serious compatibility issues for developers.

In the last few years, the European Computer Manufacturers Association (ECMA) developed a standardized version of JavaScript, which became known as ***ECMAScript***, although the language is still commonly referred to as "JavaScript." Due to this effort, the JavaScript language has become much more standardized, eliminating most compatibility issues between different browsers. This language became (and remains) the standard client-side scripting language.

Including a Script on a Page

The `<script>` tag is an addition to HTML that allows scripts to be inserted directly into HTML documents. The script tag can be used for a number of different scripting languages on a basic level and takes on the following appearance:

```
<script language="JavaScript" type="text/javascript">

    (your script goes here)

</script>
```

When you write your code within `<script<>/script>` tags, a browser that understands scripting does not display the content within those tags; instead, the browser checks the content within the tags for instructions, and then executes those instructions appropriately.

The `<script>` tag is designed to work with a number of different languages. For example, you can use the statement `<script language="VBScript" type="text/VBScript">` to insert a script written in VBScript, which is a scripting language based loosely on Microsoft's Visual Basic programming language. The list of available scripting languages varies with each browser.

If you use the `<script>` tag without specifying a language or `type` attribute, most browsers assume you mean JavaScript — since it is the most popular scripting language for browsers. We recommend that you always specify a language and `type` attribute, however, as most professional Web designers consider it sloppy programming to overlook these important elements. Both of these elements are required to ensure full XHTML compliance.

Basic JavaScript: alert()

An ***alert box*** is a message that the user must acknowledge before they can continue. You can enter any text you prefer into an alert box, but you can't modify its appearance (the browser dictates the appearance of the alert box). Typically, you use an alert box to tell users something important, such as a change to a site's policies or a problem with a form.

To create an alert box, you use the **alert()** method. A ***method*** is an action that JavaScript can perform. You place the **alert()** method between **<script> </script>** tags. This command passes an argument (information) to the script. In this instance, the information is the text to display in the alert box. For example:

```
<script language="JavaScript" type="text/javascript">
     alert ("Hi there!");
</script>
```

FIGURE 11.4

The alert part of the script is a command that tells the browser what method to carry out — in this case, to create an alert box. The alert box must display a message (the argument), which you place between the parentheses, "( )", within the code. In the sample code, **"Hi there!"** is the argument, which displays in the alert box. The double quotes surrounding the argument tell the browser it's a string of text, not a command. The code can also be written with a pair of single quotes instead of a pair of double quotes. The semicolon ends the line of code.

If you included this code within the content of a page, the browser would render the page up to that point and then display an alert box. To continue, the user must click the OK button (by default, every alert box includes an Acknowledge/OK button).

Add Alert Boxes to a Web Page

1   **Copy the contents of your Chapter_11 folder to your WIP_11 folder.**

2   **In your text editor, open start.htm from your WIP_11 folder.**

This is a simple transitional XHTML Web page that has no current content.

3   **Type the following code between the <body> and </body> tags.**

```
<!DOCTYPE html PUBLIC "-//W3C//DTD XHTML 1.0 Transitional//EN"
"http://www.w3.org/TR/xhtml1/DTD/xhtml1-transitional.dtd">

<html xmlns="http://www.w3.org/1999/xhtml">

<head>

<title>start.htm</title>

</head>

<body>
```

```
<script language="JavaScript" type="text/javascript">
alert("Hello");
alert("How are you?");
</script>
</body>
</html>
```

The **<script>** tag allows you to insert JavaScript code into an HTML document. You can use the **<script>** tag in the head or body section of an HTML document. Notice how semicolons are used at the end of JavaScript statements. Semicolons help the interpreter to understand the JavaScript code in the same way that periods help us to read sentences.

4   **Save your file in the text editor and open it in your Web browser.**

FIGURE 11.5

An alert box appears.

5   **Click OK to acknowledge the alert box that appears.**

FIGURE 11.6

A second alert box appears. Notice how the alert boxes appear in the same order they appear in the code.

| **6** | Click OK to acknowledge the second alert box. |

| **7** | Close the file in your browser and text editor. |

To Extend Your Knowledge . . .

HIDING SCRIPTS FROM OLDER BROWSERS

Older browsers may not be able to understand JavaScript code. HTML was designed to ignore unknown tags, so the `<script>` tag will be ignored by browsers. However, older browsers can mistake JavaScript for content that should be displayed on the screen. Developers can use a combination of HTML comment tags and a JavaScript comment (//) to force older browsers to ignore script commands.

```
<script language="JavaScript" type="text/javascript">

<!--

    (your script goes here)

//-->

</script>
```

JavaScript has been well integrated into browsers for several years, so this convention is rarely needed, if at all. However, many Web pages using JavaScript may still use this method.

LESSON 2 Using Inline JavaScript

Inline JavaScript refers to JavaScript code used within an HTML tag. *Inline code* appears within quotes, the same as HTML tag attributes. With inline JavaScript, you do not use the `<script>` tag.

Inline JavaScript is triggered by an *event*, which is an action the user performs, such as clicking an image or a button. An *event handler* allows the computer to detect an event. JavaScript event handlers can appear as HTML tag attributes or properties.

The event handler tells JavaScript when to carry out a command. In the following example, the **alert()** command activates when the user clicks the mouse (onclick is the event handler).

FIGURE 11.7

Onclick is probably the most popular event handler, but many other event handlers exist. **Onmouseover** is often used to create rollover buttons. For example, a designer can place an image for a button on the page using an image tag. Using the **onmouseover** event handler, we can detect when a user moves their mouse over the button; then we can change the source of the image to a different filename.

This creates a rollover effect that is impossible in HTML. The user sees one image on the page, then another one when they move over the button. JavaScript also allows us to preload the rollover image, so the user does not have to wait for the image to load when they move over the first image. When the user moves their mouse off the button, the **onmouseout** event handler allows us to restore the original image.

Use Inline JavaScript in an HTML Tag

In this exercise, you use inline JavaScript within a single HTML tag.

1   **In your text editor, open event.htm from your WIP_11 folder.**

FIGURE 11.8

The page is a very simple XHTML document.

2   **Change the `<body>` tag to read as follows:**

```
<head>
<title>event.htm</title>
</head>
<body onload="alert('Welcome to my Web site!');">
</body>
</html>
```

You attached an event handler to the **`<body>`** tag as inline JavaScript. Notice how the message within the alert is enclosed within single quotes. This keeps the HTML interpreter from confusing the HTML attribute (within double quotes) with the alert argument (within single quotes).

3   **Between the `<body>` and `</body>` tags, enter the following:**

```
<title>event.htm</title>
</head>
<body onload="alert('Welcome to my Web site!');">
<p>Once the page is loaded, you will see a welcome message!</p>
</body>
</html>
```

FIGURE 11.9

These text instructions create a user-friendly page.

4 Save the file and open it in your Web browser to view the result.

FIGURE 11.10

5 Choose OK to acknowledge the alert box.

6 Close the file in your text editor and browser.

To Extend Your Knowledge . . .

EVENT HANDLERS AND INLINE JAVASCRIPT

Most practical uses of JavaScript involve event handlers that are used inline in HTML. Usually, developers want to trigger chunks of scripting code when a specific event occurs in HTML, such as the submission of a form or the user rolling over an image. Inline event handlers are part of both HTML and JavaScript and show the close integration of the two technologies.

LESSON 3 Understanding Functions

Functions are named, reusable sections of code that exist in the head or body section of an HTML document or in an external file. Functions allow developers to reuse code without having to retype it every time they use it. For instance, when you place a function in an external file, all the documents in a Web site can access (share) the function. In addition, information can be sent to a function and a function can send information back to other scripts or other functions.

Functions are often triggered by event handlers that appear as HTML tag attributes. In the following example, the function triggers when the user clicks the image.

```
triggerfunction.htm - Notepad
File  Edit  Format  View  Help
<!DOCTYPE html PUBLIC "-//W3C//DTD XHTML 1.0 Transitional//EN"
"http://www.w3.org/TR/xhtml1/DTD/xhtml1-transitional.dtd">
<html xmlns="http://www.w3.org/1999/xhtml">
<head>
<title>triggerfunction.htm  - triggers a function when a button is
clicked</title>
<!-- insert function here -->
<script language="JavaScript" type="text/javascript">
function triggerAlert() {
alert("function is activated");
}
</script>
</head>
<body>
<!-- display the trigger button -->
<img src="images/triggerbutton.jpg" alt="button" onclick="triggerAlert();"
/>
</body>
</html>
```

FIGURE 11.11

Use a Simple Function

In this exercise, you create a simple function in the head of the HTML document.

1   **Navigate to your WIP_11 folder. Open triggerfunction.htm in your text editor.**

```
triggerfunction.htm  - Notepad
File  Edit  Format  View  Help
<!DOCTYPE html PUBLIC "-//W3C//DTD XHTML 1.0 Transitional//EN"
"http://www.w3.org/TR/xhtml1/DTD/xhtml1-transitional.dtd">
<html xmlns="http://www.w3.org/1999/xhtml">
<head>
<title>triggerfunction.html - triggers a function when a button is
clicked</title>
<!-- insert function here -->
</head>
<body>
<!-- display the trigger button -->
<img src="images/triggerbutton.jpg" alt="button" />
</body>
</html>
```

FIGURE 11.12

This simple HTML page displays an image. You use the image as a button.

2   **Open the file in your browser.**

FIGURE 11.13

The button hasn't yet been programmed to do anything.

3 **Return to your text editor. Find the following code in the head section of the document between the `<head>` and `</head>` tags.**

```
<!-- insert function here -->
```

4 **Insert the following code before the `</head>` tag.**

```
<head>

<title>triggerfunction.htm - triggers a function when a button is
clicked</title>

<!-- insert function here -->

<script language="JavaScript" type="text/javascript">

function triggerAlert() {

alert("function is activated");

}

</script>

</head>

<body>
```

This code contains a basic function that triggers an alert box when activated. Next, you add the code to trigger the function.

5 **Find the following code in your text editor.**

```
<!-- display the trigger button -->

<img src="images/triggerbutton.jpg" alt="button" />
```

6 **Change the `<img>` tag to read as follows:**

```
<body>

<!-- display the trigger button -->

<img src="images/triggerbutton.jpg" alt="button"
onclick="triggerAlert();" />

</body>

</html>
```

Adding an event handler to the `<img>` tag triggers a JavaScript function when the user clicks the object.

7 **Save the file in your text editor. Refresh the file in your browser.**

8   **Click the button image.**

The alert box displays on the screen. You may also notice that the mouse pointer does not change to a hand to indicate you can click the image (which happens when the content appears within an `<a>` tag).

FIGURE 11.14

9   **Click OK to close the alert box.**

10   **Close the file in your Web browser and text editor.**

To Extend Your Knowledge . . .

FUNCTIONS AND EVENT HANDLERS

Inline JavaScript can contain multiple code statements, which can quickly lead to cumbersome code that becomes difficult to read. It is much more common to use inline JavaScript to trigger a single function. This allows the code statements to be placed in the function instead of within the inline JavaScript code.

LESSON 4 Case Sensitivity

Case sensitivity refers to a language's ability to distinguish between uppercase (capital) and lowercase (small) letters. Languages that distinguish between uppercase and lowercase letters are *case sensitive*. A case-sensitive program that expects you to enter all commands in uppercase does not respond correctly if you enter one or more characters in lowercase. For example, the word "Document" is viewed differently than the word "document." Languages that do not distinguish between uppercase and lowercase letters are *case insensitive*.

JavaScript is a case-sensitive language. It is different than HTML, which ignores differences between upper- and lowercase letters. For this reason, users must be aware of the proper spelling of JavaScript commands. Errors in case often cause difficult-to-find problems in JavaScript code.

Add Errors to Your Code

In this exercise, you purposely introduce script errors by changing the capitalization of a JavaScript command. Depending on your browser and its configuration, this may create an error, the browser may ignore it, or it may display correctly — despite the capitalization error. To ensure the best results in real-world situations, follow the JavaScript standard guidelines for capitalization.

1 | **In your text editor and browser, open errors.htm from your WIP_11 folder.**

2 | **Change the "d" in the `document.write()` command to "D". Your code should resemble the following:**

```
<body>
<script language="JavaScript" type="text/javascript">
<!-- this line starts an HTML comment to hide JavaScript code
Document.write("Hello");
// this line ends the HTML comment block -->
</script>
```

3 | **Save the change to the file.**

4 | **Make sure the file is open in your browser. Click the Refresh button to reload the page.**

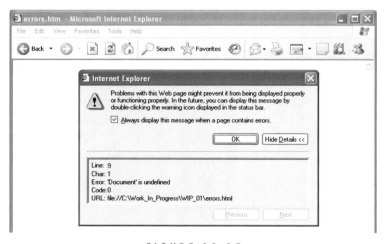

FIGURE 11.15

Most browsers ignore the **`Document.writeln()`** statement. Depending on which browser you use and how it is configured, the JavaScript interpreter may display an error message. Let's correct the capitalization error.

5   Return to the text editor and change the uppercase "D" to a lowercase "d".

Your statement should now read `document.write("Hello");`.

6   Save the document in your text editor. Refresh the file in the browser.

You should no longer see the error.

7   Close the file in your text editor and browser.

To Extend Your Knowledge . . .

MORE ABOUT CASE SENSITIVITY

In older browsers, event handlers used in HTML commands aren't case sensitive because they appear as HTML attributes — and as you know, HTML is not case sensitive. In many older pages, for example, `onclick` is spelled as `onClick`. XHTML compliance now requires that all HTML attributes be written in lower case, including JavaScript event handlers.

To complicate matters, some browsers ignore some case mistakes in JavaScript code or even require case errors. For example, older versions of Internet Explorer for the Mac require the `onclick` event to be written as `onClick`. This often creates problems since the developer doesn't notice the error until the code is tested in another browser. For best results, always consult a reference book (such as this one) to confirm your use of upper or lowercase.

LESSON 5   Embedding Flash Movies into an HTML Document

An HTML page is required to correctly display a Macromedia Flash movie in a browser. This HTML page must contain tags that reference the actual Macromedia Flash movie file to be opened and played. These tags are the ***OBJECT*** and ***EMBED tags***. The OBJECT tag is used by Internet Explorer on Windows, and the EMBED is used by Netscape Navigator (Macintosh and Windows) and Internet Explorer (Macintosh) to direct the browser to load the Macromedia Flash Player.

Internet Explorer on Windows uses an ***ActiveX*** control to play Macromedia Flash content, while all other browser and platform combinations use the Netscape plug-in technology to play Macromedia Flash content. ActiveX is a technology from Microsoft that allows the integration of sound, animation, and other items into Web pages using reusable software components. This explains the need for two tags.

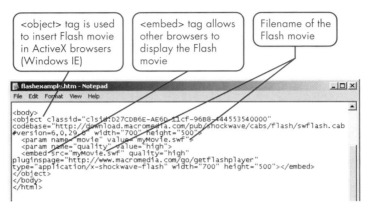

FIGURE 11.16

Hand-coding HTML pages with OBJECT and EMBED tags is not necessary when using Macromedia Flash 4 or later. The Publish feature present in those versions of Flash will automatically create an HTML document that contains the required HTML tags for browsers to access a Flash movie on the Web. To use the Publish feature in the Flash editor, choose File > Publish Settings.

Web design software packages, such as Macromedia Dreamweaver, can easily embed a Flash movie (.swf) into an HTML document. Dreamweaver also provides more control over layout and design of the page that contains the Macromedia Flash movie than the Publish feature in Flash.

A number of parameters are present in this code that are normally not changed or modified by the designer. For the **<object>** tag, these include:

classid	specifies which version of the plug-in to use
codebase	specifies where the browser plug-in can be downloaded if it is not installed
<param> tag	specifies parameters to be used with the object (in this case, the Flash movie)

The **width** and **height** attributes specify the size in which the movie can be displayed. Flash movies can be scaled to fit the available space, but it is generally recommended to use the size specified when the movie was created to maintain the best appearance.

Configure a Flash Movie

1   **In your text editor and browser, open flashstart.htm from your WIP_11 folder.**

Assuming you have the Flash plug-in installed, you should see an animation playing that says "This is my Movie".

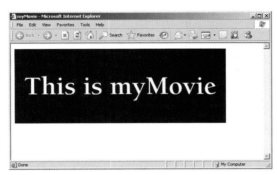

FIGURE 11.17

2   **Change the width of the movie to 250 pixels in the source code in both the `<object>` and `<embed>` tags.**

```
...

<meta http-equiv="Content-Type" content="text/html;
charset=iso-8859-1" />

</head>

<body>

<object classid="clsid:D27CDB6E-AE6D-11cf-96B8-444553540000"
codebase="http://download.macromedia.com/pub/shockwave/cabs/
flash/swflash.cab

#version=6,0,29,0" width="250" height="200">

  <param name="movie" value="myMovie.swf">

  <param name="quality" value="high">

  <embed src="myMovie.swf" quality="high"
pluginspage="http://www.macromedia.com/go/getflashplayer"

type="application/x-shockwave-flash" width="250"
height="200"></embed>

</object>

</body>

</html>

...
```

3 **Save the file and refresh your browser.**

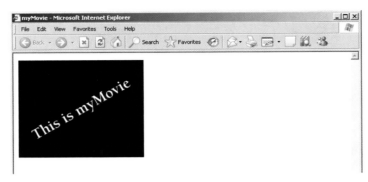

FIGURE 11.18

The movie plays as before, but the width has been reduced. Notice how the height is the same as before, since we did not change it in the code.

4 **Close the file in your browser and text editor.**

SUMMARY

In this chapter, you explored many of the commonly used aspects of client-side scripting. Client-side scripting has become very popular because it allows interactivity without using the server or requiring a new page to load. This results in a faster, better user experience when used correctly.

You discovered how to embed a client-side script into a Web page. You learned how to use events and methods to perform commands when the user does something, such as moving their mouse pointer over a button. You also learned how to insert an object that requires a plug-in into your HTML pages, in this case, a Flash movie.

You learned the benefits of preloading images, and you found that doing so saves time and enhances the user's experience. This experience has helped you to understand the limitations of HTML and how other technologies can be integrated with HTML. As you continue to learn new technologies that integrate with HTML, you will be able to make your pages more feature-rich for your viewers.

KEY TERMS

ActiveX	Event	Language attribute
Case insensitive	Event handler	Method
Case sensitive	Flash movie	Object tag
Client-side scripting	Function	Server-side scripting
ECMAScript	Inline code	Type attribute
Embed tag	Jscript	VBScript

CHECKING CONCEPTS AND TERMS

MULTIPLE CHOICE

Circle the letter that matches the correct answer for each of the following questions.

1. Why are client-side scripts useful?
   a. They provide ways to interact with the user.
   b. They provide methods of completing complex tasks without requiring the use of a server.
   c. They allow designers to perform commands based on user actions such as moving their mouse over an image or submitting a form.
   d. All of the above

2. What was the first scripting language designed specifically for browsers?
   a. ECMAScript
   b. JScript
   c. VBScript
   d. LiveScript

3. Which one of these answers is NOT a task JavaScript can be used to complete?
   a. Check a form for errors
   b. Create an image rollover effect
   c. Play a video
   d. Compute a calculation

4. The _____ method creates an alert box.
   a. confirm()
   b. popup()
   c. alert()
   d. None of the above

5. You can use the _____ event/s to create a rollover effect for a button.
   a. onmouseover
   b. onmouseout
   c. onclick
   d. Both a and b

6. Why is JavaScript useful in forms?
   a. It allows you to control form submission and field value entry.
   b. It allows you to format the form field's properties.
   c. It allows you to create a border around a form.
   d. None of the above

7. Why is it beneficial to preload images?

   a. Preloading images for rollovers helps to decrease download time when the user hovers his mouse over an image.

   b. Preloading images for rollovers helps to increase download time when the user hovers his mouse over an image.

   c. You do not have to use the height and width attributes.

   d. The images display on the screen while downloading.

8. How are Flash files inserted into HTML pages?

   a. With the <flashobject> or <flashembed> tags

   b. With the <flash> tag

   c. With the <object> and <embed> tags

   d. Through the <script> tag

9. The `onclick()` event _____.

   a. opens a new window

   b. opens a menu option

   c. can be used to trigger a command when a user clicks an object

   d. None of the above

10. You can use multiple scripts in one document.

   a. True

   b. False

DISCUSSION QUESTIONS

1. Why are functions useful when using client-side scripting?

2. Why do JavaScript event handlers appear to be part of both HTML and JavaScript? How does this demonstrate the close integration of the two languages?

3. List three ways you might use JavaScript to enhance a Web site that does not currently use JavaScript or a similar technology.

SKILL DRILL

Skill Drills reinforce project skills. Each skill that is reinforced is the same as, or nearly the same as, a skill presented in the lessons. We provide detailed instructions in a step-by-step format. You should work through these exercises in order.

1. Add an alert() Method

In the following Skill Drills, you create several scripts that allow the user to interact with the page. In the first exercise, you include an alert box with a message to the user. You also add a script that displays the current date and time.

1. Open freestyle.htm from the WIP_11>FreeStyle folder in your text editor and browser.

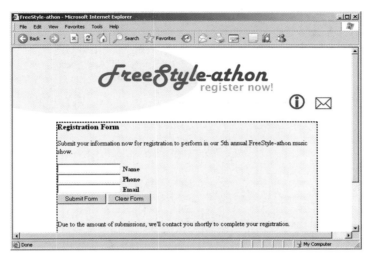

FIGURE 11.19

2. Add an alert box to the bottom of the page.

```
. . .
</td>
</tr>
</table>
<script language="JavaScript" type="text/javascript">
     alert("Hurry! Registration ends soon!");
</script>
</body>
</html>
```

3. Save the file in your text editor and refresh your browser.

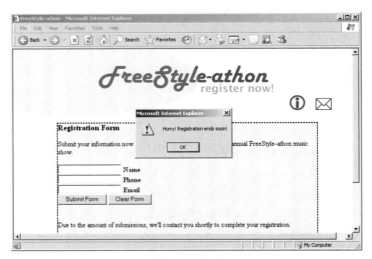

FIGURE 11.20

When the document finishes loading, the alert box displays with a message.

4. Choose OK to acknowledge the alert message.

5. Keep this file open in your text editor and browser for use in the next drill.

2. Add a Date() Method

In this drill, you use the Date() method to add the current date and time to the document. Notice how this method has the "D" capitalized. The Date() method is a special type of method that can create a new object — in this case, the current day and time.

1. In freestyle.htm in your text editor, insert the code necessary to create another script just above the Registration Form heading.

    ```
    . . .

    <!-- body -->

    <div style="height:300px; width:600px; position:absolute;

    top:175; left: 100;background-color: #E6E6FA; border-width: 2px;
    border-style: dashed; border-color: black;">

    <script language="JavaScript" type="text/javascript">

    </script>

    <h3>Registration Form</h3>

    . . .
    ```

2. Add the Date() method above the heading to display the current date.

    . . .

    ```
    <div style="height:300px; width:600px; position:absolute;
    top:175; left: 100;background-color: #E6E6FA; border-width: 2px;
    border-style: dashed; border-color: black;">
    <script language="JavaScript" type="text/javascript">
         document.write("<b>Today is ");
         document.write(Date());
         document.write(".</b>");
    </script>
    <h3>Registration Form</h3>
    ```

    . . .

3. Save the file in your text editor and refresh your browser.

    The current time and date appears above the heading.

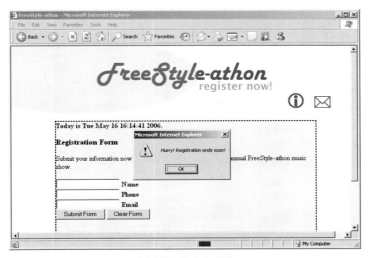

FIGURE 11.21

4. Choose OK to acknowledge the alert message.

5. Close the file in your text editor and browser.

3. Use a Mouse Event

In this exercise, you use an event handler and create inline JavaScript. The event handler triggers JavaScript code when the user chooses a text link in an HTML page.

1. In your text editor and browser, open skillmouse.htm from your WIP_11 folder.

2. Create a hyperlink by placing the following code in the body section of your document:

    ```
    <title>skillmouse.html</title>

    </head>

    <body>

    <a href="#">link text</a>

    </body>

    </html>
    ```

    Notice the link uses a placeholder (#) instead of an actual URL. When you use a placeholder, your link does not go anywhere when clicked but appears and acts as any other hyperlink.

3. Add inline JavaScript to the hyperlink to create an alert box when the user clicks the hyperlink text. Use the **onclick** event handler to accomplish this task. The alert box should say, "you clicked".

4. Save the file. Refresh the file in your browser and click on the link.

    An alert box should appear when you click the text.

FIGURE 11.22

5. Return to the document in your text editor. Change the **onclick** event handler to **onmouseover**.

6. Save the file and refresh it in the browser.

    The message should now appear when you move the mouse over the hyperlink text.

7. Change the placeholder (#) in the **href** attribute of the **<a>** tag to the following URL:

    ```
    http://www.web-answers.com
    ```

8. Save the file and refresh it in the browser. Roll your mouse over the hyperlink.

Does the action still work?

9. Change the event handler back to **onclick**. Click the link.

Does the page change to the new URL? Does the alert box appear? Do both actions take place when you click the text?

10. Close the file in your browser and text editor.

4. Use the confirm() Method

Assume that you have created an alert to notify a user that a change has been made in their binder order. Assume this can create a bad user experience and that it would work better to allow user's to decide whether they wanted to accept the proposed change. In the following drill, you create a file to confirm the change.

1. Open skillconfirm.htm in your text editor and browser.

2. Change the text of the alert message to, "You must choose a glossy finish with a 3-ring binder. Would you like to change to a glossy finish?"

3. In the code, change the word **alert** to **confirm** to change to the new method.

4. Save the file and refresh it in your browser.

The file should now ask a question the user can confirm by clicking OK or cancel by clicking Cancel, as shown here.

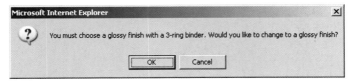

FIGURE 11.23

5. Choose Cancel to deny the confirmation.

6. Close the file in your browser and text editor.

5. Insert a Flash File into an HTML Page

In the following drill, you insert a Flash file into a Web page.

1. Open skillflash.htm from the WIP_11 folder in your text editor and browser.

This is essentially the same file you modified in a previous exercise.

2. Modify the source code to use a different Flash file.

   . . .

   ```
   <meta http-equiv="Content-Type" content="text/html; charset=iso-
   8859-1" />

   </head>

   <body>

   <object classid="clsid:D27CDB6E-AE6D-11cf-96B8-444553540000"

   codebase="http://download.macromedia.com/pub/shockwave/cabs/
   flash/swflash.cab

   #version=6,0,29,0" width="250" height="200">

     <param name="movie" value="flashNav.swf">

     <param name="quality" value="high">

     <embed src="flashNav.swf" quality="high"

   pluginspage="http://www.macromedia.com/go/getflashplayer"

   type="application/x-shockwave-flash" width="250"
   height="200"<>/embed>

   </object>

   </body>

   </html>
   ```

   . . .

   The file name is case sensitive in most browsers and must be typed correctly.

3. Save your file and refresh in the browser.

   The new file appears.

FIGURE 11.24

4. Close the file in your text editor and browser.

CHALLENGE

Challenge exercises expand on, or are somewhat related to, skills presented in the lessons. Each exercise provides a brief introduction, followed by numbered-step instructions that are not as detailed as those in the Skill Drill exercises. You should work through these exercises in order.

1. Create a Confirm Box

In this exercise, you replace the alert box with a confirm box. A confirm box is different from an alert box — a confirm box can return either a **true** or **false** value to a more advanced script.

1. In your text editor and browser, open challengefreestyle.htm from your WIP_11>FreeStyle folder.

2. Click OK to acknowledge the alert box and find the code that triggers the alert box that displays when the page loads.

3. Modify the alert method to create a confirmation box instead.

4. Modify the confirm box to convey the following message: "Are you ready for the FreeStyle-athon?!".

5. Save the file in your text editor and refresh the document in your browser.

FIGURE 11.25

6. Choose OK to accept the confirmation message.

7. Close the file in your text editor and browser.

2. React to Customer Choices

You are a Web developer designing an ordering system for users who book cruises online. On the ordering page, the user can choose the package she wants to book. Based on the user's choice, a script will process certain price details and perform other actions. In this exercise, you develop the functions that will be applied when the user makes a choice.

1. Open challengecruise.htm in your browser.

   This is a basic version of the ordering page you create in this exercise. When you click a link, a function processes the order.

   FIGURE 11.26

2. Open the file in your text editor. In the head of the document, create the first function by inserting the following code:

```
<script language="JavaScript" type="text/javascript">

function pickBahamas () {

}

</script>
```

3. Place an alert command in the function that says, "You have picked the Bahamas package".

   This tells the user which package she chose. It also allows you to make sure the function works properly.

4. In the function you created in Step 2, add a comment to explain the purpose of the function.

5. Find the **<a>** tag for the Bahamas Cruise. Add inline code to trigger the function when the user clicks the link.

```
<a href="#" onclick="pickBahamas()">Bahamas Cruise</a> | <a
href="#">Alaska Cruise</a> | <a href="#">Caribbean Cruise </a>
```

6. Save the file and test it in your browser.

   Assuming you completed the steps correctly, the alert box appears when you click the Bahamas Cruise link.

7. Return to your text editor. Create a function named "pickAlaska" and another named "pickCaribbean". Place a comment in each function to explain its purpose. Place an alert command in each function to tell the user which package she chose.

8. Insert inline code to trigger the pickAlaska function when a user clicks the Alaska Cruise link.

9. Insert inline code to trigger the pickCaribbean function when a user clicks the Caribbean Cruise link.

10. Save and test your file.

11. Keep the file open for the next exercise.

3. Change Flash Parameters

In this challenge, you correct problems with the source code used to display a Flash movie.

1.   Open challengeflash.htm from the WIP_06 folder in your text editor and browser.

     This is the same file you modified in a previous exercise.

2.   Find the code that displays the Flash file.

     The file is displayed at a size that is too small.

3.   Change the width of the file to 550 pixels.

4.   Change the height of the file to 100 pixels.

5.   Make sure the changes you made in Steps 3 and 4 have been made for all browsers and not just browsers that use the `<object>` tag.

6.   Save your file and refresh your browser. You should see the file displayed at the correct size.

7.   Close the file in your browser and text editor.

4. Correct an Error with an Embedded Flash File

A friend has asked you to help him with a Web page problem. He has embedded a Flash file into a Web page. When he views the page on a Windows machine using IE, the page shows up correctly. When he views the page using a Mac, the Flash file does not show up correctly. In this exercise, you help him find and correct this problem.

1.   In your text editor and browser, open challengeerror.htm from your WIP_11 folder.

     Assuming you are using IE on a Windows machine, the file displays correctly; other browsers will not display the code correctly.

2.   Look at the `<object>` tag in the code. The code links to the "myMovie.swf" file.

3.   If you have another browser installed, such as Mozilla Firefox or Netscape Navigator, open the file in this browser to see the problem.

4.   Find and correct the error, which is somewhere within the `<embed>` tag.

5.   Save and refresh your file. If you have a Navigator-based browser such as Firefox or Navigator, or IE on the Mac, try to open the file on this machine to confirm that it now works correctly.

6.   Close the file in your text editor and browser.

PORTFOLIO BUILDER

Correct Script and Embedded Object Errors

You've been asked to help a local delivery company correct minor problems with the Web site they use to distribute information to delivery drivers. The site uses a Flash file on the front page. A simple script is used to note the last date the page was updated. The front page is called testpage.htm and can be found in your WIP_11>Portfolio_Builder_11 folder.

In this Portfolio Builder, your task is to correct minor errors and update the code within this Web page.

- Review the source code of the page. The site has a Flash file (named animation.swf) that is supposed to serve as a navigation structure. One of the driver's reported they are unable to see the Flash animation on their Apple Macintosh computer.

- A simple script at the bottom of the page indicates the date the page was last updated so drivers can make sure they are looking at the most up-to-date version. The script tag used for this script was written a few years ago and does not contain the **type** or **language** attributes that are required for XHTML compliance.

- Add an alert box that displays when the page is loaded and reminds users of the last date to turn in their driver logs (which is also written on the page).

INTEGRATING PROJECT

This Integrating Project is designed to reflect a real-world XHTML programming job, drawing on the skills you learned throughout this book. The files you need to complete this project are located in the RF_XHTML_L1>IP folder.

Build the Backwater's Web Site

In this Integrating Project, you create a three-page Web site for a restaurant. The home page includes information about the restaurant; the menu page allows viewers to see the variety of foods offered at the restaurant; and the form page allows users to submit inquiries to the owner of the restaurant. Once the site is complete, you prepare it for publishing by providing meta information for search engines, as well as validate the document.

Plan a Site and Create a Home Page

1 Copy the contents of the RF_XHTML_L1>IP folder to your WIP_IP folder.

The images you need to complete this project are in the RF_XHTML_L1>IP folder. If you were hired to complete an actual project such as this one, the client or a graphic artist would provide the necessary images.

2 Open your text editor. Create a new XHTML document by adding the following document tags to the text file:

```
<html>
<head>
<title></title>
</head>
<body>
</body>
</html>
```

3 Save the file as "index.htm" in your WIP>IP>BackWater_Web folder.

Index.htm is the home page.

4 Open your browser. Navigate to the WIP>IP>BackWater_Web folder and open index.htm.

Index.htm displays in the browser as a blank document.

5 Switch to the text editor. Position your cursor between the **<title></title>** tags, enter the title, and then add the content shown beneath the **<body>** tag, as follows:

```
<html>
<head>
<title>The Backwaters on Sand Key Dining</title>
</head>
<body>
<p>Dining on the coastal waters <br />of the Gulf of Mexico!</p>
<p>Relax and enjoy the Backwater's on Sand Key dining</p>
The Backwater's experience offers:<br />
Indoor/outdoor dining and bar<br />
Full liquor and fine wines<br />
Wonderful selection of seafood dishes<br />
Steak entrees and nightly specials<br />
Lunch and sandwich menu selections<br />
```

```
<p>We welcome everyone in and around the Tampa Bay area and
tourists visiting our sunny beaches.

Take a look at our menu and come visit us soon.</p>

</body>

</html>
```

6 Save the changes to index.htm. Refresh the document in your browser.

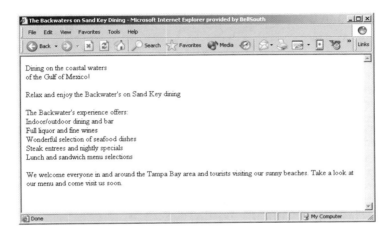

The text displays in paragraphs with single line breaks. Now you are ready to format the content.

7 Leave both applications open for the next exercise.

Format the Home Page

1 In the open document, switch to the text editor.

2 Format the document by adding and replacing tags, as follows:

```
<title>The Backwaters on Sand Key Dining</title>

</head>

<body>

<h2>Dining on the coastal waters <br />of the Gulf of Mexico!
</h2>

<p>Relax and enjoy the <b>Backwater's on Sand Key</b> dining</p>

<b>The Backwater's experience offers: </b>

<ul>

   <li>Indoor/outdoor dining and bar</li>

   <li>Full liquor and fine wines</li>
```

```
<li>Wonderful selection of seafood dishes</li>
<li>Steak entrees and nightly specials</li>
<li>Lunch and sandwich menu selections</li>
</ul>
<p>We welcome everyone in and around the Tampa Bay area and
tourists visiting our sunny beaches.
Take a look at our menu and come visit us soon.</p>
</body>
</html>
```

3 Save the changes in the text editor. Refresh the document in the browser.

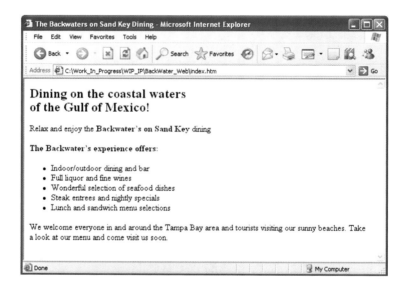

The formatting changes the display dramatically.

4 Switch to the text editor. Change the color and font style, as follows:

```
<title>The Backwaters on Sand Key Dining</title>
</head>
<body>
<h2><font color="#808080">Dining on the coastal waters <br>of
the Gulf of Mexico!</font></h2>
<p><font size="2" face="Arial" color="#808080"> Relax and enjoy
the <b>Backwater's on Sand Key</b> dining</font></p>
```

```
<b><font size="2" face="Arial" color="#000000">The Backwater's
experience offers:</font></b>

<ul>

  <li><font size="2" face="Arial" color="#808080">Indoor/outdoor
dining and bar</font></li>

  <li><font size="2" face="Arial" color="#808080">Full liquor and
fine wines</font></li>

  <li><font size="2" face="Arial" color="#808080">Wonderful
selection of seafood dishes</font></li>

  <li><font size="2" face="Arial" color="#808080">Steak entrees
and nightly specials</font></li>

  <li><font size="2" face="Arial" color="#808080">Lunch and
sandwich menu selections</font></li>

</ul>

<p><font size="2" face="Arial" color="#808080">We welcome
everyone in and around the Tampa Bay area and tourists visiting
our sunny beaches.

Take a look at our menu and come visit us soon.</font></p>

</body>

</html>
```

5 Save the changes in the text editor. Refresh the document in the browser.

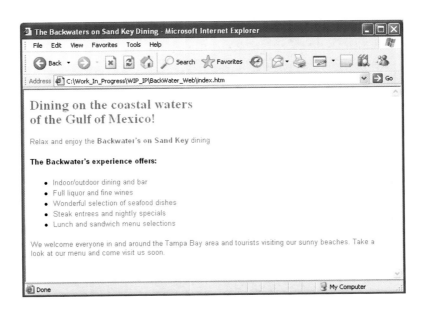

The font style displays as Arial and the color as gray. The text size displays as XHTML Level 2.

6 Leave both applications open for the next exercise.

Place an Image and Provide a Background

1 In the open document, switch to the text editor.

2 Add an image to the main page.

```
<body>

<h2><font color="#808080">Dining on the coastal waters <br>of
the Gulf of Mexico!</font></h2>

<p><font size="2" face="Arial" color="#808080">Relax and enjoy
the <b>Backwater's on Sand Key</b> dining</font></p>

<img border="0" alt="Backwaters Dining" src="images/outside.jpg"
width="200" height="149" />

<b><font size="2" face="Arial" color="#000000">The Backwater's
experience offers:

</font> </b>

<ul>
```

3 Save the changes to the text file. Refresh the document in the browser.

The image displays in the default location on the page.

4 Switch to the text editor. Right-align the image to the text on the Web page.

```
<body>

<h2><font color="#808080">Dining on the coastal waters <br>of
the Gulf of Mexico!</font></h2>

<p><font size="2" face="Arial" color="#808080">Relax and enjoy
the <b>Backwater's on Sand Key</b> dining</font></p>

<img border="0" alt="Backwaters Dining" src="images/outside.jpg"
width="200" height="149" align="right" />

<ul>

  <li><font size="2" face="Arial" color="#808080">Indoor/outdoor
dining and bar</font></li>

  <li><font size="2" face="Arial" color="#808080">Full liquor and
fine wines</font></li>
```

5 Include a background image for the Web page.

```
<head>

<title>The Backwaters on Sand Key Dining</title>

</head>

<body background="images/bkg.gif">

<h2><font color="#808080">Dining on the coastal waters <br>of
the Gulf of Mexico!</font></h2>

<p><font size="2" face="Arial" color="#808080">Relax and enjoy
the <b>Backwater's on Sand Key</b> dining</font></p>
```

6 Save the changes to the text file. Refresh the document in the browser.

The background image displays, and the main image aligns on the right side of the Web page.

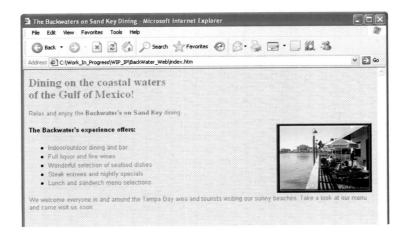

7   Leave both applications open for the next exercise.

Create a Navigational System

1   In the open file, add navigational links to the bottom of the page.

```
<li><font size="2" face="Arial" color="#808080">Lunch and
sandwich menu selections</font></li>

</ul>

<p><font size="2" face="Arial" color="#808080">We welcome
everyone in and around the Tampa Bay area and tourists visiting
our sunny beaches.

Take a look at our menu and come visit us soon.</font></p>

<p align="center">

<a href="index.htm">Home</a>   |

<a href="menu.htm">Our Menu</a>   |

<a href="contact.htm">Contact Us</a>

</p>

</body>

</html>
```

Before you begin creating a Web site, you typically know how many pages to include and the names of the pages (Home, About, Contact). Once you know this information, you can begin building the navigational system and the links to documents that you'll create later. Designers often include text links along the page's bottom to provide an alternative navigational system.

2   Save the changes to the text file. Refresh the document in the browser.

The links display at the bottom of the page, even though they do not yet link to anything.

3   Switch to the text editor. Add names to all of the links.

```
<p>We welcome everyone in and around the Tampa Bay area and
tourists visiting our sunny beaches.

Take a look at our menu and come visit us soon.</p>

<p align="center">

<a href="index.htm" title="Our home page">Home</a>   |

<a href="menu.htm" title="Our Menu">Our Menu</a>   |

<a href="contact.htm" title="Feel free to contact us.">Contact
Us</a>

</p>

</body>

</html>
```

4   Save the changes to the text file. Refresh the document in the browser. Hover your cursor over the links.

A tool tip displays the text contained in the **title=""** attributes.

5   Leave both applications open for the next exercise.

Use Tables for the Layout

1   In the open file, create a table at the top of the page, above the existing content.

```
<html>

<Head><title>The Backwaters on Sand Key Dining</title></head>

<body background="images/bkg.gif">

<table width="747" border="0" cellpadding="0" cellspacing="0">

  <tr>

  <td rowspan="2">

  <img src="images/tophead_01.jpg" width="81" height="83" /></td>

  <td rowspan="2">

  <img src="images/tophead_02.gif" width="256" height="83" /></td>

  <td rowspan="2">

  <img src="images/tophead_03.gif" width="86" height="83" /></td>

  <td>
```

```
    <img border="0" src="images/3top.jpg" width="63" height="63" />
</td>

    <td>

    <img src="images/tophead_05.jpg" width="16" height="63" /></td>

    <td>

    <img border="0" src="images/1top.jpg" width="63"
height="63"></td>

    <td>

    <img src="images/tophead_07.jpg" width="16" height="63" /></td>

    <td>

    <img border="0" src="images/2top.jpg" width="63" height="63" />
</td>

    <td>

    <img src="images/tophead_09.gif" width="100" height="63" /></td>

    </tr>

    <tr>

    <td colspan="6">

    <img src="images/tophead_10.gif" width="324" height="20" /></td>

    </tr>

    <tr>

    <td colspan="9">

    <img src="images/tophead_11.gif" width="747" height="7" /></td>

    </tr>

</table>
<h2><font color="#808080">Dining on the coastal waters <br>of the
Gulf of Mexico!</font></h2>

<p><font size="2" face="Arial" color="#808080">Relax and enjoy
the <b>Backwater's on Sand Key</b> dining</font></p>
```

This table displays a top header that consists of some images. Study the rows and cells in this advanced table to see how the table creates an image layout.

2   Save the changes. Refresh the document in the browser.

The table displays on the page's left side, above the rest of the content. Next, format the table so it aligns with the rest of the content.

3   Switch to the text document. Center-align the table.

```
<title>The Backwaters on Sand Key Dining</title>

</head>

<body background="images/bkg.gif">

<table width="747" border="0" cellpadding="0" cellspacing="0"
align="center">

<tr>

  <td rowspan="2">

  <img src="images/tophead_01.jpg" width="81" height="83" /></td>

  <td rowspan="2">
```

4   Save the changes to the text file. Refresh the document in the browser.

The table center-aligns on the Web page. The page would look more appealing if the content was the same width as the table.

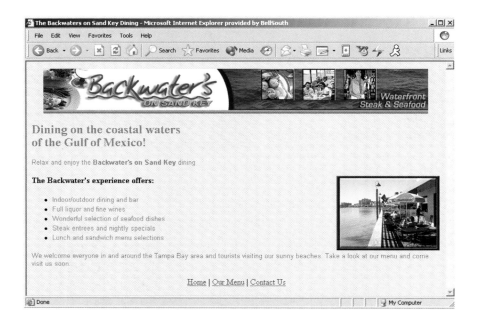

5 Leave both applications open for the next exercise.

Nest and Format Tables

You need to create another table below the header table — use the section on the left for the menu, and use the section on the right for the body content.

1 Add a new table and cell.

```
<td colspan="9">

  <img src="images/tophead_11.gif" width="747" height="7" /></td>

  </tr>

</table>

<table width="747" border="0" cellpadding="0" cellspacing="0"
align="center">

<tr>

<td width="150" valign="top" bgcolor="#001b49">
```

```
<img src="images/wine3.jpg" alt="Backwaters Dining" border="0"
width="150" height="112" />

<h2><font color="#808080">Dining on the coastal waters <br>of
the Gulf of Mexico!</font></h2>

<p><font size="2" face="Arial" color="#808080">Relax and enjoy
the <b>Backwater's on Sand Key</b> dining</font></p>
```

The new table contains an image. This image displays above the menu. You will create the closing tags for this table later in the exercise.

2   Create a table within this new cell and table of links.

```
<table width="747" border="0" cellpadding="0" cellspacing="0"
align="center">

<tr>

<td width="150" valign="top" bgcolor="#001b49">

<img src="images/wine3.jpg" alt="Backwaters Dining" border="0"
width="150" height="112" />

<table border="0" cellspacing="0" cellpadding="0">

<tr>

   <td rowspan="6">

   <img src="images/spacer.gif" width="8" height="1"
alt="Backwaters Dining" border="0" /></td>

   <td valign="top">

   <img src="images/spacer.gif" width="1" height="2"
alt="Backwaters Dining" border="0" /><img src="images/fork1.gif"
alt="Backwaters Dining" border="0" alt="Backwaters Dining"
width="12" height="12" />

   </td>

   <td> <a href="menu.htm"><font color="#FFFFFF">Our
Menu</font></a></td>

</tr>

<tr>

   <td valign="top">

   <img src="images/spacer.gif" width="1" height="2"
alt="Backwaters Dining" border="0"><img
src="images/fork1.gif" alt="Backwaters Dining"
border="0" name="ab" width="12" height="12" />
```

```
     </td>

     <td><a href="contact.htm"><font color="#ffffff"> Contact
Us</font></a></td>

</tr>

<tr>

     <td valign="top">

     <img src="images/spacer.gif" width="1" height="2"
alt="Backwaters Dining" border="0" /><img src="images/fork1.gif"
alt="Backwaters Dining" border="0" name="ac" width="12"
height="12" />

     </td>

     <td><a href="index.htm"><font
color="#ffffff"> Home</font></a></td>

</tr>

</table>

</td>

<blockquote>

<h2><font color="#808080">Dining on the coastal waters <br />of
the Gulf of Mexico!</font></h2>

<p><font size="2" face="Arial" color="#808080">Relax and enjoy
the <b>Backwater's on Sand Key</b> dining</font></p>
```

3   Open a new cell in the table. Enclose the body content within it.

```
<img src="images/spacer.gif" width="1" height="2" alt="Backwaters
Dining" border="0" /><img src="images/fork1.gif" alt="Backwaters
Dining" border="0" name="ac" width="12" height="12" />

     </td>

     <td><a href="index.htm"><font
color="#ffffff"> Home</font></a></td>
```

```
</tr>

</table>

</td>

<blockquote>

<td bgcolor="#FFFFFF">

<h2><font color="#808080">Dining on the coastal waters <br>of
the Gulf of Mexico!</font></h2>

<p><font size="2" face="Arial" color="#808080">Relax and enjoy
the <b>Backwater's on Sand Key</b> dining</font></p>

<b><font size="2" face="Arial" color="#000000">The Backwater's
experience offers:

</font>   </b>

<p align="center">

<a href="index.htm" title="Our home page">Home</a>   |

<a href="menu.htm" title="Our Menu">Our Menu</a>   |

<a href="contact.htm" title="Feel free to contact us.">Contact
Us</a>

</p>

<br />

</blockquote>

</tr>

</td>

</table>

</body>

</html>
```

4   Save the changes in the text file. Refresh the document in the browser.

The new nested tables provide a layout for the entire page.

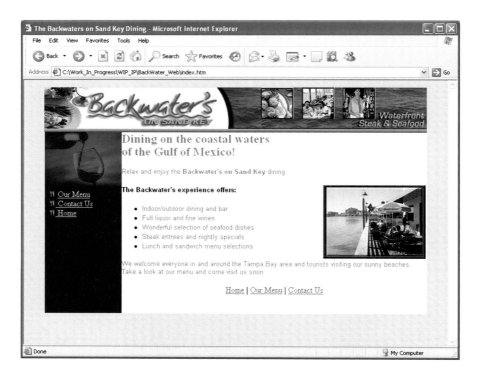

5   Close the file in your text editor and browser.

Create a Form

1   In your text editor and browser, open contact.htm from your WIP_IP>BackWater_Web folder.

This page is essentially the same as the home page, but the page's primary content has been removed.

2 Insert the following code:

```
<td bgcolor="#FFFFFF">

<blockquote>

<!-- ***** insert code here ***** -->

<h2><font color="#808080">Contact &amp; Comments </font></h2>

<p><font color="#808080">Help us serve you better. Let us know
what you think.

<br />

Please take a moment to fill out our contact form. </font></p>

<p><font color="#808080">* required fields </font></p>

<p align="center">

<a href="index.htm" title="Our home page">Home</a>  |

<a href="menu.htm" title="Our Menu">Our Menu</a>  |

<a href="contact.htm" title="Feel free to contact us.">Contact
Us</a>
```

Notice how a comment was used to help you find the proper place in the code.

3 Save the changes in the text file. Refresh the document in the browser.

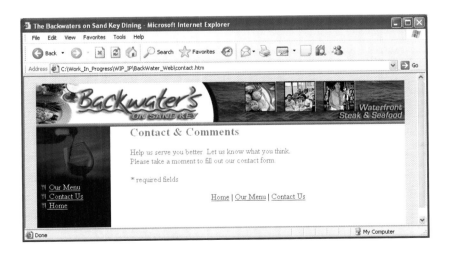

4 Create the following form:

```
<h2><font color="#808080">Backwater's Contact &amp; Comments
</font></h2>

<p><font color="#808080">Help us serve you better. Let us know
what you think.

<br />

Please take a moment to fill out our contact form. </font></p>

<p><font color="#808080">* required fields</font></p>

<p>

<form action="mailto:test@yourdomain.com" method="post">

<input type="text" size="24"
name="firstname" /> First Name <br />

<input type="text" size="24" name="lastname" /> Last Name <br />

<input type="text" size="24" name="email" />  Email Address <br />

<input type="text" size="24" name="phone" />  Phone Number <br />

Comments:<br />

<textarea rows="5" cols="24" name="comments"></textarea>

</form>

</p>

<p align="center">

<a href="index.htm" title="Our home page">Home</a>  |

<a href="menu.htm" title="Our Menu">Our Menu</a>   |

<a href="contact.htm" title="Feel free to contact us.">
Contact Us</a>

</p>
```

5   Save the changes to the text file and refresh the document in the browser.

The form displays below the text you entered in Step 2. Use your own e-mail address so you can test the form.

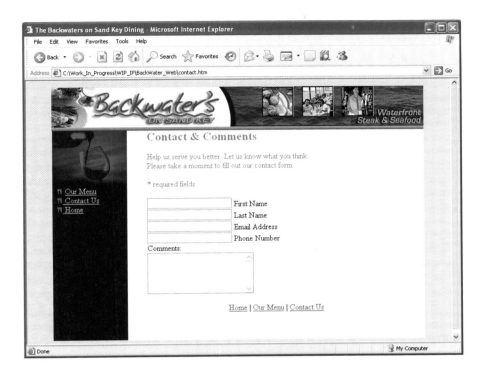

6   Close the file in both applications.

Add Meta Information and Comment Lines

1   Open index.htm in both the text editor and browser.

2   Provide keywords for the file.

```
<html>

<head>

<title>The Backwaters on Sand Key Dining</title>

<meta name="keywords" content="Dining, seafood, fine, fine
dining, eat, backwaters steak and seafood, indoor and outdoor
dining" />

</head>
```

3   Provide a description for the document.

```
<title>The Backwaters on Sand Key Dining</title></head>

<meta name="keywords" content="Dining, seafood, fine, fine
dining, eat, backwaters steak and seafood, indoor and outdoor
dining" />

<meta name="description" content="Dining on the coastal waters of
the Gulf of Mexico!" />

</head>
```

4   Provide comments for each section of the document.

```
<body background="images/bkg.gif">

<!--TOP HEADER BANNER-->

<table width="747" border="0" cellpadding="0" cellspacing="0"
align="center">

  <tr>

    <td rowspan="2">

...

<!--LEFT NAVIGATION MENU-->

<table width="747" border="0" cellpadding="0" cellspacing="0"
align="center">

...

</table>

</td>

<!--CONTENT-->

<blockquote>

<td bgcolor="#FFFFFF">

<h2><font color="#808080">Dining on the coastal waters <br>of
the Gulf of Mexico!</font></h2>

<p><font color="#808080">Relax and enjoy the <b>Backwater's on
Sand Key</b> dining</font></p>

...
```

5   Save the changes. Refresh the document in the browser.

6   Leave both applications open for the next exercise.

Include DTD and Validate the Document

1   Switch to the text editor of the open document.

2   You used presentational elements in this Web site, so you must include the XHTML Transitional DTD at the top of the page, before the **`<html>`** tag.

```
<!DOCTYPE html PUBLIC "-//W3C//DTD XHTML 1.0 Transitional//EN"

"http://www.w3.org/TR/xhtml1/DTD/xhtml1-transitional.dtd" />

<html>

<Head>

<title>The Backwaters on Sand Key Dining</title>
```

Type this as a single line of code, without clicking the Return or Enter key until you reach the end of the line.

3   Save index.htm in the text editor.

4   Log on to http://www.htmlhelp.com/tools/validator. Follow the instructions for uploading and validating the page.

The validator returns a list of errors. The errors may differ from one person to the next, depending on how well each person followed the steps in this project.

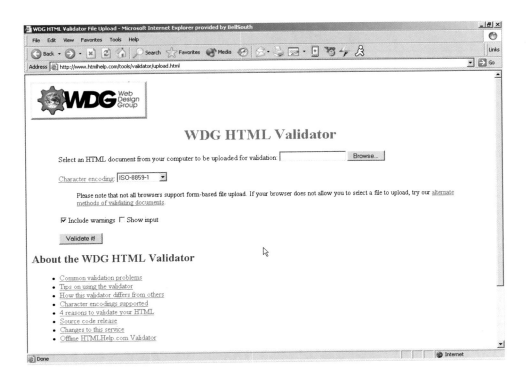

5 Address each error according to the XHTML Transitional standards. Continue to validate until all the errors are resolved.

6 Test all links and images.

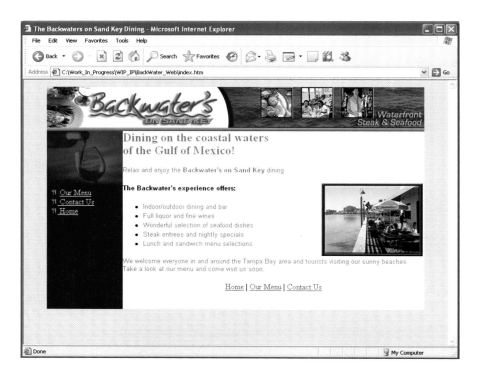

7 Close all applications.

TASK GUIDE

Element	Strict	Transitional	Frameset	Basic	XHTML1.1	Empty
a	X	X	X	X	X	
abbr	X	X	X	X	X	
acronym	X	X	X	X	X	
address	X	X	X	X	X	
applet		X	X			
area	X	X	X		X	X
b	X	X	X		X	
base	X	X	X	X	X	X
basefont		X	X			X
bdo	X	X	X		X	
big	X	X	X		X	
blockquote	X	X	X	X	X	
body	X	X	X	X	X	
br	X	X	X	X	X	X
button	X	X	X		X	
caption	X	X	X	X	X	
center		X	X			
cite	X	X	X	X	X	
code	X	X	X	X	X	
col	X	X	X		X	X
colgroup	X	X	X		X	
dd	X	X	X	X	X	
del	X	X	X		X	
dfn	X	X	X	X	X	
dir		X	X			
div	X	X	X		X	
dl	X	X	X	X	X	
dt	X	X	X	X	X	
em	X	X	X	X	X	
fieldset	X	X	X		X	
font		X	X			
form	X	X	X	X	X	
frame			X			X

Element	Strict	Transitional	Frameset	Basic	XHTML1.1	Empty
frameset			x			
h1	x	x	x	x	x	
h2	x	x	x	x	x	
h3	x	x	x	x	x	
h4	x	x	x	x	x	
h5	x	x	x	x	x	
h6	x	x	x	x	x	
head	x	x	x	x	x	
hr	x	x	x		x	x
html	x	x	x	x	x	
i	x	x	x		x	
iframe	x	x	x		x	
img	x	x	x	x	x	x
input	x	x	x	x	x	x
ins	x	x	x		x	
isindex		x	x			x
kbd	x	x	x	x	x	
label	x	x	x		x	
legend	x	x	x		x	
li	x	x	x	x	x	
link	x	x	x	x	x	x
map	x	x	x		x	
menu		x	x			
meta	x	x	x	x	x	x
noframes			x			
noscript	x	x	x		x	
object	x	x	x	x	x	
ol	x	x	x	x	x	
optgroup	x	x	x		x	
option	x	x	x	x	x	
p	x	x	x	x	x	
param	x	x	x	x	x	x
pre	x	x	x	x	x	
q	x	x	x	x	x	
rb					x	

Element	Strict	Transitional	Frameset	Basic	XHTML1.1	Empty
rbc					X	
rp					X	
rt					X	
rtc					X	
ruby					X	
s		X	X			
samp	X	X	X	X	X	
script	X	X	X		X	
select	X	X	X	X	X	
small	X	X	X		X	
span	X	X	X		X	
strike		X	X			
strong	X	X	X	X	X	
style	X	X	X		X	
sub	X	X	X		X	
sup	X	X	X		X	
table	X	X	X	X	X	
tbody	X	X	X		X	
td	X	X	X	X	X	
textarea	X	X	X	X	X	
tfoot	X	X	X		X	
th	X	X	X	X	X	
thead	X	X	X		X	
title	X	X	X	X	X	
tr	X	X	X	X	X	
tt	X	X	X		X	
u		X	X			
ul	X	X	X	X	X	
var	X	X	X	X	X	

GLOSSARY

absolute path   The location of a file or Web page beginning with the root. Includes all necessary information to find the file or page. In the case of a Web page, called "absolute URL." See *relative path*.

absolute positioning   Using CSS to specify precise coordinates to position any element in an exact position on the screen.

accessibility   The ability for a disabled user to use a Web site.

action   The location that receives data from a form.

ActiveX   A technology from Microsoft that allows the integration of sound, animation, and other items into Web pages using reusable software components.

algorithm   A specific sequence of steps to process data. A portion of a computer program that calculates a specific result.

alignment   Positioning content to the left, right, center, top, or bottom.

alt text   Alternate Text. In Web page design, text that can be displayed in lieu of an image.

anchor   In a Web page, a type of hyperlink destination in which the destination is a specific location on a page.

animated GIF   A type of sequential file format where multiple bitmap images are displayed one after another.

animated graphics   Images of any type that move.

anonymous FTP   FTP protocol that allows users access to files for downloading. The user ID is anonymous, and the password is any valid e-mail address.

ARPANET   Advanced Research Projects Agency Network. Developed by the U.S. Department of Defense during the cold war to survive nuclear attacks, authority was distributed over a number of geographically dispersed computers. This concept was the basis of the Internet.

ASCII   American Standard Code for Information Interchange. Worldwide, standard ASCII text does not include formatting, and therefore can be exchanged and read by most computer systems.

ASP   Active Server Pages. A specification for a dynamically created Web page that contains either Visual Basic or JavaScript code. When a browser requests an ASP page, the Web server generates a page with HTML code. Only available on NT servers.

asset   An image, sound, video, or other file that may be used in a Web page.

attribute   Information included in the start tag of an element.

background   A static object or color that lies behind all other objects.

bandwidth   The transmission capacity, usually measured in bits per second (*see* BPS), of a network connection.

banner   Common form of Web advertisement. Most banner ads are animated GIFs.

basefont   The default size of the text that is displayed in a document window.

baud   The speed of a modem. Although not technically accurate, baud rate is commonly used to mean bit rate (the number of bits transmitted per second).

bitmap image   An image constructed from individual dots or pixels set to a grid-like mosaic. The file must contain information about the color and position of each pixel, so the disk space needed for bitmap images can be very large.

blank   When using frames, a value for the target attribute. This value causes the browser to create a new window for the linked content when the user follows the associated link.

boldface   A heavier, blacker version of a typeface.

border   A continual line that extends around an element.

BPS   Bits Per Second. A measurement of how fast data is moved from one place to another, usually in thousands of bits per second (Kbps) or million of bits per second (Mbps). A 28.8 modem can transport 28,800 bits per second.

browser   Software program that allows you to surf the Web. The most popular browsers are Netscape Navigator and Microsoft Internet Explorer. The very first browsers, such as Lynx, only allowed users to see text. Also called "Web browser."

browser compatibility   A term that compares how a Web page functions on different browsers. Incompatibilities often exist due to how a browser interprets the HTML. The differences may be very slight or significant.

bullet   A marker preceding text, usually a solid dot, used to add emphasis; generally indicates the text is part of a list.

button   An element a user can click to cause an effect, such as the submission of a form.

caps   An abbreviation for capital letters.

caps and small caps   A style of typesetting in which uppercase letters are used in the normal way, while the type that would normally be in lowercase is changed to uppercase letters of a smaller point size. A true small-caps typeface does not contain any lowercase letters.

Cascading Style Sheets (CSS)   Part of a Web page file listing properties that affect the appearance of content, the content to which those properties apply, and their values.

case insensitive   When a computer language does not distinguish between upper- and lowercase versions of the same letter.

case sensitive   When a computer language can distinguish between upper- and lowercase versions of the same letter.

client-side language   A computer language, markup language, or scripting language that is interpreted by the user's computer.

CD-R/CD-RW   A recordable CD disc and drive, also known as a "burner." A CD-R drive can write to a CD-R disc once; afterward, the disc cannot be erased or rewritten. CD-RW allows a CD-RW disc to be erased and rewritten. A CD-RW drive can also "burn" a CD-R disc.

CD-ROM   A device used to store approximately 600 MB of data. Files are permanently stored on the device and can be copied to a disk, but not altered directly.

cell   A unit of information within a table.

cellpadding   The margin around the inside of a table cell.

cellspacing   The margin between table cells.

CGI   Common Gateway Interface. Interface that allows scripts to run on a Web server. CGI scripts can be used to put the content of a form into an email message, to perform a database query, or to generate HTML pages on the fly.

CGI script   A CGI program used to process a form or provide other dynamic content.

CGI-bin   The most common name of a directory on a Web server in which CGI scripts are stored.

check box   A square the user can click to cause the form to send a name-value pair to the action; a form element that allows a user to choose zero or more choices.

client   A computer system or application that requests a service of another computer system on the network.

client-side   Scripting or other actions that take place within the browser, as opposed to the server.

clip art   Collections of predrawn and digitized graphics.

clipboard   The portion of computer memory that holds data that has been cut or copied. The next item cut or copied replaces the data already in the clipboard.

colgroup tag   Used to modify the alignment of a group of columns within a table.

column   1. A vertical area for type; used to constrain line length to enhance design and readability. 2. A series of cells arranged vertically.

comment   A line in a piece of programming code that is intended to be read, not executed.

contrast   The relationship and degree of difference between the dark and light areas of an image.

cookie   Information a Web server writes to your computer hard disk via your browser, containing data such as login information and user preferences. This data can be retrieved so Web pages can be customized before they are sent to the visiting browser.

compression   The process of making a file or data smaller to use less disk size or to transfer more quickly.

copyright   Ownership of a work. Permits the owner of material to prevent its use without express permission or acknowledgement. Copyrights may be sold, transferred, or given up contractually.

custom class   A rule (or rules) that tells the browser how to display any item to which the selector is applied. In other words, any member assigned to the class takes on the characteristics of the class.

declaration   Chunks of CSS code that consist of selectors and rules.

default   A specification for a mode of computer operation that occurs if no other is selected. The default font size might be 12 point, or a default color for an object might be white with a black border.

deprecated   The status of a tag or attribute that can still be used, but will eventually be removed, and so should be avoided, if possible.

DHTML (Dynamic HTML)   A term used to describe the combination of CSS, JavaScript, and XHTML.

DNS   Domain Name Server or Domain Name System. Maps IP numbers to a more easily remembered name. When you type http://www.somedomain.com into a browser, the DNS searches for a matching IP address (228.28.202.95).

DOCTYPE   Specification of the DTD that applies to a page.

document   The general term for a computer file containing text and/or graphics.

document root   The main directory for a Web site.

domain name   A unique name that is used to identify a Web site, FTP site, and/or email server. A domain name always points to one specific server, even though the server may host many domain names.

download   Transferring data from a server to your computer's hard disk.

DSL   Digital Subscriber Line. A means for gaining high-speed access to the Internet using phone wiring and a specialized phone connection.

dynamic   Content that changes according to client-side or server-side scripting.

ECMAScript   Standardized version of the JavaScript language.

e-commerce   Electronic Commerce. Conducting business online, including product display, online ordering, and inventory management. The software, which works in conjunction with online payment systems to process payments, resides on a commerce server.

element   The smallest unit of a graphic, or a component of a page layout or design. Any object, text block, or graphic might be referred to as a design element.

email address   An electronic mail address. Email addresses are in the form of user@domain.com (for example, chris@webguest.net).

email alias   Email address that points to another email address. All messages sent to an email alias are automatically redirected (forwarded) to the specified email address.

embedding   Including a complete copy of a text file or image within a document, with or without a link. See *linking*.

embed tag   Tag used by Netscape Navigator-based browsers that allows external content such as animation, sound, or video to be presented in a Web browser using reusable software components.

embedded style sheet CSS rules defined in the HTML document using the <style> tag.

empty element tag A tag that has no closing element tag.

empty tag A tag that has no text between the opening and closing tags. Empty tags carry all information in attributes. There is no content to enclose, so empty tags are abbreviated with a "/" within the opening tag and have no closing tag.

encryption Procedure that scrambles the content of a file before sending it over the Internet. The recipient must have software to decrypt the file. PGP (Pretty Good Privacy) is a commonly used encryption program.

end user The person(s) who will view and use your Web pages and designs.

event An action performed by a user than can be detected by a computer language.

event handler A word in a computer language that can be used to detect the occurrence of a particular event, such as a mouse click.

external style sheet Formatting rules saved in other files rather than the current HTML document.

file A specific collection of information stored on the computer disk, separate from all other information. Can be randomly accessed by the computer.

file extension The suffix used to identify file types under the Macintosh and Windows operating systems, separated from the rest of the file name by a period.

file:/// A protocol used by browsers to access information available on the local computer.

fixed positioning When an element does not change position when the page on which it resides scrolls up or down.

Flash movie Files created by the Macromedia Flash web-authoring tool or similar software that can be inserted into Web pages to create interfaces, animation, video, sound, or any combination of these items.

flow chart A block diagram representing the major steps of an event. Used by computer programmers to translate events into computer logic.

font The complete collection of all the characters (numbers, uppercase and lowercase letters, and in some cases, small caps and symbols) of a given typeface in a specific style; for example, Helvetica Bold.

font family In Web design, a grouping of (supposedly) similar fonts, which will be used to display text in the Web page. See *Cascading Style Sheets*.

form A page that enables a user to enter information and send it to a site via form elements, such as text boxes, radio buttons, and pull-down menus.

form validation The process of making certain a Web form contains all required data and no invalid data.

frame A section of the browser window displaying content; independent of all other areas within the browser window. This window-within-a-window can be referenced by links in other frames.

frameset The document defining the layout on a framed page and breaking it into one or more frames.

function A reusable set of instructions that are activated within a computer program.

GIF Graphics Interchange Format. A popular graphics format for online clip art and drawn graphics. Graphics in this format are acceptable at low resolution. See *JPEG*.

hard disk A magnetic storage medium consisting of specially coated metal disks, and associated mechanical and electronic equipment. Found inside most personal computers; can store a tremendous amount of information, and is sometimes removable or portable.

hardware The physical components of a computer and its auxiliary equipment.

header information Information at the beginning of a Web page file that defines the content and characteristics of the page.

hex values Numbers specified in the hexadecimal system, commonly used for specifying colors on Web pages.

hexadecimal color code Colors expressed as hexadecimal numbers.

hexadecimal number A number expressed using sixteen possible values for each digit. Hexadecimal numbers are popular with computer scientists because they allow computer memory values to be written in an easy to understand fashion.

hidden field Data not shown to the user, but submitted with the rest of the form data.

home page Main page of a Web site. A Web site containing only one page is also called a home page.

HREF Hyperlink Reference. HTML code that specifies a URL as the linked resource.

HTML Hypertext Mark-Up Language. A tagging language that allows content to be delivered over the World Wide Web and viewed by a browser.

HTTP Hypertext Transfer Protocol. The method used by browsers and Web servers to communicate, such as to request and deliver content, respectively.

hyperlink An HTML tag that directs the computer to a different anchor or URL. A hyperlink can be a word, phrase, sentence, graphic, or icon. A hyperlink can also cause an action, such as opening or downloading a file.

hypertext An organization of content that enables the user to select related content.

hypertext reference attribute The location of the information to which a browser should link.

ID selector Designed for one-time usage; you create an ID selector for a single element.

inline code JavaScript code placed inside of an attribute of an HTML tag. The attribute is usually an event handler, such as onclick.

inline style sheet CSS formatting that works as an attribute within an HTML tag.

interface   The design with which users interact.

Internet   A global system of interconnected computers.

Internet Explorer   A common Web browser, developed by Microsoft.

InterNIC   Internet Network Information Center. The entity that keeps track of domain names. Recently, the right to register domain names has been widely granted to private companies, so the cost and services associated with obtaining a new domain can vary.

IP   Internet Protocol. The rules that provide basic Internet functions. IP allows computers to find each other.

IP address   A unique, 32-bit Internet address consisting of four numbers, separated by dots and sometimes called a "dotted quad" (90.0.0.95). Every client computer and every server computer connected to the Internet has a unique IP number that is assigned by the ISP.

JavaScript   A scripting language that can be embedded into HTML documents.

JPEG   A compression algorithm that reduces the file size of bitmapped images. Named for the Joint Photographic Experts Group, which created the standard. JPEG is "lossy" compression; image quality is reduced in direct proportion to the amount of compression.

keywords   A word or words that identifies the content of a Web page and can be used by search engines as part of their process of determining the results of searches.

language attribute   A parameter of an HTML tag, typically used with the <script> tag to specify the language to be used within the tag.

layer   A term many Web designers use to describe the use of CSS elements with absolute positioning and z-index values.

layout   The arrangement of text and graphics on a page, usually produced in the preliminary design stage.

left alignment   Text having a straight left edge and a ragged or uneven right edge.

linked style sheet   See *external style sheet*.

linking   The act of placing a reference to one file (sound, graphic, or video) into another file. When the referenced file is modified, the placed reference is automatically (or manually, depending on the application) updated.

list   A series of items.

location   The address of a particular Web page or file.

lossless compression   Compression that does not reduce the quality of the file when reducing the file size.

lossy compression   Compression that reduces the quality of the file when reducing the file size.

mailto: A protocol used to tell the browser to create a new email message.

method   A command designed to perform an action within a code sequence. Within a computer program, a method is similar to a verb within a spoken language.

meta tag   An optional HTML tag that is used to specify information about a Web document. Some search engines index Web pages by reading the information contained within the meta tags.

monospace   A font in which all characters occupy the same amount of horizontal width regardless of the character.

Mosaic   The first Web browser (developed by NSCA) with the ability to display graphics. The Mosaic browser caused a major breakthrough in the way people could access the resources of the World Wide Web.

named target   A frame that has a designated name, allowing links to specify that content should be displayed within that frame.

name-value pair   A combination of two elements: a name that identifies the information, and a value (the actual information).

nested frameset   A frameset that is the content of the frame of another frameset.

nested tag   A tag contained within another tag.

nesting   Placing graphic files or tables within other graphic files or tables.

Netscape Navigator   A common Web browser.

no frames section   Content provided for browsers that does not support frames contained within a noframes element.

object tag   Used within Microsoft Internet Explorer-based browsers to load external content such as Flash movies, which require a separate software component that is not included within the browser.

one-line text box   This field allows the viewer to insert a single line of data, such as a name or address. This form element is commonly used to gather basic demographic information from a user, or to act as a password field.

online   Currently connected to a computer network.

opening tag   The indication of the start of an element containing the name of the element and any attributes.

operating system (OS)   The software that allows your computer to function. Examples of operating systems are Mac OS X and Microsoft Windows.

page properties   In Web design, the characteristics of a layout page, including default background and text colors, page width, and background image.

page title   Text that appears in the Title bar of the user's browser when the page is viewed.

parent   The master element to which secondary "child" elements are related. Can refer to styles, graphic elements or objects, layers, folders, and Web site frames.

password box   A text box that replaces all characters with a bullet or asterisk to hide their identity.

Perl   Practical Extraction and Report Language. A powerful computer language, especially used for writing CGI scripts that handle input/output actions on Web pages.

PHP   A server-side, HTML-embedded scripting language used to create dynamic Web pages. The strength of PHP lies in its compatibility with many types of databases. PHP can talk across networks using IMAP, SNMP, NNTP, POP3, or HTTP.

pixel Picture element. One of the tiny rectangular areas or dots generated by a computer or output device to constitute images. A greater number of pixels per inch results in higher resolution on screen or in print.

PNG Portable Network Graphics. PNG is a new graphics format similar to GIF. It is a relatively new file format, and is not yet widely supported by most browsers.

POP Post Office Protocol. Internet protocol used by ISPs to handle email for its subscribers. A POP account is a synonym for an email account.

property A characteristic of an object.

pseudo-class A set of rules that refer to situations that do not exist in HTML code. As an example, consider the a:hover property in CSS which affects the colors of links when mouse pointers move over the links.

pseudo-code A plain English translation of an actual code statement.

pull-down menu A menu that displays additional options.

radio button A single round button a user can click to cause a form to send a name-value pair to the action.

radio group A group of radio buttons with the same name. Only one radio button may be selected at a time within a radio group.

RAM Random access memory. The "working" memory of a computer that holds files in process. Files in RAM are lost when the computer is turned off, whereas files stored on the hard drive or floppy disks remain available.

redefining HTML tags When HTML tag names are used as CSS selectors, the rule applied overwrites the default display styles of the tag.

redirect To cause the browser to load a different page without intervention from the user. A particular HTML code in the heading of a Web page that can seamlessly redirect the visitor to another Web page.

refresh To reload a Web page.

relative positioning Using CSS to offset the position of an element relative to where it would normally appear in the document.

reset button A button that, when clicked, causes a form to return to the state it was in when the page was first loaded.

resolution The density of graphic information expressed in dots per inch (dpi) or pixels per inch (ppi).

RGB 1. The colors of projected light from a computer monitor that, when combined, simulate a subset of the visual spectrum. 2. The color model of most digital artwork.

right alignment Text having a straight right edge and a ragged or uneven left edge.

rule A guideline for how the selector will display on the page.

script Instructions that tell the computer what to do.

scripting The process of adding programming capabilities to a program (e.g., AppleScript), file (e.g., Action-Script), or Web page (e.g., JavaScript).

search engine A Web site that allows users to search for keywords on Web pages. Every search engine has its own strategy for collecting data.

select list A list of potential choices, displayed as a menu that appears when the user clicks it, or as a box with its own scroll bar.

select option A potential choice listed in a select list.

selection The currently active object/s in a window. Often made by clicking with the mouse or dragging a marquee around the desired object/s.

selector The class (an item or items) to which CSS rules are applied.

_self When using frames, a value for the target attribute. This value causes the browser to place the linked content into the frame containing the current document when the user follows the associated link.

server-side language A computer language, markup language or scripting language that is interpreted by a remote computer (server).

SGML Standard Generalized Markup Language. The predecessor to Hypertext Markup Language; a means for creating universally available content using tagging.

site See *Web site*.

site root directory The parent folder that contains all other files and directories for a Web site.

slicing The act of converting a large image into smaller images that can be constructed into a Web page.

SMTP Simple Mail Transfer Protocol. Primary protocol to send and receive email between servers on the Internet.

source The actual text that makes up the Web page received by the browser, including HTML/XHTML, client-side scripting, and other information.

spider Program, also known as an orbit or a bot, used by some search engines to index Web sites. Spiders search the Web to find URLs that match the given query string.

static positioning When the browser positions elements on the Web page in the order they appear in the source code.

storyboard A series of sketches of the key visualization points of a Web page.

string A unit of text.

style guide A list of standardized formatting requirements required for a Web site, book, or other project.

submit button A button that, when clicked, causes the browser to send form data to the server.

tags An indication of the start and end of an element.

target The page or part of a page to which a link points.

TCP/IP Transmission Control Protocol/Internet Protocol. A suite of communications protocols that defines how information is transmitted over the Internet.

template   A document file containing layout, styles, and repeating elements (such as logos) by which a series of documents can maintain the same look and feel. A model publication you can use as the basis for creating a new publication.

text   The characters and words that form the main body of a publication or Web page.

text attribute   A characteristic applied directly to a letter or letters in text, such as bold, italic, or underline.

text box   A box into which users can type.

text editor   An application used to create or make changes to text files.

text effects   Means by which the appearance of text can be modified, such as bolding, underlining, and italicizing.

text string   Any sequence of alphanumeric characters that are not code commands.

text wrap   The ability of a browser to automatically continue text on the next line.

TIFF   Tagged Image File Format. A common format used for scanned or computer-generated bitmapped images.

top   When using frames, a value for the target attribute. This value causes the browser to place the linked content into the current browser window, rather than an individual frame, when the user follows the associated link.

transparency   The quality of an image element that allows background elements to partially or entirely show through.

type attribute   Parameter of an HTML <script> tag that tells the browser the type of information included within the <script> tag.

type family   1. A set of typefaces created from the same basic design but in different variations, such as bold, light, italic, book, and heavy. 2. In Web design, a list of fonts that will be used to display text in a Web page. See *Cascading Style Sheets*.

type size   Typeface as measured (in points) from the bottom of descenders to the body clearance line, which is slightly higher than the top of ascenders.

typeface   A unique and distinctive design of a font alphabet; the combined group of all the letters, figures, and punctuation of a specific font.

uploading   The process of sending a file from one computer to a remote server.

uppercase   The capital letters of a typeface as opposed to the lowercase (small) letters. When type was hand composited, the capital letters resided in the upper part of the type case.

URL   Uniform Resource Locator. Address of any resource on the Web.

usability   The ease with which a user can access, navigate, and achieve goals on a Web site.

user ID   Unique identifier you must enter every time you want to access a particular service on the Internet. The user ID is always accompanied by a password.

validate   To analyze a file to ensure the structure, tag names, and attributes are correct, according to the DTD selected.

validation   Making certain input fields, particular types of information, or information in a specific format mandatory for a form to be successfully submitted.

value   The current nature of a property. In CSS, a value is assigned to a property. For example, background color can be set to a value of "red."

W3C   The World Wide Web Consortium. The group responsible for defining HTML Standards (http://www.w3c.org).

WAI   An acronym for the Web Accessibility Initiative.

Web Accessibility Initiative   A project at the W3C to create guidelines for actions that developers should take to increase the accessibility of their sites and applications.

Web designer   An individual who is the aesthetic and navigational architect of a Web site, determining how the site looks, how it is designed, and what components it contains.

Web developer   A person who builds the technical architecture of Web sites, providing the programming required for a particular Web product to work.

Web directory   A site that contains categorized listings of Web sites.

Web host   A company that provides access to a server on which you can place your Web site content. This server is connected to the Internet, allowing the general public to access your Web site.

Web page   A single file or Web address containing HTML or XHTML information. Web pages typically include text and images, but may include links to other pages and other media.

Web site   A collection of HTML files and other content that visitors can access by means of a URL and view with a Web browser.

Webmaster   The person who is responsible for the Web server (usually the sysadmin).

Web-safe color   A color palette used for images that will be displayed on the Internet. The Web-safe color palette is a specific set of colors that can be displayed by most computer-operating systems and monitors.

World Wide Web   Client/server hypertext system for retrieving information across the Internet.

wrap   Type set on the page so it wraps around the shape of another element.

WYSIWYG Web-page editor   A Web-page editor that allows an author to directly manipulate items on a page, so that What You See Is What You Get.

XForms   An emerging specification defining advanced functionality for Web forms.

XHTML   An acronym for eXtensible HyperText Markup Language. The reformulization of HTML 4.01 in XML.

XHTML Elements   An emerging specification for defining the handling of events on a Web page.

XHTML Frameset   A version of XHTML that includes all tags that are part of HTML 4.01, including those involving frames.

XHTML Strict   A version of XHTML that does not include any presentational tags or attributes.

XHTML Transitional   The most common version of XHTML. Includes all tags and attributes that are part of HTML 4.01, except those involving frames.

XML   An acronym for eXtensible Markup Language.

z-index property   CSS property used to specify the stacking order of positioned elements.

INDEX